A Da Capo Press Reprint Series

FRANKLIN D. ROOSEVELT AND THE ERA OF THE NEW DEAL

GENERAL EDITOR: FRANK FREIDEL
Harvard University

INTERCITY DIFFERENCES IN COSTS OF LIVING IN MARCH, 1935—59 CITIES

Division of Research
Work Projects Administration

Research Monographs

I. Six Rural Problem Areas, Relief—Resources—Rehabilitation
II. Comparative Study of Rural Relief and Non-Relief Households
III. The Transient Unemployed
IV. Urban Workers on Relief
V. Landlord and Tenant on the Cotton Plantation
VI. Chronology of the Federal Emergency Relief Administration May 12, 1933, to December 31, 1935
VII. The Migratory-Casual Worker
VIII. Farmers on Relief and Rehabilitation
IX. Part-Time Farming in the Southeast
X. Trends in Relief Expenditures, 1910-1935
XI. Rural Youth on Relief
XII. Intercity Differences in Costs of Living in March 1935, 59 Cities
XIII. Effects of the Works Program on Rural Relief
XIV. Changing Aspects of Rural Relief
XV. Rural Youth: Their Situation and Prospects
XVI. Farming Hazards in the Drought Area
XVII. Rural Families on Relief
XVIII. Migrant Families
XIX. Rural Migration in the United States
XX. State Public Welfare Legislation
XXI. Youth in Agricultural Villages
XXII. The Plantation South, 1934-1937
XXIII. Seven Stranded Coal Towns
XXIV. Federal Work, Security, and Relief Programs
XXV. Vocational Training and Employment of Youth
XXVI. Getting Started: Urban Youth in the Labor Market

Works Progress Administration
Division of Social Research
Research Monograph XII

INTERCITY DIFFERENCES IN COSTS OF LIVING IN MARCH, 1935 — 59 CITIES

By Margaret Loomis Stecker

DA CAPO PRESS • NEW YORK • 1971

A Da Capo Press Reprint Edition

This Da Capo Press edition of *Intercity Differences in Costs of Living in March 1935 — 59 Cities* is an unabridged republication of the first edition published in Washington, D.C., in 1937. It is reprinted by permission from a copy of the original edition owned by the Harvard College Library.

Library of Congress Catalog Card Number 79-165689

ISBN 0-306-70344-0

Published by Da Capo Press, Inc.
A Subsidiary of Plenum Publishing Corporation
227 West 17th Street, New York, N.Y. 10011

Manufactured in the United States of America

INTERCITY DIFFERENCES IN COSTS OF LIVING IN MARCH, 1935—59 CITIES

WORKS PROGRESS ADMINISTRATION
Harry L. Hopkins, *Administrator*
Corrington Gill, *Assistant Administrator*

DIVISION OF SOCIAL RESEARCH
Howard B. Myers, *Director*

INTERCITY DIFFERENCES IN COSTS OF LIVING IN MARCH 1935, 59 CITIES

By

Margaret Loomis Stecker

•

RESEARCH MONOGRAPH XII

1937

UNITED STATES GOVERNMENT PRINTING OFFICE, WASHINGTON

Letter of Transmittal

WORKS PROGRESS ADMINISTRATION,
Washington, D. C., July 23, 1937.

Sir: I have the honor to transmit the findings of a study of the costs of living of industrial, service, and other manual workers at a basic maintenance level and under emergency conditions, initiated by the Federal Emergency Relief Administration and completed by the Works Progress Administration. The figures show the dollars and cents outlay necessary in each of 59 cities in the United States with a population of over 25,000 and relative costs among these cities. The findings provide a large body of basic information which will be of value not only in handling the unemployment relief problem but also in many other fields where facts are required regarding the costs of living and intercity cost differences.

The average cost of living for a 4-person family at the maintenance level in the 59 cities combined was $1,261 per year in 1935. Costs were so nearly alike in the separate cities that only in five did the difference from the average exceed 10 percent. The budget of goods and services priced does not represent the content of a satisfactory American standard of living, nor does its cost indicate what families would have to spend to secure an American standard. It should be noted, however, that according to studies by the Brookings Institution, 4 out of every 10 families in the United States had annual incomes of less than $1,500 in 1929 at the period of our greatest productivity, and 1 out of 5 had less than $1,000.

The study was made in the Division of Social Research under the direction of Howard B. Myers, Director of the Division. Margaret Loomis Stecker supervised the investigation, analyzed the data, and wrote the report. The field work, which was done in cooperation with the United States Bureau of Labor Statistics, was under the supervision of John H. Cover, who also had charge of tabulating the data. Henry B. Arthur, then Assistant Director of the Division of Social Research, supervised the tabulations. John N. Webb, Coordinator of Urban Surveys, assisted in editing the report.

Acknowledgment is made of the assistance of Elizabeth K. Morrison and Glenn Steele in preparing the quantity budgets which were priced; of Harry D. Wilson, Francis E. Wilcox, and Wilson E. Sweeney in conducting the field work and tabulating the data; and of Joel C. Hawkins in checking the analysis. Many others, too numerous to mention separately, assisted in collecting and analyzing the data; their services are acknowledged with appreciation.

Respectfully submitted.

CORRINGTON GILL,
Assistant Administrator.

Hon. HARRY L. HOPKINS,
Works Progress Administrator.

Contents

FIGURES

Intercity Differences in Costs of Living in March 1935, 59 Cities

VII

FIG. 1-SIZE AND LOCATION OF 59 CITIES INCLUDED IN THE STUDY OF COSTS OF LIVING

March 1935

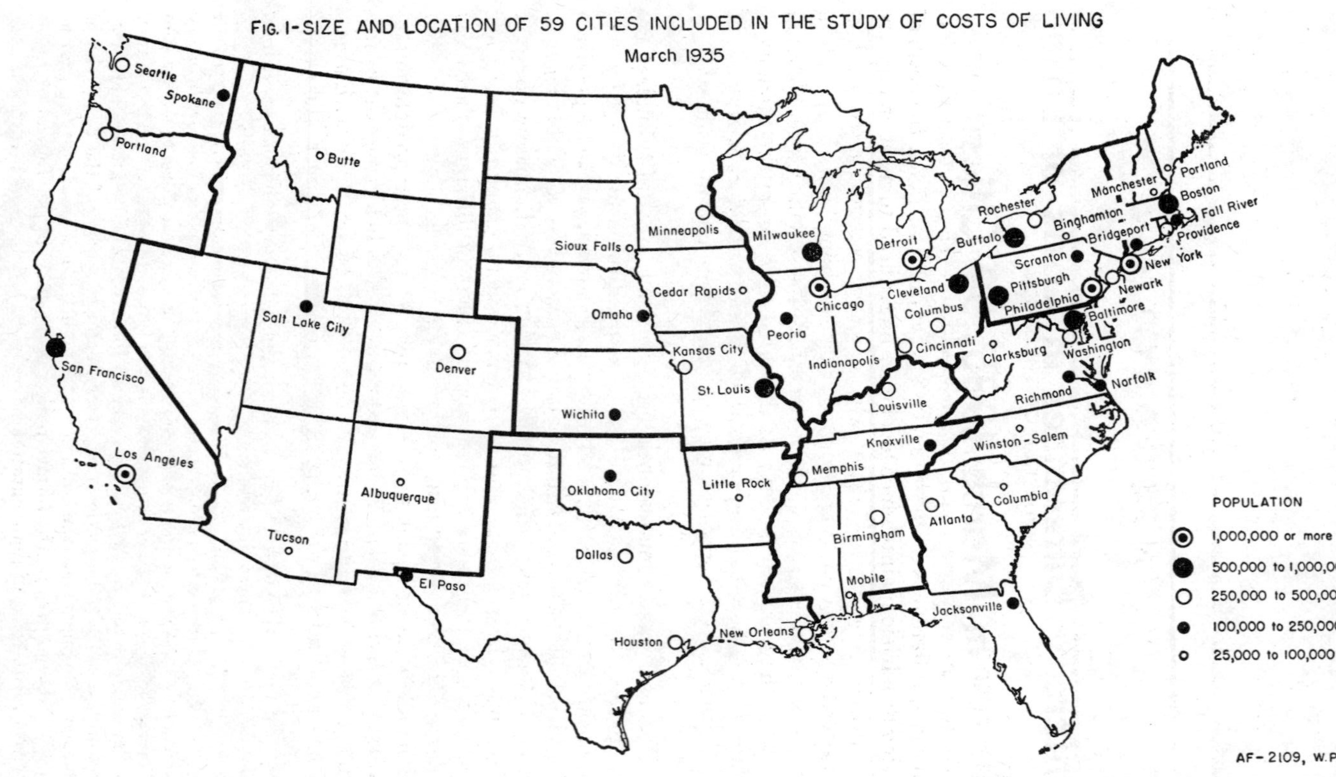

INTRODUCTION

PURPOSE OF THE STUDY

THE PURPOSE of this investigation is to determine the costs of family living in 59 separate cities at two specified levels;[1] to measure intercity cost differences at these levels; to find out how much the costs of living at a basic maintenance level may be reduced to meet emergency conditions; and to ascertain what factors contribute to explain observed intercity cost variations. "Costs of living" is defined as retail prices of the goods and services essential at a specified level of living in more than one community at the same time, or in the same community at different times, or both, combined with such quantities of each item as will represent normal or average consumption at that level.[2]

Cost of living estimates obtained by pricing a quantity budget are not necessarily identical with actual expenditures for living by real families. Expenditures depend on tastes, customs, and local practices as well as on prices and are definitely restricted by available income. In cost measurements the content of living is fixed, income does not enter into the problem, and variations depend primarily on price. Expenditure studies show how much is spent in different places and what is received in return; cost of living studies show how much would have to be spent in different places to buy a predetermined content of living which, as far as practicable, is held constant everywhere. By comparing the results of a cost of living study with ascertained expenditures for living in the same place, however, the extent

[1] Data were not collected to show the costs of living for individuals apart from a family group. These differ in many ways from group living costs.

[2] Commodity prices and service fees were analyzed only as city averages for the purpose of interpreting group costs; no attempt was made to measure intracity variations. Analysis of the problems of sampling in retail price reporting and of price differences between neighborhoods and types of stores, as well as between similar stores in different cities, is part of an Illinois Works Progress Administration project under the direction of Professor John H. Cover, of the University of Chicago, who supervised the collection and tabulation of prices for the present study. One purpose of the former project is to provide the Bureau of Labor Statistics with a list of representative stores in each city, to be used in choosing additional outlets in its collection of retail prices.

to which families in fact are able to obtain the level specified may be measured, with resulting knowledge as to where existing consumption patterns are superior or deficient.[3]

The present study attempts to provide a solution to one of the hitherto unsolved problems of cost of living measurements. Information has often been collected to show how much families spend to live and what they obtain for their money;[4] differences from year to year in the costs of living have been measured in this country for two decades;[5] the same or different levels of living have been priced by a variety of agencies in different places at different times.[6] Until this study was made, however, data were not available to show how much is required

[3] The United States Department of Labor and its predecessors in the Federal Government have made several investigations of family expenditures at approximately the same time, in different communities. A large body of facts relating to expenditures by wage earners and lower-salaried clerical workers in 92 cities in 1917–1919 was published in 1924. See *Cost of Living in the United States*, Bulletin No. 357, United States Department of Labor, Bureau of Labor Statistics, 1924. In 1934 the Bureau started a new series of studies of money disbursements of wage earners and lower-salaried clerical workers in 55 cities. Results of these have been published from time to time in *Monthly Labor Review*, beginning in March 1936. More comprehensive than any such studies made previously is the investigation of consumer purchases carried on with Works Progress Administration funds in 1936 by the Bureau of Labor Statistics in the Department of Labor and the Bureau of Home Economics in the United States Department of Agriculture, in cooperation with the National Resources Committee and the Central Statistical Board.

[4] Williams, Faith M. and Zimmerman, Carle C., *Studies of Family Living in the United States and Other Countries: An Analysis of Material and Method,* Miscellaneous Publication No. 223, United States Department of Agriculture, December 1935.

[5] Index numbers showing cost of living changes over a period of time are computed regularly by the United States Bureau of Labor Statistics, the National Industrial Conference Board, and the Massachusetts Department of Labor and Industries. The Bureau's figures relate to the outlay necessary for a specified list of goods and services in 32 cities separately and in all combined; prices are collected 4 times a year, and the index numbers are printed in *Monthly Labor Review*. The National Industrial Conference Board's index numbers are computed each month as an average for the country as a whole and are printed in *Conference Board Service Letter*. The series for Massachusetts was started in 1919 by the Special Commission on the Necessaries of Life, and figures are now computed each month by the Division on the Necessaries of Life in the Department of Labor and Industries. They are mimeographed in *Memorandum Relative to the Cost of Living in Massachusetts*.

[6] The Bureau of Labor Statistics in 1919 constructed minimum quantity budgets for a "health and decency" level of living for a clerical worker's family and for a wage earner's family. The Bureau priced the former in Washington (D. C.), in August 1919. See *Monthly Labor Review*, December 1919. The wage earner's budget was printed in *Monthly Labor Review*, June 1920, and has been priced a number of times by the Labor Bureau, Inc., a private research group serving the interests of organized labor.

The National Industrial Conference Board used the same technique but different quantity budgets in investigating the minimum cost of a "fair American" standard

for support at a uniform level of living in a large number of places at the same time, or how these costs compare on an intercity basis.[7] Cost differentials between two well-defined levels of living had not been so completely analyzed, and such a volume of detail had not been assembled for comparing estimated costs and actual expenditures.

The reason for this paucity of facts so obviously useful in many fields of economic and social life does not lie in lack of interest in the subject. Delay in investigation, rather, is to be accounted for by the numerous technical difficulties involved in setting up a study which would supply the materials desired and by the expense of its execution. As the relief and work programs of the Federal Government progressed, the need for detailed information relating to costs of living became increasingly apparent. The investigation of which this monograph is a report was made to supply the necessary figures, as part of the broad research programs of the Federal Emergency Relief Administration and the Works Progress Administration.[8]

of living among wage earners. The first of these studies was made in Fall River in October 1919; the most recent of which a report has been published covered 12 industrial cities in August–October 1927. See National Industrial Conference Board, *The Cost of Living Among Wage Earners, Fall River, Massachusetts, October 1919*, Research Report No. 22, Boston, November 1919; and National Industrial Conference Board, *The Cost of Living in Twelve Industrial Cities*, New York, 1928.

Other private organizations have proceeded along more or less similar lines. See, for example, Heller Committee for Research in Social Economics, *Quantity and Cost Budgets* * * *, University of California, Berkeley, Calif., February 1937. See also Visiting Housekeeper Association, *Scale for Estimating Minimum Budgets* * * *, Detroit, Mich.

[7] The National Industrial Conference Board priced an identical level of living in the 5 separate boroughs of the city of New York in 1926 and in 12 industrial cities in 1927. In 1935 the Board covered 69 cities in a comparative cost of living survey, but it has not published figures for the separate communities. See National Industrial Conference Board, *The Cost of Living in New York City*, New York, 1926; National Industrial Conference Board, *The Cost of Living in Twelve Industrial Cities*, New York, 1928; and *Conference Board Bulletin*, December 10, 1935. For such findings of the study in 69 cities as may be compared with those of the present investigation, see pp. 136–138.

The International Labour Office made a study of the costs of living in 14 cities in Europe in 1931, as compared with the cost of living in Detroit, by pricing a sample of goods and services which were representative of local consumption habits and differed, therefore, in the separate cities. International Labour Office, *A Contribution to the Study of International Comparisons of Costs of Living*, Studies and Reports, Series N (Statistics) No. 17, second revised edition, Geneva, 1932. Certain findings of the study are noted on pp. 138, 146, and 147.

[8] The Bureau of Labor Statistics, the Federal agency vested with responsibility for collecting and analyzing data related to prices and urban costs of living, cooperated in the field work and computed the city average food prices. Thus, duplication of effort was avoided and the Bureau was able to extend its retail price reporting system. The Bureau collects retail food prices each month, and prices of other goods and services quarterly. To the 51 cities in which food prices were collected prior to 1935, 13 others have been added as a result of the

QUANTITY BUDGETS

The content of a standard of living is not subject to exact measurement. Even at a minimum level it is not easy to say what is essential and what is not. Construction of quantity budgets for pricing purposes is accomplished, therefore, through many compromises. These are multiplied as the number and variety of communities to be represented are increased. Purchases in the course of a year, moreover, cover a wider variety than it is either feasible or necessary to price. Hence, the goods and services which are priced must be included in the budgets in such quantities as will represent others which are not priced, in order to obtain a balanced total cost.[9]

Research in nutrition has determined necessary food consumption, and minimum housing standards are fairly well established.[10] There is no authority for the other essentials of family living, and budget allowances must be constructed by well-reasoned estimates. Actual consumption by families whose purchases seem to supply the needs of health and self-respect forms the basis for certain budget allowances. If it appears, however, that some goods and services are being obtained through skimping on other essentials, a synthetic budget must bring the other essentials up to satisfactory standards. If, on the other hand, it is apparent that certain expenditures cannot be made at the level specified without the sacrifice of others more necessary from a common-sense viewpoint, synthetic budgets will not include them.

Thus, synthetic budgets of a balanced content of living at a minimum level in some respects are superior to the consumption habits of the class they represent and in others they are inferior. Through careful planning, nutrition can be purchased for less than families usually spend for food. Housing occupied by families of modest means at the present time frequently is below accepted standards of adequacy. Group pressure often dictates purchases whose principal justification lies in the intangible satisfactions they afford.

THE TWO LEVELS OF LIVING

In the present investigation quantity budgets were constructed as an itemization of the content of two levels of living.[11] The basic *maintenance* level represents normal or average minimum requirements

present study. These 13 cities are in sections of the country or are representative of local characteristics not previously so completely covered.

[9] Popular comparisons of intercity cost differences are sometimes made on the basis of rents, food prices, or some other single budget item prices. These may represent, in fact, only a small part of the total cost of living.

[10] There is a conflict in housing standards between what is desirable and what is practical. Those specified for this study take into account the necessity for pricing what exists, but in no sense constitute specifications for the future.

[11] Quantity budgets for the two levels of living are given in complete detail in Stecker, Margaret L., *Quantity Budgets for Basic Maintenance and Emergency Standards of Living*, Research Bulletin Series I, No. 21, Division of Social Research, Works Progress Administration, 1936.

for industrial, service, and other manual workers; the *emergency* level takes into account certain economies which may be made under depression conditions. The maintenance level provides not only for physical needs but also gives some consideration to psychological values. The emergency level allows more exclusively, though not entirely, for material wants, but it might be questioned on the grounds of health hazards if families had to live at this level for a considerable period of time.

The family whose costs of living are measured in this investigation is best described as the unskilled manual worker type. It consists of a moderately active man, a moderately active woman, a boy age 13, and a girl age 8.[12] The man wears overalls at his work. No household assistance of any kind is employed.

At the maintenance level, these four persons live in a four- or five-room house or apartment with water and sewer connections. Their dwelling is in at least a fair state of repair and contains an indoor bath and toilet for their exclusive use. They have gas, ice, electricity, and a small radio, but no automobile. They read a daily newspaper, go to the movies once a week, and enjoy other simple leisure-time activities. Their food is an adequate diet at minimum cost. They pay for their own medical care. Clothing, furniture, furnishings, and household equipment are provided with some regard for social as well as material needs. Carfare, taxes, and numerous incidental expenses are included in their budget.

At the emergency level this four-person family has cheaper kinds of food to secure the same nutritive values as the maintenance budget provides. Housing is less desirable. There is less frequent replacement of clothing, furniture, furnishings, and household equipment. Household supplies are less plentiful; other services are reduced in quantity or eliminated entirely.

All the essentials of living are to be purchased at market prices; the budgets make no provision for home-grown food or home dressmaking.

[12] The size and composition of this family was selected as the nearest approach to the average census private family, which consists of 4.01 persons. The census distribution is such that the median size of all families is 3.40, and of urban families, 3.26. *Fifteenth Census of the United States: 1930*, Population Vol. VI, pp. 10 and 16. Less than one-third of the census families in 1930 had more than four members; in urban areas the proportion was only slightly in excess of one-fourth. *Ibid.*, pp. 13 and 14. Sixty-two percent of all census families and sixty percent of urban census families contained only one gainful worker. *Ibid.*, pp. 22–23. The average number of children under age 15 per family was 1.2 and per urban family, 1.02. The latter figures were obtained by dividing all children in this age group by total number of families. *Fifteenth Census of the United States: 1930*, Population Vol. II, p. 567. The sex and age of the two children in the present study were assigned arbitrarily for the purpose of representing a diversity of cost elements. In the matter of housing certain complications are implied which disappear if the family is considered as representative rather than as an exact replica of real families.

Complete self-support in all respects is provided for, but only on a current cost basis, since there is no allowance for carrying or liquidating debts or for necessary future expenditures, except small life insurance policies.

It is probable that neither of these levels of living has been defined before. The maintenance budget is not so liberal as that for a "health and decency" level which the skilled worker may hope to obtain, but it affords more than a "minimum of subsistence" living. The emergency budget, restricted as it is, represents a better level of living than most relief budgets allow.

Neither of these budgets approaches the content of what may be considered a satisfactory American standard of living, nor do their costs measure what families in this country would have to spend to secure "the abundant life." Such a standard would include an automobile, better housing and equipment, a more varied diet, and preventive medical care. Provision would be made for future education of the children and for economic security through saving. These and other desirable improvements above a maintenance level of living would necessitate annual expenditures considerably in excess of the money values of the budgets used in this investigation.

From a realistic point of view, however, little is to be gained for the present purpose by constructing quantity budgets whose contents do not reasonably portray existing expenditure habits. Only on this basis are they of practical use in determining prevailing costs of living. At the same time it should be understood that the budgets priced are neither ideal nor static and that as consumption itself is raised to higher levels, budgets must take account of the improved standards of living thus manifested.

CITIES SURVEYED

Selecting the 59 cities in which to make the study required consideration of geographic location, size, and socio-economic characteristics of various kinds. These considerations are discussed in some detail in Chapter VII, Techniques and Procedures. The 59 cities, their location and population in 1930, are shown in table 1 and figure 1.

COMPUTING THE COSTS OF LIVING

The quantity budgets at both levels were uniform, in the main, in all communities studied in order that the cost estimates might approximate a measure of the outlay necessary for the same goods and services in each community. Absolute identity of budget content, however, could be maintained throughout only by the sacrifice of reality. Some items cannot be priced in certain communities at all; average requirements overstate or understate needs in given instances. The outstanding examples of budget needs which cannot be completely standardized are housing, fuel, ice, and transportation.

***Table 1.*—59 Cities Included in the Study of Costs of Living, March 1935**

City and geographic division	Population 1930
New England:	
Boston, Mass	781, 188
Providence, R. I	252, 981
Bridgeport, Conn	146, 716
Fall River, Mass	115, 274
Manchester, N. H	76, 834
Portland, Maine	70, 810
Middle Atlantic:	
New York, N. Y	6, 930, 446
Philadelphia, Pa	1, 950, 961
Pittsburgh, Pa	669, 817
Buffalo, N. Y	573, 076
Newark, N. J	442, 337
Rochester, N. Y	328, 132
Scranton, Pa	143, 433
Binghamton, N. Y	76, 662
East North Central:	
Chicago, Ill	3, 376, 438
Detroit, Mich	1, 568, 662
Cleveland, Ohio	900, 429
Milwaukee, Wis	578, 249
Cincinnati, Ohio	451, 160
Indianapolis, Ind	364, 161
Columbus, Ohio	290, 564
Peoria, Ill	104, 969
West North Central:	
St. Louis, Mo	821, 960
Minneapolis, Minn	464, 356
Kansas City, Mo	399, 746
Omaha, Nebr	214, 006
Wichita, Kans	111, 110
Cedar Rapids, Iowa	56, 097
Sioux Falls, S. Dak	33, 362
South Atlantic:	
Baltimore, Md	804, 874
Washington, D. C	486, 869
South Atlantic—Continued.	
Atlanta, Ga	270, 366
Richmond, Va	182, 929
Norfolk, Va	129, 710
Jacksonville, Fla	129, 549
Winston-Salem, N. C	75, 274
Columbia, S. C	51, 581
Clarksburg, W. Va	28, 866
East South Central:	
Louisville, Ky	307, 745
Birmingham, Ala	259, 678
Memphis, Tenn	253, 143
Knoxville, Tenn	105, 802
Mobile, Ala	68, 202
West South Central:	
New Orleans, La	458, 762
Houston, Tex	292, 352
Dallas, Tex	260, 475
Oklahoma City, Okla	185, 389
El Paso, Tex	102, 421
Little Rock, Ark	81, 679
Mountain:	
Denver, Colo	287, 861
Salt Lake City, Utah	140, 267
Butte, Mont	39, 532
Tucson, Ariz	32, 506
Albuquerque, N. Mex	26, 570
Pacific:	
Los Angeles, Calif	1, 238, 048
San Francisco, Calif	634, 394
Seattle, Wash	365, 583
Portland, Oreg	301, 815
Spokane, Wash	115, 514

Source: *Fifteenth Census of the United States: 1930*, Population Vol. I, pp. 10 and 22 ff.

Most of the essentials of living in urban communities in this country are acquired through private purchase; some are not a direct charge to the consumer but are supplied by the community from the tax fund. Prices of those goods and services to be purchased individually, plus specified taxes, were obtained in each city studied in the present investigation. City average prices of each item were then combined with the quantity allowances of each per year, as given in the budgets, to obtain budget group costs. If there was a sales tax, its amount was added and aggregates for the cost of living as a whole were computed.

RESULTS

The findings of the study measure in dollars and cents the costs of self-support at 2 levels of living for a 4-person manual worker's family in each of 59 cities. They do not show what families were spending or what their purchases should be. Component elements of the costs of living are analyzed and compared to indicate their relative importance within a given city and to explain intercity cost differences. Such inferences as may be drawn regarding relative costs must be considered with a view to the fact that uniform budgets were priced, in the main, with only minor allowances for differences in local needs and habits. Comparative group costs, either on a geographic or size of city basis, relate only to costs in the cities of which each group is composed.

It is possible that the levels of living specified can be obtained in the separate cities with smaller outlays than the results of this study show to be necessary through substitution of commodities locally less expensive but serving the same purpose as those specified in the quantity budgets. Likewise, some savings may be effected by home production, patronage of special sales, and various forms of thrift and superior household management. On the other hand, waste of various kinds may more or less offset these savings. Such factors are impossible of statistical measurement, especially in an appraisal of intercity costs on a comparable basis.

It would be too much to expect that all details for every city are exact representations of definite local needs or that even for the budgets as a whole the values are accurate to the last penny. Accepting the figures for what they are—namely, a generalized statement of the amounts required for the purpose specified, not to be taken too literally with reference to any one family or group of families—there is reason to believe that a contribution has been made to cost of living knowledge, not only with reference to the money values of a given level but also to the techniques by which these values were obtained. Extension of these figures for comparative purposes to other communities, other levels of living, and families of different size and composition should proceed with caution.

SUMMARY

THIS STUDY was instituted to determine the annual costs of self-support in 59 cities for a 4-person manual worker's family at 2 levels of living. The first level has been designated as the basic *maintenance* level and the second as the *emergency* level.

The terms "maintenance level" and "emergency level" have been defined in the Introduction. For purposes of this summary it may be said that the cost of the maintenance level measures necessary current outlay, including some allowance for psychological as well as material needs. The cost of the emergency level provides more exclusively, but not entirely, for physical wants.

The Works Progress Administration urges that in considering the findings of this study two facts be clearly understood.

(1) That neither the maintenance nor the emergency level represents a desirable living standard. Neither level will permit families to enjoy the full fruits of what we have come to call the American standard of living. Indeed, those forced to exist at the emergency level for an extended period may be subjected to serious health hazards. From the point of view of the long-time well-being of workers' families, a desirable standard of living would be one in which the concepts of maintenance and emergency have no place. Moreover, as a basis for a national volume of consumption sufficient to keep pace with the increasing output of industry, the two levels are inadequate. Those interested in improving our standards of living will find the information in this study useful as a description of 2 limited levels which the workers in 1935 could achieve at various costs in 59 cities, rather than as a statement of desirable objectives.

(2) That the costs of the two levels of living which are to be outlined are those of March 1935. Since that time costs of living have advanced throughout the country. In March 1937 the costs of living had increased in 31 of the 59 cities studied; facts are not available for the other 28 cities. Thus, it does not follow that the estimates presented in this study would be adequate at the present time to support even the low standards represented by the basic maintenance and emergency levels.

The costs of living at the maintenance level ranged from a high of $1,415 in Washington [1] to a low of $1,130 in Mobile, at March 1935 prices. The average cost in the 59 cities combined was $1,261. The cost of living at the emergency level also was highest in Washington, $1,014; but was lowest in Wichita, $810. The average was $903. At both levels necessary outlays in the most expensive city averaged about 25 percent above those in the least expensive. In more than half the cities living costs were within a range of $100 per year.

These cost of living figures relate to the requirements of a family consisting of a man, a woman, a boy age 13, and a girl age 8. They were obtained by pricing a list of goods and services essential for this family at each level of living; they do not show family expenditures. The budgets priced were uniform in all cities except for a few items. For instance, allowances for transportation had to be adjusted to take account of city size and area; and allowances for fuel and ice had to be adjusted to take account of differences in climate.[2] Prices of the separate items obtained in each city, combined with their quantity allowances, constitute the local costs of support at the levels of living specified.

The quality of goods and services priced was the same in both budgets. The cost differential between the two was obtained by substituting a larger proportion of the cheaper kinds of food at the emergency than at the maintenance level to meet the same nutritive requirements, by allowing for less frequent replacement of clothing, furniture, furnishings, and household equipment, by curtailing the supply of certain household necessities, by providing less expensive housing, and by reducing the allowances of certain other services.

The average cost of the emergency budget on this basis was 72 percent of the average cost of the maintenance budget; there was little difference in this respect among the separate cities. Household operation costs were most nearly alike at the two levels, and costs of miscellaneous family needs differed most.

Twice as much of the average cost of living in the 59 cities combined was required for food as for housing, and the outlay necessary for household operation was less than for clothing, clothing upkeep, and personal care. The difference between maintenance and emergency budget costs was greater for clothing, clothing upkeep, and personal care than for household operation, and miscellaneous family needs took one-fifth of the average maintenance budget cost but only one-sixth of the average emergency budget cost.

---

[1] In this summary all aggregate values and percentages are rounded to the nearest whole number; in the text of the report and the tables exact figures are given.

[2] Quantity budgets for the two levels of living are given in complete detail in Stecker, Margaret L., *Quantity Budgets for Basic Maintenance and Emergency Standards of Living*, Research Bulletin, Series I, No. 21, Division of Social Research, Works Progress Administration, 1936.

	Maintenance level		Emergency level	
	Amount	*Percent*	*Amount*	*Percent*
Total	$1, 261	100	$903	100
Food	448	35	340	37
Clothing, clothing upkeep, and personal care	184	15	128	14
Housing	222	18	168	19
Household operation	154	12	122	14
Miscellaneous	253	20	145	16

Intercity variations in the costs of living as a whole resulted from all manner of combinations of separate commodity and service costs. Relatively large outlays often were necessary for some items and relatively small outlays for others in the same place.

Among the 10 most expensive cities in which to live at the maintenance level when this study was made, for example, only San Francisco, Chicago, and Boston reported all major budget group costs well above the 59-city average. In the other most expensive cities some group costs were high and some were low. Food costs were less than the average in Minneapolis, Milwaukee, Cleveland, and Detroit; clothing, clothing upkeep, and personal care costs were relatively low in New York, Washington, and St. Louis; household operation costs were low in Washington, Cleveland, and St. Louis. On the other hand, all 10 of these highest cost cities reported rents and the costs of miscellaneous family needs above the average.

In the 10 lowest cost cities rents were less than the average in the 59 cities combined; but only in Mobile, Wichita, Little Rock, and Knoxville were all costs relatively low. Food was relatively expensive in Clarksburg and Dallas; and clothing, clothing upkeep, and personal care costs slightly exceeded the average in Clarksburg, Columbus, and Cedar Rapids. Household operation costs were above the average in Cedar Rapids and El Paso; and the cost of miscellaneous family needs was above the average in Birmingham.

Though it cannot be said as a general proposition that geographic location alone determines relative costs of living, there are some sections where costs are undoubtedly low, and some where they seem to be high, with reference to the general average. In the South Central States, for example, every city reported less than average costs for the budget as a whole and for most of the major budget groups. Less was required per year for support at the maintenance level in the most expensive South Central city than in the cheapest New England or Middle Atlantic city. None of these South Central cities had as many as 500,000 population. The costs of living seemed to be high in the East North Central Division as well as in the New England and Middle Atlantic States, but there were exceptions to the general tendency in each area. More large cities are located in these sections of the country than in any others, and the costs of living in the large cities often exceeded the average.

On the other hand, size of city, as such, does not account entirely for cost variations, though for the budget as a whole costs declined with population. Families in the two largest cities in the Pacific Division required more for support at the maintenance level of living than in the three smaller cities in that area, but in the Mountain Division costs in the two largest cities were less than in the smaller places. All cities with a population of 500,000 or more were more expensive places in which to live than the average, and costs were much alike in most of them. Costs in some of the smaller cities were relatively high and in others, relatively low, depending on a variety of local circumstances, the influence of which may be guessed but not measured quantitatively.

The greatest similarity in major budget group costs,[3] which together constitute the cost of living as a whole, was found in combined food prices; and the greatest difference, in rents. Clothing, clothing upkeep, and personal care cost dispersion more nearly approached that of food; household operation and miscellaneous family needs cost dispersions more nearly resembled that of rent. Some of the widest cost variations were found for subgroups within these classifications, and individual commodity and service prices differed most of all.

FOOD

When prices of the 44 commodities in the maintenance food budget were combined with the quantities of each required per year by the 4-person family of this investigation and totaled, there was a difference of less than 17 percent between Cedar Rapids, where cost was least, and Bridgeport, where cost was most. This cost similarity for food as a group resulted from partial cancellation of differences for separate commodities when all were combined. Prices of lard, sugar, ham, bacon, raisins, cheese, and most can and package goods, for example, showed ranges of less than 50 percent between lowest and highest city averages. Highest city averages for carrots, cabbage, spinach, and apples, on the other hand, were over four times as much as lowest city averages. Prices of other food commodities varied from city to city within a range between the extremes for the two groups just cited. In no city, however, were prices of all 44 commodities relatively high or relatively low.

As compared with the average cost of food in the 59 cities combined, costs in the New England, Middle Atlantic, South Atlantic, and Mountain cities averaged high, and in all other areas averaged low. There were relative degrees to the variations, however, and they were caused by differing cost relationships among the separate commodity groups. Only in New England were all group costs high, and only

[3] All cost comparisons are based on prices and quantities allowed in the maintenance budget, plus sales tax where levied. Relatives for the costs of the emergency budget were nearly but not quite identical, owing to differences in the quantity allowances in the two; prices were the same.

in the East North Central States were all group costs low. Size of city was not so important a factor in food cost differences as was geographic location, and group averages for the five population classifications were much alike.

CLOTHING, CLOTHING UPKEEP, AND PERSONAL CARE

The costs of the clothing, clothing upkeep, and personal care budget for the maintenance level of living varied nearly twice as much as the costs of food; that is, slightly more than 32 percent between Dallas, the cheapest city, and Butte, the most expensive city. Whereas only commodities comprise the food list, certain local services in addition to commodities are required for clothing, clothing upkeep, and personal care. Prices of these services, such as cleaning and pressing, shoe repairs, and haircuts and waves, differed more than most commodity prices. On the other hand, prices of many clothing commodities were twice as high in some cities as in others. This spread in prices was particularly noticeable for girls' clothing. Price differentials, however, tended to cancel in each city, as was the case with food prices, producing a much narrower range for the costs of the clothing, clothing upkeep, and personal care budget as a whole.

Highest costs for clothing, clothing upkeep, and personal care were found in the Pacific, Mountain, and East North Central Divisions, where all but 2 of the 18 cities were above the average in the 59 cities combined. Only 2 among the 20 cities in the 3 groups of Southern States had more than average costs for this major budget group. These costs also were relatively low in the Middle Atlantic States, with the exception of two cities.

The relative positions of costs for clothing, clothing upkeep, and personal care as a whole in cities in the separate areas were also found for its subgroups, save for clothing upkeep in the East North Central Division and personal care in the West North Central. Clothing upkeep was one of the few groups of budget items whose cost seemed to be closely related to size of city; it definitely increased as population decreased.

HOUSING

Rent of dwellings specified for the maintenance level of living in Washington was 116 percent higher than in Portland (Oreg.). This housing was required to have four or five rooms and a private indoor bath and toilet for each family. It was described as safely constructed, in at least a fair state of repair, without serious fire hazards, and conforming to existing housing and building codes. It had normal size rooms and windows, and sewer and water connections or equivalent services. Such accommodations were found in big apartment or smaller flat buildings, in row houses, or detached cottages, depending on the usual type of working class dwelling in the separate cities. Despite the great variety of building types priced, rents in 36 cities were between $15 and $20 per month, and in 14 more they were between $20 and $25.

Rents, in general, seemed to be highest in sections of the country where the most substantial buildings are required because of weather conditions and lowest where frame cottages on piers provide entirely adequate shelter. Size of city affected rent levels to a greater extent than it did most other essentials of living. Thus, the average of rents in cities with a population of 500,000 or more greatly exceeded the average in smaller places and the average in the 59 cities combined. Rents were relatively high in 15 of the 19 largest cities studied, and they were below the average in 9 of the 13 cities with less than 100,000 population.

HOUSEHOLD OPERATION

At the maintenance level of living approximately two-fifths of the average outlay necessary for household operation was required for fuel; one-fifth for replacement of furniture, furnishings, and household equipment; one-sixth for ice, refuse disposal, and unspecified essentials; and one-eighth each for electricity and household supplies. Intercity differences in the costs of the household operation budget as a whole were the result of a wide variety of differences in costs of the budget subgroups. No city had highest cost or lowest cost for more than one of these household operation budget subgroups.

The cost of the household operation budget as a whole was nearly 68 percent more in Sioux Falls than in Houston. The cost of winter fuel, however, was 6 times as much in the city where it was most expensive as where it was least expensive; the largest annual gas budget cost was over 13 times as much as the smallest. Differences in costs of the budget allowances of ice, electricity, and refuse disposal also greatly exceeded the differences for the entire household operation group combined. For household supplies and for furniture, furnishings, and household equipment, on the other hand, the cost spreads between the extreme cities were very much less. The cost of unspecified essentials in the household operation budget was practically identical in all cities.

Marked differences in the costs of the household operation budget as a whole appeared in separate sections of the country. All but 1 of the 16 cities in the New England, Pacific, and Mountain States were above the average in the 59 cities combined; and all but 1 of the 11 South Central cities were below. In the other geographic divisions household operation costs were relatively high in some places and low in others; but, except in the West North Central States, the group averages were less than in the 59 cities combined. In the areas where household operation budget costs were highest, everything was above the average except ice in New England, fuel in the Mountain States, and both fuel and electricity in the Pacific States. In the lowest cost areas everything was less than the average except the budget allowance of gas in the East South Central cities and of ice and electricity in the West South Central cities. Size of city apart from geographic location seemed not to account for any differences in the costs of household operation as a whole or of its component subgroups.

MISCELLANEOUS FAMILY NEEDS

None of the miscellaneous family needs provided for in the budgets are supplied by commodities, except drugs and appliances in the medical care list, school supplies, and certain items in the recreation list. At the maintenance level of living, recreation of all sorts required three-tenths of the average cost of miscellaneous family needs; life insurance, church contributions, other contributions, and taxes,[4] one-quarter; medical care and transportation, one-fifth each; and school attendance, three one-hundredths.

Most of these miscellaneous costs are conditioned largely by local circumstances. Their intercity relationships, like those for household operation, result from the balancing of costs of a number of unrelated items. The cost of miscellaneous family needs was highest in Cleveland, where 63 percent more was needed to purchase the budget allowance than in El Paso.

The variety of miscellaneous family needs probably explains the absence of any consistent cost tendencies which may be attributed to geographic location, except as these are brought about by the size of cities in different sections of the country. There is a definite relationship between size of city and cost of miscellaneous family needs, owing primarily to the fact that the allowance of transportation in the separate cities was based directly on population and city area.

It is impossible to forecast how much any one family will need to spend in a given year for medical care. Requirements over a considerable period of time for a large number of families, however, can be estimated with reasonable accuracy. The annual cost of minimum medical care per 1,000 persons constitutes the starting point of the medical care cost estimates in the present study. Thus computed, there was a difference of 72 percent between cities with the lowest and highest costs. The outlay necessary in each city was largely determined by relative doctors', dentists', nurses', and hospital fees, inasmuch as together they required about 90 percent of the total; eyeglasses and frames, proprietary medicines, and prescriptions took 10 percent.

Variations in what families needed to spend for transportation were greater than for any other budget subgroup, except refuse disposal, school attendance, and taxes. Thirteen and one-half times as much

[4] Exclusive of sales tax.

was required for transportation where cost was highest as where it was lowest. This range occurred because more rides were allowed in the largest than in the smallest places, rather than because of any such wide diversity in streetcar or bus fares. The maximum spread for adult cash fares was from 5 cents to 10 cents; prices of tickets or tokens were less widely dispersed.

Some cities provided all the books, supplies, and gymnasium equipment needed by children in the public schools; in others these items required nearly 2 percent of the total cost of living for a family with a boy age 13 and a girl age 8. Hence, intercity differences in costs were very wide.

Recreation is provided in the maintenance budget by allowances for newspapers, motion picture theater admissions, organization memberships, tobacco, toys, and other leisure-time accessories. The difference in the total recreation cost between the city where least was required to purchase the recreation budget allowance and the one where most was required was 40 percent.

The spread in newspaper costs was 87 percent and in motion picture theater admission costs, 76 percent. By budget definition, the costs of tobacco, toys, and other leisure-time accessories were identical in all cities. The amounts involved are small and prices are practically the same wherever these items are sold, except for sales taxes where levied. Identical allowances also were made in all cities for organization dues, life insurance premiums, church contributions, and other contributions.

In 18 of the 59 cities there was a sales tax in March 1935, representing from 2 percent to one-half of 1 percent of the total cost of living. Personal property taxes were assessed in 22 cities; capitation taxes, in 25; and both, in 11. There were 13 cities where families at the economic level with which this study is concerned were not assessed direct taxes.

COST VARIATIONS

Differences in service charges and other costs which for the most part are locally determined seem to be more accountable for intercity cost of living variations than differences in commodity prices. What must be paid to the landlord and the utility companies, together with outlays necessary for medical services, refuse disposal, taxes, and similarly determined local needs differed more among the 59 cities included in this investigation than the amounts required for food, clothing, household replacements, and supplies. Costs which are determined largely by local conditions cannot be measured so accurately as commodity costs, and it is possible that their intercity range is overstated. The effect of the greater dispersion of locally determined costs on the relative costs of the budget as a whole was reduced somewhat by the fact that they required slightly under two-fifths of the average annual cost of living. The less varied commodity costs exclusive of coal or wood and ice, together with the outlays necessary for life insurance, postage, and other essentials whose prices are identical everywhere, required slightly over three-fifths.

Costs differed most for those services which were supplied from the tax fund in some communities, but which were a direct charge on the individual or family in others. These services are refuse disposal and public school attendance. Direct taxes, which were levied in some places and not in others, likewise belong in the group of widely dispersed budget costs. Extensive cost variations among the 59 cities also occurred for those necessities supplied through a diversity of sources, or for which the budget allowance for a given purpose differed with natural circumstances. The widely dispersed costs of transportation, gas, coal or wood, and ice are to be explained not only by price differences but also by the fact that a larger quantity is required in some places than in others at the same level of living. For example, less natural gas than manufactured gas as a rule is necessary for a given purpose; at the same time, the rate per 1,000 cubic feet of natural gas usually is lower. The quantity budgets allow gas for cooking and water heating only during the months when coal or wood for room warming is not necessary. The period of use thus provided varies from 5 to 9 months per year. All these factors contributed to explain annual gas cost variations.

The costs of newspapers, electricity, housing, motion picture theater admissions, clothing upkeep, and medical services are attributable in varying degrees to peculiar circumstances in each locality. Size of city affects some, geographic location affects others, but all are the product of a variety of local forces past or present which fix the going rate. For none of these did necessary annual outlays differ so much as did costs of the first groups of items mentioned, but they were considerably more dispersed than the costs of the groups composed mostly of commodities; the latter showed the smallest range.

These groups composed mostly of commodities are household supplies; personal care; clothing; drugs and appliances; furniture, furnishings, and household equipment; and food. National advertising, chain merchandising, and concentration of manufacturing and processing many commodities in relatively few hands seem to make for commodity cost uniformity. Considerations related to seasonality, the kind of goods locally sold, and the distance from the source of supply constitute perhaps the outstanding factors in commodity cost dispersion. Local trade practices and their influence on retail quotations, though important, were not studied in the present investigation.

COSTS OF LIVING AND FAMILY EXPENDITURES

Lowest income self-supporting white families in 10 cities were spending an average of $10 less per year at the time the present study was made than the average cost of the maintenance budget in the same 10 cities. The expenditures with which the budget costs are compared were made by wage earners and lower-salaried clerical workers during a period of 1 year between 1933 and 1936. The facts were collected and analyzed by the Bureau of Labor Statistics.

Families allowed relatively more of their total expenditures for food, personal care, household operation, furniture, furnishings, household equipment, and transportation than appeared in the distribution of quantity budget costs; and they allowed relatively less for clothing, housing, medical care, recreation, and all other needs. The distributions of average annual cost and average annual expenditure are shown below.

10-city average	*W. P. A. cost of living study*	*B. L. S. expenditure study*
Number of persons per family	4. 00	4. 75
Cost of living or expenditure	$1, 267	$1, 257
Total percent	100. 0	100. 0
Food	35. 8	38. 5
Clothing and clothing upkeep	12. 6	10. 6
Personal care	1. 9	2. 1
Housing	16. 9	16. 6
Household operation	9. 8	12. 2
Furniture, furnishings, and household equipment	2. 4	2. 6
Medical care	4. 1	3. 5
Transportation	5. 0	5. 6
Recreation	6. 0	4. 8
All other	5. 5	3. 5

Families studied by the Bureau averaged larger than the four-person family whose costs of living were measured in the present investigation, and they were not of the same composition. What constitute current charges also differed in the two sets of figures. These facts explain some of the differences between distribution of expenditures and distribution of costs among the separate budget items. Differences also occurred because the quantity budget priced in the present study was designed to provide a balanced plan for spending, regardless of individual tastes or local circumstances, or the managerial ability of any family or group of families, whereas all these factors play some part in the actual spending pattern.

Chapter I

TWO LEVELS OF LIVING

THE ANNUAL costs of living for a 4-person manual worker's family at a maintenance level in 59 cities in the United States in March 1935 ranged from a high of $1,414.54 in Washington to a low of $1,129.81 in Mobile (appendix table 2).[1] The cost of living at a level reduced somewhat to meet temporary emergency conditions was also highest in Washington, $1,013.98, but the lowest cost city at the emergency level was Wichita, where the amount required was $809.64 (appendix table 8).[2]

At both levels highest costs exceeded lowest costs by slightly more than 25 percent. The spread was $285 at the maintenance level and $204 at the emergency level, but costs were so similar in the separate cities that in more than half of the 59, the money value of the maintenance budget averaged between $1,200 and $1,300 per year (table 2); for the emergency budget between $850 and $950 was required in 41 of the 59 cities. The cost of living in the least expensive city at the maintenance level was more than $100 greater than in the most expensive city at the emergency level.

The costs of living at the maintenance level exceeded the average for the group in 29 cities, and they were less in 30 cities (fig. 2); comparable numbers at the emergency level were 28 and 31, respectively. Washington costs were about 12 percent above the average; Mobile and Wichita costs were about 10 percent below (appendix tables 3 and 9).

The cost of the emergency budget averaged 71.7 percent of the cost of the maintenance budget (table 3). Ratios varied only slightly

---

[1] See table 7, p. 10, for changes in the costs of living between March 1935 and March 1937.

[2] Quantity budgets for the two levels of living are given in complete detail in Stecker, Margaret L., *Quantity Budgets for Basic Maintenance and Emergency Standards of Living*, Research Bulletin, Series I, No. 21, Division of Social Research, Works Progress Administration, 1936. For the methods used in collecting quotations and computing city average prices and aggregate costs, see ch. VII.

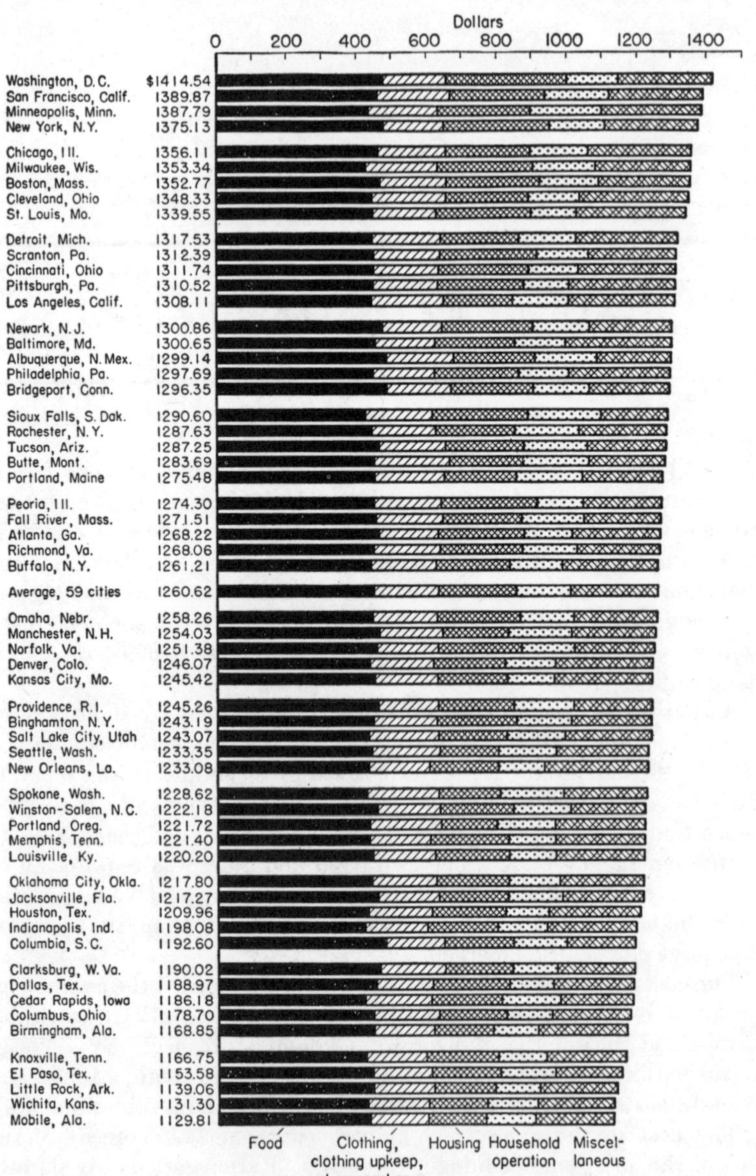

FIG. 2 - ANNUAL COSTS OF LIVING, BY MAJOR BUDGET GROUPS,
4-PERSON MANUAL WORKER'S FAMILY,
59 CITIES, MARCH 1935

Maintenance Level

AF-2111, W.P.A.

among the 59 cities. The smallest differential between the maintenance and the emergency budget costs was found in Minneapolis, where the latter was 73.1 percent of the former, and the largest was in Binghamton and Fall River, 70.6 percent. The range in clothing cost differentials was narrowest, from a ratio of 70.6 percent in Salt Lake City to 68.5 percent in Scranton; that for miscellaneous costs was the widest, from 63.8 percent in Kansas City (Mo.) to 50.5 percent in El Paso.

Table 2.—Annual Costs [1] of Living, 4-Person Manual Worker's Family, 59 Cities, March 1935

Annual cost	Number of cities	
	Maintenance level	Emergency level
Total	59	59
$800.00–$849.99	—	9
$850.00–$899.99	—	21
$900.00–$949.99	—	20
$950.00–$999.99	—	6
$1,000.00–$1,049.99	—	3
$1,050.00–$1,099.99	—	—
$1,100.00–$1,149.99	3	—
$1,150.00–$1,199.99	9	—
$1,200.00–$1,249.99	15	—
$1,250.00–$1,299.99	16	—
$1,300.00–$1,349.99	9	—
$1,350.00–$1,399.99	6	—
$1,400.00–$1,449.99	1	—
Average,[1] 59 cities	$1, 260. 62	$903. 27

[1] Include sales tax where levied (appendix tables 15 and 16).

Owing to differences in the quantities of specific goods and services included in the maintenance and emergency budgets, relative positions of only 11 cities were identical in the separate cost of living arrays. Nineteen were different by one place, ten by two places, six by three places, six by four places, two by five places, three by seven places, and two by eight places.

Discussion of cost differences is based on data relating to the maintenance level of living except where factors of significance make reference to the emergency level desirable. A complete set of figures for the emergency level is included in the text and appendix B. For all practical purposes, however, it may be assumed that under most circumstances calculating the cost of the emergency budget as between 70 percent and 75 percent of the cost of the maintenance budget will provide adequately for the emergency level of living.

Table 4 summarizes the costs of living per year, per month, and per week at the maintenance level and at the emergency level, in each of the 59 cities separately, and as averages of the costs in all cities combined.

Table 3.—Costs [1] of Emergency Level of Living as Percents of Costs of Maintenance Level, by Major Budget Groups, 4-Person Manual Worker's Family, 59 Cities, March 1935

City	Major budget group					
	Total	Food	Clothing, clothing upkeep, and personal care	Housing, including water	Household operation [2]	Miscellaneous [3]
Maintenance level cost	100.0	100.0	100.0	100.0	100.0	100.0
Average, 59 cities	71.7	75.9	69.5	75.6	79.4	57.5
Albuquerque, N. Mex.[1]	72.9	77.6	70.0	78.0	79.9	53.9
Atlanta, Ga	71.9	75.0	68.9	76.8	79.4	59.1
Baltimore, Md	71.2	75.3	68.9	76.3	78.0	59.7
Binghamton, N. Y	70.6	75.1	69.2	75.0	80.2	52.5
Birmingham, Ala	71.5	75.4	69.6	76.7	79.1	58.8
Boston, Mass	70.9	74.6	69.5	75.0	78.8	56.3
Bridgeport, Conn	71.0	74.5	69.2	74.4	79.9	55.9
Buffalo, N. Y	71.5	75.4	69.7	74.3	79.1	60.1
Butte, Mont	72.6	77.4	70.2	78.6	79.7	54.1
Cedar Rapids, Iowa [1]	71.6	76.2	69.5	76.2	79.8	53.7
Chicago, Ill.[1]	71.7	75.6	69.4	75.0	80.1	60.1
Cincinnati, Ohio [1]	71.3	75.7	69.3	75.5	78.0	58.6
Clarksburg, W. Va.[1]	71.7	76.5	69.1	76.6	76.2	56.8
Cleveland, Ohio [1]	71.5	76.0	68.7	75.6	78.5	61.1
Columbia, S. C	70.8	75.0	68.6	75.8	79.1	51.2
Columbus, Ohio [1]	71.3	76.7	68.7	75.0	76.6	56.9
Dallas, Tex	71.8	76.0	69.9	76.4	78.7	57.2
Denver, Colo.[1]	71.0	76.1	70.0	73.5	77.7	58.7
Detroit, Mich.[1]	71.6	74.8	69.4	75.7	80.4	60.7
El Paso, Tex	72.1	77.2	70.1	78.5	79.0	50.5
Fall River, Mass	70.6	74.3	68.9	75.7	78.5	53.8
Houston, Tex	71.8	76.1	69.6	75.7	78.6	60.2
Indianapolis, Ind	71.7	76.1	69.2	77.6	78.0	58.3
Jacksonville, Fla	71.4	75.2	69.8	75.8	79.8	55.7
Kansas City, Mo	72.3	75.6	69.3	75.8	78.0	63.8
Knoxville, Tenn	72.4	77.2	69.5	76.7	80.2	56.9
Little Rock, Ark	72.0	76.6	69.7	77.6	78.5	56.5
Los Angeles, Calif.[1]	71.5	76.0	69.0	74.2	79.4	60.9
Louisville, Ky.[1]	71.4	76.2	69.3	77.1	77.3	56.9
Manchester, N. H	70.9	75.1	70.3	74.2	79.9	54.3
Memphis, Tenn	71.8	76.8	68.8	75.7	78.5	59.0
Milwaukee, Wis	71.7	75.5	68.7	75.6	80.5	58.7
Minneapolis, Minn	73.1	76.7	70.3	75.0	82.3	61.2
Mobile, Ala	72.1	76.2	68.8	78.0	79.8	57.7
Newark, N. J	70.8	75.1	69.4	74.4	78.7	53.7
New Orleans, La	71.6	76.6	69.7	74.2	78.2	60.7
New York, N. Y.[1]	71.4	75.3	69.5	74.0	79.6	58.2
Norfolk, Va	71.2	75.0	69.6	74.8	79.8	56.0
Oklahoma City, Okla.[1]	71.8	76.9	69.7	76.6	79.7	55.3
Omaha, Nebr	72.2	76.6	70.0	76.1	79.7	57.4
Peoria, Ill.[1]	71.7	76.2	69.7	75.9	77.2	56.3
Philadelphia, Pa	71.2	76.1	69.4	75.0	78.2	58.7
Pittsburgh, Pa	71.0	75.2	69.3	74.4	78.1	60.1
Portland, Maine	72.3	76.2	69.6	76.5	81.6	56.2
Portland, Oreg	72.4	76.8	70.4	75.4	80.7	59.5
Providence, R. I	71.1	74.1	68.9	75.0	79.8	56.5
Richmond, Va	71.8	75.6	69.1	77.1	79.1	57.0
Rochester, N. Y	71.8	75.2	70.1	74.7	81.3	58.1
Salt Lake City, Utah [1]	71.7	76.8	70.6	73.8	78.2	57.7
San Francisco, Calif.[1]	72.0	76.7	69.4	75.6	81.1	56.7
Scranton, Pa	71.0	76.1	68.5	75.0	77.8	55.7
Seattle, Wash	71.9	76.8	69.2	75.0	80.2	58.5
Sioux Falls, S. Dak	72.7	77.7	69.9	75.7	81.8	51.0
Spokane, Wash	72.8	78.1	69.3	75.9	80.4	58.3
St. Louis, Mo	71.4	75.4	69.4	75.6	77.8	60.7
Tucson, Ariz.[1]	71.5	76.9	69.4	74.3	78.8	54.0
Washington, D. C	71.7	74.9	69.3	75.4	79.1	58.8
Wichita, Kans	71.6	75.7	70.3	74.5	80.0	56.7
Winston-Salem, N. C.[1]	71.4	75.0	69.3	75.6	80.3	55.0

[1] Include sales tax where levied (appendix tables 15 and 16).

[2] Includes coal or wood, gas, electricity, ice, household supplies, furniture, furnishings, household equipment, refuse disposal, and unspecified essentials. In those cities where water was a direct charge on the tenant, its cost was added to rent.

[3] Includes medical care, transportation, recreation, school attendance, church contributions, other contributions, life insurance, and taxes exclusive of sales tax.

Table 4.—Costs[1] of Living per Year, per Month, and per Week, 4-Person Manual Worker's Family, 59 Cities, March 1935

City	Maintenance level			Emergency level		
	Per year	Per month	Per week	Per year	Per month	Per week
Average, 59 cities	$1, 260. 62	$105. 05	$24. 24	$903. 27	$75. 27	$17. 37
Albuquerque, N. Mex.[1]	1, 299. 14	108. 26	24. 98	947. 57	78. 96	18. 22
Atlanta, Ga	1, 268. 22	105. 69	24. 39	911. 25	75. 94	17. 52
Baltimore, Md	1, 300. 65	108. 39	25. 01	926. 71	77. 23	17. 82
Binghamton, N. Y	1, 243. 19	103. 60	23. 91	878. 10	73. 18	16. 89
Birmingham, Ala	1, 168. 85	97. 40	22. 48	835. 81	69. 65	16. 07
Boston, Mass	1, 352. 77	112. 73	26. 01	958. 45	79. 87	18. 43
Bridgeport, Conn	1, 296. 35	108. 03	24. 93	920. 39	76. 70	17. 70
Buffalo, N. Y	1, 261. 21	105. 10	24. 25	901. 72	75. 14	17. 34
Butte, Mont	1, 283. 69	106. 97	24. 69	932. 11	77. 68	17. 93
Cedar Rapids, Iowa[1]	1, 186. 18	98. 85	22. 81	849. 35	70. 78	16. 33
Chicago, Ill.[1]	1, 356. 11	113. 01	26. 08	972. 59	81. 05	18. 70
Cincinnati, Ohio[1]	1, 311. 74	109. 31	25. 23	935. 54	77. 96	17. 99
Clarksburg, W. Va.[1]	1, 190. 02	99. 17	22. 89	852. 87	71. 07	16. 40
Cleveland, Ohio[1]	1, 348. 33	112. 36	25. 93	964. 71	80. 39	18. 55
Columbia, S. C	1, 192. 60	99. 38	22. 93	844. 92	70. 41	16. 25
Columbus, Ohio[1]	1, 178. 70	98. 23	22. 67	840. 68	70. 06	16. 17
Dallas, Tex	1, 188. 97	99. 08	22. 86	853. 98	71. 17	16. 42
Denver, Colo.[1]	1, 246. 07	103. 84	23. 96	885. 24	73. 77	17. 02
Detroit, Mich.[1]	1, 317. 53	109. 79	25. 34	944. 00	78. 67	18. 15
El Paso, Tex	1, 153. 58	96. 13	22. 18	832. 05	69. 34	16. 00
Fall River, Mass	1, 271. 51	105. 96	24. 45	898. 09	74. 84	17. 27
Houston, Tex	1, 209. 96	100. 83	23. 27	869. 23	72. 44	16. 72
Indianapolis, Ind	1, 198. 08	99. 84	23. 04	859. 04	71. 59	16. 52
Jacksonville, Fla	1, 217. 27	101. 44	23. 41	868. 57	72. 38	16. 70
Kansas City, Mo	1, 245. 42	103. 79	23. 95	899. 85	74. 99	17. 30
Knoxville, Tenn	1, 166. 75	97. 23	22. 44	844. 37	70. 36	16. 24
Little Rock, Ark	1, 139. 06	94. 92	21. 91	819. 97	68. 33	15. 77
Los Angeles, Calif.[1]	1, 308. 11	109. 01	25. 16	935. 85	77. 99	18. 00
Louisville, Ky.[1]	1, 220. 20	101. 68	23. 47	871. 62	72. 64	16. 76
Manchester, N. H	1, 254. 03	104. 50	24. 12	889. 61	74. 13	17. 11
Memphis, Tenn	1, 221. 40	101. 78	23. 49	877. 27	73. 11	16. 87
Milwaukee, Wis	1, 353. 34	112. 78	26. 03	970. 64	80. 89	18. 67
Minneapolis, Minn	1, 387. 79	115. 65	26. 69	1, 013. 88	84. 49	19. 50
Mobile, Ala	1, 129. 81	94. 15	21. 73	814. 92	67. 91	15. 67
Newark, N. J	1, 300. 86	108. 41	25. 02	920. 54	76. 71	17. 70
New Orleans, La	1, 233. 08	102. 76	23. 71	882. 80	73. 57	16. 98
New York, N. Y.[1]	1, 375. 13	114. 59	26. 44	982. 11	81. 84	18. 89
Norfolk, Va	1, 251. 38	104. 28	24. 07	891. 57	74. 30	17. 15
Oklahoma City, Okla.[1]	1, 217. 80	101. 48	23. 42	874. 17	72. 85	16. 81
Omaha, Nebr	1, 258. 26	104. 86	24. 20	908. 71	75. 73	17. 48
Peoria, Ill.[1]	1, 274. 30	106. 19	24. 51	913. 39	76. 12	17. 57
Philadelphia, Pa	1, 297. 69	108. 14	24. 96	924. 56	77. 05	17. 78
Pittsburgh, Pa	1, 310. 52	109. 21	25. 20	930. 45	77. 54	17. 89
Portland, Maine	1, 275. 48	106. 29	24. 53	921. 94	76. 83	17. 73
Portland, Oreg	1, 221. 72	101. 81	23. 49	884. 81	73. 73	17. 02
Providence, R. I	1, 245. 26	103. 77	23. 95	885. 17	73. 76	17. 02
Richmond, Va	1, 268. 06	105. 67	24. 39	910. 36	75. 86	17. 51
Rochester, N. Y	1, 287. 63	107. 30	24. 76	925. 16	77. 10	17. 79
St. Louis, Mo	1, 339. 55	111. 63	25. 76	956. 48	79. 71	18. 39
Salt Lake City, Utah[1]	1, 243. 07	103. 59	23. 91	890. 84	74. 24	17. 13
San Francisco, Calif.[1]	1, 389. 87	115. 82	26. 73	1, 001. 12	83. 43	19. 25
Scranton, Pa	1, 312. 39	109. 37	25. 24	932. 21	77. 68	17. 93
Seattle, Wash	1, 233. 35	102. 78	23. 72	886. 58	73. 88	17. 05
Sioux Falls, S. Dak	1, 290. 60	107. 55	24. 82	938. 27	78. 19	18. 04
Spokane, Wash	1, 228. 62	102. 39	23. 63	894. 02	74. 50	17. 19
Tucson, Ariz.[1]	1, 287. 25	107. 27	24. 75	920. 05	76. 67	17. 69
Washington, D. C	1, 414. 54	117. 88	27. 20	1, 013. 98	84. 50	19. 50
Wichita, Kans	1, 131. 30	94. 28	21. 76	809. 64	67. 47	15. 57
Winston-Salem, N. C.[1]	1, 222. 18	101. 85	23. 50	873. 04	72. 75	16. 79

[1] Include sales tax where levied (appendix tables 15 and 16).

COSTS OF MAJOR BUDGET GROUPS AND PRINCIPAL SUBGROUPS

The cost of living is composed of the prices of a large number of goods and services, combined with the quantities of each required at a specified level. The average budget cost in the 59 cities was so distributed that food took more than twice as much as housing, and considerably less was necessary for household operation than for clothing, clothing upkeep, and personal care (table 5). One-fifth was required for miscellaneous family needs at the maintenance level, and one-sixth, at the emergency level. These budget cost distributions differed in the separate cities in response to a variety of local circumstances (appendix tables 17, 18, 19, 20, 21, and 22).

Table 5.—Percent Distribution of the Average Annual Costs [1] of Living Among the Major Budget Groups and Principal Subgroups, 4-Person Manual Worker's Family, 59 Cities, March 1935

Budget group	Maintenance level	Emergency level
Average,[1] 59 cities: Amount	$1, 260. 62	$903. 27
Percent	100. 0	100. 0
Food	35. 6	37. 6
Clothing, clothing upkeep, and personal care	14. 6	14. 2
Clothing	11. 6	11. 1
Clothing upkeep	1. 0	1. 3
Personal care	2. 0	1. 8
Housing, including water	17. 6	18. 6
Household operation	12. 2	13. 5
Fuel	4. 6	5. 3
Ice	1. 8	2. 1
Electricity	1. 5	1. 6
Household supplies	1. 5	1. 9
Furniture, furnishings, and household equipment	2. 5	2. 1
Refuse disposal	0. 1	0. 2
Unspecified essentials	0. 2	0. 3
Miscellaneous	20. 0	16. 1
Medical care	4. 2	5. 1
Transportation	4. 3	5. 0
School attendance	0. 5	0. 8
Recreation	5. 9	1. 4
Life insurance	3. 7	2. 3
Church contributions and other contributions	1. 2	1. 2
Taxes [2]	0. 2	0. 3

[1] Include sales tax where levied (appendix tables 15 and 16).
[2] Exclusive of sales tax.

The greatest uniformity in budget group costs among the 59 cities was found in combined food prices; the greatest difference, in house rents (table 62). The cost of the budget for clothing, clothing upkeep, and personal care more nearly approached that for food in its dispersion; household operation and miscellaneous cost differences were more like that for rent. The widest dispersions for any subgroups were found in the costs of certain items of which the household operation and miscellaneous groups are composed.

The relative cost of living in one city as compared with all others is fixed by various combinations of separate commodity and service costs. Among the 10 most expensive cities in which to live at the maintenance level, for example, only San Francisco, Chicago, and Boston reported all major budget group costs well above the 59-city average (appendix table 3). In the others some were high and some were low. Food costs were less than the average in Minneapolis, Milwaukee, Cleveland, and Detroit; clothing, clothing upkeep, and personal care costs were relatively low in New York, Washington, and St. Louis; and household operation costs were low in Washington, Cleveland, and St. Louis. On the other hand, all 10 of these highest cost cities reported rents and the costs of miscellaneous family needs above the average.

In the 10 lowest cost cities rents were considerably less than the average but only in Mobile, Wichita, Little Rock, and Knoxville were all costs relatively low. Food was expensive in Clarksburg and Dallas; and clothing, clothing upkeep, and personal care costs slightly exceeded the average in Clarksburg, Columbus, and Cedar Rapids. Household operation costs were above the average in Cedar Rapids and El Paso, and the cost of miscellaneous family needs was high in Birmingham.

These combinations of high and low costs of various magnitudes appear throughout the array of the 59 cities and require study to ascertain how they, in turn, were made up and what elements in the group totals account for their respective ranking. This analysis is contained in the chapters which follow.

INFLUENCE OF GEOGRAPHIC LOCATION AND SIZE OF CITY ON COSTS OF LIVING[3]

The section of the country in which families live influences to some extent the amount which they must spend to secure a specified level of living (appendix tables 5 and 11). The effect of geographic location is modified by other circumstances, notably size of city, and it is difficult to say with assurance that any one causal factor is most important. Costs were undoubtedly low in the South Central States. Every city in these areas reported less than average values for the budget as a whole and for most of the major budget groups; in the most expensive places less was required per year for support at the maintenance level than in the cheapest New England or Middle Atlantic city (table 6). None of these South Central cities had as many as 500,000 population. Costs of living seemed to be high in the Middle Atlantic, New England, and East North Central States. There are more large cities in these sections than in any other geographic division, however, and it was in the more populous centers, for

[3] See table 1, p. XV, for list of cities in each geographic division and their population and table 62, p. 128, for cost variations within separate geographic divisions and size of city classifications.

the most part, that costs exceeded the average. The two large California cities had greater budget costs than the other three cities in the Pacific Division. The average in the South Atlantic States was slightly below the average in the 59 cities combined, but in the largest places in this area the costs of living were above the 59-city average. On the other hand, though the costs of living in the Mountain States averaged more than in the group of 59 cities as a whole, the 2 largest communities therein reported below average figures. In the West North Central cities costs were high and low in about equal proportion, with the average in the area just above the average in the 59 cities combined.

Table 6.—Average Annual Costs[1] of Living in 9 Geographic Divisions and 5 Size of City Classifications, Ratio of Highest to Lowest Cost in Each Group, and Highest and Lowest Deviations from Group Averages, 4-Person Manual Worker's Family, 59 Cities, March 1935

MAINTENANCE LEVEL
[Average cost, 59 cities=$1,260.62]

Geographic division and size of city classification	Annual cost of living					Percent deviation from group average cost	
	Percent group average is of 59-city average	Group average	Highest cost in each group	Lowest cost in each group	Percent highest cost is of lowest cost in each group	Highest	Lowest
Geographic division							
New England	101.7	$1,282.57	$1,352.77	$1,245.26	108.6	+5.5	−2.9
Middle Atlantic	103.0	1,298.58	1,375.13	1,243.19	110.6	+5.9	−4.3
East North Central	102.5	1,292.27	1,356.11	1,178.70	115.1	+4.9	−8.8
West North Central	100.2	1,262.73	1,387.79	1,131.30	122.7	+9.9	−10.4
South Atlantic	99.8	1,258.32	1,414.54	1,190.02	118.9	+12.4	−5.4
East South Central	93.7	1,181.40	1,221.40	1,129.81	108.1	+3.4	−4.4
West South Central	94.4	1,190.41	1,233.08	1,139.06	108.3	+3.6	−4.3
Mountain	100.9	1,271.84	1,299.14	1,243.07	104.5	+2.1	−2.3
Pacific	101.2	1,276.33	1,389.87	1,221.72	113.8	+8.9	−4.3
Size of city classification							
1,000,000 or more	105.6	$1,330.92	$1,375.13	$1,297.69	106.0	+3.3	−2.5
500,000 to 1,000,000	105.7	1,332.03	1,389.87	1,261.21	110.2	+4.3	−5.3
250,000 to 500,000	99.3	1,251.68	1,414.54	1,168.85	121.0	+13.0	−6.6
100,000 to 250,000	98.0	1,235.05	1,312.39	1,131.30	116.0	+6.3	−8.4
25,000 to 100,000	97.6	1,230.25	1,299.14	1,129.81	115.0	+5.6	−8.2

[1] Include sales tax where levied (appendix table 15).

All places with a population of 500,000 or more had costs of living definitely above the average in the 59 cities combined (appendix tables 7 and 13). There are 13 cities in this population classification in the United States, and all were included in the study. The average in localities with a population between 250,000 and 500,000 was slightly less than the average in all cities included in the study, but in 4 of the 6 largest places in this population classification costs were higher than either the group or total average. Thus, in 17 of these 19 largest cities costs of living for manual workers were above the average in the 59 cities. Costs were so much lower in the other cities between 250,000 and 500,000 population, however, that the group dispersion was the widest found in any size of city classification.

Group costs in the smallest cities averaged markedly less than in the largest cities. At the maintenance level the highest reported cost in the smallest city group exceeded by less than $1.50 per year the lowest cost in the largest city group (table 6). Within the groups, however, cost tendencies were irregular, and variations were nearly twice as wide as among the two largest city groups. In 5 of the 14 places where the population was 100,000 to 250,000 and in 5 of the 13 in the group with 25,000 to 100,000, reported costs were above the average in the 59 cities combined. These intragroup differences among the smallest cities may be attributable to the absence of stabilizing cost factors which were common to the larger places. Without them, geographic location seemed to be a more important cost of living determinant than it was in cities of greater size.

COSTS OF LIVING AND THE SALES TAX

In this group of 59 cities 18 had a nonabsorbed sales tax of some kind on the retail price of one or more budget items in March 1935 (appendix tables 15 and 16).[4] Of the 10 cities at the top of the list in costs of living, 5 had a sales tax; of these, Detroit would be eliminated from the top group if costs were computed without the tax, and the positions of some of the others would change. Louisville, which had the largest sales tax, was 16th from the least expensive city among the 59 and would drop 4 places without the tax. Columbus, Clarksburg, and Cedar Rapids, which were among the 10 cheapest cities in which to live at the maintenance level, each had a sales tax.

CHANGES IN COSTS OF LIVING MARCH 1935–MARCH 1937

During the 2 years since the date of this study costs of living increased in all 32 of the cities where the Bureau of Labor Statistics measures price changes.[5] The greatest difference between March 1935 and March 1937 occurred in Detroit, an increase of 8.9 percent; the least was reported from Boston, an increase of 1.6 percent (table 7). In the 32 cities combined the average increase was 4 percent.

The most spectacular changes reported were certain rent increases, but in a few cities rents decreased within the 2 years. The budget groups made up of commodity prices, on the other hand, were more

[4] This tax may be levied on occupation or gross income of the vendor, but where it is supposed to be collected from the consumer as a separate charge, not absorbed by the vendor or concealed in prices, it has been treated as a direct sales tax. New Orleans levied a tax on motion picture theater admissions exceeding 10 cents, but this has not been treated as a sales tax.

[5] The Bureau of Labor Statistics computes cost of living changes quarterly in 32 cities; 31 of these were included in the present study.

costly in each of the 32 cities in 1937 than in 1935. Increases for food and for furniture, furnishings, and household equipment varied somewhat among the cities, but for food the difference exceeded 10 percent in 7 cities, and for furniture, furnishings, and household equipment it exceeded 10 percent in 11 cities. The average increase in all cities for both major budget groups was greater than the net

Table 7.—Changes in Costs [1] of Living, by Major Budget Groups, 32 Cities, March 1935—March 1937

City	Cost of living (maintenance level)		Percent cost in 1937 was of cost in 1935 [2]						
	March 1937	March 1935	Total	Food	Clothing	Housing	Fuel and light	Furniture, furnishings, and household equipment	Miscellaneous
Average, 32 cities	(3)	(3)	104.0	[4] 107.0	103.8	105.3	98.7	109.3	100.5
Minneapolis, Minn.	$1,480.77	$1,387.79	106.7	113.6	103.1	106.4	98.9	110.8	102.7
Washington, D. C.	1,455.56	1,414.54	102.9	102.9	105.6	104.2	96.7	109.4	100.9
Detroit, Mich.[1]	1,434.79	1,317.53	108.9	109.0	103.0	131.5	96.8	109.9	103.3
Chicago, Ill.[1]	1,422.56	1,356.11	104.9	107.2	103.7	105.3	104.5	109.4	101.9
San Francisco, Calif.[1]	1,421.84	1,389.87	102.3	102.8	105.2	101.6	97.1	108.5	100.4
Cleveland, Ohio [1]	1,418.44	1,348.33	105.2	105.8	106.5	114.1	100.9	108.4	100.2
New York, N. Y.[1]	1,399.88	1,375.13	101.8	104.2	103.5	100.1	96.3	107.7	99.7
St. Louis, Mo.	1,395.81	1,339.55	104.2	110.0	102.8	102.1	95.7	110.4	100.2
Los Angeles, Calif.[1]	1,382.67	1,308.11	105.7	108.9	104.2	116.8	94.6	113.3	100.5
Boston, Mass.	1,374.41	1,352.77	101.6	103.5	102.7	98.7	98.2	107.7	100.3
Cincinnati, Ohio [1]	1,365.52	1,311.74	104.1	107.7	105.1	103.9	92.5	113.1	100.9
Pittsburgh, Pa.	1,359.01	1,310.52	103.7	107.3	103.5	102.5	101.5	108.6	99.8
Baltimore, Md.	1,347.47	1,300.65	103.6	107.5	101.8	103.6	97.0	109.4	100.6
Philadelphia, Pa.	1,345.70	1,297.69	103.7	108.8	102.9	102.5	99.2	108.2	99.8
Scranton, Pa.	1,345.20	1,312.39	102.5	108.1	103.8	98.4	91.2	107.3	98.9
Atlanta, Ga.	1,334.17	1,268.22	105.2	106.9	103.9	111.0	104.6	106.0	101.9
Richmond, Va.	1,323.85	1,268.06	104.4	109.2	104.0	103.2	102.6	106.8	100.2
Portland, Oreg.	1,318.24	1,221.72	107.9	113.9	105.7	114.6	107.3	106.9	101.7
Buffalo, N. Y.	1,312.92	1,261.21	104.1	106.4	105.6	106.1	97.7	112.4	99.8
Seattle, Wash.	1,309.82	1,233.35	106.2	110.9	106.5	108.7	101.2	108.7	101.8
Denver, Colo.[1]	1,305.88	1,246.07	104.8	109.5	101.8	110.7	96.3	107.2	99.7
Portland, Maine	1,304.82	1,275.48	102.3	107.7	100.6	98.1	97.6	103.6	[5] 100.0
Kansas City, Mo.	1,303.95	1,245.42	104.7	110.6	105.1	103.4	98.4	105.4	100.3
Norfolk, Va.	1,291.42	1,251.38	103.2	107.5	103.6	99.5	98.3	106.9	100.8
Jacksonville, Fla.	1,274.48	1,217.27	104.7	108.5	104.4	107.5	98.3	105.2	102.1
Memphis, Tenn.	1,271.48	1,221.40	104.1	106.7	103.5	109.3	102.6	110.3	99.6
Houston, Tex.	1,269.25	1,209.96	104.9	107.4	103.4	111.0	102.4	113.2	99.0
Indianapolis, Ind.	1,266.37	1,198.08	105.7	113.5	106.4	111.5	94.0	111.9	98.1
New Orleans, La.	1,262.67	1,233.08	102.4	103.5	105.5	99.9	98.7	110.3	100.7
Birmingham, Ala.	1,250.67	1,168.85	107.0	111.5	105.2	118.5	102.0	110.1	100.1
Mobile, Ala.	1,156.93	1,129.81	102.4	107.4	102.7	101.7	[6] 100.0	110.2	96.9
Savannah, Ga.	(7)	(7)	102.3	107.1	103.0	103.3	101.3	107.1	96.7

[1] Include sales tax where levied (appendix table 15).
[2] The groupings are those of the Bureau of Labor Statistics but the terminology is that of the present report.
[3] Aggregates were not computed.
[4] Includes 51 cities.
[5] Increased less than 0.05 percent.
[6] Decreased less than 0.05 percent.
[7] Savannah was not included in the Works Progress Administration's study; therefore, aggregates are not available.

Source: The percent changes were computed by the Bureau of Labor Statistics from data collected in its quarterly enumeration. The aggregates for March 1935 are the results of the present study; those for March 1937 were computed by adding or subtracting the appropriate percent changes to or from the aggregates for March 1935. Were the aggregates for March 1937 computed by totaling the costs of the separate budget groups, slightly different figures would appear, because of differences in the samples and quantity allowances used in the present study and by the Bureau of Labor Statistics. The aggregates do not show the costs of the Bureau of Labor Statistics' sample.

change in average rent. Price increases for the clothing group, while not so large, nevertheless, were general. In nearly two-thirds of the cities fuel and light combined was less expensive than 2 years earlier, and the average difference was a small decrease. The cost of miscellaneous items changed very little anywhere.

These cost of living changes reported by the Bureau of Labor Statistics are based on prices of goods and services which are not necessarily identical with those used in this study of the costs of living in 59 cities. They represent purchases of wage earners and lower-salaried clerical workers, however, and the percentages probably are sufficiently representative of differences between the costs of the maintenance budget in March 1935 and March 1937.

If the March 1935 cost of living figures obtained in the present study are recomputed to bring the figures up to March 1937 in the 31 cities where the changes can be taken into account,[6] certain shifts occur in the cost array. Minneapolis advances ahead of Washington and San Francisco to top place. Detroit moves up to 3d from 9th place among the 31 cities; San Francisco goes down to 5th, and New York to 7th, from 2d and 4th, respectively. The cost ranks of Boston, Portland (Maine), Scranton, Norfolk, and New Orleans become several places lower, and of Los Angeles, Portland (Oreg.), and Seattle, several places higher. The cheapest cities in this group of 31 in 1935 are still the cheapest in 1937: Mobile and Birmingham.

These cost of living changes in 31 cities separately and the average change in 32 combined provide no data by means of which the relative standing in March 1937 of all the 59 cities included in this investigation can be computed. It is apparent that some changes must have occurred in most if not all of the remaining 28 cities, and it is probable that the effect of any increases or decreases would be to rearrange the relative positions of the separate cities.

[6] Savannah, the 32d city, was not included in the present study.

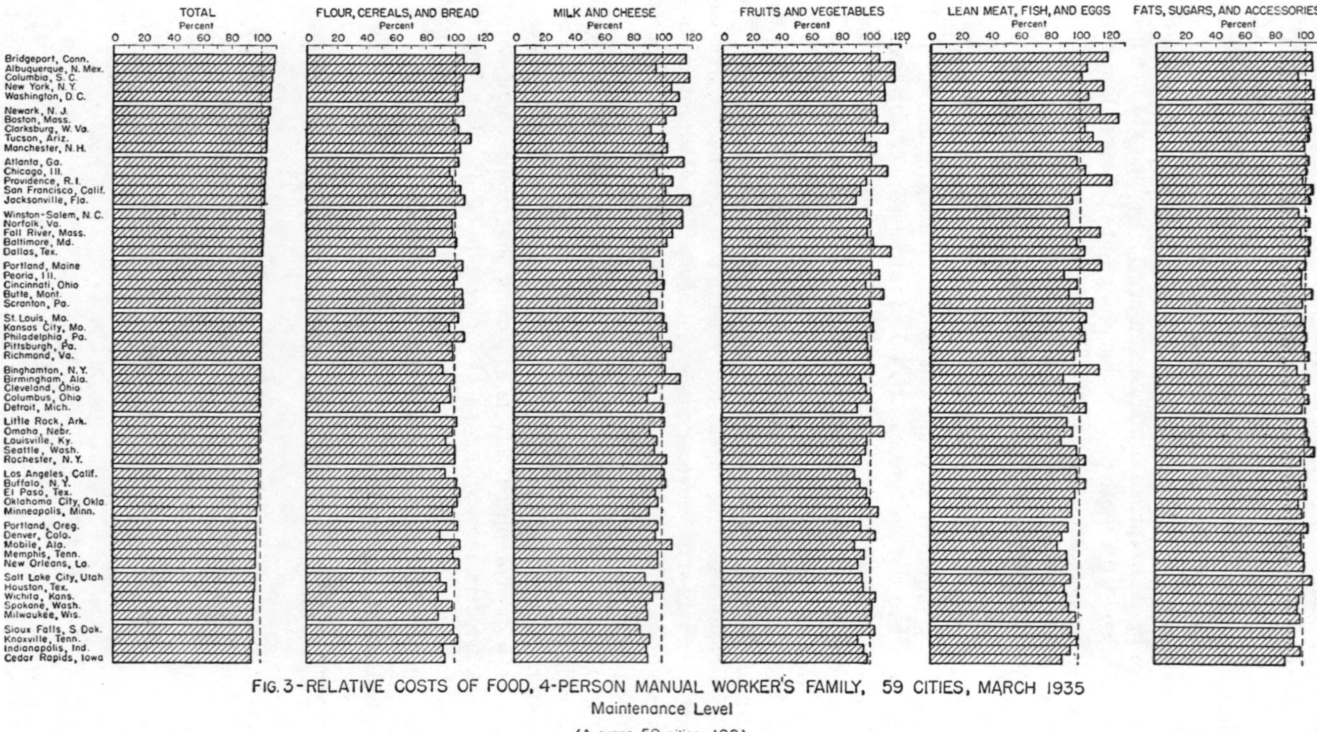

FIG. 3-RELATIVE COSTS OF FOOD, 4-PERSON MANUAL WORKER'S FAMILY, 59 CITIES, MARCH 1935
Maintenance Level
(Average, 59 cities = 100)

AF-2113, W.P.A.

Chapter II

FOOD

THE COSTS of the maintenance food budget for a 4-person manual worker's family varied among the 59 cities from $487.51 per year in Bridgeport to $418.28 in Cedar Rapids (appendix table 2). Thus, 16.6 percent more was required in Bridgeport than in Cedar Rapids. The average annual outlay necessary for food in the 59 cities combined was $448.18. Twenty-seven cities were above this average and thirty-two were below (fig. 3). In no case was the deviation from the average as much as 10 percent (appendix table 3). The annual costs of food at the maintenance level were between $430 and $460 in more

Table 8.—Annual Costs [1] of Food, 4-Person Manual Worker's Family, 59 Cities, March 1935

Annual cost	Number of cities	
	Maintenance level	Emergency level
Total	59	59
$310.00–$319.99	—	2
$320.00–$329.99	—	5
$330.00–$339.99	—	25
$340.00–$349.99	—	18
$350.00–$359.99	—	6
$360.00–$369.99	—	2
$370.00–$379.99	—	1
$380.00–$389.99	—	—
$390.00–$399.99	—	—
$400.00–$409.99	—	—
$410.00–$419.99	2	—
$420.00–$429.99	5	—
$430.00–$439.99	8	—
$440.00–$449.99	23	—
$450.00–$459.99	9	—
$460.00–$469.99	6	—
$470.00–$479.99	3	—
$480.00–$489.99	3	—
Average,[1] 59 cities	$448.18	$340.30

[1] Include sales tax where levied (appendix tables 15 and 16).

than two-thirds of the cities (table 8). Costs at the emergency level were even more narrowly concentrated.[1]

The ranks of cities with reference to the cost of the emergency food budget (appendix tables 8, 9, 11, and 13) differed somewhat from their ranks for the maintenance budget, because the quantities of the commodities included in each budget were different. The cost range was only slightly wider, however, though in brackets about $100 less per year. The amount required to purchase the emergency food budget averaged 75.9 percent of the cost of the maintenance food budget in the 59 cities combined, but ratios varied from 78.1 percent in Spokane to 74.1 percent in Providence (table 3).

The average cost of food in the 59 cities combined was distributed as shown in table 9. These percentages differed slightly among the separate cities as the cost of one group or another was more or less than the average. In all the cities, however, the larger share required for starches, sugars, and fats at the emergency than at the maintenance level reflects differences in quantity allowances in the two budgets to meet the needs of nutrition with less expensive foods. Milk, cheese, fruits, vegetables, lean meat, fish, and eggs took a proportionately smaller share of emergency than of maintenance budget cost.

Table 9.—Percent Distribution of the Average Annual Costs[1] of Food Among the Principal Commodity Groups, 4-Person Manual Worker's Family, 59 Cities, March 1935

Group	Maintenance level	Emergency level
Total	100.0	100.0
Flour, cereals, and bread	16.3	23.7
Milk and cheese	23.5	16.3
Fruits and vegetables	23.2	21.4
Lean meat, fish, and eggs	13.9	9.3
Fats, sugars, and accessories	23.1	29.3
Average,[1] 59 cities	$445.52	$338.24

[1] Do not include sales tax where levied.

Food of all kinds was relatively expensive in Bridgeport and relatively cheap in Cedar Rapids, but the milk and cheese group and the lean meat, fish, and egg group were well toward the extremes in the two cities. Their costs covered a wider range among the 59 cities than any others. Except for eggs and one meat item, however, prices of the commodities making up these groups were more uniform than were many other food prices. Some groups which as a whole varied least in cost, on the other hand, were composed of commodities whose price spreads were widest.

[1] Quantity budgets for the two levels of living are given in complete detail in Stecker, Margaret L., *Quantity Budgets for Basic Maintenance and Emergency Standards of Living*, Research Bulletin, Series I, No. 21, Division of Social Research, Works Progress Administration, 1936. For the methods used in collecting quotations and computing city average prices and aggregate costs, see ch. VII.

Prices of 17 of the 44 separate commodities listed averaged over twice as much in one city as in another (table 10).[2] Each of the nine kinds of fresh fruits and vegetables [3] priced was more than twice as

Table 10.—Food Commodity Price Ratios,[1] 59 Cities, March 1935

Commodity	Number of cities where prices exceeded ±10 percent with reference to the 59-city average [1]			Percent highest price is of lowest price [1]
	Total	Above average	Below average	
Total food	(2)	(2)	(2)	116.6
Flour, cereals, and bread	5	2	3	133.5
White flour	11	5	6	157.5
Corn meal	40	23	17	288.5
Rolled oats	11	8	3	147.8
Rice	28	15	13	209.6
Macaroni	18	9	9	183.5
White bread	21	12	9	171.6
Rye bread	13	5	8	185.7
Whole wheat bread	13	6	7	182.0
Milk and cheese	13	8	5	130.7
Fresh milk	26	12	14	166.7
Can evaporated milk	(2)	(2)	(2)	119.4
Cheese	10	6	4	143.8
Fruits and vegetables	7	5	2	129.7
Potatoes	42	18	24	387.5
Cabbage	37	19	18	452.0
Carrots	34	21	13	523.5
Spinach	38	24	14	424.2
Lettuce	30	19	11	302.5
Onions	21	11	10	215.2
Oranges	30	17	13	206.3
Bananas (dozen)	[3] 15	8	7	205.5
Bananas (pound)	[4] 11	7	4	170.9
Bananas (dozen and pound)	27	13	14	243.1
Apples	25	8	17	416.7
Black-eyed peas	30	14	16	214.3
Navy beans	34	16	18	224.4
Peanut butter	17	7	10	147.8
Prunes	15	8	7	172.0
Raisins	5	3	2	143.8
Can tomatoes	17	10	7	160.7
Can string beans	24	11	13	164.5
Can corn	10	4	6	153.1
Lean meat, fish, and eggs	15	9	6	146.3
Plate beef	18	9	9	240.4
Chuck beef	30	15	15	184.0
Breast of lamb	25	11	14	184.9
Picnic ham	14	7	7	139.9
Can pink salmon	10	7	3	137.2
Eggs	36	14	22	210.4
Fats, sugars, and accessories	1	(2)	1	120.9
Butter	9	3	6	147.0
Lard	3	3	(2)	128.4
Oleomargarine	16	6	10	207.6
Bacon	12	6	6	141.6
Salt pork	18	10	8	160.3
Granulated sugar	10	7	3	134.0
Can corn syrup	23	10	13	144.0
Can molasses	29	14	15	217.1
Tea	31	14	17	174.4
Coffee	20	11	9	150.9

[1] Ratios for all totals were computed from maintenance level costs for a 4-person manual worker's family. The total cost of food includes sales tax where levied (appendix table 15); the group totals and commodity prices are without sales tax.
[2] In no city was deviation from the average as much as 10 percent.
[3] Number of cities where prices exceeded ±10 percent with reference to the average in 29 cities.
[4] Number of cities where prices exceeded ±10 percent with reference to the average in 30 cities.

[2] Prices in all instances are compared without sales tax in order that the two may not be confused in the measurement of intercity differences. Were the tax where levied added to prices, the spread often would be greater than appears in the comparison without tax. The total cost of food includes sales tax where levied.

[3] Except bananas sold by the pound.

expensive in some cities as in others; for some of them, the top prices were four or five times the bottom. Highest egg prices were more than double the lowest. Corn meal and rice were so cheap in some places and so dear in others that the spread from bottom to top in the array of 59 cities was over 100 percent. Greatest price uniformity was found for evaporated milk and such staples as lard and granulated sugar; most can and package goods could be bought for amounts differing from the average by less than 50 percent wherever they were sold; and bacon, cheese, and ham prices were fairly similar in all cities.

INFLUENCE OF GEOGRAPHIC LOCATION AND SIZE OF CITY ON COSTS OF FOOD[4]

The cost of food was higher in New England than in any other geographic division (appendix table 5). All commodities were relatively expensive but the group composed of meat, fish, and eggs was outstandingly above the average in the 59 cities combined. Almost as much would have to be spent for food in the South Atlantic cities as in New England, largely because of the high cost milk and cheese group; all group costs except meat, fish, and eggs also exceeded the average. The meat, fish, and egg group in the Middle Atlantic cities averaged well above the 59-city average; this is the only section except New England where this situation was found. The East North Central cities, on the other hand, reported less than average costs for every food group, and in several sections of the country all were low except one group.

Most cities within each geographic division reported high or low food costs in keeping with the area average. All the New England cities were above the average in the group of 59 combined, and so were all the South Atlantic cities except Richmond. Less than average costs were reported in all the East South Central cities. On the other hand, food prices in two of the eight Middle Atlantic cities were so high that they raised the average in that section to third place among the geographic divisions. Among the North Central cities there were more with low than with high costs.

Size of city apparently affects the costs of food less than does its geographic location (appendix table 7). In 2 of the 5 cities with 1,000,000 or more population, food costs were above the average, and in 8 of the 13 with 25,000 to 100,000 population they were also above the average. No one size of city classification was consistently high or consistently low, though the tendency was downward until the smallest cities were reached. The average for this group of 13 was higher than for any of the other classifications with less than 1,000,000 population.

[4] See table 1, p. XV, for list of cities in each geographic division and their population and table 62, p. 128, for cost variations within separate geographic divisions and size of city classifications.

COST DIFFERENCES

The relatively slight dispersion of food costs as a whole among the 59 cities has 2 principal explanations. First, national advertising of trade-marked goods, widely operating chain store systems, and the concentration of processing and distributing functions within relatively few hands tend to standardize retail charges for certain commodities. Second, though intercity price differences for other commodities were wide, high prices were not all found in the same place, nor were low prices similarly concentrated. When the price of each commodity was combined with its budget allowance and annual costs were computed, high and low prices tended to counterbalance each other to produce much more uniform aggregates. These two influences on food costs are seen in the fact that group costs which varied most were composed of the most similar separate commodity prices (table 10), while commodities which showed the widest price scattering were combined into groups whose costs were relatively homogeneous. Food group costs as a rule did not differ so much as the prices of any of the commodities of which the groups were composed. Assembling the separate costs of 44 food commodities produced totals which were only 16.6 percent greater in the most expensive than in the least expensive city.

Variations in the costs of the entire food budget in different sections of the country are related to more or less all-pervasive influences. The high cost of food in New England, for example, suggests that, in general, not enough is produced in that area to supply the needs of its population and that charges for getting most commodities to market are greater than in, say, the States where the production of meats, grains, or fruits and vegetables is a major industry. Costs in the South Atlantic, Middle Atlantic, and Mountain cities showed the effect of conflicting price influences—some local and some of a more general nature. These sections as a whole were above the average in food costs.

It cannot be said, however, that the prices of foods nationally distributed from more or less centrally located production points, or standardized by brand, as a class were dispersed less than the prices of commodities not so regulated, though the tendency was in that direction.[5] Bread prices, for example, varied somewhat more than prices of the flour from which bread is made; can and package goods were more uniform in price than were fresh vegetables and fruits, fresh milk, and fresh meats, home output of which competes in varying degrees with the supply shipped in from distant points. Local factors which are combined with those of more general application to create the level of food prices are so numerous that an attempt to classify them would require a study of its own, which is no part of the

[5] No attempt was made to compare prices of identical brands in the separate cities.

present investigation.[6] These local phases of price behavior play their part, however, in determining the cost of food in any given city. Some food cost differences cannot be explained at all in any generalization.

Seventeen cities reported a nonabsorbed direct consumers' tax on all or most food commodities sold at retail in March 1935 (appendix tables 15 and 16).[7] The most common exemptions were fresh milk and breadstuffs, which were excluded from the tax in five and four cities, respectively. In sections of the country where, in general, food costs were highest there was no sales tax, and in Cedar Rapids where food was cheapest there was a sales tax. Food requires so large a part of the total cost of living, however, and its costs were so similar in the separate cities that the addition of a sales tax to food prices resulted in a different order in the array of food costs in the 59 cities from that shown without the sales tax.

Though no part of the present study contemplates an analysis of commodity prices sufficiently refined to indicate exact causal relationships, certain phases of the investigation bearing on commodity prices must be noted to explain the dispersion of food costs as a whole. These circumstances relate to specifications, to the seasonal factor in food prices, and to the problem arising in some cities because the date to which prices relate was some weeks earlier than the date on which they were collected.

All commodities were priced by specification. Specifications for food have been standardized more definitely than for most consumers' goods. Alternatives which were permitted in this study for certain articles, however, might well account for some of the price spread. For example, certain States have standards of their own for strictly fresh eggs, which were used instead of the U. S. grades; prices of plate beef were for the best cut of the best grade of beef handled, with the bone in, but such a specification covers a wide range of meat grade as well as a varying proportion of bone, depending on the method of cutting used.[8] A diversity of grades was possible within many of the other specifications. Oleomargarine [9] might be either animal or

[6] An analysis of intracity price variations, which takes into account factors connected with marketing, has been made as a special Works Progress Administration project by Professor John H. Cover, of the University of Chicago, who supervised the collection and tabulation of prices for the present study.

[7] The local sales tax in the city of New York is not levied on food, except meals in restaurants costing $1 or more.

[8] The methods of cutting meat for retail sale vary considerably in different parts of the country.

[9] An oleomargarine tax varying from 5 cents to 15 cents per lb. was effective in 23 cities, but in only 7 of them did the price of this commodity vary 10 percent or more from the average in the 59 cities combined, suggesting that the tax accounted but little for price differentials. Failure to secure any quotations for oleomargarine in three cities, on the other hand, may have been caused by prohibitive taxes or license fees which excluded this commodity from the market.

nut vegetable; prices of commodities sometimes sold in bulk and sometimes in packages or cans, such as lard, butter, coffee, tea, molasses, cereals, and dried fruits, were obtained in units of varying size, according to the usual method of sale. Some fresh fruits and vegetables were priced by size rather than by weight: number of oranges, of heads of lettuce, or of bunches of carrots to the crate; and not one number but a limited range was specified. That the size of these commodities must have varied considerably is suggested by the fact that the price spread of bananas sold by the pound was considerably less than of bananas sold by the dozen (table 10).

Most food dealers carry only one kind of certain merchandise at a time, and the price quoted was necessarily for the commodity in stock on the day of the report. Often neither the shopkeeper nor the field agent could tell exactly what its specifications were. Prices of fresh fruits and vegetables varied most among the separate cities; quotations for these commodities on any day depend almost entirely on the available supply, for such perishables soon lose all value if they are not sold. Supply in turn is related to the seasons and to shipments received in the market each day. Prices were obtained in March 1935 in cities where summer had already come as well as in those where winter still lingered. Thus, various degrees of seasonality were embodied in the quotations reported from different parts of the country.

To those circumstances which genuinely influence food prices as paid by the consumer there must be added, as an explanation of the very wide spread in quotations for some commodities, the fact that prices were not taken on an identical day in all 59 cities. Reports in 46 of them were secured on March 12 by the Bureau of Labor Statistics through its regular channels; in some of the 13 others, where prices were collected for the first time for this investigation, the study started 6 weeks or 2 months after the middle of March, to which date prices referred. Food prices vary greatly from day to day and few dealers have a record of what the customer paid on any given date; when queried on the subject they must depend largely on memory for the answer. It is significant that the spread of prices among the 13 cities where quotations were not collected on March 12 was much greater, for the most part, than among the 46 where quotations were furnished on the identical day to which they applied. The apparent biases did not run in the same direction for all commodities in several cities, with the result that their reported intercity price ranges were very wide. The resulting price dispersions may overstate the true spread for the separate commodities.

In the last analysis, however, so sensitive are retail food prices to the influence of any circumstance which affects the flow of commodities to the dealer's shelves and so quickly can changes in his costs be passed on to the consumer that quotations for a single item on a given day may in no sense be representative. Prices of a large number of items combined with their quantity allowances, however, are likely to measure satisfactorily prevailing food costs. The in-season period is not identical for all commodities, and seldom do all prices tend to be high or low at the same time. The inclusion of 44 separate foods in the quantity budgets provides a wide field within which high and low prices may cancel, so that the cost of all combined is fairly uniform.

Under some circumstances home production of certain commodities may reduce food costs, but in urban communities property occupied by working class families as a rule does not provide facilities for either gardens or livestock. It should be remembered, however, that the foodstuffs listed in the quantity budgets are samples for which substitutions can and will be made at no sacrifice of nutritive satisfaction. Thus, individual families may keep down their expenditures for food by purchasing each day those articles in the separate food groups which at the time offer the best value.[10] No other necessity of living can be supplied through so varied a choice.

[10] Sometimes a small percentage of the cost of a synthetic food budget is added to provide for waste, unwise purchases, and the like. This procedure was not followed in the present calculations, both because the allowances in the budgets for food accessories are liberal and because prices were obtained from all kinds of stores rather than from only those where quotations usually are cheapest.

Chapter III

CLOTHING, CLOTHING UPKEEP, AND PERSONAL CARE

THE ANNUAL costs of clothing, clothing upkeep, and personal care covered a wider range among the 59 cities included in this investigation than the comparable outlays necessary for food, but still varied within relatively narrow limits. The most expensive city was Butte, where $214.54 was required to purchase the maintenance budget for a four-person manual worker's family, and the cheapest was Dallas, where $162.09 was necessary (appendix table 2); relatively, these goods and services together cost 32.4 percent more in Butte than in Dallas. Their average cost in the 59 cities combined was $184.35, an amount which was exceeded in 27 cities and not reached in 32 (fig. 4). The highest cost exceeded the average by 16.4 percent and the lowest was less by 12.1 percent (appendix table 3). In 47 of the 59 cities the costs of the maintenance clothing, clothing upkeep, and personal care budget were between $170 and $200 per year (table 11). Emergency budget costs had a similar range in lower cost groups.[1]

The average cost of the emergency budget for clothing, clothing upkeep, and personal care in the 59 cities combined was about $56 less per year than the average cost of the maintenance budget, a ratio of 69.5 percent (table 3). The percentage which the emergency budget cost was of the maintenance budget cost varied only slightly among the 59 cities, from 70.6 percent in Salt Lake City to 68.5 percent in Scranton. Ranks of cities in the emergency cost array (appendix tables 8, 9, 11, and 13) were not always identical with those in the maintenance cost array, owing to the differences in quantity allowances of the goods and services in the two budgets, but such shifts were slight.

[1] Quantity budgets for the two levels of living are given in complete detail in Stecker, Margaret L., *Quantity Budgets for Basic Maintenance and Emergency Standards of Living*, Research Bulletin, Series I, No. 21, Division of Social Research, Works Progress Administration, 1936. For the methods used in collecting quotations and computing city average prices and aggregate costs see ch. VII.

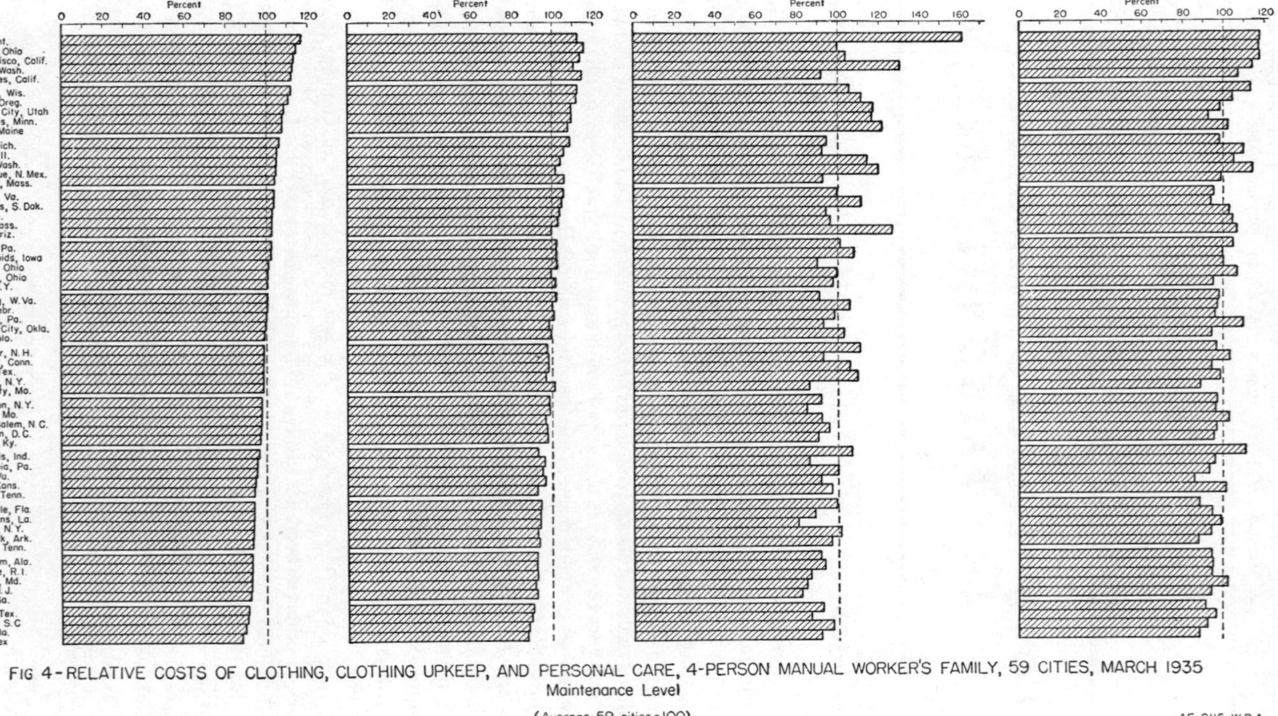

FIG 4—RELATIVE COSTS OF CLOTHING, CLOTHING UPKEEP, AND PERSONAL CARE, 4-PERSON MANUAL WORKER'S FAMILY, 59 CITIES, MARCH 1935
Maintenance Level
(Average, 59 cities = 100)

Table 11.—Annual Costs [1] of Clothing, Clothing Upkeep, and Personal Care, 4-Person Manual Worker's Family, 59 Cities, March 1935

Annual cost	Number of cities	
	Maintenance level	Emergency level
Total	59	59
$110.00–$119.99	—	11
$120.00–$129.99	—	27
$130.00–$139.99	—	13
$140.00–$149.99	—	7
$150.00–$159.99	—	1
$160.00–$169.99	5	—
$170.00–$179.99	18	—
$180.00–$189.99	19	—
$190.00–$199.99	10	—
$200.00–$209.99	5	—
$210.00–$219.99	2	—
Average,[1] 59 cities	$184.35	$128.05

[1] Include sales tax where levied (appendix tables 15 and 16).

The proportions of average annual cost of this major budget group attributable to each of its subgroups are shown in table 12. Clothing includes 90 commodities separately priced in all cities plus an identical money allowance in each for articles usually sold for the same amount everywhere in the chain limited price variety stores; clothing upkeep includes 7 services separately priced and an identical allowance in each city for other items; personal care includes 1 commodity and 4 services separately priced and an identical allowance in each city for other items. The percentages taken by the different subgroups were not the same in all cities, but the range within which they varied as prices varied was limited. Identical money allowances accounted for 10.8 percent of the average cost of the group as a whole at the maintenance level in the 59 cities, 7.1 percent of clothing cost, 11.5 percent of clothing upkeep cost, and 32.4 percent of personal care cost.

Table 12.—Percent Distribution of the Average Annual Costs [1] of Clothing, Clothing Upkeep, and Personal Care Among the Principal Commodity and Service Groups, 4-Person Manual Worker's Family, 59 Cities, March 1935

Group	Maintenance level	Emergency level
Total	100.0	100.0
Clothing	79.1	78.3
Clothing upkeep	7.4	9.3
Personal care	13.5	12.4
Average,[1] 59 cities	$184.35	$128.05

[1] Include sales tax where levied (appendix tables 15 and 16).

CLOTHING

Clothing costs considered separately showed practically the same spread as when combined with outlays necessary for clothing upkeep and personal care. The most expensive city for this subgroup was Cleveland, in which 31.9 percent more was required for clothing at the maintenance level than in Dallas. Thirty dollars per year measures most of the cost variation among the cities (table 13).

Table 13.—Annual Costs[1] of Clothing, 4-Person Manual Worker's Family, 59 Cities, March 1935

Annual cost	Number of cities	
	Maintenance level	Emergency level
Total	59	59
$80.00–$89.99	—	3
$90.00–$99.99	—	28
$100.00–$109.99	—	19
$110.00–$119.99	—	9
$120.00–$129.99	2	—
$130.00–$139.99	15	—
$140.00–$149.99	25	—
$150.00–$159.99	10	—
$160.00–$169.99	7	—
Average,[1] 59 cities	$145.93	$100.23

[1] Include sales tax where levied (appendix tables 15 and 16).

The annual costs of clothing in the 59 cities combined averaged $145.93; 26 cities exceeded this amount and 33 were less. Men's, women's, boys', and girls' budgets showed varying degrees of cost similarity, and quotations for individual articles varied most of all (table 14).[2]

Prices of most men's garments differed by less than 100 percent between the lowest and highest cities. Work socks, house slippers, and wool work shirts, however, which had the widest price ranges, showed average spreads of about 167 percent, 121 percent, and 104 percent, respectively. The dearest city for business shirts, overalls, winter union suits, and cotton pajamas, on the other hand, was not 50 percent above the cheapest. When the entire men's clothing budget for a year is considered, the difference between its smallest and largest value was only 36 percent.

A price range of 100 percent or more between the least expensive and most expensive cities appeared for the following articles in the women's clothing budget: kimonos, handbags, wool sweaters, wool dresses, cotton house dresses, and summer hats; quotations for several other garments approached 100 percent differentials. A combination of the prices of all women's garments and accessories with the quantity of each necessary per year produced a cost difference of only 37.3 percent between the lowest and the highest cities.

[2] Prices in all instances are compared without sales tax in order that the two may not be confused in the measurement of intercity differences. Were the tax where levied added to prices, the spread often would be greater than appears in the comparison without tax. All totals except for men's, women's, boys', and girls' clothing include sales tax where levied.

Table 14.—Clothing, Clothing Upkeep, and Personal Care Commodity and Service Price Ratios,[1] 59 Cities, March 1935

Commodity or service	Number of cities where prices exceeded ±10 percent with reference to the 59-city average [1]			Percent highest price is of lowest price [1]
	Total	Above average	Below average	
Total [2] clothing, clothing upkeep, and personal care	9	7	2	132.4
Clothing [2]	10	7	3	131.9
Men's clothing	9	7	2	136.0
Winter overcoat	22	13	9	158.6
Winter suit	20	10	10	173.2
Summer suit	19	10	9	158.4
Wool sweater	29	13	16	192.6
Work trousers	32	15	17	170.0
Business shirt	6	4	2	141.3
Cotton work shirt	18	9	9	153.3
Wool work shirt	26	10	16	204.3
Overalls	12	5	7	148.4
Jumper	13	6	7	153.5
Winter union suit	18	8	10	142.1
Summer union suit	29	13	16	166.5
Flannelette pajamas	16	6	10	174.8
Cotton pajamas	9	5	4	133.3
Cotton dress socks	18	9	9	152.8
Cotton work socks	40	19	21	267.3
Felt hat	28	13	15	161.3
Straw hat	23	11	12	170.8
Wool cap	23	13	10	162.4
Leather street gloves	21	12	9	161.3
Cotton work gloves	28	15	13	184.7
Oxfords	19	10	9	156.5
Work shoes	15	7	8	165.9
House slippers	28	13	15	221.0
Rubbers	4	3	1	163.4
Women's clothing [2]	16	10	6	137.3
Winter coat	27	14	13	190.8
Spring coat	21	11	10	174.1
Wool sweater	38	18	20	224.6
Wool dress	34	13	21	212.7
Silk dress	32	17	15	177.4
Cotton street dress	31	13	18	186.5
Cotton house dress	13	5	8	210.9
Dress slip	36	16	20	188.8
Corset	27	13	14	186.9
Brassiere	28	11	17	196.4
Bloomers or panties	30	15	15	184.4
Winter union suit	23	10	13	163.8
Flannelette nightgown	19	9	10	148.4
Cotton nightgown	32	16	16	190.9
Bathrobe	25	11	14	181.6
Kimono	21	10	11	237.2
Cotton stockings	22	11	11	174.2
Silk stockings	38	17	21	193.8
Winter hat	28	12	16	172.2
Summer hat	23	13	10	205.2
Fabric gloves	19	9	10	157.8
Street shoes	23	12	11	165.7
House slippers	15	10	5	161.6
Galoshes	7	5	2	164.2
Cotton umbrella	19	9	10	155.2
Handbag	32	16	16	229.2
Boys' clothing [2]	8	6	2	134.9
Sheep-lined jacket	9	3	6	132.4
Raincoat	25	12	13	167.6
Winter suit	32	17	15	190.9
Wool sweater	14	7	7	152.2
Corduroy slacks	29	16	13	233.3

See footnotes at end of table.

Table 14.—Clothing, Clothing Upkeep, and Personal Care Commodity and Service Price Ratios, 59 Cities, March 1935—Continued

Commodity or service	Number of cities where prices exceeded ±10 percent with reference to the 59-city average [1]			Percent highest price is of lowest price [1]
	Total	Above average	Below average	
Boys' clothing [2]—Continued.				
Cotton slacks	19	6	13	190.9
Cotton shirt	10	6	4	150.8
Overalls	15	7	8	148.8
Winter union suit	17	8	9	163.6
Summer union suit	16	9	7	156.8
Flannelette pajamas	14	6	8	145.3
Cotton pajamas	20	12	8	183.1
Winter cap	27	13	14	200.3
Wool gloves	38	20	18	319.2
Oxfords	15	10	5	157.9
Canvas sport shoes	8	4	4	134.2
Rubbers	6	3	3	147.6
Girls' clothing [2]	11	6	5	137.7
Winter coat	22	10	12	219.6
Spring coat	22	12	10	216.2
Wool sweater	28	13	15	210.4
Silk dress	35	15	20	253.1
Cotton dress	27	14	13	197.1
Wool skirt	39	16	23	219.3
Cotton blouse	31	12	19	231.8
Cotton dress slip	24	10	14	187.2
Bloomers or panties	23	11	12	208.1
Winter union suit	27	12	15	168.2
Summer union suit	18	7	11	203.8
Flannelette nightgown	27	11	16	224.8
Cotton nightgown	32	16	16	252.9
Cotton stockings	22	12	10	169.9
Socks	16	8	8	196.5
Winter hat	40	18	22	257.8
Summer hat	34	18	16	252.7
Wool gloves	29	15	14	272.8
Oxfords	16	9	7	161.6
Pumps	19	9	10	170.6
Sneakers	9	5	4	144.4
Galoshes	6	4	2	203.9
Clothing upkeep [2]	21	11	10	200.7
Cleaning and pressing:				
Men's suit	39	16	23	327.2
Women's dress	36	14	22	299.1
Women's coat	36	15	21	255.7
Shoe repairs:				
Men's half soles and heels	30	13	17	210.6
Women's half soles and heels	30	13	17	200.3
Women's heels only	34	16	18	224.0
Girls' half soles and heels	24	9	15	234.2
Personal care [2]	13	8	5	137.3
Haircut:				
Men's	35	16	19	192.3
Women's	24	11	13	192.3
Girls'	34	12	22	230.4
Hair wave:				
Women's	30	13	17	239.4
Toilet soap	9	6	3	155.0

[1] Ratios for all totals were computed from maintenance level costs for a 4-person manual worker's family. Except for men's, women's, boys', and girls' clothing, the group totals include sales tax where levied (appendix table 15); commodity and service prices are without sales tax. Prices of commodities or services used in valuing more than 1 budget are shown only once.

[2] Includes an identical allowance in all cities for items not separately priced, as well as prices for the items listed which were priced in each city, combined with their quantity allowances in the maintenance budget.

The widest price variation among the 59 cities for any single garment in the 4 separate clothing budgets appeared for boys' wool gloves; the largest city average was 219.2 percent more than the smallest. Corduroy slacks and winter caps were conspicuous in the breadth of their price ranges. Such commodities as canvas sport shoes and sheep-lined jackets, on the other hand, showed relatively small price differences among the cities. For the boys' clothing budget as a whole, the highest annual cost was 34.9 percent above the lowest.

More items in the girls' wearing apparel budget showed wide price ranges than in the other three clothing budgets. Of the 22 commodities priced, 14 cost more than twice as much in the highest as in the lowest city; and of the other 8, prices of 7 varied nearly as much. Only girls' sneakers cost less than half as much again in the most expensive as in the least expensive city. When combined with annual quantity allowances, these wide commodity price differences were so compensated, however, that for the girls' clothing budget as a whole 37.7 percent more was required in the highest than in the lowest cost city.

CLOTHING UPKEEP

The costs of clothing upkeep covered a much wider range, relatively, than the original costs of the garments, judged by the amounts which would have to be spent for shoe repairs, cleaning and pressing, and such supplies as shoe polish, thread, pins, and the like. Most was required for this purpose in Butte, $21.82, where annual outlay necessary was practically twice that required in New York, $10.87, the least expensive city. The average annual cost in the 59 cities combined was $13.55. As appears from table 15, Butte prices were not repre-

Table 15.—Annual Costs [1] of Clothing Upkeep, 4-Person Manual Worker's Family, 59 Cities, March 1935

Annual cost	Number of cities	
	Maintenance level	Emergency level
Total	59	59
$9.00–$9.99	—	4
$10.00–$10.99	1	15
$11.00–$11.99	7	19
$12.00–$12.99	19	9
$13.00–$13.99	14	6
$14.00–$14.99	7	3
$15.00–$15.99	6	2
$16.00–$16.99	2	—
$17.00–$17.99	2	—
$18.00–$18.99	—	1
$19.00–$19.99	—	—
$20.00–$20.99	—	—
$21.00–$21.99	1	—
Average, [1] 59 cities	$13.55	$11.88

[1] Include sales tax where levied (appendix tables 15 and 16).

sentative, and clothing upkeep costs, as a rule, fell within a narrow range. There were more cities in which prices were below the average than above.

Prices charged for shoe repairs were extremely diverse and highest quotations exceeded lowest by 100 percent or more (table 14). For cleaning and pressing services even wider price ratios were common.

PERSONAL CARE

Prices of barber and hairdressing services, soap, and other toilet supplies combined with their quantity allowances produced an average annual personal care cost in the 59 cities combined of $24.87. The highest city was Butte, $29.32, and the lowest, Wichita, $21.36. The excess was 37.3 percent, and many more cities reported below than above average costs (table 16). Only two of the five items separately priced were at least twice as high in the most expensive as in the least expensive city (table 14).

Table 16.—Annual Costs[1] of Personal Care, 4-Person Manual Worker's Family, 59 Cities, March 1935

Annual cost	Number of cities	
	Maintenance level	Emergency level
Total	59	59
$14.00–$14.99	—	9
$15.00–$15.99	—	24
$16.00–$16.99	—	17
$17.00–$17.99	—	7
$18.00–$18.99	—	2
$19.00–$19.99	—	—
$20.00–$20.99	—	—
$21.00–$21.99	2	—
$22.00–$22.99	4	—
$23.00–$23.99	18	—
$24.00–$24.99	13	—
$25.00–$25.99	6	—
$26.00–$26.99	7	—
$27.00–$27.99	3	—
$28.00–$28.99	3	—
$29.00–$29.99	3	—
Average,[1] 59 cities	$24.87	$15.93

[1] Include sales tax where levied (appendix tables 15 and 16).

INFLUENCE OF GEOGRAPHIC LOCATION AND SIZE OF CITY ON COSTS OF CLOTHING, CLOTHING UPKEEP, AND PERSONAL CARE[3]

Larger sums were required to purchase the clothing, clothing upkeep, and personal care budgets in the Mountain and Pacific Areas than in any other section of the country (appendix table 5). Every city in these geographic divisions except Denver reported costs ex-

[3] See table 1, p. XV, for list of cities in each geographic division and their population and table 62, p. 128, for cost variations within separate geographic divisions and size of city classifications.

ceeding the average in the 59 cities combined, and 5 of the 7 cities with total annual maintenance budget values above $200 per year were located here. The costs of this major budget group were low in all sections of the South. Of the 20 cities in the South Atlantic, East South Central, and West South Central Divisions only 2 had costs as great as or more than the average in the 59 cities combined.

Outlays necessary for the principal subgroups showed much the same dispersions as for the three combined. Clothing was definitely expensive in the Pacific States and definitely cheap in the Southern cities. In other sections of the country high and low cost clothing was found, though in the North Central and Mountain States there were more places where it was above than below the average.

The cost of clothing upkeep was high everywhere west of the Rockies except in Los Angeles and was correspondingly low in most of the Southern cities. Costs in the other geographic divisions varied.

Personal care was uniformly more expensive than the 59-city average in all the Pacific and the smaller Mountain cities. Charges were high in the East North Central cities except in Detroit. Costs in the West North Central cities as a group averaged the lowest found anywhere, and all cities in the group except Cedar Rapids were below the average in the 59 cities combined. Personal care for the most part was cheap in the South.

Size of city apparently had no effect on the combined or separate costs of clothing, clothing upkeep, and personal care, except that the outlay necessary for clothing upkeep went up as the size of the cities went down (appendix table 7). Clothing and personal care costs were erratic among the five size of city classifications. Services were relatively less expensive than commodities in the largest cities, but for the group as a whole no relationship of any significance apparently can be attributed to size of city as such.

COST DIFFERENCES

The costs of outfitting a four-person manual worker's family with clothing and keeping its members clean and presentable varied slightly less than twice as much as did the costs of food. The considerable uniformity in the outlays necessary for these goods and services, wherever purchased, seems to have occurred because similar stocks of certain commodities at comparable prices are found everywhere in chain limited price variety stores; and because no matter how widely dispersed prices of other goods and services were, they never were all low or all high in the same place. Tendencies toward dispersion result from regional differences in charges for shipping commodities from producers to retailers, and from the existence of natural differentials based on climate and the standard of living whose influence was not eliminated by specifications. These general suggestions for explaining cost differences do not preclude the possible existence of peculiar local situations connected with the cost of doing business, intracity competition, and the like, which in a particular community may go far toward determining whether or not it is an expensive place in which to buy.

About one-tenth of the average cost of the maintenance budget for clothing, clothing upkeep, and personal care in the 59 cities combined was accounted for by $19.80, plus sales tax where levied, to cover the cost of chain limited price variety store merchandise and incidentals which were not specified. The stabilizing effect of being able to purchase the same commodities for the same price in any part of the country is particularly noticeable in the case of personal care; nearly one-third of the average annual cost of this maintenance budget subgroup was for such items.

A total of 102 goods and services [4] in the budgets for clothing, clothing upkeep, and personal care was separately priced in each city; for many of them city averages varied widely from place to place. Specifications for these items described inexpensive merchandise, such as usually is purchased by industrial, service, and other manual workers of small means. Some of these specifications were more exact than others, in the nature of the case, and it is possible that part of the intercity price diversity of clothing, just as of food, is attributable to the fact that quotations for identical goods and services were not always obtained. It never happened that all prices were extreme in any one place, however, no matter how much more or less than the average in the 59 cities combined the purchaser might have to pay for specific items. When the city average price of each was combined with its designated annual allowance as given in the quantity budgets and these costs were totaled, the spread between cities was greatly reduced. Hence, there was more cost uniformity for the group than was found for any of its separately priced component elements.[5]

All differences were not obliterated by this tendency toward high-low cost balancing, which was not half so effective as in the case of food, though prices of more than twice as many items were combined. Families in Butte or Cleveland required nearly one-third more for clothing and its upkeep and for the personal care of four individuals than in Dallas or Mobile, but among most of the cities cost differences were limited to a range of only half this ratio.

The great centers of the clothing industry for the most part are east of the Mississippi River, but production of garments in which fashion is not a primary consideration and no great skill is required

[4] Excluding duplications used in more than one subgroup.

[5] Except for sheep-lined jackets, for which the price spread without the sales tax was identical with that for the costs of the group as a whole, which include the tax.

is more generally scattered. Thus, advertised "prices slightly higher west of the Mississippi" or "west of Denver," to cover the greater cost of bringing garments or materials from factory to retailer, are indicated in the somewhat larger outlays for clothing quite generally found to be necessary west of the Rockies and in certain of the West North Central cities. Possibly, also, some of the cheapest merchandise sold in or near the places where it is made never finds its way to remote places because of high shipping costs.

Above average clothing costs reported in most of the cities in the two North Central Divisions and in certain New England and Middle Atlantic cities may result, however, more from their winter weather than from their distance from the wholesale markets. Even with the quantity budgets priced everywhere by uniform specifications, clothing locally sold seems to be adapted to probable need, for its cost was often high where winters are long and severe and low where they are short and mild, except on the Pacific Coast.[6] Differences not only in climate but also in standards of dress and personal care may be reflected in these prices. For example, the consistently lower prices of winter garments in the South than elsewhere, which largely account for low clothing costs in that section, seem to indicate that the quality is poorer or that when the period of use of warm clothing is relatively short only a small investment will be made in such apparel. Higher prices in the Northern cities may reflect the opposite situation. Thus, clothing prices seem to reflect local choice differentials which were not eliminated by specifications, as well as differential charges for sending merchandise from the producer to the consumer.

Clothing upkeep and personal care require services for the most part rather than commodities, and their prices are controlled more largely than commodity prices by local circumstances. These are not standardized among cities and tend to produce a wide range of cost differentials. Commodity prices totaling an identical amount in all cities somewhat limited the cost range for clothing upkeep as a whole, but not so much as in the case of personal care.

A sales tax in 18 cities (appendix tables 15 and 16) accounted for some differences in the relative costs of the budgets for clothing, clothing upkeep, and personal care. Services usually were exempt from the sales tax, but commodities quite generally were covered. Most cities with a sales tax were located in sections of the country where clothing costs would have been high had there been no tax. The cost of

[6] Instructions for pricing took account of the fact that March is a different season in various sections of the country by including only in-season quotations, no mark-down or clearance-sale prices. In none of the cities where the costs of clothing were high were the price collection periods far removed from the date to which prices referred. Even were prices quoted at a later date, however, recorded prices are more apt to be available from clothing stores than from food stores.

clothing in one of the Southern cities with a sales tax, however, was raised above the average because of its inclusion.

All costs of clothing, clothing upkeep, and personal care were computed from in-season prices. Families may not buy exactly the contents of the quantity budgets as listed, but any substitutions on the same basis would probably necessitate an equivalent outlay. Certain savings may be effected, however, by purchasing at special sale or mark-down values. Home making of some garments instead of purchasing them ready made as provided for in the budgets may also reduce clothing costs.

Chapter IV

HOUSING

RENTS OF houses or apartments meeting the qualifications specified in the maintenance budget for a 4-person manual worker's family in the 59 cities ranged from $342 per year in Washington to $158.40 in Portland (Oreg.) (appendix table 2). The former, therefore, was 115.9 percent more than the latter. Rents averaged $221.89 in all cities combined, with 29 cities above and 30 cities below this amount (fig. 5). Washington rent exceeded the average by 54.1 percent and Portland (Oreg.) rent was less by 28.6 percent (appendix table 3). These comparisons are based on quotations of house or apartment rents for four or five rooms and bath, plus the water rate in cities where the tenant pays this as a separate charge.[1] If reported rents be compared, there

Table 17.—Annual Rents,[1] 4 or 5 Rooms and Bath, 59 Cities, March 1935

MAINTENANCE LEVEL

Annual rent	Number of cities		
	All rents adjusted to include water cost	Reported rents include water cost	Reported rents do not include water cost
Total	59	33	26
$150.00–$174.99	7	2	5
$175.00–$199.99	10	6	10
$200.00–$224.99	17	8	4
$225.00–$249.99	13	8	4
$250.00–$274.99	9	6	3
$275.00–$299.99	1	1	—
$300.00–$324.99	1	1	—
$325.00–$349.99	1	1	—
Average,[1] 59 cities	$221.89	—	—

[1] Include sales tax where levied (appendix table 15).

[1] It is the custom in some cities for the owner of low rent houses to pay the water rate; in others, the tenant pays; in some cities, both procedures are found. In order to make all comparisons on the same basis, the cost of water was added to the average of reported rents in each city where the tenant pays this charge.

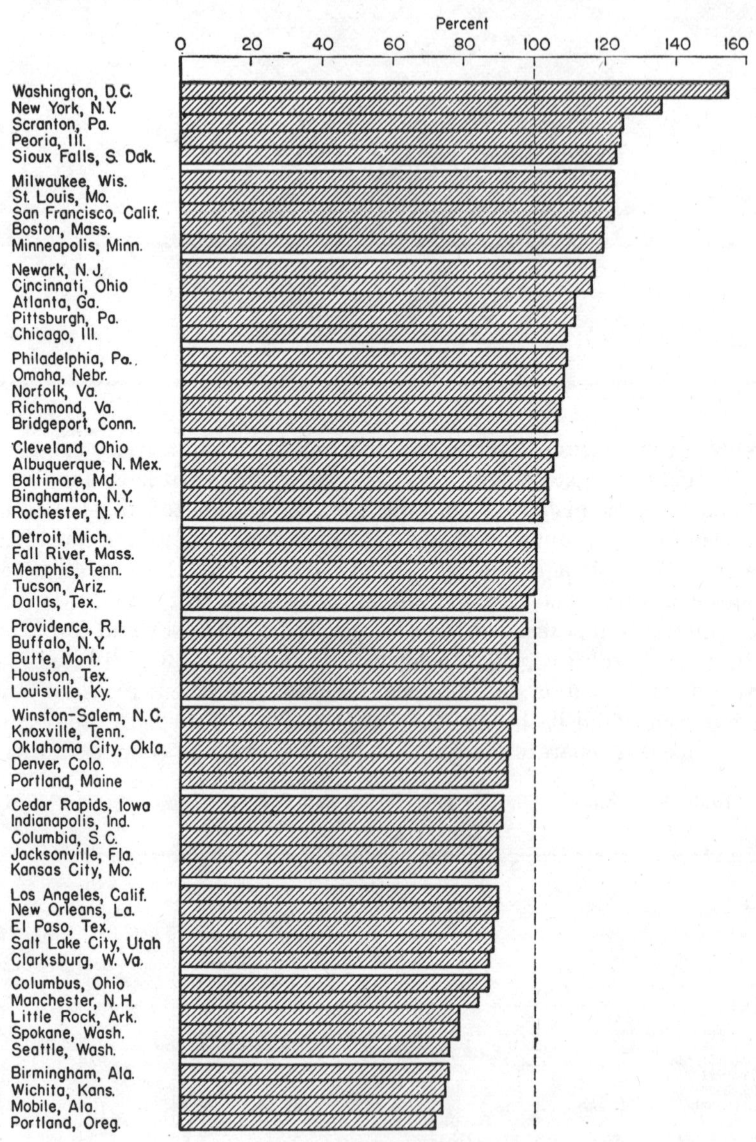

FIG. 5–RELATIVE RENTS, 4-PERSON MANUAL WORKER'S FAMILY, 59 CITIES, MARCH 1935

Maintenance Level

(Average 59 cities = 100)

AF-2117, W.P.A.

is a slightly different cost distribution between those which do and do not include the service of water. Nonpayment of the water rate, however, did not necessarily mean lower rents. Among the seven lowest rent cities in this study, five were thus classified after the water rate had been added (table 17). Highest reported rents do not seem to be in this position because they covered the water rate.

Rents at the emergency level of living were computed as 75 percent of reported rents at the maintenance level, plus the water rate where it was paid by the tenant. With local adjustments for water and other considerations in a few places, the average ratio was 75.6 percent (table 3). The smallest ratio, 73.5 percent, was found in Denver and the largest, 78.6 percent, in Butte.[2]

In most cities between $15 and $20 per month was required to secure satisfactory accommodations of four or five rooms with private bath (table 18). For less desirabe but habitable dwellings $10 to $15 per month was necessary.[3] The positions of the cities with reference to rents at the emergency level of living (appendix tables 8, 9, 11, and 13) were practically identical with those shown at the maintenance level.

Table 18.—Monthly Rents,[1] 4-Person Manual Worker's Family, 59 Cities, March 1935

Monthly rent	Number of cities	
	Maintenance level	Emergency level
Total	59	59
$5.00–$9.99	—	1
$10.00–$14.99	7	39
$15.00–$19.99	36	18
$20.00–$24.99	14	1
$25.00–$29.99	2	—
Average,[1] 59 cities	$18.49	$13.98

[1] Include the cost of water plus sales tax where levied (appendix tables 15 and 16).

INFLUENCE OF GEOGRAPHIC LOCATION AND SIZE OF CITY ON RENTS[4]

There was a tendency for rents to average highest in the Middle Atlantic, North Central, and South Atlantic States and lowest in the South Central, Mountain, and Pacific States (appendix table 5). Owing to the fact that water was not billed separately in any city studied in New England or the Middle Atlantic States, rents actually

[2] See p. 106 for discussion of the reason why emergency level rents actually were sometimes more and sometimes less than 75 percent of maintenance level rents.

[3] Quantity budgets for the two levels of living are given in complete detail in Stecker, Margaret L., *Quantity Budgets for Basic Maintenance and Emergency Standards of Living*, Research Bulletin, Series I, No. 21, Division of Social Research, Works Progress Administration, 1936. For the methods used in collecting quotations and computing city average prices and aggregate costs, see ch. VII.

[4] See table 1, p. XV, for list of cities in each geographic division and their population and table 62, p. 128, for cost variations within separate geographic divisions and size of city classifications.

paid for the housing listed showed a wider variation than when the charge for water was added to rents which did not cover this. All Middle Atlantic cities except Buffalo and all East North Central cities except Indianapolis and Columbus reported rents above the average in the 59 cities combined. Rents in every city [5] in the two South Central Divisions were low. Rents in the largest cities in the South Atlantic Division were above the average and in the smaller cities were below. The opposite situation appeared in the Mountain States. In the Pacific Area only San Francisco rents exceeded the average, and 3 of the 7 lowest rent cities among the 59 studied were in this section.

Size of city seems to have made more difference in rents than in the costs of any other major budget requirement (appendix table 7), but it is difficult to separate the factor of urbanization from that of climate. Thus, in cities with 375,000 or more population rents averaged considerably higher than they did in most of the smaller places, and rents reported in 15 of them were above the average in the group of 59. Fifteen of these nineteen largest cities, however, were in the high rent sections of the country; and two of the four which were in low rent areas had rents well above the area average. All the low rent smaller cities were not in the milder climates, but many were.

RENT DIFFERENCES

The very wide range of rents for working class housing which met certain specifications was no greater than the price ranges for many separate commodities and services in the other major budget groups. Because these commodity price extremes tended to cancel when combined to measure the group costs, the spreads for the other major budget groups were much less than the spread for rents, for which only housing and water were priced. Even so, $75 per year marked the limits of rent variations among most of the cities. This relationship is perhaps more remarkable than are the wide differences shown for a few cities at either extreme of the array, considering the great variety of housing which prevails throughout the country, the general nature of the specifications used in pricing, and the fact that most factors responsible for rents are of local origin. These matters cannot be analyzed in detail but a few generalizations seem to be warranted.

For the most part, more substantial and, therefore, more costly buildings are required in those sections of the country [6] where rents were

[5] Rent in Memphis including the water rate was just above the average in the 59 cities combined; water was a separate charge, however, so that rent as paid was well below the average.

[6] Rents in the South Atlantic Division would average slightly below the average in the 59 cities combined were it not for Washington, where an abnormal market had pushed rents to the highest reported in this study. Rents above the average were required in several other cities in this area, however, to obtain standard accommodations.

found to be highest. Brick or wood houses with basements, plumbing insulated against freezing temperatures, and other devices for insuring comfort during severe winter weather, however, may provide no more desirable shelter in the Northern cities than frame bungalows on piers in a warmer climate. Where less substantial houses are built of materials available nearby, low rents are common unless other circumstances more than counteract this advantage.

Rents were neither consistently high nor consistently low in all the geographic divisions, however; nor were all the high rents in the high rent areas or vice versa. This circumstance suggests that the situation in each city plays a considerable part in establishing relative rent levels. Land values apart from the improvements thereon, cost of municipal operation, and fiscal policy with reference to the tax burden are related to size of city to a considerable extent. Communities hard hit by the depression, those where working class dwellings have been overbuilt in relation to the demand, or those where other circumstances have kept a large supply of houses on the market may have low rents. In other cities, however, rents may be maintained at a higher level because of the diversified nature of their economic life or a shortage of low price housing.

Cities where home ownership is more common than the average sometimes lack proper rentable homes. A shortage of four- and five-room dwellings in comparison with available accommodations of other size may explain relatively high rents for four- and five-room units in some places. Working class housing, in general, is so poor in some cities that to get reports of rents for accommodations meeting the specifications it was necessary to price dwellings not customarily occupied by industrial, service, and other manual workers of small means.[7]

Thus, to climatic conditions and degree of urbanization as factors in rent differentials must be added the local supply of working class housing which meets certain specifications. Where such dwellings are usual, the reported average rent may be less, relative to the average in cities of the same size or in the same geographic location, than where unskilled laborers as a rule live in substandard houses. This is not to say that substandard housing commands a higher rent, but that it was not considered in the cost of living estimates. In such cities rents allowed were for houses not usually occupied by industrial, service, and other manual workers of small means.

Another factor in intercity rent differentials which cannot be measured with the data at hand is concerned with the relative acceptability

[7] A check with the Real Property Inventory in certain cities, where at first glance the rent allowances as calculated for this study appear to be high, shows that while many houses might be had for less than the amounts allowed, the proportions of these without private indoor bath and toilet or in poor condition were so large that the higher rents were required to obtain the standard specified.

of the housing priced. Specifications were necessarily general, and criteria for establishing the extent of adequacy were few. Hence, the four or five rooms and bath provided by the reported rents might be of varying size and convenience of layout, with a diversity of equipment ranging from old-fashioned to modern improvements. Single cottages, row houses, flats, and apartments might provide these accommodations. The age of the buildings and their construction materials were not homogeneous; size of building plots, desirability of neighborhoods, and location of the dwellings with reference to the social and industrial life of the city were not always the same. Any of these circumstances may account for ascertained rent differentials, apart from other considerations.

The rents used in the cost of living estimates are average figures for housing which met certain specifications in each city. Beyond conformity with these specifications, which were necessarily very general, it cannot be claimed that identical or even completely comparable accommodations were priced.

Except for a sales tax on water in 3 cities, the tenant paid no direct tax on his housing in any of the 59 cities studied (appendix tables 15 and 16).

Chapter V

HOUSEHOLD OPERATION

HOUSEHOLD OPERATION costs were computed from outlays necessary for the following items: fuel; ice; electricity; household supplies; furniture, furnishings, and household equipment; refuse disposal; and unspecified essentials.

The combined costs of all these goods and services in the maintenance budget for a 4-person manual worker's family averaged $153.54 per year in the 59 cities (appendix table 2). The disperson among the separate cities ran from $208.08 in Sioux Falls to $123.98 in Houston. This excess of 67.8 percent of greatest over least cost somewhat exaggerates the normal spread, because of the very large outlays necessary in two cities. Were Sioux Falls and Minneapolis with their unusual fuel costs omitted, the range would measure only 49.2 percent difference from lowest to highest. Twenty-nine cities exceeded the average and thirty cities reported less than the average cost of the household operation budget, but the lowest cost was more representative than the highest (fig. 6). The most expensive city cost exceeded the average in the 59 combined by 35.5 percent [1] and the cheapest was 19.3 percent below the average (appendix table 3).

Household operation costs were less narrowly concentrated than those for certain other budget groups previously considered (table 19), even leaving out the two extreme cities. Forty dollars per year marked the range within which more than half the city average costs fell.[2]

The spread between top and bottom emergency household operation budget costs (appendix tables 8, 9, 11, and 13) was somewhat greater

[1] Were it not for Sioux Falls and Minneapolis, the highest cost would have been only 20.5 percent above the average.

[2] Quantity budgets for the two levels of living are given in complete detail in Stecker, Margaret L., *Quantity Budgets for Basic Maintenance and Emergency Standards of Living*, Research Bulletin, Series I, No. 21, Division of Social Research, Works Progress Administration, 1936. For the methods used in collecting quotations and computing city average prices and aggregate costs, see ch. VII.

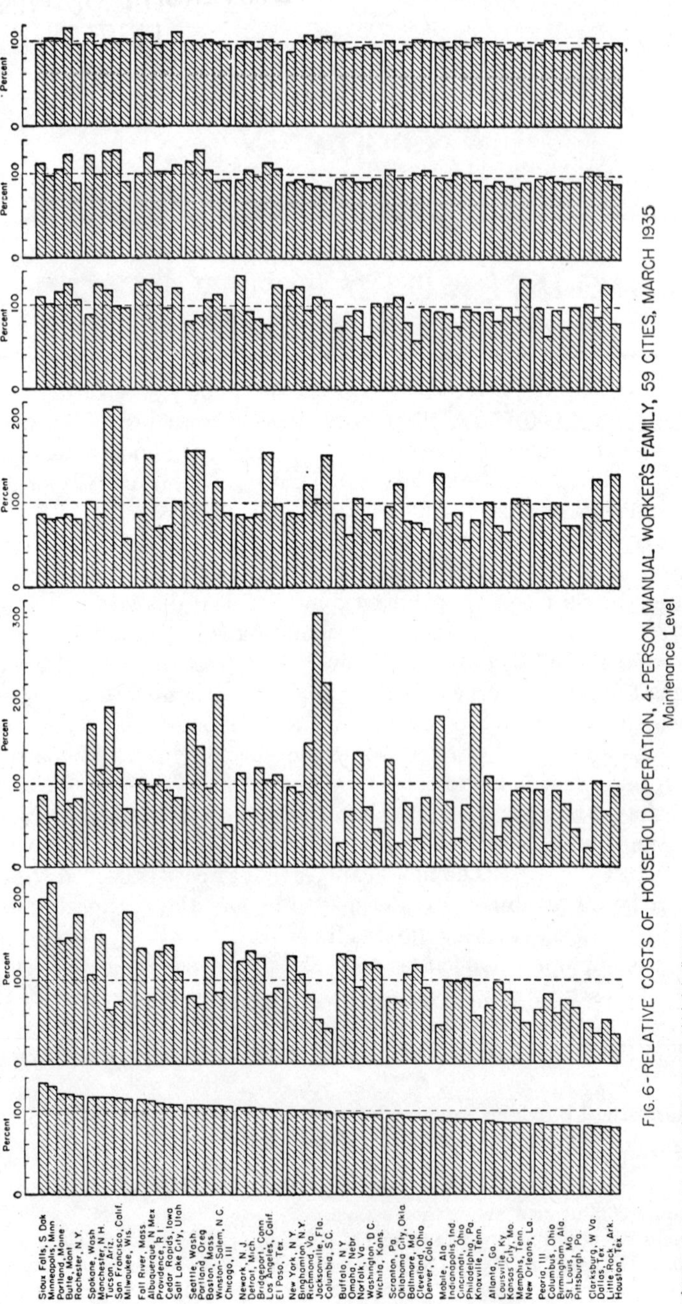

FIG. 6 - RELATIVE COSTS OF HOUSEHOLD OPERATION, 4-PERSON MANUAL WORKER'S FAMILY, 59 CITIES, MARCH 1935
Maintenance Level
(Average, 59 cities = 100)

* Relatives for the total computed from aggregates which include allowance for certain minor needs not itemized separately.

than the spread between maintenance budget costs. The ranks of certain cities also were shifted because of the existence of minimum charges for gas and electricity, which sometimes made the necessary emergency level bills for these services higher than would application of the rates alone to the quantity allowances. The two most expensive cities were identical in both arrays, but the lowest emergency budget cost was found in Clarksburg, as compared with Houston for the maintenance budget. The average difference was less than $32. Emergency budget cost averaged 79.4 percent of maintenance budget cost (table 3), and ratios varied from 82.3 percent in Minneapolis to 76.2 percent in Clarksburg.

Table 19.—Annual Costs[1] of Household Operation, 4-Person Manual Worker's Family, 59 Cities, March 1935

Annual cost	Number of cities	
	Maintenance level	Emergency level
Total	59	59
$90.00–$99.99	—	7
$100.00–$109.99	—	10
$110.00–$119.99	—	13
$120.00–$129.99	8	12
$130.00–$139.99	9	7
$140.00–$149.99	10	7
$150.00–$159.99	10	1
$160.00–$169.99	10	1
$170.00–$179.99	6	1
$180.00–$189.99	4	—
$190.00–$199.99	—	—
$200.00–$209.99	2	—
Average,[1] 59 cities	$153.54	$121.84

[1] Include sales tax where levied (appendix tables 15 and 16).

The average cost of the household operation budget was divided among the different goods and services which make it up as shown in table 20. Inasmuch as the annual costs of some of these items varied widely from city to city, the distributions of costs also showed wide differences. The saving in operating expenses at the emergency level of living through a curtailment of furniture, furnishings, and household equipment replacements is apparent. The cost of water, which logically is chargeable as a household operation expense, has been considered in connection with rent.[3]

Marked differences in the costs of the household operation budget appeared in different sections of the country (appendix table 5).[4] All New England, Pacific, and Mountain cities were high except Denver, and all South Central cities were low except El Paso. But in New England everything except ice and in the Mountain States

[3] See pp. 105–106.

[4] See table 1, p. XV, for list of cities in each geographic division and their population and table 62, p. 128, for cost variations within separate geographic divisions and size of city classifications.

everything except fuel, required more than the average outlay in the 59 cities combined, whereas in the Pacific States fuel and electricity took less. Necessary outlays for gas averaged high in the East South Central cities and for ice and electricity, in the West South Central cities; otherwise all annual costs were low in these areas.

Household operation costs declined with size of city until the middle classification was reached and then rose to the highest level in the smallest cities (appendix table 7). All household operation costs in cities with a population 250,000 to 500,000 were less than the average in the 59 cities combined, and all were more than the average in those cities where the population was 25,000 to 100,000. In the other size of city classifications some costs were high and others were low.

Table 20.—Percent Distribution of the Average Annual Costs[1] of Household Operation Among the Principal Commodity and Service Groups, 4-Person Manual Worker's Family, 59 Cities, March 1935

Group	Maintenance level	Emergency level
Total	100.0	100.0
Coal or wood	30.5	31.8
Gas	7.2	8.3
Electricity	12.2	11.9
Ice	14.6	15.3
Household supplies	12.3	13.9
Furniture, furnishings, and household equipment	20.2	15.3
Refuse disposal	1.0	1.2
Unspecified essentials	2.0	2.3
Average,[1] 59 cities	$153.54	$121.84

[1] Include sales tax where levied (appendix tables 15 and 16).

To interpret the cost of household operation as a whole, it is necessary to analyze the costs of its component elements. Except for the fact that the quantity budgets prescribe complementary periods of use for coal or wood and gas, and that ice is allowed for the same number of months as gas, these budget subgroups bear no relationship to each other and can be considered as entirely separate entities. On the other hand, since the complementary fuel and ice allowances are necessarily arbitrary there is an advantage in discussing fuel and ice costs together, in that a deficient allowance of one may be counterbalanced by an excessive allowance of the other. Hence, the cost of coal or wood, gas, and ice combined presents a better value for these items, to be apportioned by local requirements, than does the cost of any one of them separately.

FUEL

The fuel budgets itemize quantity requirements for anthracite, bituminous coal, or wood for room warming, cooking, and water heating throughout the coldest months, and gas for cooking and water heating during the remainder of the year. An identical amount of money was allowed everywhere for kindling, matches, and other fuel accessories. Coal or wood and accessories required about four-fifths of the average annual fuel cost and gas about one-fifth. There was a great variation among the separate cities.

The spread in total fuel costs between the most expensive and the least expensive city was greater than for any item of comparable importance in the family budget except transportation, and only three of lesser significance exceeded it.[5] In Minneapolis, where the outlay necessary per year for a four-person manual worker's family was $108.28 at the maintenance level of living, 326.8 percent more was required than in Clarksburg, with its annual fuel cost of $25.37 (appendix table 2). The average cost of the fuel budget in the 59 cities combined was $57.98; this was exceeded in 28 and not reached in 31. The highest cost exceeded the average by 86.8 percent and the lowest cost was less by 56.2 percent (appendix table 3). The classification of city costs (table 21) shows a considerable variation as well as a wide range between extremes, indicating that necessary annual fuel bills in the separate cities were not so uniform as were those for food, clothing, or housing.

Table 21.—Annual Costs[1] of Fuel, 4-Person Manual Worker's Family, 59 Cities, March 1935

Annual cost	Number of cities	
	Maintenance level	Emergency level
Total	59	59
$10.00–$19.99	—	1
$20.00–$29.99	3	5
$30.00–$39.99	5	10
$40.00–$49.99	13	18
$50.00–$59.99	16	13
$60.00–$69.99	8	6
$70.00–$79.99	8	3
$80.00–$89.99	2	2
$90.00–$99.99	2	1
$100.00–$109.99	2	—
Average,[1] 59 cities	$57.98	$48.80

[1] Include sales tax where levied (appendix tables 15 and 16).

Emergency fuel budget costs (appendix tables 8, 9, 11, and 13) averaged about $9 less per year than maintenance budget costs, but the differentials varied among the separate cities with the total cost of each fuel budget. The average ratio of 84.2 percent results from the fact that little economy in fuel is possible if modest comfort is to be secured. Differences in the ranks of cities in the two arrays are caused by the existence of minimum gas bills in some places. These often were greater than the costs of the emergency budget allowance

[5] Refuse disposal, school attendance, and taxes might or might not require a direct charge; hence, the spread in annual costs of these items varied from nothing to several dollars per year.

would have been had it been possible to consider rates alone, as usually was the case in computing maintenance gas budget costs.

The range in costs of the separate fuel items (tables 22 and 23), especially of gas, was much wider than of fuel as a whole. The

Table 22.—Annual Costs [1] of Coal or Wood, 4-Person Manual Worker's Family, 59 Cities, March 1935

Annual cost	Number of cities	
	Maintenance level	Emergency level
Total	59	59
$10.00–$19.99	3	6
$20.00–$29.99	7	13
$30.00–$39.99	15	15
$40.00–$49.99	9	11
$50.00–$59.99	11	9
$60.00–$69.99	8	1
$70.00–$79.99	2	3
$80.00–$89.99	2	1
$90.00–$99.99	1	—
$100.00–$109.99	1	—
Average,[1] 59 cities	$47.00	$38.66

[1] Include sales tax where levied (appendix tables 15 and 16).

Table 23.—Annual Costs [1] of Gas, 4-Person Manual Worker's Family, 59 Cities, March 1935

Annual cost	Number of cities	
	Maintenance level	Emergency level
Total	59	59
$0.00–$4.99	7	7
$5.00–$9.99	20	28
$10.00–$14.99	21	15
$15.00–$19.99	6	5
$20.00–$24.99	4	3
$25.00–$29.99	—	—
$30.00–$34.99	1	1
Average,[1] 59 cities	$10.98	$10.14

[1] Include sales tax where levied (appendix tables 15 and 16).

allowance of bituminous coal and fuel accessories at the maintenance level in Minneapolis was over six times as expensive as the comparable allowance of wood and fuel accessories at the same level in Houston (fig. 6). The outlay necessary for manufactured gas in Jacksonville was more than 13 times as much as that for natural gas in Clarksburg.

Influence of Geographic Location and Size of City on Costs of Fuel [6]

Fuel costs varied noticeably among the different sections of the country (appendix table 5). Every New England city was 20 percent

[6] See table 1, p. XV, for list of cities in each geographic division and their population and table 62, p. 128, for cost variations within separate geographic divisions and size of city classifications.

or more above the average in the group of 59. Four of seven West North Central cities exceeded the average by a wide margin; the two highest cost fuel cities studied were in this area. Though the outlays necessary for coal averaged about the same in New England and the West North Central States, the quantity of gas allowed in the budget was so much more expensive in the former than in the latter that the cost of the total fuel budget in New England was greater. The costs of fuel as a whole were uniformly low in both South Central Divisions, despite the large requirements for gas in several cities. In the Pacific Area every city except Spokane had a low total fuel cost, though the costs of the gas budget were high in all of them.

Size of city as such had no influence on the costs of fuel (appendix table 7). These costs declined as population decreased until the classification 250,000 to 500,000 was reached. In the two groups of smallest cities costs were higher than in the middle group. These relationships seem to depend on the geographic location of the cities, however, both with reference to climatic needs for winter fuel and distance from the source of supply.

Cost Differences

The family necessities whose costs were considered in the preceding chapters were allowed in equal quantity in all 59 cities on the theory that, though identical goods and services might not be universally consumed, the value of those priced would provide adequately for substitutes in local use. For fuel, however, average quantity allowances would be too much in some places and not enough in others, owing to the great extremes in the American climate. Moreover, no one fuel is in such general use that its price would be significant everywhere, even if quotations for it could be obtained. On the contrary, consumption of different kinds of fuel serving identical purposes is quite definitely localized. For these reasons alternative means of providing for room warming, cooking, and water heating were included in the quantity budgets; and the fuel priced in each city was the one most commonly used by industrial, service, and other manual workers of small means.[7]

The necessity for recognizing that quantity allowances of fuel for room warming depend on winter temperatures and that identical fuel is not used everywhere for a given purpose inevitably injected elements into fuel cost calculations which had nothing to do with the price of fuel as such. To get at the factor of price in fuel cost, therefore, as contrasted with quantity allowances and the kinds of fuel used, such an analysis is necessary as will eliminate the effects of

[7] As will be noted later, quantity allowances for the fuel most popular in a few cities are not contained in the budgets, and fuel costs were computed from prices of those which the budgets list. See pp. 52 and 108.

differential allowances and of pricing a variety of fuels in the separate cities. This is accomplished by classifying the cities in four groups according to their average winter temperatures: "A," cities with winters long or cold or long and cold; "B," average; "C," short or mild or short and mild; and "D," very short or very mild or very short and very mild. All cities in each climate group were allowed identical or comparable [8] quantities of fuel per year, but between the climate groups quantities were graduated by the number of months of use required in each. The number of cities in each of the four climate groups,[9] classified as to fuel priced for room warming, cooking, and water heating during the colder months and for cooking and water heating throughout the remainder of the year, is shown in table 24.

Table 24.—Kinds of Fuel Priced in 59 Cities in 4 Separate Climate Groups [1]

Kind of fuel	Number of cities in climate group [1]				
	Total	"A"	"B"	"C"	"D"
Total for colder months	59	13	24	13	9
Anthracite	13	3	10	—	—
Bituminous coal	40	[2] 10	13	10	7
Wood	6	—	1	3	2
Total for remainder of year	59	13	24	13	9
Natural gas	27	3	11	6	7
Manufactured gas	26	6	11	7	2
Mixed gas	6	4	2	—	—

[1] See text, above, for definition of these 4 climate groups, and p. 107 for list of cities in each group.
[2] Includes coke in 1 city.

The largest outlay for fuel generally, but not always, was found to be necessary where long, cold winters require the most extensive use of artificial heat for room warming, but at the other end of the scale the reverse was not true. There was a spread of 80.6 percent between the least expensive city and the most expensive city in the "A" group. Nine cities in the "B" group and even one "C" group city had average annual fuel costs exceeding that of the cheapest "A" city. The latter, however, ranking 23d from the highest cost city among the 59, was near the anthracite fields and coal prices were correspondingly low; the gas cost there was also less than the average in the 59 cities combined. Coal prices were so high in a few "A" cities that the average annual cost for the group was exceeded in only four, while costs were less than the average in nine. All cities with excessive fuel costs in the "A" group owed their positions to high coal prices. Only in New England were high coal prices combined with above average rates for the gas budget allowance.

[8] Based on consumption equivalents for anthracite, bituminous coal or coke, and wood, and on calorific values for natural, manufactured, or mixed gas.

[9] See p. 107 for list of the cities in each climate group.

Among the "B" cities largest annual fuel costs were uniformly found in New England and the Middle Atlantic anthracite using centers, where manufactured gas was the common cooking fuel and rates were relatively high. There was a wide range, however, among the cities in this average climate group. In Fall River, using anthracite, the cost of fuel was three times as much as in Clarksburg, using run-of-mine bituminous coal. Fall River is several hundred miles from the anthracite fields, whereas bituminous coal mining is one of Clarksburg's leading industries. Clarksburg, with its natural gas, reported the lowest cost for the budget allowance among the 59 cities studied; but manufactured gas in Fall River was more costly than the average.

The annual cost of fuel in Winston-Salem exceeded costs in all other "C" cities, ranking 21st from the top in the array of 59 and 94 percent above Little Rock where the cost of fuel was the lowest in the group. Coal prices in Winston-Salem averaged next to the highest in any of these 13 mild winter climate cities, and the gas rate for the budget allowance was highest of all. Little Rock fuel was inexpensive, not only because wood was most commonly used and its price was low but also because cheap natural gas made tho outlay necessary for cooking fuel next to the smallest in the "C" group.

The cost of fuel was greater in Jacksonville than in any other "D" city, owing largely to the high rate for the budget allowance of gas; the price of coal was about average in the group. In Houston, on the other hand, the gas rate was as low as any in the "D" city group; wood for room warming required a smaller outlay for winter fuel than in any other city among the 59 studied; and the total cost of fuel was less than in any other city except Clarksburg.

As table 26 shows, the only winter fuel priced in all sections of the country is bituminous coal.[10] From the equivalents for other fuels included in the quantity budgets, however, a comparison can be made of relative fuel costs, exclusive of sales tax where levied, in cities in the separate climate groups, with relative annual allowances of the same fuels in the same climate groups (table 25). Budget allowances are based on the assumption that needs in the "B" climate are average. The cost of winter fuel in the "B" cities combined averaged 101.4 percent of its cost in the 59 cities combined, with half above and half below. Thus, fuel budget costs in the "B" cities were very nearly representative of the average necessary outlay for fuel. In the "D" cities the cost of fuel was 76.6 percent more than the relative fuel requirement for that climate; in the "A" cities, 38.3 percent more; and in the "C" cities, 15.4 percent more. In other words, prices in the "B" cities were relatively low in the ratios shown.

[10] Bituminous coal was priced in some cities in each climate group, but it was not priced in all because it was not the usual domestic fuel.

Table 25.—Relative Quantity Allowances and Relative Fuel Costs in 4 Separate Climate Groups, 4-Person Manual Worker's Family, 59 Cities, March 1935 [1]

Climate group	Coal or wood	
	Annual quantity allowance [2]	Average annual cost [1]
"A"	115.4	159.6
"B"	100.0	100.0
"C"	61.5	71.0
"D"	26.9	47.5

[1] This comparison is based on maintenance budget quantity allowances and costs. The cost figures include neither the allowance for kindling and matches in all cities nor the sales tax where levied.
[2] Bituminous coal only. No other fuel was priced in all sections of the country.

Average prices of both anthracite and wood were much alike in the separate areas where these fuels are used, but bituminous coal prices covered a wider range (table 26). Among the separate cities bituminous coal prices were even more varied. The highest city average where bituminous coal is commonly used,[11] $12.89 per ton, was in the "A" group; three other cities reported average prices exceeding $10; and only two reported $7.50 or less. City average prices per ton were less than $8 in all "B" cities; the lowest were in three important bituminous coal centers. The 10 cities in the "C" group using bituminous coal reported average prices ranging from less than $6 in 2 cities near bituminous coal mines to $9.60 at Atlantic tidewater. Prices were $10.50 or more per ton in five of the seven "D" cities using bituminous coal.

Table 26.—Average Prices [1] of Coal and Wood in 4 Separate Climate Groups, 59 Cities, March 1935

Climate group	Average price		
	Coal per ton		Wood per cord
	Anthracite	Bituminous	
"A"	$12.55	[2] $9.42	—
"B"	12.39	5.59	$5.64
"C"	—	7.58	5.76
"D"	—	12.79	5.28

[1] Prices are without sales tax. [2] Includes coke in 1 city.

Anthracite quotations averaged $10, $12.65, and $15 per ton in the separate "A" cities. In the "B" group they ranged from $7.90 in Scranton, the center of the industry, to $15 in one of the New England cities; all except two reported more than $11 per ton. City average prices of wood per cord varied from $4 to $7.50 in the separate localities where this fuel is commonly used for room warming.

Common qualities which can be specified for pricing even a given kind of coal or wood wherever it is sold are almost entirely lacking,

[11] Highest prices were found in the "D" cities on the Pacific Coast and the Southwest, but coal is not the usual domestic fuel in these cities.

except for the size standardization of anthracite; nor is any one kind of coal or wood in general use. The range of calorific values, however, is probably more limited for anthracite than for bituminous coal or wood. Anthracite sizes are standardized, and the chestnut size as a rule was priced. There are no such universally accepted specifications for marketing bituminous coal or wood, and quotations necessarily were obtained for the grade and size popular as domestic fuel in each community. The area of anthracite mining and use is small, but bituminous coal is found in several parts of the country and its consumption is Nation-wide. Anthracite prices vary little at the mines, because of the generally uniform quality of the veins and the standardization of production costs through labor contracts.[12] The greater range of quality of bituminous coal and its scattered production centers make for greater price differentiation. Wood is the customary domestic fuel only where it is readily available and marketing costs are low. Part of the sectional uniformity of wood and anthracite prices no doubt reflects more nearly similar distribution charges than are embodied in bituminous coal prices, but part of it may be due to other circumstances peculiar to the industries.

Fuel prices during the heating season preceding March 1935 were collected. This period was not the same in all cities, nor were prices collected on the same date in all cities. A slight price variation may be attributable to these circumstances. The price of fuel is essentially seasonal, rising during the period of greatest use and falling during the warmer months.

Turning to an analysis of gas costs, a procedure may be followed somewhat similar to that employed in the discussion of outlays necessary for coal and wood. The quantity of gas allowed per year in each city depends on the number of months it is required for cooking and water heating and the kind of gas used, as given in the budgets. In both the "A" and "B" cities, where the allowance was for 5 months, annual group costs averaged $8.57; in the "C" cities, for 7 months, $13.52; and in the "D" cities, for 9 months, $17.24.

Even when reduced to a monthly basis and the sales tax is omitted, the budget allowances of gas averaged nearly 13 percent more expensive in the "C" cities than in the "B" cities and nearly 12 percent more in the "D" cities than in the "B" cities. Though differentials based on annual requirements play no part in necessary monthly bills, the kind of gas used is still present as a cost factor.

Costs of the monthly budget allowance of gas in the cities in the "A" and "B" groups covered a wide range. Spokane, where manu-

[12] Labor costs constitute nearly 60 percent of the total cost of mining anthracite. *Fifteenth Census of the United States, Mines and Quarries: 1929*, p. 11. Wages throughout the industry are regulated by agreement with the United Mine Workers of America.

factured gas is consumed and the largest outlay per month in any city among the 59 was required, is in the "B" group, as are several other cities with high rates for manufactured gas. On the other hand, many cities in or near the middle western oil fields are also in the "B" group. They use natural gas or mixed gas with a high B. T. U. content [13] and were among those having lowest monthly gas costs.

Six of the thirteen cities in the "C" group have manufactured gas whose monthly costs exceeded the group average. Manufactured gas also is consumed in Birmingham but its cost was below the group average. In the other six cities in the "C" group use of natural gas at low rates made for relatively low monthly gas costs. The smallest monthly bill required in any of the 59 cities for the quantity of gas allowed in the maintenance budget was for natural gas in Oklahoma City.

Among the 9 "D" cities the 2 which use manufactured gas were the 2d and 7th from the top of the array of monthly budget costs in the 59 cities. The two most expensive natural gas cities also were in this group of "D" cities. Natural gas is used in the 2 cheapest cities in the "D" group; these cities were 12th and 13th from the lowest in monthly cost among the 59 cities. Hence, whether manufactured or natural gas is supplied to the "D" cities, their monthly budget allowance costs were high in comparison with most of the other cities among the 59 studied.

The part played by kind of gas used in determining how much a family needs to spend a month for cooking and water heating fuel is suggested by the figures in table 27. Thermal content of gas varies, and necessary monthly bills to a considerable extent reflect these differences in calorific values because the monthly budget allowances

***Table* 27.—Monthly Costs [1] of Gas, 4-Person Manual Worker's Family, Classified by Kind of Gas, 59 Cities, March 1935**

Monthly cost	Kind of gas			
	All kinds	Natural	Manufactured	Mixed
Total	59	27	26	6
\$0.00–\$0.49	1	1	—	—
\$0.50–\$0.99	6	5	—	1
\$1.00–\$1.49	15	10	3	2
\$1.50–\$1.99	15	7	5	3
\$2.00–\$2.49	12	4	8	—
\$2.50–\$2.99	6	—	6	—
\$3.00–\$3.49	2	—	2	—
\$3.50–\$3.99	2	—	2	—
Average,[1] 59 cities	\$1.79	\$1.35	\$2.33	\$1.38

[1] All costs refer to the maintenance level and are without sales tax. Inasmuch as this table is included only for illustrative purposes, comparable data for the emergency level were not assembled.

[13] B. T. U. is the abbreviation for British thermal unit, the quantity of heat required to raise 1 pound of water through 1 degree Fahrenheit. The more B. T. U.'s contained per 1,000 cu. ft. of gas, the fewer cu. ft. are required for any given service.

for manufactured gas are greater than those for natural or mixed gas. Arraying the estimated necessary monthly gas bills at the maintenance level of living in the 59 cities, 27 were above the average and 32 were below. Of those above, 19 have manufactured, 7 have natural, and 1 has mixed gas. Of those below, 7 have manufactured, 20 have natural, and 5 have mixed gas. The 12 cities where largest monthly bills were required use manufactured gas. Manufactured gas is used in 18 of the 20 cities where gas costs were highest, and natural gas or mixed gas approaching a natural gas B. T. U. content is used in 18 of the 20 cities where gas costs were lowest.

When reduced to the common basis of outlay necessary per month to obtain approximately equivalent calorific values, it is apparent, therefore, that natural gas was less expensive than manufactured gas. This is true because basic rates for a specified quantity of natural gas usually were lower than those of manufactured gas,[14] and also because the B. T. U. content of natural gas is greater, with a consequently smaller allowance for a given purpose.

The largest annual outlays for gas were required in the two cities where its use for 9 months was allowed, where manufactured gas is consumed, and where the rates for the monthly allowance were high. The combination of 9 or 7 months' use and high price manufactured gas explains all annual gas costs exceeding $15, except in three cities. In Tucson and Mobile, which have natural gas, the budget allowance called for 9 months' use, but the rates were higher than in any other city in which natural gas was priced. In Spokane for 5 months' use of manufactured gas the rate for the monthly budget allowance was the highest reported.

From the foregoing analysis it appears that local fuel price differences depend for the most part on the kind of fuel consumed and distance from the source of supply. Coal grade variations cannot be measured, but they account for some of the diversity of reported prices. The B. T. U. content of gas plays a large part in determining how much the monthly bill will be. Natural gas is used in the locality of its source and often it is piped long distances. Manufactured gas usually is consumed within a small radius of the place where it is made, and to a large extent its price is related to the price of the coal from which it is produced. Shipping costs, therefore, may enter into gas rates as well as into coal and wood prices. The demand for gas and the location of its customers in each locality also determine the price of the service rendered. Gas rates, like charges for other public utilities, are subject to government regulation; and peculiarities of a given local situation, unrelated to any other community, often are embodied in the rate structure.

[14] Basic rates have not been discussed because of the great variety of factors of which they are composed.

Inasmuch as annual outlay necessary for fuel depends on quantity allowance, kind of fuel, and price, its amount in the separate cities is determined by different combinations of three variables. Places which require more than average fuel for room warming because of their long and cold winters frequently are far removed from the coal fields. Prices, therefore, are high, since often only the better grade of coal is shipped and freight charges are heavy. If manufactured gas is used for cooking and water heating in these same cities, its costs may be greater for 5 months' use than the costs of natural gas consumed over a longer period of time in cities where rates are lower. Where rates are high and gas is required for 7 or 9 months, even with low price coal or wood necessary for only 5 or 3 months, costs of the total fuel budget may exceed costs where more fuel for room warming is required. These are only examples of possible combinations of gas rates, coal or wood prices, and quantity allowances which determine the annual cost of fuel in a given community.

The fuel included in the quantity budgets was more expensive than possible substitutes in a few cities, and use of these alternatives was sometimes reported. For example, range oil may take the place of anthracite in New England, and homes are warmed by natural gas in Los Angeles. Families of small means do not use gas in certain cities, but coal, wood, or oil takes its place. Thus, in Columbia, Portland (Oreg.), Spokane, and Winston-Salem wood is the customary cooking and water heating fuel the year around; in Seattle wood is used in summer, and coal, in winter. Both oil and wood are used for this purpose in Jacksonville and Mobile; coal, in Butte, Knoxville, and Salt Lake City; and oil, in Portland (Maine).

A smaller quantity of fuel may be required to warm rooms in apartments or other compact units than is included in the budgets for a stove heated house. The total cost of fuel is not likely to be much reduced, however, because coal for apartment use frequently is purchased in small units at high rates. The smaller quantity required, therefore, may be counterbalanced by the higher prices paid.

A factor making for greater uniformity in fuel costs than would exist otherwise is the inclusion of an identical money allowance in all cities to provide for kindling, matches, and other fuel accessories not subject to quantity itemization. The cost of coal and gas alone, without this stabilizing element, was over 400 percent greater in the highest cost city than in the lowest, as contrasted with 327 percent difference when the allowance for accessories was added.

The sales tax as such played a minor part in accounting for intercity differences in the costs of the fuel budget. Consumers paid a tax on coal or wood and accessories in 18 cities and on gas in 11 cities (appendix tables 15 and 16). Among the cities where fuel costs were highest, the top 7 in the array of 59 had no sales tax; and Clarksburg, at the bottom of the scale, had a sales tax.

ICE

Few families at the economic level with which this study is concerned own mechanical refrigerators. Ice is commonly used for food preservation during part of the year, however, in most sections of the country.

The average cost of ice in the 59 cities included in this study was $22.40 per year for a 4-person manual worker's family living at the maintenance level (appendix table 2); 21 cities were above this average, and 38 were below (fig. 6). Highest costs were $47.97 in San Francisco [15] and $47.50 in Tucson; lowest costs were $12.96 in Milwaukee and Philadelphia. The cost of ice in San Francisco was 270.1 percent more than in Milwaukee or Philadelphia; the former exceeded the average by 114.2 percent and the latter were less than the average by 42.1 percent (appendix table 3). In nearly three-quarters of the cities the costs of the maintenance ice budget were between $15 and $25 per year (table 28); emergency budget costs were similarly concentrated, at a lower level.

***Table 28.*—Annual Costs [1] of Ice, 4-Person Manual Worker's Family, 59 Cities, March 1935**

Annual cost	Number of cities	
	Maintenance level	Emergency level
Total	59	59
$10.00–$14.99	3	14
$15.00–$19.99	31	32
$20.00–$24.99	12	4
$25.00–$29.99	4	5
$30.00–$34.99	2	2
$35.00–$39.99	5	2
$40.00–$44.99	—	—
$45.00–$49.99	2	—
Average,[1] 59 cities	$22.40	$18.67

[1] Include sales tax where levied (appendix tables 15 and 16).

The emergency ice budget allowance is 83.3 percent of the maintenance budget allowance. The annual costs of ice, therefore, showed this ratio in all cities (appendix tables 8, 9, 11, and 13), and the ranks of cities were identical in both series.

Influence of Geographic Location and Size of City on Costs of Ice [16]

Ice costs averaged highest in the South Atlantic, West South Central, Mountain, and Pacific cities. They were well below the average in all other areas except the East South Central, and here

[15] See p. 55 for comment on the representativeness of this ice cost.

[16] See table 1, p. XV, for list of cities in each geographic division and their population and table 62, p. 128, for cost variations within separate geographic divisions and size of city classifications.

they were 99.7 percent of the average in the 59 cities combined (appendix table 5). Every New England, Middle Atlantic, and North Central city was low; every Pacific city was high; in other sections above and below average costs accounted for the relative positions of the areas as a whole.

Size of city was without significance as a factor in ice costs (appendix table 7). The group average in the smallest places was well above that in the 59 cities combined, but in 8 of the 13 smallest cities costs were below the 59-city average.

Cost Differences

The annual cost of ice is dependent on the quantity allowance and the price for which it is sold. Ice is allowed in the budgets for the months when fuel for room warming is not necessary: namely, 5, 7, or 9 per year. The high average cost of ice in the group of 59 cities results from the fact that in a few places where most ice was allowed its price was the highest recorded. All cities where ice costs exceeded $25 per year were in the group for which the budget allowed a period of 7 or 9 months' use.

Table 29.—Prices[1] of Ice per 100 Pounds, 59 Cities, March 1935

Price	Number of cities
Total	59
$0.40–$0.44	7
$0.45–$0.49	5
$0.50–$0.54	13
$0.55–$0.59	5
$0.60–$0.64	21
$0.65–$0.69	2
$0.70–$0.74	1
$0.75–$0.79	1
$0.80–$0.84	4
Average,[1] 59 cities	$0.57

[1] Prices are without sales tax and are based on a sales unit of 25 lbs.

Most ice for city consumption today is manufactured rather than winter cut and stored, but plants are located where the product is used and only the peculiarities of the local situation control its price. The rate per 100 pounds computed from quotations for a 25-pound piece delivered can be used to separate the price of ice from its annual allowances in the budgets. This rate ranged from 40 cents to 80 cents (table 29). The most frequent quotations for 25 pounds were 13 cents and 15 cents. Prices varied within the cities but the average in each would purchase ice at a representative rate.

Average prices of ice per 100 pounds, when purchased in a 25-pound piece delivered, were almost identical in the four climate groups for which quantity allowances differed (table 30).[17] The large allowances

[17] Quantity allowances of ice in the "A" and "B" cities were identical. See pp. 108 and 110.

assigned to the 22 cities in the "C" and "D" groups, therefore, were more accountable for the fact that their ice costs ranked at the top of the array of the 59 cities than was the price of ice. A comparison of average prices with annual costs in different parts of the country (table 31) indicates that high prices and high annual costs or vice versa seldom went together.

Table 30.—Average Prices [1] of Ice per 100 Pounds in 4 Separate Climate Groups, 59 Cities, March 1935

Climate group	Average price
Average, 59 cities	$0.57
"A"	.55
"B"	.56
"C"	.58
"D"	.57

[1] Prices are without sales tax and are based on a sales unit of 25 lbs.

Except for Tucson and Albuquerque, where quotations were among the highest reported, the price of ice, in general, was low where most is required and high where least is required. This relationship does not appear from the tabulations, because employing winter temperature as a criterion for city grouping resulted in large ice allowances in several places where use of artificial refrigeration is uncommon at any time. In San Francisco, Portland (Oreg.), and Seattle ice was 80 cents per 100 pounds when purchased in 25-pound units, but 85 percent of the families interviewed in San Francisco, 77 percent in Portland (Oreg.), and 55 percent in Seattle reported that they used neither ice nor mechanical refrigeration. This custom may be due partly to the high price of ice and partly to the fact that summers are not warm enough to make ice a necessity.[18] The latter is probably the more important reason, because in Tucson, where ice also was 80 cents per 100 pounds and summer temperatures are high, more than half the reporting families purchased ice, and all but three of the remainder had mechanical refrigerators. In Albuquerque, with ice at 76 cents per 100 pounds, 53 percent of the families used it, but 31 percent reported they used no refrigeration of any kind. Thus, it is not unlikely that in San Francisco and Portland (Oreg.), and possibly in Seattle, the estimated costs of living are high by the amounts that have been allowed for ice, if inadequate provision for other essentials did not absorb these surpluses. From the information collected on the family schedule, it appears that ice is a necessity in the other cities.

[18] That ice is not a necessity in San Francisco is indicated by the fact that in the Heller Committee budgets only the executive is allowed refrigeration. His cost of living averaged $6,025 per year in November 1935. Budgets for a clerk and for a wage earner make no provision for ice or refrigeration. See Heller Committee for Research in Social Economics, *Quantity and Cost Budgets * * * Prices for San Francisco, November 1935*, University of California, Berkeley, Calif., February 1936.

A sales tax was levied on ice in all 18 cities where there was such a tax (appendix tables 15 and 16). Without the tax the ice cost spread would be somewhat reduced.

The budget allowances of fuel and ice were based on the assumption that the periods of their use within a year were complementary. It is perhaps best, therefore, to consider costs also as complementary. The annual outlay necessary for coal or wood, gas, and ice in each city would then be considered in the aggregate rather than separately. In such a combination dispersion was greatly narrowed as compared with the cost spread of any one of these items alone (table 62),[19] and a better comparison of intercity variations is obtained.

Table 31.—Relative Prices of Ice per 100 Pounds and Relative Annual Costs[1] of Ice in 9 Separate Geographic Divisions, 59 Cities, March 1935

Geographic division	Percent of 59-city average [1]	
	Price	Annual cost
New England	102.1	83.4
Middle Atlantic	100.5	82.4
East North Central	97.7	81.5
West North Central	89.9	73.7
South Atlantic	97.7	107.8
East South Central	86.4	99.7
West South Central	85.8	112.3
Mountain	117.9	125.7
Pacific	131.0	160.1

1 Prices are without sales tax and are based on a sales unit of 25 lbs.; annual costs include sales tax where levied (appendix tables 15 and 16).

ELECTRICITY

Electricity is generally consumed for light and operation of small household appliances.[20] Hence, electric energy was priced in all cities, and provision for lamp replacements and other electrical accessories was included in annual electricity cost. At rates in operation March 15, 1935, the outlays necessary for energy and accessories in the 59 cities combined averaged $18.68 per year for a 4-person manual worker's family at the maintenance level of living. Twenty-five cities exceeded this average and thirty-four were lower, suggesting that high rates for the budget allowance in a few places somewhat raised the average (fig. 6).

19 This phenomenon appears for many combinations of items. The present one is significant because of the complementary allowances in the quantity budgets, not because of canceling price differentials. The latter may play a part, however, in the greatly reduced dispersion of combined costs as compared with any one separately.

20 In a few cities families of small means reported using oil for illumination, because they either had found it cheaper than electricity or had failed to deposit the necessary guarantee with the utility companies.

In Newark where $25.37 was required, the annual necessary electricity bill was 127.9 percent more than the $11.13 required in Cleveland (appendix table 2). For energy only, the difference was 145.1 percent. Newark's cost exceeded the average by 35.8 percent and Cleveland's was less than the average by 40.4 percent (appendix table 3). Costs within a range of $8 per year provided for necessary energy and accessories in most places (table 32).

Table 32.—Annual Costs[1] of Electricity, 4-Person Manual Worker's Family, 59 Cities, March 1935

Annual cost	Number of cities	
	Maintenance level	Emergency level
Total	59	59
$7.00–$8.99	—	1
$9.00–$10.99	—	4
$11.00–$12.99	3	11
$13.00–$14.99	4	19
$15.00–$16.99	10	11
$17.00–$18.99	18	9
$19.00–$20.99	9	4
$21.00–$22.99	7	—
$23.00–$24.99	6	—
$25.00–$26.99	2	—
Average,[1] 59 cities	$18.68	$14.52

[1] Include sales tax where levied (appendix tables 15 and 16).

Emergency electricity budget costs (appendix tables 8, 9, 11, and 13) averaged about $4 per year less than maintenance budget costs. Cities ranked somewhat differently at the two levels of living, however, owing to the fact that minimum bills, meter, and similar charges carried greater weight with the smaller allowance in the emergency than in the maintenance budget.

Influence of Geographic Location and Size of City on Costs of Electricity[21]

Electricity rates for the budget allowance, in general, were high in the New England, Middle Atlantic, West South Central, and Mountain Divisions (appendix table 5); all but 7 of the 25 cities studied in these 4 areas reported costs considerably above the average in the 59 cities combined. Below average costs, on the other hand, were reported from every East North Central, East South Central, and Pacific city. High and low rates were found in the other sections.

Electricity rates seem to have increased as the size of cities decreased, except that where the population was a million or more they were higher than in cities where the population was between 250,000 and 1,000,000 (appendix table 7).

[21] See table 1, p. XV, for list of cities in each geographic division and their population and table 62, p. 128, for cost variations within separate geographic divisions and size of city classifications.

Cost Differences

Factors influencing the cost of electricity are largely local in character. Kind and density of the population served, and diversity of their requirements both as to time of day and amount of energy used, accessibility to fuel or water power, and seasonal consumption probably condition the price necessarily charged. Inasmuch as the distribution of electric energy is virtually a monopoly in most communities, State regulation has attempted to control rates for the benefit of the consumer, but the force of tradition has kept many variations of which some depend on circumstances no longer in operation.[22]

The inclusion of an identical amount in all cities to pay for accessories which can be purchased everywhere for the same price resulted in a smaller cost spread than was shown for energy alone.

A sales tax was added to the total cost of energy and accessories in 11 cities and to the cost of accessories only, in 7 cities (appendix tables 15 and 16). The amounts required were small but contributed a little to the variation in electricity costs among the separate cities.

HOUSEHOLD SUPPLIES

The annual costs of soap and other cleaning and laundry supplies for a 4-person manual worker's family in each of the 59 cities studied ranged from a high of $23.93 in Tucson to a low of $16.10 in Columbia, at the maintenance level of living (appendix table 2); the former was 48.6 percent more than the latter. The outlays necessary for household supplies in the 59 cities combined averaged $18.82. More cities reported low costs than high costs, however, for extreme prices in a few produced an arithmetic mean which only 24 exceeded while 35

Table 33.—Annual Costs[1] of Household Supplies, 4-Person Manual Worker's Family, 59 Cities, March 1935

Annual cost	Number of cities	
	Maintenance level	Emergency level
Total	59	59
$14.00–$14.99	—	5
$15.00–$15.99	—	17
$16.00–$16.99	8	13
$17.00–$17.99	16	13
$18.00–$18.99	13	3
$19.00–$19.99	11	2
$20.00–$20.99	2	4
$21.00–$21.99	3	2
$22.00–$22.99	3	—
$23.00–$23.99	3	—
Average,[1] 59 cities	$18.82	$16.94

[1] Include sales tax where levied (appendix tables 15 and 16).

[22] Federal Power Commission, *Electric Rate Survey, Preliminary Report, Domestic and Residential Rates in Effect January 1, 1935, Cities of 50,000 Population and Over,* Rate Series No. 1, p. 14.

were less (fig. 6). The most expensive city was above the average by 27.2 percent but the cheapest was only 14.4 percent below (appendix table 3). Differences of $3 per year marked the range among two-thirds of the cities (table 33).

Inasmuch as the cost of the emergency household supplies budget was computed as 90 percent of the cost of the maintenance budget (appendix tables 8, 9, 11, and 13), relative costs of both were identical.

Eleven commodities constitute the household supplies budget. Five were separately priced in each city; for the other six, an identical amount of money was allowed in all cities, based on chain limited price variety store quotations which are likely to be the same everywhere.

Though the costs of household supplies as a group differed but slightly among most of the cities, the spread was much greater for some of the separate commodities of which it is composed (table 34).[23]

Table 34.—Household Supplies Commodity Price Ratios,[1] 59 Cities, March 1935

Commodity	Number of cities where prices exceeded ±10 percent with reference to the 59-city average[1]			Percent highest price is of lowest price[1]
	Total	Above average	Below average	
Total[2] household supplies	17	10	7	148.6
Soap powder	45	24	21	417.4
Kitchen soap	44	19	25	282.0
Soap flakes	30	11	19	250.9
Starch	10	5	5	189.9
Laundry soap	14	11	3	149.2

[1] The ratio for the total is identical for a 4-person manual worker's family at both the maintenance and emergency levels. The total cost of household supplies includes sales tax where levied (appendix tables 15 and 16); commodity prices are without sales tax.

[2] Includes an identical allowance in all cities for items not separately priced, as well as prices for the items listed which were priced in each city, combined with their quantity allowances in the maintenance budget.

Prices of soap flakes, for example, were so high in a few cities that the average in the 59 combined was greater than in 42 of them separately. Laundry soap quotations were more uniform, but in 33 cities the prices were below the average for this item, in 2 they were at the average, and in 24 they were above the average.

Influence of Geographic Location and Size of City on Costs of Household Supplies[24]

Nine of the ten highest cost cities for household supplies were in the group of ten in the Pacific and Mountain States (appendix table 5).

[23] Prices in all instances are compared without sales tax in order that the two may not be confused in the measurement of intercity differences. Were the tax where levied added to prices, the spread often would be greater than appears in the comparison without tax. The total cost of household supplies includes sales tax where levied.

[24] See table 1, p. XV, for list of cities in each geographic division and their population and table 62, p. 128, for cost variations within separate geographic divisions and size of city classifications.

The lowest cost cities were geographically more scattered, but 5 of the 10 in this class were found among the 14 South Atlantic and East South Central cities.

No cost variation for household supplies appears to be directly connected with size of city (appendix table 7). The largest deviation from the average was observed in the excessive cost in the smallest cities. Three of these are located in the Mountain Division, however, where prices were the highest in the country.

Cost Differences

The dispersion of costs of household supplies among the 59 cities exceeded that for certain other commodity groups, but was less than might have been expected, considering the few items of which the group is composed and the extremely general specifications by which these goods were priced. Average prices per pound in the separate cities reflect differences in brand, in weight of the commodity unit, and in unit of sale, as well as price differentials of specific commodities on a unit price basis. For the most part, however, field agents obtained samples of strong and mild cleansing materials in a range of prices so that when quotations were averaged, combined with quantity allowances, and totaled, the costs of the budget as a whole showed no such spread as the prices of the separate items displayed. In the highest cost cities better brands of merchandise were more uniformly priced, and quotations for these brands were higher than the average. A preponderance of yellow soaps and powders in the sample kept down the cost of household supplies in the South.

The relatively narrow range in the costs of household supplies as a group is also to be accounted for by the inclusion of an identical amount of money in all cities for a few items, the prices of which tend to be the same everywhere. This identical allowance totaled 30.5 percent of the average cost in the 59 cities, 24.2 percent in the highest, and 35.4 percent in the lowest.

A sales tax in 18 cities (appendix tables 15 and 16) had little effect on the variation in costs of the household supplies budget.

Had it been possible to set up a balanced budget of cleaning supplies by brand name, identical size of commodity unit, and uniform unit of sale, prices might not have been so widely dispersed as happened where a variety of articles meeting each specification was priced, but some differences would have appeared. Each locality seems to have its own group of best sellers, however, and these are not the same the country over.

Thus, though the variation in prices of individual commodities was wide, the very greatly reduced differences observed when all were combined probably represent what families in the separate localities had to pay for household supplies in the course of a year. To analyze commodity price differentials separately, brand, size of commodity unit, and unit of sale would necessarily be segregated, and comparisons would be made only to the extent that prices could be related to a completely homogeneous sample.

FURNITURE, FURNISHINGS, AND HOUSEHOLD EQUIPMENT

The annual costs of necessary replacements of furniture, furnishings, and household equipment for a 4-person manual worker's family living at the maintenance level averaged $31.10 in the 59 cities combined and ranged from a high of $36.27 in Butte to a low of $27.53 in New York (appendix table 2). This difference of 31.7 percent represents rather extreme variations, with the excess somewhat on the side of high costs; 28 cities were above the average and 31 were below (fig. 6). Necessary outlay in the most expensive city was 16.6 percent more than the average, but in the least expensive it was only 11.5 less (appendix table 3). Five dollars per year marked the difference in costs of necessary replacements of furniture, furnishings, and household equipment among most of the cities (table 35); emergency budget costs were within narrower limits.

The cost of the emergency furniture, furnishings, and household equipment budget (appendix tables 8, 9, 11, and 13) was computed as 60 percent of the cost of the maintenance budget. Intercity differences, therefore, were identical at both levels of living.

More than 150 commodities constitute the requirements for housekeeping listed in the quantity budgets; their prices represent the

Table 35.—Annual Costs[1] of Furniture, Furnishings, and Household Equipment, 4-Person Manual Worker's Family, 59 Cities, March 1935

Annual cost	Number of cities	
	Maintenance level	Emergency level
Total	59	59
$16.00-$16.99	—	2
$17.00-$17.99	—	14
$18.00-$18.99	—	19
$19.00-$19.99	—	17
$20.00-$20.99	—	5
$21.00-$21.99	—	2
$22.00-$22.99	—	—
$23.00-$23.99	—	—
$24.00-$24.99	—	—
$25.00-$25.99	—	—
$26.00-$26.99	—	—
$27.00-$27.99	1	—
$28.00-$28.99	7	—
$29.00-$29.99	9	—
$30.00-$30.99	12	—
$31.00-$31.99	13	—
$32.00-$32.99	9	—
$33.00-$33.99	2	—
$34.00-$34.99	4	—
$35.00-$35.99	1	—
$36.00-$36.99	1	—
Average,[1] 59 cities	$31.10	$18.66

[1] Include sales tax where levied (appendix tables 15 and 16).

initial cost of furniture, furnishings, and household equipment from which annual replacement cost was calculated. About one-third of these commodities were separately priced in each city and two-thirds were quoted everywhere at prevailing chain limited price variety store

Table 36.—Furniture, Furnishings, and Household Equipment Commodity Price Ratios,[1] 59 Cities, March 1935

Commodity	Number of cities where prices exceeded ± 10 percent with reference to the 59-city average[1]			Percent highest price is of lowest price[1]
	Total	Above average	Below average	
Total[2] furniture, furnishings, and household equipment	5	4	1	131.7
Living room rug	25	13	12	185.7
Living room heater	36	15	21	475.6
Living room table	28	14	14	180.0
Upholstered chair	35	19	16	260.7
Rocker or arm chair	24	11	13	179.3
Straight wood chair	34	17	17	220.7
Table lamp	31	15	16	204.0
Radio	27	15	12	236.9
Small bedroom rug	39	19	20	305.8
Bureau with mirror	14	8	6	136.3
Chest of drawers	18	8	10	157.3
Double bed	15	8	7	156.1
Cot	24	12	12	179.0
Double bed spring	24	12	12	179.6
Bedroom chair	44	21	23	311.8
Double bed mattress	21	10	11	183.5
Cot mattress	29	14	15	216.0
Bed pillow	22	11	11	229.6
Double bed sheet	16	9	7	154.2
Cot sheet	21	8	13	191.3
Pillow case	24	13	11	207.0
Wool blankets	34	15	19	292.6
Cotton comforter	26	11	15	211.1
Bedspread	30	14	16	206.1
Couch cover	40	18	22	333.3
Table cloth	22	12	10	193.0
Napkins	38	16	22	375.4
Felt base rug	16	9	7	164.8
Kitchen range	37	16	21	308.8
Coal scuttle	21	9	12	177.0
Ash can	33	13	20	242.6
Gas plate	34	11	23	343.2
Portable oven	42	18	24	356.3
Refrigerator	26	11	15	226.0
Kitchen table	27	12	15	190.6
Kitchen chair	18	10	8	150.0
Garbage pail	23	10	13	189.3
Bread box	21	9	12	182.4
Tea kettle	23	12	11	158.5
Large kettle	19	10	9	208.3
Wash tub	10	5	5	158.1
Wash board	24	13	11	180.2
Clothes wringer	26	12	14	205.7
Clothes boiler	29	14	15	229.3
Electric iron	37	17	20	214.2
Ironing board	25	11	14	210.5
Clothes basket	20	10	10	170.4
Broom	30	14	16	236.4
Hatchet	32	16	16	209.7

[1] The ratio for the total is identical for a 4-person manual worker's family at both the maintenance and emergency levels. The total cost of furniture, furnishings, and household equipment includes sales tax where levied (appendix tables 15 and 16); commodity prices are without sales tax.

[2] Includes an identical allowance in all cities for items not separately priced, as well as prices for the items listed which were priced in each city, combined with their quantity allowances in the maintenance budget.

figures. The identical amount of money allowed for these items in all cities, however, averaged only 12.1 percent of total cost, varying from 10.3 percent in Butte to 13.8 percent in New York.

Of the 49 commodities separately priced, the highest city average quotation for 27 was more than twice the lowest (table 36), [25] but no city reported consistently high or consistently low prices.[26] Commodities showing the greatest price variations were living room heaters, with an intercity price variation of nearly 500 percent, and kitchen ranges, napkins, portable ovens, gas plates, couch covers, bedroom rugs, and bedroom chairs, with price variations of 300 to 400 percent. The smallest differences between lowest and highest prices for any of the 49 commodities in the separate cities were 36.3 percent for bureaus with mirror and 50 percent for kitchen chairs. For 20 other items the ranges in prices from lowest to highest were less than 100 percent.

Influence of Geographic Location and Size of City on Costs of Furniture, Furnishings, and Household Equipment [27]

Though furniture, furnishings, and household equipment costs were found to be highest in the Pacific and Mountain States and lowest in the West Central Areas, the differences between sections were relatively small (appendix table 5). All geographic divisions except those where costs were highest contained cities both above and below the average. Costs seemed to go up as population decreased (appendix table 7), except for the middle group. High and low cost cities appeared in the separate size of city classifications.

Cost Differences

The explanation of the relative similarity in the annual costs of replacing furniture, furnishings, and household equipment in the 59 cities lies in the large number of commodities making up the list. City average prices of the separate items were never all high or all low in the same place, and the extremes tended to cancel when combined to obtain the total cost. The allowance of $3.73 in each city, plus sales tax where levied, as the annual cost of articles which can be purchased for the same amount everywhere in the chain limited price variety stores also acted as a cost stabilizer. Constituting less than one-eighth of the average outlay necessary for this budget sub-

[25] Prices in all instances are compared without sales tax in order that the two may not be confused in the measurement of intercity differences. Were the tax where levied added to prices, the spread often would be greater than appears in the comparison without tax. The total cost of furniture, furnishings, and household equipment includes sales tax where levied.

[26] It so happens that in New York most prices were low and in Fall River most were high, but these situations were unusual.

[27] See table 1, p. XV, for list of cities in each geographic division and their population and table 62, p. 128, for cost variations within separate geographic divisions and size of city classifications.

group, however, its influence in this direction was relatively unimportant.

Omission of the sales tax on furniture, furnishings, and household equipment in 18 cities (appendix tables 15 and 16) would make for a greater rather than smaller cost range among the 59 cities studied, because New York, the cheapest city for this budget subgroup, had a sales tax. The largest amounts added as sales tax were found in the 3 Ohio cities where the rate was 3 percent; without the tax the position of Cleveland would drop 10 places and this city would no longer be among the 10 with highest costs for this budget subgroup.

The tendency toward higher prices in the Pacific and Mountain Divisions observable for other commodities appeared also for furniture, furnishings, and household equipment. This reflects perhaps higher charges for shipping from factory to market, perhaps a superior quality of merchandise, perhaps above average costs of doing business. Specifications for many of these items were necessarily somewhat general and could be met by articles of wide quality range. Some of the commodities whose price ranges were widest, however, appear to be more adapted to exact specification than others whose price ranges were less. To the extent that quotations were obtained for commodities in popular use, they indicate the sums required annually for replacement of the items listed in the quantity budgets or for obtaining equivalent commodities serving the same purpose.

REFUSE DISPOSAL

A variety of customs governs the disposal of refuse. In some cities the householder is responsible for this service; in others, the city collects garbage, ashes, and other trash, either charging directly for this service or covering its cost in the tax rate. Provision for refuse disposal is made in the quantity budgets if it involves a direct expense to the family.

In 18 cities included in this study, the householder assumed all or part of the cost of refuse disposal. There was a direct charge for garbage removal and none for ashes in one city, and in nine the opposite practice was found. In general, the smallest outlays were reported where it was necessary to pay for the removal of ashes for a few months or for some other part of complete service.

Maintenance and emergency budget provisions for refuse disposal are identical, hence costs at the two levels of living were identical (appendix tables 2 and 8). Cost relatives were computed (appendix tables 3, 5, 7, 9, 11, and 13), but they are without significance because the costs of refuse disposal were direct charges in only 18 cities.

UNSPECIFIED ESSENTIALS

The quantity budgets for a four-person manual worker's family include $3.05 at the maintenance level and $2.75 at the emergency level in all cities to cover the cost of a number of minor family needs, such as writing materials, postage, telephone calls, twine, glue, tacks, and similar essentials. Where a sales tax was applicable to that part of the allowances included for commodities as contrasted with postal, telephone, and other services,[28] its amounts (appendix tables 15 and 16) were added to annual costs; in all other cities the allowances noted above were included for unspecified household essentials (appendix tables 2 and 8).

[28] Telephone calls were taxed in one city, but no effort was made to apply the rate to that part of total annual allowances of $1.90 and $1.65 in the maintenance and emergency budgets, respectively, which might be expected to be necessary for telephone calls.

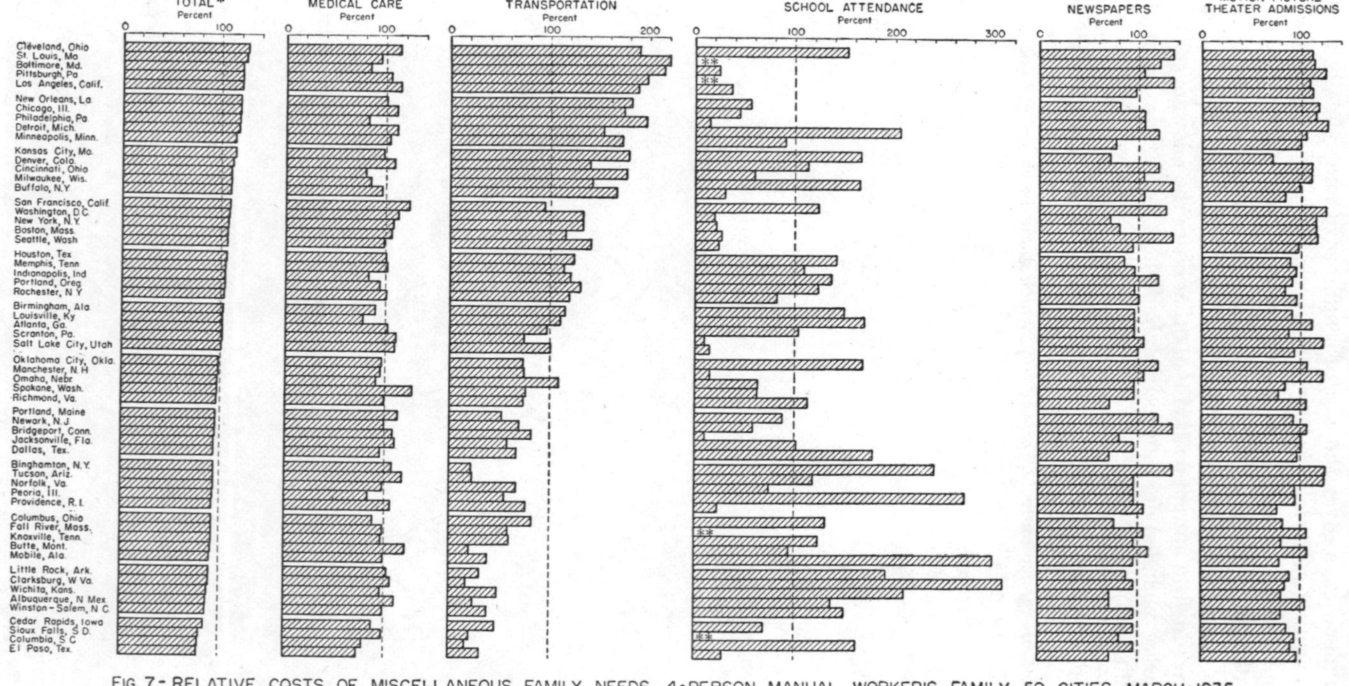

FIG. 7 - RELATIVE COSTS OF MISCELLANEOUS FAMILY NEEDS, 4-PERSON MANUAL WORKER'S FAMILY, 59 CITIES, MARCH 1935
Maintenance Level
(Average, 59 cities=100)

* Relatives for the total computed from aggregates which include allowance for certain minor needs not itemized separately.

** Not a direct charge.

AF-2121, W.P.A.

Chapter VI

MISCELLANEOUS FAMILY NEEDS

IN THE group of budget items combined under the classification "Miscellaneous" is included a number of unrelated family needs grouped together for convenience of summary. Specifically, these are medical care, transportation, school attendance, recreation, life insurance, church contributions, other contributions, and taxes.[1]

Miscellaneous items as a group required the largest annual outlay in Cleveland, $316.41 for the maintenance budget, and the smallest in El Paso, $193.72 (appendix table 2). The former averaged 63.3 percent more than the latter. The average in the 59 cities combined was $252.67, with budget costs above this figure in 29 cities and below it in 30 (fig. 7). The highest exceeded the average by 25.2 percent and the lowest was less by 23.3 percent (appendix table 3). Thirty cities reported annual costs of miscellaneous items between $220 and $260 at the maintenance level of living (table 37), and thirty-eight were between $120 and $160 at the emergency level.[2]

The average outlay necessary for the emergency budget of these goods and services was only 57.5 percent of the maintenance budget cost, a smaller ratio by far than was shown for any other major budget group (table 3). The content of the 2 budgets for miscellaneous family needs differed considerably in some respects; hence, the relative positions of the 59 cities in the 2 cost arrays often were not identical (appendix tables 8, 9, 11, and 13).

---

[1] Sales taxes have been computed as part of the costs of specified groups of goods and services. They are aggregated and discussed in this chapter, but the only taxes included in miscellaneous expenses as a separate item are personal property and capitation taxes.

[2] Quantity budgets for the two levels of living are given in complete detail in Stecker, Margaret L., *Quantity Budgets for Basic Maintenance and Emergency Standards of Living,* Research Bulletin, Series I, No. 21, Division of Social Research, Works Progress Administration, 1936. For the methods used in collecting quotations and computing city average prices and aggregate costs, see ch. VII.

***Table 37.*—Annual Costs [1] of Miscellaneous Family Needs, 4-Person Manual Worker's Family, 59 Cities, March 1935**

Annual cost	Number of cities	
	Maintenance level	Emergency level
Total	59	59
$80.00–$99.99	—	1
$100.00–$119.99	—	5
$120.00–$139.99	—	22
$140.00–$159.99	—	16
$160.00–$179.99	—	8
$180.00–$199.99	3	7
$200.00–$219.99	4	—
$220.00–$239.99	18	—
$240.00–$259.99	12	—
$260.00–$279.99	9	—
$280.00–$299.99	8	—
$300.00–$319.99	5	—
Average,[1] 59 cities	$252.67	$145.30

[1] Include sales tax where levied (appendix tables 15 and 16).

The goods and services making up the group of miscellaneous family needs are a heterogeneous lot. Certain items in the maintenance budget are omitted entirely in the emergency budget; for some, smaller allowances are made and for others, identical allowances are made. The proportions of the total miscellaneous costs required for each item, therefore, were different (table 38). The average distribution in the 59 cities combined varied considerably among them separately, not only with prices but also with differential transportation allowances and public policy as to school costs and taxes.

Certain items whose costs are the same everywhere and certain needs which cannot be definitely specified were covered by money allowances of $92.20 at the maintenance level and $36 at the emergency level in all cities, plus sales tax where levied. These sums were

***Table 38.*—Percent Distribution of the Average Annual Costs [1] of Miscellaneous Family Needs Among the Principal Commodity and Service Groups, 4-Person Manual Worker's Family, 59 Cities, March 1935**

Group	Maintenance level	Emergency level
Total	100.0	100.0
Medical care	20.7	32.5
Transportation	21.4	30.9
School attendance	2.7	4.7
Recreation	29.8	8.7
Motion picture theater admissions	13.4	5.4
Newspapers	4.3	(2)
Organizations	3.8	(2)
Tobacco and toys	8.3	3.3
Life insurance	18.3	14.3
Church contributions and other contributions	6.1	7.2
Taxes [3]	1.0	1.7
Average,[1] 59 cities	$252.67	$145.30

[1] Include sales tax where levied (appendix tables 15 and 16).
[2] Not included in emergency budget.
[3] Exclusive of sales tax.

designed to provide for organization memberships, tobacco, toys, and other leisure-time accessories, life insurance, church contributions, and other contributions. The maintenance allowance constituted 36.5 percent of the average miscellaneous cost in the group of 59 cities combined and varied from slightly more than 29 percent in Cleveland to slightly less than 48 percent in El Paso. Though the inclusion of an identical amount in all cities for so large a part of the total cost of miscellaneous family needs apparently tended to limit the range between cities, the procedure depicts a situation which exists and its use does not misrepresent the true spread.

The variety and unrelated character of the items grouped as miscellaneous family needs (table 38) explain the absence of any consistent cost tendency among the separate geographic areas (appendix table 5), except as these were influenced by the size of cities making up the groups. There was a definite relationship between the size of city and costs of miscellaneous items (appendix table 7), due primarily to the fact that the quantity of transportation allowed in the separate cities decreased with population and area.[3] The analysis proceeds, therefore, to consideration of the various budget subgroups as a means of explaining miscellaneous costs.

MEDICAL CARE

Neither the kind nor the quantity of medical care required by any one individual or family can be predicted in advance; hence, its cost in any one year cannot be estimated. Requirements by large groups of persons, over a period of years, however, can be calculated. Such estimates on a minimum basis constitute the quantity budgets for medical care priced in the present study. The amounts obtained measure the costs of the minimum medical care required during a life time, prorated to an annual basis for a four-person family. They should be regarded only as a means of accounting for this necessity in the annual costs of living for average families. They are without significance as a measure of the necessary cost of medical care for any one family.

The amounts required each year to provide minimum medical care when needed for a four-person manual worker's family were computed from reported charges for a representative sample of medical services, and drugs and appliances in such volume as would represent minimum requirements per 1,000 persons of small means. Prices of 11 services and 9 commodities were used in the cost calculations. In 29 cities costs were above and in 30, below the average of $52.32 in the 59 cities combined (fig. 7). Thirty-seven cities reported maintenance budget costs within a range of $10 (table 39). There were extremes, however, which resulted in Spokane, the highest cost city,

[3] See pp. 116–117.

with a budget cost of $66.10 per year, being 71.9 percent above El Paso, the lowest cost city, where $38.46 was required (appendix table 2); the former was 26.3 percent more than the average and the latter, 26.5 percent less (appendix table 3).

Inasmuch as the cost of the emergency budget for medical care (appendix tables 8, 9, 11, and 13) was computed as 90 percent of the maintenance budget cost in all cities, intercity relationships in the two series were identical.

Table 39.—Annual Costs[1] of Medical Care, 4-Person Manual Worker's Family, 59 Cities, March 1935

Annual cost	Number of cities	
	Maintenance level	Emergency level
Total	59	59
$30.00-$34.99	—	1
$35.00-$39.99	1	7
$40.00-$44.99	8	9
$45.00-$49.99	8	24
$50.00-$54.99	22	14
$55.00-$59.99	15	4
$60.00-$64.99	4	—
$65.00-$69.99	1	—
Average,[1] 59 cities	$52.32	$47.08

[1] Include sales tax where levied (appendix tables 15 and 16).

The average annual cost of medical care in the group of 59 cities was so distributed that services accounted for 90.5 percent and commodities, 9.5 percent (appendix table 14). Hence, the costs of medical care in the separate cities tended to be fixed largely by combined local charges for physicians', dentists', nurses', and hospital services, though the relative positions of these items separately were not identical in the same place.[4] For example, Spokane, where medical care as a whole cost most, also reported the largest outlay necessary for all services combined and highest physicians' fees; but dentists' charges ranked 30th from the top; hospital care cost, 25th; and drugs and appliances cost, 23d. The least expensive city for medical care, El Paso, on the other hand, was lowest for all services combined, and for physicians separately, 41st from the top for dentists, 53d for hospital care, and 38th for drugs and appliances.

Among the 59 cities 29 reported more than average costs for services and 30 reported less; the excess of highest over lowest was 81.4 percent. The spread for drugs and appliances, including eyeglasses and

[4] Necessary substitutions of quotations for eye refractions by optometrists and for nursing care by public health nurses in 22 and 36 cities, respectively, resulted in identical costs for the first service in 36 cities, and for the second, in 59 cities. The amounts involved were $1.80 per year in the maintenance and $1.62 per year in the emergency budget costs in 36 cities, and $1.60 and $1.44, respectively, in 23 cities. See pp. 114–115 and 115.

frames, was from 15.6 percent above the average to 14.9 percent below, with the highest cost city 35.9 percent more than the lowest. The separate services and commodities showed still wider cost ranges (table 40).[5]

Table 40.—Medical Care Commodity and Service Price Ratios,[1] 59 Cities, March 1935

Commodity or service	Number of cities where prices exceeded ± 10 percent with reference to the 59-city average [1]			Percent highest price is of lowest price [1]
	Total	Above average	Below average	
Total medical care	22	11	11	171.8
Services	23	12	11	181.4
Physician [2]	25	12	13	216.4
Dentist	37	16	21	214.6
Hospital	32	12	20	235.9
Nurse [3]	(3)	(3)	(3)	(3)
Drugs and appliances	6	3	3	135.9
Iodine	9	2	7	140.7
Cough syrup	4	4	(4)	128.6
Cold ointment	9	4	5	143.3
Milk of magnesia	9	4	5	164.8
Laxative	10	1	9	179.2
Aspirin	4	1	3	177.6
Prescription	14	8	6	153.3
Eyeglasses and frame	45	19	26	382.3

[1] Ratios for all totals are identical for a 4-person manual worker's family at both the maintenance and emergency levels of living. The total cost of medical care includes sales tax where levied (appendix tables 15 and 16); the group totals and commodity and service prices are without sales tax.
[2] Includes optometrist.
[3] The fees for nurses' services were the same in all cities. See footnote 4, p. 70, and p. 115.
[4] In no city was the deviation from the average as much as 10 percent.

Influence of Geographic Location and Size of City on Costs of Medical Care[6]

Medical care was notably expensive in the Mountain and Pacific Divisions (appendix table 5). All cities in the former and three of the five in the latter group reported both service and commodity costs well above the average; drugs and appliances were relatively cheaper, however, than services. In all but one of the East South Central cities and in all but one of the West North Central cities medical care costs were below the average, but high price services often were combined with low price drugs and vice versa; in general, charges for services in these areas were relatively lower than for commodities.

The costs of the medical care budget tended to decline with decreased city size (appendix table 7), at least until the 250,000 population group

[5] Prices in all instances are compared without sales tax in order that the two may not be confused in the measurement of intercity differences. Were the tax where levied added to prices, the spread would be no different than that shown, inasmuch as neither of the extreme cities had a sales tax. The total cost of medical care includes sales tax where levied.

[6] See table 1, p. XV, for list of cities in each geographic division and their population and table 62, p. 128, for cost variations within separate geographic divisions and size of city classifications.

was reached. Highest costs were found in the smallest cities, but these may be influenced more by geographic location than by size.

Cost Differences

Physicians' and dentists' fees and charges for hospital care did not all rank in the same direction in many places; where some were relatively high, others were relatively low, with numerous intermediate ratios. Thus, when all service prices in each city were combined, variations were not nearly so great as were those for any one separately. After the outlay necessary for drugs and appliances was added to service fees, the tendency toward cost uniformity was further narrowed. As already noted, however, services everywhere required so much more of the total cost of medical care than commodities that the ranks of the cities in total medical care costs were somewhat similar to their ranks in service costs alone.

When causal factors are considered, it is logical that there should be a considerably greater spread between the costs of services than the costs of commodities. Charges for most services depend on local circumstances past or present which vary widely and on a diversity of influences within a given community. Quotations obtained in cities with well-defined working class neighborhoods, for example, may represent a fee scale somewhat below the general level for the community. In places where physicians serve patients of small means along with those of larger resources, on the other hand, the reported charges may not be those usually paid by unskilled laborers, owing to the custom of adjusting prices to what the patient can afford. Check of fees reported in the separate cities indicates, however, that this factor was relatively unimportant as an explanation of cost differences. The fact that the costs of nurses' and optometrists' services were identical in most cities only slightly counteracted the general tendency toward wide medical service cost variations, because the allowances for these two items were small.

The influences which determine commodity prices are more alike than are those which account for service charges. Specifications for drugs and appliances permitted inclusion of several brands of some proprietary medicines in the sample, however, and a variety of other circumstances served to produce a diverse range of city average prices. The dispersion of commodity costs as a group was less than half that of service costs and tended to reduce somewhat the spread in costs of the medical care budget as a whole.

Except in one city the sales tax on medical care was applicable only to drugs and appliances, and not to all these in every city. In New York, for example, only physicians' prescriptions for drugs were exempt; in Oklahoma City only eyeglasses and frames were taxed. Thus, the existence of a sales tax in 18 cities (appendix tables 15 and 16) contributed little to medical care cost differences.

TRANSPORTATION

Transportation requirements are largely an individual matter. They depend on the location of each family's home in relation to the place of employment of its members and the children's school, as well as on shopping, visiting, and other social demands. Average transportation needs are without significance, therefore, except to provide for this item in a balanced measure of the cost of living. In general, requirements may be presumed to differ somewhat with the area of a city and the size of its population. Quantity allowances based on these factors varied among the cities; but even though they were taken into account in computing necessary transportation costs, these costs must be regarded primarily as representative for groups of families, rather than for any one family.

Table 41.—Annual Costs[1] of Transportation, 4-Person Manual Worker's Family, 59 Cities, March 1935

Annual cost	Number of cities	
	Maintenance level	Emergency level
Total	59	59
$0.00–$9.99	2	5
$10.00–$19.99	7	6
$20.00–$29.99	6	9
$30.00–$39.99	9	9
$40.00–$49.99	5	5
$50.00–$59.99	5	9
$60.00–$69.99	7	4
$70.00–$79.99	5	5
$80.00–$89.99	2	5
$90.00–$99.99	5	2
$100.00–$109.99	4	—
$110.00–$119.99	2	—
Average,[1] 59 cities	$53.96	$44.97

[1] Include sales tax in 1 city (appendix tables 15 and 16).

Charges on public conveyances commonly patronized by industrial, service, and other manual workers of small means were used as a basis for computing annual transportation costs; an automobile is not included in the quantity budgets. If the costs as computed permit transportation in an automobile[7] the same purpose will be served.

Owing to the wide range in the quantities of transportation allowed in the separate cities, annual costs of this service for a four-person manual worker's family also were widely dispersed; the largest outlay necessary on the basis of March 15, 1935, rates was more than 13.5 times the smallest (appendix table 2). In St. Louis where most was needed to purchase the quantity allowed at the maintenance level, $118.44 per year was required; in Columbia where annual cost was lowest, a smaller quantity was allowed and $8.75 was required. The

[7] It is not uncommon for several men to share the cost of transportation to and from work in an automobile owned by one of them.

average cost of the transportation budget in the 59 cities combined was $53.96 annually; 27 cities exceeded this amount and 32 cities were less (fig. 7). In the city where most was required, cost was 119.5 percent more than the average, and in that with smallest necessary outlay, its amount was 83.8 percent less (appendix table 3). There was no well-defined concentration of transportation costs (table 41), such as was found for most other items of family consumption, but rather a fairly even grouping in $10 intervals.

Emergency transportation budget cost (appendix tables 8, 9, 11, and 13), by definition, averaged 83.3 percent of maintenance budget cost everywhere; relatives, therefore, were identical in all arrays.

Influence of Geographic Location and Size of City on Costs of Transportation [8]

Geographic location as such had little to do with car and bus fares or with the annual costs of transportation, except as costs were influenced by the size of cities in the separate areas. Costs were perhaps somewhat higher in the Middle Atlantic and North Central States than in other sections (appendix table 5), save for the Pacific Division where high costs in three of the larger cities brought up the average for the area.

Because quantity allowances were largely based on the population factor, transportation costs were more dependent on size of city than were the costs of any other budget group and declined as cities decreased in size (appendix table 7).

Cost Differences

The quantity budgets set certain basic standards for the calculation of transportation costs and provide for modification of the basic allowance to represent local needs. These adjustments were made for each city on a percentage basis adapted to local population and city area.[9] Three elements, therefore, entered into the annual cost of transportation as computed for this study: the lowest rate of fare on public conveyances for each purpose specified, the basic allowance in the quantity budgets, and the percentage of the basic budget allowance applicable in each city.

Street railway and bus fares were sufficiently varied to account for most of the range in unmodified transportation costs in the 59 cities: namely, from 5 cents cash fare or reduced ticket or token rate where the cash fare itself exceeded 5 cents, to 10 cents cash and no reduction by ticket or token. Some cities had special fares for children under 12 years of age or for all children within certain hours on school days, while others charged children the same rates as adults. Cash fares

[8] See table 1, p. XV, for list of cities in each geographic division and their population and table 62, p. 128, for cost variations within separate geographic divisions and size of city classifications.

[9] See pp. 116–117.

Table 42.—Adult Cash Fares and Annual Costs[1] of Transportation, 4-Person Manual Worker's Family, 59 Cities, March 1935

City	Percent modification of basic budget allowance	Aggregate cost[1]			Relative cost[1]		
		Basic budget allowance	Basic budget allowance modified for population and city area	Adult cash fare	Basic budget allowance	Basic budget allowance modified for population and city area	Adult cash fare
Average, 59 cities	—	$96.48	$53.96	$0.087	100.0	100.0	100.0
Kansas City, Mo	72.0	132.83	95.63	.10	137.7	177.2	114.9
Pittsburgh, Pa	84.0	126.50	106.26	.10	131.1	196.9	114.9
Buffalo, N. Y	72.0	124.00	89.28	.10	128.5	165.5	114.9
Peoria, Ill	24.0	124.00	29.76	.10	128.5	55.2	114.9
St. Louis, Mo	96.0	123.38	118.44	.10	127.9	219.5	114.9
Bridgeport, Conn	36.0	121.50	43.74	.10	125.9	81.1	114.9
Omaha, Nebr	48.0	121.50	58.32	.10	125.9	108.1	114.9
Baltimore, Md	96.0	120.30	115.49	.10	124.7	214.0	114.9
Portland, Maine	24.0	118.80	28.51	.10	123.1	52.8	114.9
Cincinnati, Ohio	84.0	112.62	94.60	.10	116.7	175.3	114.9
Salt Lake City, Utah	48.0	112.39	53.95	.10	116.5	100.0	114.9
Scranton, Pa	36.0	111.83	40.26	.08	115.9	74.6	92.0
Philadelphia, Pa	96.0	110.48	106.06	.08	114.5	196.6	92.0
Manchester, N. H	36.0	110.25	39.69	.10	114.3	73.6	114.9
Atlanta, Ga	48.0	109.35	52.49	.10	113.3	97.3	114.9
Minneapolis, Minn	84.0	109.35	91.85	.10	113.3	170.2	114.9
Rochester, N. Y	60.0	106.50	63.90	.10	110.4	118.4	114.9
Cleveland, Ohio	96.0	105.75	101.52	.10	109.6	188.1	114.9
Milwaukee, Wis	72.0	105.75	76.14	.10	109.6	141.1	114.9
Albuquerque, N. Mex	12.0	[2]105.57	[2]12.67	.10	[2]109.4	[2]23.5	114.9
Los Angeles, Calif	96.0	105.53	101.30	.10	109.4	187.7	114.9
Denver, Colo	72.0	103.95	74.84	.10	107.7	138.7	114.9
Cedar Rapids, Iowa	24.0	103.50	24.84	.10	107.3	46.0	114.9
Tucson, Ariz	12.0	102.75	12.33	.10	106.5	22.9	114.9
Birmingham, Ala	60.0	102.48	61.49	.07	106.2	114.0	80.5
Memphis, Tenn	60.0	102.06	61.24	.07	105.8	113.5	80.5
New Orleans, La	96.0	101.85	97.78	.07	105.6	181.2	80.5
Norfolk, Va	36.0	99.50	35.82	.10	103.1	66.4	114.9
Louisville, Ky	60.0	99.25	59.55	.10	102.9	110.4	114.9
Binghamton, N. Y	12.0	97.35	11.68	.10	100.9	21.6	114.9
Chicago, Ill	96.0	97.20	93.31	.07	100.7	172.9	80.5
Portland, Oreg	72.0	97.14	69.94	.10	100.7	129.6	114.9
Houston, Tex	72.0	92.61	66.68	.10	96.0	123.6	114.9
Sioux Falls, S. Dak	12.0	91.13	10.94	.10	94.5	20.3	114.9
Indianapolis, Ind	72.0	90.56	65.21	.07	93.9	120.8	80.5
Butte, Mont	12.0	90.19	10.82	.10	93.5	20.1	114.9
Seattle, Wash	84.0	89.85	75.47	.10	93.1	139.9	114.9
Knoxville, Tenn	36.0	89.28	32.14	.10	92.5	59.6	114.9
Fall River, Mass	36.0	87.38	31.46	.10	90.6	58.3	114.9
Winston-Salem, N. C	24.0	87.38	20.97	.07	90.6	38.9	80.5
Mobile, Ala	24.0	87.23	20.93	.08	90.4	38.8	92.0
Providence, R. I	48.0	86.10	41.33	.08	89.2	76.6	92.0
Jacksonville, Fla	36.0	85.86	30.91	.10	89.0	57.3	114.9
Spokane, Wash	48.0	85.86	41.21	.10	89.0	76.4	114.9
Detroit, Mich	96.0	85.50	82.08	.06	88.6	152.1	69.0
Washington, D. C	84.0	85.05	71.44	.10	88.2	132.4	114.9
Richmond, Va	48.0	83.16	39.92	.07	86.2	74.0	80.5
Oklahoma City, Okla	48.0	82.35	39.53	.10	85.4	73.3	114.9
Clarksburg, W. Va	12.0	76.67	9.20	.07	79.5	17.0	80.5
New York, N. Y	96.0	74.40	71.42	.05	77.1	132.4	57.5
Columbus, Ohio	60.0	74.10	44.46	.06	76.8	82.4	69.0
Boston, Mass	84.0	73.50	61.74	.05	76.2	114.4	57.5
Columbia, S. C	12.0	72.90	8.75	.07	75.6	16.2	80.5
Wichita, Kans	36.0	72.90	26.24	.07	75.6	48.6	80.5
El Paso, Tex	24.0	71.28	17.11	.06	73.9	31.7	69.0
Little Rock, Ark	24.0	68.58	16.46	.06	71.1	30.5	69.0
Newark, N. J	60.0	62.91	37.75	.05	65.2	70.0	57.5
San Francisco, Calif	84.0	60.45	50.78	.05	62.7	94.1	57.5
Dallas, Tex	60.0	59.94	35.96	.07	62.1	66.6	80.5

[1] All costs refer to the maintenance budget. Inasmuch as this table is included only for illustrative purposes, comparable data for the emergency budget were not assembled. Emergency transportation budget cost, by definition, is 83.3 percent of maintenance budget cost; aggregate and relative annual costs are shown in appendix tables 8 and 9.

[2] Includes sales tax (appendix tables 15 and 16).

varied 100 percent from lowest to highest: in 36 cities the rate was 10 cents; in 11 cities, 7 cents; in 4 cities, 8 cents; in 4 cities, 6 cents; and in 4 cities, 5 cents (table 42). The total spread between the lowest and highest annual costs of transportation in the 59 cities, obtained by combining minimum charges for specified services with the basic allowance for transportation in the quantity budgets, was 121.6 percent.

The basic budget allowance of transportation for the man to work, 612 rides, is identical in all cities, but for the boy to school it varies with the number of school days per year. Twenty-one separate numbers were reported.[10] They ranged from 156 days in Dallas to 200 days in St. Louis;[11] the median and the mode were 180 days. Assuming that all cities had a school year of 180 days, the maximum differences in total transportation costs attributable to variations in the number of school days would be $4.03 per year reduction in St. Louis and $1.30 addition in Dallas. Thus, differences in the annual transportation costs among the separate cities were not closely related to differences in the basic budget allowances.

Modifications of the basic budget allowance in the separate cities to provide for local transportation requirements ranged from 96 percent in the largest to 12 percent in the smallest places. Applying the appropriate local percentage to the basic budget allowance cost in each city produced a transportation cost range of 1,253.6 percent between lowest and highest cost cities, as compared with 121.6 percent unmodified cost range. It is apparent, therefore, that the great spread in transportation costs among the 59 cities in this study was due primarily to differential needs based on population and area. Without this modifying factor of differential needs, the cost dispersion would have been wider than for many other items, but not nearly so great as the final calculations show.

To illustrate the effect of these three elements in transportation cost computation, attention may be directed to Kansas City (Mo.) and Dallas, the extreme cities for basic budget allowance costs unmodified by local differentials (table 42). In Kansas City (Mo.), where the basic budget allowance cost was highest, fares were at the rate of 4 rides for 35 cents on a token basis for adults and children over 12 years of age; cash, 10 cents; and a weekly pass, $1.10. Neither cash fare nor weekly pass was used in computing costs. The cost of the basic budget allowance in Kansas City (Mo.) was modified to 72 percent to provide for local requirements, and that city then ranked 8th from the top in the cost of this service as finally calculated for the 59 cities. In Dallas, at the other end of the scale of basic budget allowance

[10] Not including three cities where 5 days were added in computing carfare to provide for midweek holidays.

[11] The school year was 200 days but owing to the use of a weekly pass 41 weeks were assumed to provide for weeks in which there were holidays.

transportation costs, the adult cash fare was 7 cents but 6 tokens were sold for 30 cents and school children rode for 3 cents. The basic budget allowance for transportation in Dallas was reduced to 60 percent to provide for local needs, but in many other cities reductions were so much greater that instead of being at the bottom of the list for carfare actually required, Dallas was 20th from the cheapest city.

Basic budget allowance transportation costs and adult cash fares were not closely related, primarily by reason of the great variety of modifications of cash fares expressed in ticket or token rates for adults and children.[12] Both happened to average highest in the 72 percent cities and lowest in the 60 percent cities (table 43). Though local differentials declined in 12 point intervals from largest to smallest, the average annual costs of transportation in the groups of cities with the same differentials did not vary so regularly. The largest local consumption differential was eight times the smallest, but the average annual cost of transportation in the group of cities with the largest percentage allowance was more than nine times that with the smallest.

***Table 43.*—Relative Car and Bus Fares and Relative Annual Transportation Costs, Classified by Local Consumption Differentials, 59 Cities, March 1935**

Local consumption differential	Percent of 59-city average		
	Adult cash fare	Basic budget allowance [1] cost	Basic budget allowance cost modified for population and city area
96 percent	92.0	106.5	182.7
84 percent	103.4	97.4	146.2
72 percent	114.9	110.6	142.4
60 percent	80.5	89.9	96.5
48 percent	103.4	100.8	86.5
36 percent	103.4	100.9	64.9
24 percent	92.0	97.9	42.0
12 percent	103.4	[2] 94.0	[2] 20.2

[1] Includes slight differentials related to number of school days in each city.
[2] Includes sales tax in 1 city (appendix tables 15 and 16).

One factor possibly affecting transportation costs in certain cities, which could not be considered in any generalized method of cost calculation, is the circumstance that reduced fares for children are good only for school use. In computing total transportation costs from these charges, payable only under certain circumstances, these totals may be slightly understated. The average fare good only on school days in 34 cities was 4.13 cents per ride, and that paid by children in cities where there were no such special rates averaged 7 cents per ride. On the basis of 180 school days per year the budget cost differences were $10.33 for school use at both the maintenance and emergency levels of living, $5.17 for other purposes at the maintenance level and

[12] Differences in the numbers of school days reflected in the basic budget allowance accounted for some, but very little, of the differences between basic budget allowance costs and adult cash fares. See p. 76.

$2.58 at the emergency level, or total average annual differences of $15.50 and $12.92, respectively, in basic budget allowance costs. Modified by local consumption differentials, reductions varying from 4 percent to 88 percent would be made.

For only 22 cities is any test available of the reliability of the local consumption differentials used in computing transportation costs. Even this probably means little because the bases for measuring local transportation use were different. The Real Property Inventory of the Department of Commerce in 1934 attempted to ascertain the number of principal income earners in areas studied who walked to work and the kind of transportation used by those who rode.[13] Assuming that all who did not walk required transportation, reducing these aggregates to percentages of all principal income earners, and comparing these percentages with the local consumption differentials used in this study, it appears that, for principal income earners only, the smaller local consumption differentials were too small and the larger ones were too large in an almost uniform progression. In other words, in the smaller cities not enough transportation to work was provided by the local percentage differentials and in the larger ones, too much. Manual workers, however, are more likely to locate their homes near the places of their employment than are all income earners as a class. This practice is especially noticeable in smaller cities, where industrial plants quite generally are surrounded by modest residential areas in which their employees live. Moreover, from such information as was obtained in this study regarding school transportation needs, location of shopping areas, and related matters, any apparent deficiency of transportation to work in the smaller cities seems to be fully counterbalanced by an excessive allowance of transportation to school. The reverse relationship probably exists in the larger cities.

Fares on public conveyances are subject to control by public service or other regulatory bodies, and a number of local circumstances determines what are reasonable rates. From this standpoint, the process of their establishment is analogous to the fixing of gas and electricity charges. The present analysis in no sense constitutes a comparison of car or bus fares. Its purpose is to measure, as accurately as possible according to a definite formula, the costs of transportation in the different cities. Inasmuch as requirements as well as fares varied, both are reflected in the costs as computed.

A sales tax was levied on bus fares in Albuquerque in March 1935 (appendix tables 15 and 16). This was the only city among the 59 which had a sales tax on car or bus fares.

[13] United States Department of Commerce, Bureau of Foreign and Domestic Commerce, *Real Property Inventory, 1934*, City Proper, Table V, "Mode of Transportation and Time for Principal Income Earners to Get to Work." There are separate reports for 64 cities.

SCHOOL ATTENDANCE

The two children in the family whose costs of living are measured here were assumed to attend public schools. Minimum requirements connected with this attendance for the boy age 13 in the 9th grade and the girl age 8 in the 3d grade are books, stationery, other supplies, and gymnasium equipment.[14] Resulting annual school costs for a four-person manual worker's family varied from nothing a year in Fall River, Pittsburgh, St. Louis, and Sioux Falls to $21.19 in Clarksburg (appendix table 2). Extremes were unusual, however, and in most places school costs were less than $12 per year (table 44). The average outlay necessary in the 55 cities where school attendance required a direct charge on the family was $7.37. In 27 cities costs were above this amount; and in 32, including the 4 in which there was no cost, they were below (fig. 7). Relative costs are shown in appendix table 3.

Table 44.—Annual Costs[1] of School Attendance, 4-Person Manual Worker's Family, 55 Cities, March 1935

Annual cost	Number of cities
Total	55
$0.00–$3.99	16
$4.00–$7.99	15
$8.00–$11.99	16
$12.00–$15.99	4
$16.00–$19.99	2
$20.00–$23.99	2
Average,[1] 55 cities	$7.37

[1] Maintenance and emergency level costs by definition are identical; sales tax included where levied (appendix tables 15 and 16).

By definition, maintenance and emergency school attendance budget costs were identical (appendix tables 8, 9, 11, and 13).

Influence of Geographic Location and Size of City on Costs of School Attendance [15]

In general, the New England and Middle Atlantic cities required the smallest direct outlays from pupils in the public schools for books, supplies, and gymnasium equipment, and the East North Central and South Central States required the largest (appendix table 5). The cost of school attendance in the South Atlantic Division also was well above the average.

Though there seemed to be a tendency for school costs to increase with decreased city size (appendix table 7), the relationship was neither uniform nor regular.

[14] Outlay necessary for school lunches is included in the cost of food, car or bus fare in the cost of transportation, and social expenses in the cost of recreation.

[15] See table 1, p. XV, for list of cities in each geographic division and their population and table 62, p. 128, for cost variations within separate geographic divisions and size of city classifications.

Cost Differences

The most significant cause of the wide range in the amounts families must pay as a direct charge for public school attendance in the separate cities, based on use of identical or comparable equipment by two children of specified sex, age, and school grade in all, lies in variations in local practices regarding expenditures for this purpose from public funds.

State laws govern the policies concerning textbooks and supplies in some cities; other cities are permitted to determine how many of these necessities the taxpayers will furnish. Between 1931 and 1934 the amounts spent for books and supplies by the public school systems in 728 cities of all sizes the country over declined about one-third, though the number of pupils increased.[16] Decreased public support means that these materials must be supplied privately. Table 45, embodying the results of a survey made in 1934 by the National Education Association,[17] suggests an important explanation of the variation in school costs reported in the present study.

Table 45.—Policy Relating to Furnishing Free Textbooks and Supplies, 800 Public School Systems, 1933

Items furnished by public funds	School systems	
	Number	Percent
Total	800	100.0
Textbooks and supplies in all classes	354	44.3
Textbooks and supplies in elementary classes only	35	4.4
Textbooks and some supplies	38	4.7
Supplies and some textbooks	25	3.1
Textbooks but no supplies	24	3.0
Supplies but no textbooks	66	8.2
Textbooks in elementary classes only	23	2.9
Neither textbooks nor supplies	128	16.0
Some materials—other policies not classifiable under above items	107	13.4

Source: National Education Association, Department of Superintendence and Research Division, *School Books and Supplies: Recent Trends in Expenditures and Policies*, Educational Research Service, Circular No. 2, February 1934, p. 5.

Some or all school materials were subject to tax in the 18 cities where a sales tax was levied (appendix tables 15 and 16). School books were frequently exempt but supplies and gymnasium equipment usually were covered.

Though in 1935 children in the public schools were paying for some of the equipment previously supplied by the community,[18] few cities

[16] National Education Association, Department of Superintendence and Research Division, *School Books and Supplies: Recent Trends in Expenditures and Policies*, Educational Research Service, Circular No. 2, February 1934, p. 1.

[17] *Ibid.*, p. 5.

[18] Some cities are attempting to return all children to a free basis. From Seattle, for example, came the report in 1935: "Students are furnishing stationery and supplies (partially) due to shortage of money for school. This condition is for this year only and, therefore, is not representative of Seattle schools."

failed to provide equipment for pupils who were too poor to furnish their own. Cost estimates in the present study are designed to cover all school needs in a self-supporting family of the specified size and composition.

RECREATION

The costs of recreation for a four-person manual worker's family at the maintenance level were $87.18 per year in Binghamton and $62.33 in Kansas City (Mo.) (appendix table 2). These were the extremes among the 59 cities studied. The average for the group as a whole was $75.18, made up of more low than high cost cities; the spread from lowest to highest was 39.9 percent. Binghamton cost exceeded the average by 16 percent and Kansas City (Mo.) cost was less by 17.1 percent (appendix table 3). While maintenance recreation budget costs covered a $25 range among the 59 cities, emergency budget costs were less than $15 a year in all of them (table 46).

Table 46.—Annual Costs[1] of Recreation, 4-Person Manual Worker's Family, 59 Cities, March 1935

Annual cost	Number of cities	
	Maintenance level	Emergency level
Total	59	59
$10.00–$14.99	—	59
$15.00–$19.99	—	—
$20.00–$24.99	—	—
$25.00–$29.99	—	—
$30.00–$34.99	—	—
$35.00–$39.99	—	—
$40.00–$44.99	—	—
$45.00–$49.99	—	—
$50.00–$54.99	—	—
$55.00–$59.99	—	—
$60.00–$64.99	1	—
$65.00–$69.99	11	—
$70.00–$74.99	22	—
$75.00–$79.99	11	—
$80.00–$84.99	12	—
$85.00–$89.99	2	—
Average,[1] 59 cities	$75.18	$12.63

[1] Include sales tax where levied (appendix tables 15 and 16).

The emergency budget contains no provision for newspapers or organization memberships, and the identical money allowance in all cities for toys, tobacco, and other leisure-time accessories is materially less than the maintenance budget allowance. Highest to lowest cost ratios in the two arrays were nearly the same, however, though ranks of the individual cities were somewhat different (appendix tables 8, 9, 11, and 13).

Newspapers accounted for 14.4 percent of the average cost of the maintenance recreation budget; motion picture theater admissions, 45 percent; and an identical allowance plus sales tax where levied amounting to 40.6 percent covered organization memberships, tobacco, toys, and other leisure-time accessories. Cost details of the items making up the recreation budget follow.

Newspapers

A daily newspaper is allowed in the maintenance budget as a means of measuring the outlay necessary for reading material of all kinds. A variety of prices and combinations of prices for newspapers was found. These ranged from a per copy rate of 3 cents daily and 10 cents Sunday on the street, at a total cost of $14.56 per year, to 15 cents weekly or 65 cents per month for delivery 7 days per week by carrier, at an annual cost of $7.80 (appendix table 2).

The spread of 86.7 percent between lowest and highest newspaper costs was so distributed that among more than half the cities differences of only $2 per year were found (table 47). The highest cost exceeded the average in the 59 cities combined, $10.84, by 34.4 percent, and the lowest cost was less by 28 percent (appendix table 3). Newspaper costs were more than the average in 24 cities and less in 35 (fig. 7).

Table 47.—Annual Costs of Daily and Sunday Newspapers, 59 Cities, March 1935

Annual cost	Number of cities
Total	59
$7.00–$7.99	7
$8.00–$8.99	6
$9.00–$9.99	2
$10.00–$10.99	21
$11.00–$11.99	10
$12.00–$12.99	—
$13.00–$13.99	7
$14.00–$14.99	6
Average, 59 cities	$10.84

The most frequently found annual newspaper costs were $10.40 in 17 cities, $11.44 in 9 cities, and $7.80 in 7 cities. These were, respectively, 20 cents per week by carrier; 2 cents per day for 6 days and 10 cents on Sunday, street sale price; and 15 cents per week or 65 cents per month by carrier.

Analysis of street or newsstand sale prices of papers selling for the weekly amounts used in computing cost estimates shows the following rates per copy daily: 3 cents, 26 cities; 2 cents, 12 cities; 5 cents, 12 cities; 3 or 5 cents, 4 cities; 2 or 3 cents, 3 cities; 1 cent, 1 city; no report, 1 city. Sunday papers most often were 10 cents on the street: 41 cities reported this price; 11 cities, 5 cents; 1 city, 5 or 10 cents; 1 city, 6 cents; 1 city, 7 cents; 1 city, no report; 3 cities had no local Sunday paper.

Motion Picture Theater Admissions

Admission charges to motion picture theaters were adopted as a generally applicable means of measuring the costs of commercial entertainment on a common basis in all cities. If necessary outlays thus computed were to be used for other kinds of recreation, the same purpose would be served.

The amounts to be spent for motion picture theater admissions by a four-person manual worker's family living at the maintenance level varied from a high of $42.54 in Philadelphia to a low of $24.13 in Kansas City (Mo.); the average was $33.80 (appendix table 2). For these amounts each member of the family could go to the theater once a week.[19] The cost of attending the movies in Philadelphia was 76.3 percent more than in Kansas City (Mo.) and 25.9 percent above the average in the 59 cities combined (appendix table 3); Kansas City (Mo.) cost was 28.6 percent below the average. Costs exceeded the average in 27 cities, were less in 31, and the cost was exactly the same as the average in 1 (fig. 7).

Maintenance budget costs of motion picture theater attendance fell within a range of $15 per year among most of the cities (table 48). The cost range for the emergency budget was $5 between lowest and highest, and in no city was as much as $10 per year required for this budget.

Table 48.—Annual Costs[1] of Motion Picture Theater Admissions, 4-Person Manual Worker's Family, 59 Cities, March 1935

Annual cost	Number of cities	
	Maintenance level	Emergency level
Total	59	59
$5.00–$9.99	—	59
$10.00–$14.99	—	—
$15.00–$19.99	—	—
$20.00–$24.99	1	—
$25.00–$29.99	13	—
$30.00–$34.99	19	—
$35.00–$39.99	19	—
$40.00–$44.99	7	—
Average,[1] 59 cities	$33.80	$7.80

[1] Include sales tax where levied (appendix tables 15 and 16).

Organizations, Tobacco, and Toys

Within this classification the quantity budgets allow certain sums of money to cover recognized needs which cannot be itemized. Children belong to character-building groups, school and church clubs, and similar organizations; adults are associated in nationality and patriotic groups, fraternities, musical and athletic groups, and the like. Their purposes are legion. To provide such memberships for a four-person manual worker's family at the maintenance level of living,

[19] The emergency budget allows one attendance per person per month.

$9.60 was included in all cities (appendix table 2). This amount does not cover labor union dues.[20]

An allowance of $20.80 in the maintenance budget (appendix table 2) and of $4.80 in the emergency budget (appendix table 8) was included in all cities, plus sales tax where levied, to meet the costs of a large number of goods and services which no two families probably would specify similarly as to details. These amounts would provide tobacco, "treats" of various kinds, games, athletic equipment, and a variety of other leisure-time accessories, serving no particular purpose but contributing something to life's more frivolous moments.

Influence of Geographic Location and Size of City on Costs of Recreation [21]

Recreation costs were above the average in the Middle Atlantic, Mountain, East North Central, and New England States in the order given and below in all other areas except the Pacific States, where exactly the average cost was found (appendix table 5). In no section, however, were all cities consistently high or consistently low.

Size of city seems to have been a more influential factor than geographic location in the establishment of recreation costs, especially with reference to the very large cities (appendix table 7). Differences in the costs of motion picture theater admissions were more accountable for this relationship than variations in newspaper charges.

In general, newspaper costs were high in the Middle Atlantic, East North Central, New England, and Pacific States; were about average in the Mountain Division; and were low in the West North and South Central Areas. The five cities included in the East South Central Division reported the same annual newspaper costs; identical outlays were necessary in six of the nine South Atlantic cities. No other sections showed such uniformity of newspaper costs. In all but 2 cities with 500,000 or more population newspaper costs were higher than the average in the 59 cities combined, and in all but 4 of the smaller places they were lower than the average.

Low cost motion picture theater admissions were usual in the West North Central and East South Central States, and costs were high in the Middle Atlantic, Mountain, and New England States, but these costs perhaps were related more definitely to size of city than to geographic area. Costs declined until the 25,000 to 100,000 population classification was reached; the smallest cities averaged slightly more than those in the next 2 larger size classifications. Among the 7 highest cost cities were 3 with a population of 25,000 to 100,000, and the lowest cost city had a population of approximately 400,000.

---

[20] Union dues for unskilled manual workers average about $12 per year.

[21] See table 1, p. XV, for list of cities in each geographic division and their population and table 62, p. 128, for cost variations within separate geographic divisions and size of city classifications.

Cost Differences

A large amount cannot be provided for recreation in a low cost family budget but simple leisure-time activities must be regarded as necessities. What these activities shall be is a matter of opinion. The quantity budgets embody those which seem most universally popular, with the idea that cost computed on the basis of the goods and services listed will supply recreation, no matter how the need is expressed in individual cases. Families will not spend what these budgets cost in the manner outlined, but the amounts thus provided should take care of minimum needs.

The fact that the range in recreation costs from lowest to highest city was only about half that shown for newspapers or motion picture theater admissions is to be attributed to the partial cancellation of extremes in combination, and to the fact that more than two-fifths of the average total annual necessary outlay was carried as an identical amount in all cities, plus sales tax where levied. Newspaper and motion picture theater admission costs together were nearly twice as far apart between the extreme cities as was the spread when the identical allowance for organizations, tobacco, toys, and other leisure-time accessories was added. The smaller difference is the more representative, however, in that the identical allowance provides for items with highly standardized prices, which normally differ little wherever sold.

Newspaper prices are largely of local origin and the fact that a range of nearly 87 percent between lowest and highest costs was found is without significance, except as a reflection of local conditions.

Average charges for admission of adults to motion picture theaters on Saturday evenings varied from 13.2 cents to 27 cents and on Saturday afternoons from 10 cents to 23.75 cents, but children's prices on Saturday afternoons ranged from 5 cents to 12 cents. City averages for each admission were not uniformly high or uniformly low in any place; hence, a narrower cost spread appeared for the entire family's theater attendance than that indicated for any individual separately.

Motion picture theater admissions were subject to a sales tax in three cities (appendix tables 15 and 16). In addition, New Orleans had a 1-cent tax on all admissions exceeding 10 cents; this was the only direct consumers' tax in the city in March 1935. Without these taxes the dispersion of motion picture theater admission costs among the 59 cities would have been slightly narrowed. Tobacco, toys, and other leisure-time accessories always were covered where there was a sales tax.

LIFE INSURANCE, CHURCH CONTRIBUTIONS, AND OTHER CONTRIBUTIONS

The amounts to be included in the total cost of living for life insurance, church contributions, and other contributions are specified in the quantity budgets and allowances were identical in all cities.

Life insurance for a four-person manual worker's family at a maintenance level of living required annual premiums totaling $46.40 (appendix table 2). These premiums would provide a death benefit of $1,000 for the man and smaller amounts for the woman and two children. The $20.80 per year premiums allowed at the emergency level (appendix table 8) would assure small death benefits for each member of the family.

Church contributions to be made by this family are allowed as $10.40 annually in both budgets, but at the maintenance level of living $5 more is included to cover support of community activities of various kinds, bringing the total necessary outlay for contributions at this level to $15.40 per year (appendix tables 2 and 8).

TAXES

Personal property and capitation taxes of various kinds may be required of industrial, service, and other manual workers of small means as well as the consumers' sales tax referred to previously. The sales tax has been treated throughout this analysis as part of the cost of the commodities and services on which it was levied, but its basis is discussed in this chapter. Personal property and capitation taxes constitute separate charges to be added to other budget costs.[22]

Reports regarding tax rates and their applicability collected for this study were not always consistent among different authorities consulted in the same State, or with available manuals.[23] This confusion probably occurred because some taxes are permissive and may or may not be levied by a given local unit, and also because rates and their application change from year to year and the dates to which the separate reports refer may not be identical. The data used relate to taxes payable as of March 15, 1935.

Personal Property and Capitation Taxes

Personal property taxes were collectible from the 4-person manual worker's family of this study in 22 cities in March 1935, and capitation taxes, in 25; 11 cities had both and 23 cities had neither (appendix tables 2 and 8). By definition maintenance and emergency budget taxes were identical. The maximum amount recorded for a personal property tax was $6.22, and sums in the neighborhood of $2 or $3 were most commonly required. Capitation taxes seldom amounted to as much as $5 per year (table 49).

Personal property and capitation taxes were most frequently found in New England and the Southern States; none of the Pacific

[22] Though many States and the Federal Government levy income taxes, exemptions and deductions were such that income taxes were not collectible from families at the economic level with which this study deals.

[23] The Tax Research Foundation, *Tax Systems of the World*, sixth edition, Chicago, 1935.

Division cities reported such taxes. Among the largest cities only Chicago reported a personal property or capitation tax, and the popularity of these taxes increased as the size of cities decreased. Geographic division and size of city relatives (appendix tables 5, 7, 11, and 13) are without significance, however, owing to the fact that not every city in the group of 59 had personal property or capitation taxes.

Table 49.—Annual Taxes [1] Exclusive of Sales Tax, 4-Person Manual Worker's Family, 36 Cities, March 1935

Annual tax	Number of cities		
	All taxes	Personal property tax	Capitation tax
Total	36	22	25
$0.00-$0.99	—	1	—
$1.00-$1.99	4	2	2
$2.00-$2.99	7	9	5
$3.00-$3.99	9	6	9
$4.00-$4.99	3	3	5
$5.00-$5.99	4	—	2
$6.00-$6.99	4	1	1
$7.00-$7.99	2	—	—
$8.00-$8.99	3	—	1
Average annual tax [2]	$4.17	$2.96	$3.40

[1] Maintenance and emergency budget taxes by definition are identical.
[2] The averages in the separate columns are based on the number of cities in which the specified tax was levied.

Sales Tax

Any tax levied as a percentage of retail prices and paid by the consumer as a charge separate from these prices was treated in this study as a sales tax. On this basis, 18 cities had a sales tax in March 1935.[24] The amounts represented by a sales tax in the aggregate cost of living of a four-person manual worker's family covered a fairly wide range (table 50).[25] In Louisville where most was required for this purpose, necessary annual outlay was $25.20 at the maintenance level of

[24] Known generally as retail sales taxes, these taxes often are excises on gross income or receipts of business, levied in exchange for the privilege of engaging in a specified occupation but designed to be paid directly by the retail purchaser. Some statutes forbid vendors to advertise that they absorb the tax or will refund the amount paid. In other States, however, the vendor may absorb the tax or add it to the purchase price, as he pleases. A third group of States have taxes on the value of retail sales which the vendor himself is required to pay. Changes in the laws of several States have been made since March 1935, but rates and other specifications in operation at that time were used in all cost calculations.

[25] This table is included for reference only; the sales tax has already been added to the costs of all items on which it is levied. A local tax of 1 cent on motion picture theater admissions exceeding 10 cents in New Orleans was also added to the charge itself in all cost calculations. It amounted to $1.56 annually at the maintenance level of living and 36 cents at the emergency level. This tax was not a sales tax and New Orleans is not included with the sales tax cities.

living; the smallest sales tax was $6.49 in New York (appendix table 15). Emergency level sales taxes were proportionately less (appendix table 16).

Table 50.—Annual Sales Tax, 4-Person Manual Worker's Family, 18 Cities, March 1935

Annual sales tax	Number of cities	
	Maintenance level	Emergency level
Total	18	18
$4.00–$5.99	—	2
$6.00–$7.99	2	—
$8.00–$9.99	—	2
$10.00–$11.99	1	5
$12.00–$13.99	1	1
$14.00–$15.99	3	6
$16.00–$17.99	3	2
$18.00–$19.99	4	—
$20.00–$21.99	2	—
$22.00–$23.99	1	—
$24.00–$25.99	1	—
Average, 18 cities	$16.76	$12.38

The sales tax accounted for 2.1 percent of the total annual cost of living in Louisville and one-half of 1 percent in New York. The average in the 18 cities combined was 1.3 percent of the maintenance budget cost and 1.4 percent of the emergency budget cost (table 51).

None of the cities in New England had a sales tax, and the local excise in the city of New York was unique in the Middle Atlantic States. Sales taxes were found in a number of cities in other sections of the country, and they were especially popular in the East North Central and Mountain Divisions. Butte was the only Mountain city which had no sales tax.

Table 51.—Sales Tax as Percent of Total Cost of Living, 18 Cities, March 1935

City	Rate of tax (percent)	Percent of cost of living	
		Maintenance level	Emergency level
Average, 18 cities	—	1.3	1.4
Albuquerque, N. Mex.	2.0	1.6	1.5
Cedar Rapids, Iowa	2.0	1.4	1.4
Chicago, Ill.	2.0	1.2	1.2
Cincinnati, Ohio	3.0	1.4	1.5
Clarksburg, W. Va.	2.0	1.3	1.3
Cleveland, Ohio	3.0	1.5	1.6
Columbus, Ohio	3.0	1.6	1.7
Denver, Colo.	2.0	1.0	1.1
Detroit, Mich.	3.0	1.8	1.9
Los Angeles, Calif.	2.5	1.5	1.5
Louisville, Ky.	3.0	2.1	2.1
New York, N. Y.	2.0	0.5	0.5
Oklahoma City, Okla.	1.0	0.6	0.6
Peoria, Ill.	2.0	1.2	1.3
Salt Lake City, Utah	2.0	1.2	1.3
San Francisco, Calif.	2.5	1.4	1.5
Tucson, Ariz.	1.5	0.9	1.0
Winston-Salem, N. C.	3.0	1.4	1.5

Tax Differences

Tax differences among the separate cities are accounted for by a number of circumstances. What personal property shall be taxed, what percentage of full valuation shall constitute the tax base, how much shall be tax free, and what rate shall be levied vary considerably and explain personal property tax differences. The difficulty of collecting these taxes from individuals of small means has resulted in entirely exempting personal property of low value in some places.

So also with capitation taxes. These are fixed amounts which vary among the separate cities. Roads, schools, poor relief, old-age pensions, general expenses, and other purposes benefit from these taxes. Several such taxes may be levied for different purposes or by different branches of the government on one person in a given community. They may be paid by men only, or by men and women, and age limits usually are specified. Some States forbid poll taxes; nowhere except in a few Southern States is their payment a prerequisite to voting.

The sales tax laws indicate the percentage of gross income or gross receipts which will be collected from the merchant and require that this be charged to the retail purchaser; but few of the statutes specify how the consumer shall pay, in the absence of legal tender of less than 1 cent.[26] A schedule of brackets usually is set up, in which purchases of less than a certain amount are tax free; within the next price grouping a tax of 1 cent is required; then a price group where the tax is 2 cents; and so on, so that an average equal to the rate per $1 of sales presumably will be collected. Unless the schedule is embodied in the law or has general application throughout the State by order of the State tax commission, a wide variety of bracket systems may be used in any one State or even in any one city.

The States differ somewhat in their application of the sales tax, varying from the procedure in New Mexico where in March 1935 all retail purchases supposedly were covered, including professional services, car and bus tokens, and telephone calls, to North Carolina where all services, public utilities, and many food commodities were exempt. The most usual exclusions from sales tax coverage were services and sales by nonprofit-making institutions. Rates also varied among the 18 cities from 3 percent of retail value in Cincinnati, Cleveland, Columbus, Detroit, Louisville, and Winston-Salem to 1 percent in Oklahoma City. In most of the others the rate was 2 percent.

These variations in applicability and rates, together with prices of the goods and services taxed, account for sales tax differences. For example, both Louisville and Detroit had a 3-percent rate. The annual

[26] Some States have adopted a system of tokens valued at fractions of 1 cent, and the exact percentage specified is collected on each purchase no matter what its price may be.

tax on the maintenance budget cost was more in Louisville, however, because a larger part of the budget was covered, than in Detroit where prices were higher but fewer items were taxed. In New York the rate was 2 percent but food and personal services were exempt, so that the tax at the same level of living amounted to less than in Oklahoma City with its 1-percent rate and lower prices but more extensive coverage.

Chapter VII

TECHNIQUES AND PROCEDURES

PROPER INTERPRETATION of the cost of living figures analyzed in the earlier chapters depends on an understanding of the methods used in obtaining them.[1] These techniques and procedures are described in the present chapter.

CITIES SURVEYED

Choosing the cities in which to make the study required consideration of geographic location, size, and socio-economic characteristics of various kinds. At the same time it was desirable to include as large a proportion of the country's population as possible. Inasmuch as 40 percent of all inhabitants of the United States live in cities of 25,000 or more,[2] and a greater body of information is available regarding the characteristics of these communities and their residents than of smaller places, the study was confined to cities of this size. Nearly 50 percent of the total population and slightly more than 63 percent of the urban population live east of the Mississippi and north of the Ohio Rivers.[3] This area is more homogeneous in climate and in social and economic life than the remainder of the country, which comprises several times as much territory, but the remainder of the country also was represented. Covering the country as a whole in the group of cities surveyed resulted in a certain amount of conflict between population and geographic criteria, in that some sections are best represented by cities of certain size; the inclusion of these reduced the proportion of cities of the same size in other areas where they are more numerous but less significant. Thus, it happens that in the present group of 59

[1] Quantity budgets for the two levels of living are given in complete detail in Stecker, Margaret L., *Quantity Budgets for Basic Maintenance and Emergency Standards of Living*, Research Bulletin Series I, No. 21, Division of Social Research, Works Progress Administration, 1936.

[2] *Fifteenth Census of the United States: 1930*, Population Vol. I, p. 14.

[3] *Ibid.*, pp. 10 and 15.

cities the smallest are perhaps more typical of the section of the country in which they are located than of their population class.[4]

In compiling the list of cities to be investigated, free use was made of earlier studies by other organizations interested in price and cost of living research [5] and of the list prepared by the Federal Emergency Relief Administration for its study of urban workers on relief.[6] Because the retail food prices collected by the Bureau of Labor Statistics were to be used as far as possible, most of the 51 cities in which these were being reported regularly in March 1935 were included.[7] Their inclusion automatically brought into the group all but 1 of the 32 cities in which the Bureau makes its quarterly study of changes in the costs of living.[8] The cities finally chosen (table 1) proved reasonably satisfactory for the purpose in hand; those least representative from an industrial point of view were included to obtain geographic coverage (fig. 1).[9] Appendix table 1 indicates that the 59 cities in which prices were obtained had 60.9 percent of the urban population living in communities of 25,000 or more in 1930 and 24.4 percent of the entire population of the United States.

NEIGHBORHOOD COVERAGE

All cities were districted and neighborhoods were spotted for price collection and other study. A variety of data formed the basis for this neighborhood selection. Census tracts, local surveys, and opinions of municipal authorities, chambers of commerce, social welfare organiza-

---

[4] For example, 7 of the 10 cities with a population of 25,000 or more in the Mountain Division are in the group 25,000 to 50,000; 3 of these were included in the investigation. The Mountain Division, with these 3 cities, is 72.4 percent covered as to population in places of 25,000 or more. There are 185 cities in the United States, however, with a population between 25,000 and 50,000. Obviously many of these are not represented by the Mountain Division cities.

[5] A list of 110 cities prepared by the Cost of Living Division of the Bureau of Labor Statistics in 1934 contained 91 with a population of 25,000 or more; 55 of these were included. A list of 237 communities prepared the same year for the Joint Committee on Government Statistics and Information Services of the American Statistical Association and the Social Science Research Council contained 119 cities within the same size range; 57 of these were included. Cover, John H., *Retail Price Behavior*, Studies in Business Administration, Vol. V, No. 2, University of Chicago, Chicago, 1935, pp. 3–4, and 69–75.

[6] Wood, Katherine D., *Urban Workers on Relief*, Research Monograph IV, Division of Social Research, Works Progress Administration, 1936.

[7] Charleston, S. C., New Haven, Conn., St. Paul, Minn., Savannah, Ga., and Springfield, Ill., were omitted because of geographic considerations.

[8] Savannah was not included because the Bureau's list is somewhat overweighted with Atlantic port cities, and another city in the same area was substituted.

[9] In the analysis in chs. I–VI involving geographic location, city groupings are made according to the census classification as shown in table 1. Size of city groupings are those of the census, except that cities with a population of 25,000 to 100,000 are combined.

tions, and other local groups were correlated to determine where in each city the industrial population lived and did its buying.

Coverage in a given city depended on the composition of its population with reference to isolation of the industrial group, on its own peculiar layout, and to a certain extent on its area. The study was confined within each city's corporate limits for the most part, but in a few places these were exceeded because the suburbs were closely integrated with the city itself. The proportion of each city's population living in the neighborhoods studied varied from city to city, but in 49 for which coverage could be estimated the average was slightly over 48 percent. These estimates are not exact and too great importance cannot be attached to them, but they serve to indicate that a representative sample was secured in each city as a basis for the cost of living analysis.[10]

COMMODITIES PRICED AND THEIR SPECIFICATIONS

The quantity budgets are made up of the kind of goods and services used by families of industrial, service, and other manual workers of small means in urban areas. The annual allowances were designed to supply the needs of such families.

A total of 251 separate commodities listed in the quantity budgets was priced in each city on 13 separate schedules.[11] Four additional schedules inquired into (1) consumer shopping habits; (2) medical, dental, nursing, and hospital care; (3) housing, fuel, light, ice, and water; and (4) such miscellaneous needs as transportation, school attendance, newspapers, motion picture theater admissions, refuse disposal, and taxes. Finally, quotations were available for 44 food commodities,[12] priced in 46 cities by the Bureau of Labor Statistics and in 13 additional cities by the Federal Emergency Relief Administration. Approximately 1,432,000 price quotations and pertinent consumption data were obtained on 93,000 schedules, together with

[10] The areas covered represent the most important industrial life of most of the cities. Where plants are located outside the city proper, as sometimes happens with mines, quarries, and similar extractive industries, or with factories which seek to obtain lower taxes by suburban locations and operate on the company village plan, some of the significant aspects of the working class life of the locality may have been missed, but the necessity for uniformity of the sample dictated that they be omitted.

[11] The goods and services priced cover requirements for men and women and for children of both sexes between the ages of 2 and 15, inclusive. Most of the material was used in estimating costs for the four-person family of this study. A few clothing, and furniture, furnishings, and household equipment items related specifically to the needs of families of different size and/or composition; rents for larger and smaller units than those used also were collected. Specifications and schedules on which quotations were collected are not reproduced in this monograph because of space considerations.

[12] Prices were collected for 87 food commodities, but only 44 of them are listed in the quantity budgets.

a large volume of supporting and interpretive facts and figures. About 175 small articles, such as handkerchiefs, tea strainers, or bluing, were not listed on the schedules, but their prices in Washington chain limited price variety stores were used in all cities. All told, prices of approximately 550 separate items went into the cost calculations in each city.

To insure comparability of standard from store to store and place to place, specification manuals were made up, embodying descriptions of most of the goods and services to be priced. Neither second-hand nor reconditioned merchandise was included. The specification for a few commodities, such as cleaning supplies or proprietary medicines,[13] was that they should be those having the largest sale. The types of housing and fuel priced were related somewhat closely to local means available for satisfying stipulated needs. Public utility rates, of which there usually was only one in a given city for a given service, required no definition beyond their relationship to the budget allowances.

Quotations were obtained for items which met the specifications as closely as possible, but where the designated commodities were not carried and comparable merchandise seemed representative of local use, the latter was priced. These deviations from specifications in all instances were to be noted by the field agents in order that noncomparable quotations might be eliminated.

Obviously, it is impossible to maintain absolute identity of budget content in 59 cities scattered throughout the country. A few items cannot be priced in some communities; average requirements overstate or understate the needs in particular localities. One kind of housing cannot be priced the country over. The same fuel is not used everywhere. Average fuel allowances would be inadequate where winters are long and cold, and excessive where they are very short and very mild. The reverse relationships would occur for refrigeration requirements. More transportation obviously is necessary for carrying on life's ordinary economic and social activities where a large population is scattered over an extensive territory than in small communities where the industrial and social life is more concentrated. Quantity allowances for these items were adjusted in the budgets to represent differential needs.

Because the costs of refuse disposal and school attendance may be paid directly by individual families in some cities while they are met from public funds in others, the outlays necessary for these purposes were included in each city's cost estimates as required, without quantity allowances. Taxes were similarly treated. Several costs were not itemized but were included in the budgets as fixed values, without provision for local pricing. These identical allowances were for such

[13] These were trade-marked or other commodities usually sold by brand names, which were not specified in the present investigation.

necessities as postage, telephone calls, and insurance, whose costs are the same everywhere; or church contributions and organization membership, which obviously are completely unstandardized.

Thus, certain departures from an identical budget were made. Despite these departures, the principle of uniform budgets was maintained by means of the substitutions and adjustments described above.

PRICE COLLECTION

Local agents under the supervision of members of the research staffs of the Federal Emergency Relief Administration and the Retail Price Division of the Bureau of Labor Statistics did the field work. They obtained reports from families regarding their buying habits, rents, and prices paid for certain items of household operation;[14] they collected commodity prices from stores at which industrial, service, and other manual workers of small means trade and service charges from those who supply such families. The 17 schedules and specifications previously described were used in this procedure.[15] The time spent in each city depended on the size of the community, its business and residential layout, and the number of persons engaged in collecting the data. The average was about 2 months.

The commodity schedules called for notation of the kind of store, such as department, specialty, variety, and the like; type of operation, such as independent or chain; type of service, such as cash and carry, credit and delivery, or installment credit; and location, such as central shopping area, neighborhood trade center, or other neighborhood location. Every city supervisor was provided with an estimate of the number of different kinds of stores in the city and the commodities sold in each, based on the 1930 Census of Distribution.[16] At least 10 quotations for each commodity in each shopping area were called for, pro rata to the census classification as far as possible, unless the commodity was not sold in 10 retail outlets. In some cities, especially the smaller places, strict adherence to established classifications was not feasible, and all stores which sold a specified commodity necessarily were visited. The resulting sample adequately covered stores which serve a working class trade, and the number of quotations obtained for each article insured a representative city average price.

---

[14] A total of more than 10,000 schedules was taken from families in the 59 cities for the purpose of obtaining certain information regarding consumer shopping habits, rents, and prices paid for fuel and ice. Price data were used in cost calculations for this study, but expenditures, reflecting consumption habits, were not analyzed.

[15] Retail food prices also were collected on 6 separate schedules in 13 cities where the Bureau of Labor Statistics had no routine price reporting system in March 1935.

[16] *Fifteenth Census of the United States: 1930*, Distribution Vol. I, Pts. II and III.

Service schedules also were assigned on a quota basis. Selecting the samples for housing, medical care, and various miscellaneous family needs required more time and presented more complications than any other phase of the study, owing to the fact that for most of them standards could not be specified in definite terms.

Quotations were obtained as of March 15, 1935, except that for certain essentially seasonal goods prices in the last preceding season were taken. Special sale values were avoided if these were markdowns, clearance prices, or other discounts from regular quotations, but stores always operating on a cut-rate basis were included. Installment prices were quoted for commodities frequently purchased on the deferred payment plan.

OFFICE PROCEDURE

Certain limitations are inherent in the use of specifications in price reporting, and the judgments of the agent who collects the quotations and the dealer who sells the goods play a large part in the procedure. Considerable discretion was required, therefore, in editing the schedules to determine which prices to admit and which to reject. The following general rule was laid down with reference to discards: quotations were to be rejected for all commodities which did not conform to specifications if apparently they would not serve the same purpose as the item specified, if the length of their service probably would be less than that called for in the quantity budgets, or if differences in size, material, or construction might result in price differences. If the specifications were not sufficiently precise to insure that they were always interpreted in the same way or that they were checked carefully, all quotations which fitted into the array of prices for commodities conforming to the specifications were used.

In the event that acceptable quotations for a given item were not obtained in a community, one of several procedures was followed to complete the cost estimates. If a similar commodity had been found to sell elsewhere for approximately the same price, this price was substituted for the one which was missing. If no such relationship was apparent, the average of prices of the missing article in cities in the same areas or prices from other reliable sources were used. The theory behind these procedures was that certain wants were to be provided for and that where the items specified were not sold, comparable merchandise at comparable prices would take their places. All told, relatively few substitutions of any kind were necessary, and city averages for the separate items are fair statements of local values.

In preparing the field data for analysis after editing and coding, both machine and hand tabulations were used, depending on the nature of the material; and two types of average were necessary because of the variety of data to be handled. It may be said that, in general, commodity price quotations were coded for machine tabulation and the average taken was the simple arithmetic mean; no adjustments whatever were made in these results.[17] Hand tabulations were necessary for service prices, and a modified median [18] was the average most frequently used. Emphasis was placed on the reasonableness of the results. Where the nature of the data, taken in connection with nonquantitative field reports and other means of checking, in a few instances suggested that the figures were not representative, they were adjusted on the basis of apparently more authentic information.

Eventually usable city average prices for every item in the budgets were available. These were then combined with their respective quantity allowances for the four-person family of this study, and the costs of the budget groups were calculated. Finally, group costs were totaled to obtain the outlays necessary for the content of living as a whole at the two levels. Where there was a sales or similar consumers' tax, its amount was computed by taking the rate percent of aggregate costs of the budget groups [19] and was added to these aggregates. This method of calculating the sales tax was used because in no two jurisdictions is it similarly applied in all respects to separate purchases. By isolating taxes from prices, the latter can be compared by themselves and the part played by sales taxes in intercity cost of living comparisons can be appraised.

In computing average costs in the 59 cities combined and in the separate geographic divisions and size of city classifications, individual city costs were not weighted by either their population or area importance, but the simple arithmetic mean was taken. The average in the 59 cities combined affords a convenient value in terms of which individual city costs can be compared.

BUDGET GROUPS AND PRICES

The procedures used in collecting and tabulating prices and in computing and analyzing costs are described below in essential detail for the separate budget groups.

Food

The quantity food budgets contain 44 commodities listed for pricing, with 1 percent of their cost added for nonpriced condiments. These foods are grouped as follows: flour, cereals, and bread, 8 commodities; milk and cheese, 3; fruits and vegetables, 17, of which 9 are

[17] City average food prices were calculated by the Bureau of Labor Statistics which used machine operations and computed the arithmetic mean. Inasmuch as the latter included a sales tax where levied, certain recalculations were necessary to obtain each price without the tax. See footnote 22, p. 99.

[18] Arithmetic mean of the three, four, five, or six central values in the array, the number of central values averaged depending on the total number in the array.

[19] Where certain commodities or services were tax exempt, they were excluded from the aggregates for tax computation purposes.

fresh, 5 are dried, and 3 are canned; lean meat, fish, and eggs, 6; fats, sugars, and accessories, 10. They were selected from among the 87 items for which the Bureau of Labor Statistics regularly collects quotations each month, on the basis of their low cost food value, in order to represent a balanced diet at minimum cost. The same foods are included in both the maintenance and emergency budgets, but the former contains a more liberal supply of the higher cost foods than does the latter. It is to be understood, of course, that the budgets are only samples of inexpensive foods, included in such quantities as to provide for consumption of the greater variety of commodities which families purchase in season, to satisfy their own tastes, and to conform with local custom.

The Bureau of Labor Statistics' regular price quotations obtained as of March 12, 1935, were used in calculating average food costs in 46 of the cities. The Bureau had no routine reporting system in the other 13, and food prices as of March 15, 1935, were collected for the first time for the present investigation. The Bureau's six food price schedules [20] and the Bureau's specifications as to type of store and kind of commodity were used.

In general, merchandise was described as "U. S. No. 1 or equal grade," "good quality," "best cut" carried, or by similar designations applicable to different types of commodities. These specifications permitted a wide choice in pricing, but the articles selected for this purpose were sold by each store visited to its working class trade. Where only one grade was carried, that commodity necessarily was priced. Potential inaccuracies resulting from the heterogeneity of the sample were overcome in the average of a considerable number of quotations. Their number varied among the separate commodities and with the retailing situation in the different cities. As a rule, at least 10 quotations were taken and sometimes as many as 20; in no instance was an average computed of fewer than 4.

The Bureau of Labor Statistics calculated all city average food prices, using the simple arithmetic mean of quotations furnished by the separate dealers in each city. All the Bureau's food price averages contain the sales tax where levied.[21] In computing the cost of food for use in the present study, the tax was abstracted from the city average price of each commodity with which it had been incorporated by the Bureau, and these revised prices were then combined with the

[20] Some commodities were priced on more than 1 schedule, and 37 items not used in this investigation also were listed. Hence, no attempt is made here to classify commodities by the schedules used in their collection.

[21] Where provision has not been made for adding the tax to the sale price on a unit basis, as, for example, through use of tokens valued at less than 1 cent, bracket systems are used. With this arrangement, prices within certain ranges call for taxes of specified amounts, so adjusted that on each dollar of sales the average rate percent will be realized. See p. 89.

quantity of each article required for the four-person family, as listed in the budgets for the maintenance and emergency levels of living.[22] One percent of the total of these amounts was added for condiments to complete the estimate of necessary annual food cost, exclusive of sales tax.

Clothing, Clothing Upkeep, and Personal Care

Commodities and services to the number of 177 were priced, on 9 schedules, 102 of which were used in computing the cost of clothing, clothing upkeep, and personal care (table 52). Those not used are listed in the quantity budgets for children outside the four-person family with which this monograph is concerned, or they were collected for special purposes not directly related to the present study.

Table 52.—Number of Commodities and Services Priced and Used in Computing Costs of Clothing, Clothing Upkeep, and Personal Care, 59 Cities, March 1935

Schedule	Number of commodities and services	
	Priced	Used [1]
Total	177	102
Men's clothing	[2] 22	[3] 21
Women's clothing	[2] 24	23
Boys' clothing	40	[4] 14
Girls' clothing	41	18
Shoes	25	14
Shoe repairs	4	[5] 4
Personal services	[2] 5	[5] 4
Dry cleaners	[2] 4	3
Cleaning supplies and sundries	12	[6] 1

[1] A few of these commodities and services were not used in computing the costs of the emergency budget.
[2] Includes 1 item not in the quantity budgets.
[3] Does not include 1 item from the women's clothing schedule, used also for the man's budgets.
[4] Does not include 2 items from the men's clothing schedule, used also for the boy's budgets.
[5] 1 item used for both man and boy.
[6] Other items on this schedule were priced either for the household supplies group or for the furniture, furnishings, and household equipment group, or were not included in the quantity budgets.

Identical money allowances were added to the cost of goods and services priced separately in each of the 59 cities to provide for commodities whose prices are likely to be the same everywhere and for unspecified clothing incidentals (table 53). Though all these items are essential, they are usually bought at chain limited price variety stores for the amounts specified, and omitting them from the schedules materially reduced the field work and other operations involved in cost computations.

[22] Because of the deletion of the sales tax, food prices used in this study differ slightly in some instances from those reported by the Bureau of Labor Statistics which include the tax. In deducting the tax from each city average price, the amount applicable to that price according to prevailing brackets was removed, unless this procedure resulted in a nontaxable price or one in another tax bracket, in which case the average of the two taxes was deducted. In cities where there was a sales tax, its amount was added to the aggregate cost of food to conform with the procedure used in calculating the annual costs of other budget groups.

The exactness of the specifications varied with the nature of the items described. They listed the appropriate size or age of each person for whom each garment was priced and designated the material and construction of "inexpensive quality" merchandise. Obtaining quotations in the stores where the families of industrial, service, and other manual workers of small means trade provided a good check on the sample, and judicious editing for prices obviously out of line insured representative city averages when all were combined.[23]

Table 53.—Identical Annual Allowances [1] for Clothing, Clothing Upkeep, and Personal Care: Commodities and Services Not Separately Priced, 4-Person Manual Worker's Family, 59 Cities, March 1935

Item	Annual allowance [1]	
	Maintenance level	Emergency level
Total	$19.80	$13.60
Men's clothing	3.50	1.75
Women's clothing	2.75	1.45
Boys' clothing	2.65	1.50
Girls' clothing	1.35	.75
Clothing upkeep	1.55	1.35
Personal care	8.00	6.80

[1] Sales tax to be added where levied (appendix tables 15 and 16).

Prices for clothing, unlike those for food which were as of a given day in mid-March, were the in-season prices. Thus, if the merchandise called for was out of season on March 15, as, for example, winter garments, the season's prices rather than mark-down values were reported. The arithmetic mean of all accepted quotations for each item was taken, and this was combined with its appropriate annual allowances as given in the quantity budgets. These processes were performed entirely by mechanical tabulators. Aggregates of these annual costs for the separate items gave annual costs for the budget subgroups and for the major budget group as a whole, exclusive of sales tax.

Housing

In studying the costs of support at comparable levels of living in 59 separate cities, few problems presented so many phases demanding special attention as arose in connection with rents. The homes of industrial, service, and other manual workers of small means are found in frame bungalows in some cities; in others, in big brick tenements. A diversity of dwelling types exists between these two extremes. Houses vary as to material, age, and state of repair; as to number, layout, and size of rooms; as to conveniences, neighborhood, and numerous other criteria of desirability. Hence, the pricing specifications were fairly general, and details were worked out in each city to meet the peculiar local situation. In computing the outlay neces-

[23] See pp. 95–97.

sary for rent, more definite criteria were set up.[24] It should be clearly understood, however, that the purpose of the study was to ascertain representative rents for dwellings meeting specified standards; all other data collected were collateral to them. In no sense was a general housing survey conducted. The relative prevalence of different types of dwellings in a given city was not necessarily ascertained, therefore, and a large sample was not always essential for proper valuation of standard accommodations.

The following excerpts from instructions for using the housing schedule in the field indicate the method of collecting the data.

* * * The schedule is designed to fulfill the requirements for studying both standard and prevalent types of housing. * * * The definitions of dwellings, standard dwellings, and typical dwellings are as follows:

Dwelling Unit: This term is designed to cover any one of several types of family residence units. It may be a single-family house; it may be part of a two- or three-family building; or it may be a suite of rooms in an apartment, tenement, etc. The term refers at all times to a residence unit in which a single family resides.

Standard Dwelling Unit: A standard dwelling unit meets the housing requirements of either a minimum decency [25] or an emergency budget. The former provides for a private bathroom; the latter only for a private toilet. Other requirements are identical for both budgets.

The building must be safely constructed and in at least a fair state of repair, clean, sanitary, and without serious fire hazards. Where there is a State or local housing code setting minimum standards for light, air, sanitation, etc., and where there is a building code setting standards for structural safety, the housing must comply with these regulations. Each room in a dwelling unit must have at least one window of normal size admitting natural light and providing ventilation. * * *

Bedrooms must be large enough to contain one double or two single beds, a chair, and chest of drawers; the living room must be large enough to permit seating all members of the family at table at the same time for meals, with additional space for a couch and easy chairs; or the living room may be large enough for a couch and easy chairs, and a kitchen large enough to permit seating all members of the family at table at meals. In all instances, space for moving about, children's play, etc., must be provided for.

The requirements for minimum decency and emergency housing are identical in the above respects. The specifications for bath, toilet, and water facilities differ between the two types of housing and are stated as follows:

Housing that meets the requirements of minimum decency must have a bathroom, running water, and a toilet for the exclusive use of one family, and these facilities must be in a separate compartment within the dwelling unit of the family. No variation, whatever, is permitted from these requirements.

The standard of emergency housing does not require a private bathroom. A private toilet is essential, however, and if sewer and water mains exist in the area being studied, both the toilet and running water must be within the dwelling unit of the family and the toilet in a separate compartment, except that if the locality being studied is one where freezing temperatures rarely occur, the toilet may be on the back porch and the water may be outside the house. The toilet may be in the yard only when a privy is the only practicable form of toilet, and

[24] See pp. 103–104.

[25] Later called "basic maintenance."

when that privy conforms to local health requirements. There may be no other variation from these standards, and under no circumstances are cellar or community toilets of any kind to be considered satisfactory.

Typical Dwelling Units: Typical dwelling units are the types of units most frequently found in the neighborhood in which the study is being made. Typical dwelling units may or may not meet the specifications for standard dwelling units.

Sources of Information: The information called for on this schedule is to be secured by interviews with a variety of informants. Health officers, building inspectors, officials of zoning boards, local research organizations, real estate agents, and social workers will supply most of the information concerning the character and cost of housing. * * *

The local health officer and the building inspector will know whether the housing in the study areas violates the sanitary and housing regulations or the building code.

Schedules will also be taken of samples of families living in various types of dwelling units in the designated neighborhoods, as a check on other sources of information. * * *

Areas: The areas inhabited by low-income families in industrial, service, or other manual worker groups will have been identified for the purpose of pricing other items, such as food and clothing. The same areas will be covered with the present schedule, * * * *except* when the standard dwelling units *do not exist* in the areas selected for survey. * * * It is anticipated that in the larger cities both standard dwelling types will be found in some of the neighborhoods studied. In some of the smaller places, however, housing which meets specifications for standard dwelling units may not exist in the neighborhoods selected, but may be found in other parts of the city. In such cases it will be necessary to price housing outside of the selected neighborhood. * * * Whenever this is done, rentals for housing which most nearly approaches working class uses and which is in areas that can be readily identified should be secured.

Interviews: All persons interviewed should be acquainted with the purpose and method of the investigation. * * * After areas have been spotted for study, the first visit should be made to those officials in the city hall who are charged with the responsibility of enforcing zoning, building, or sanitary codes. They will be able to tell the extent to which housing in the areas selected conforms to building and sanitary codes, and to designate specific blocks which are acceptable from that point of view. This will enable the interviewer to complete the detailed specifications for standard dwelling units. Social workers familiar with the neighborhood will also be informed on this point and will provide much background material as the basis for further work. They also are likely to know of particular studies made of the neighborhoods by research organizations, from which information may be secured regarding the housing situation. Real estate agencies handling housing in the area should then be visited, for the purpose of obtaining definite information regarding rentals of specific groups of houses. * * *

Finally, families living in houses of the types determined to be standard and/or typical will be visited to obtain information regarding rents * * * actually paid by them. * * *

If there are variations in housing in the neighborhood based not on standards of adequacy or bath and toilet facilities but on variations in the kind of housing, such as single-family dwelling units, flats, and/or apartment houses or tenements, and these are not covered in any of the dwelling units already scheduled, as many additional schedules should be taken as will properly represent them, also. * * *

In interviewing families, select several specific dwelling units or blocks of standard and typical dwellings with the help of health officers, real estate agents, social workers, etc. The number of dwellings of each type interviewed should be approximately in proportion to the percentage which such types are of all types in the neighborhood. * * *

Total Number of Schedules: The total number of schedules to be filled for any one city varies with the number of different types of housing existent, with the size of the city, with the presence or absence of standard dwelling units, with the extent to which these units are typical units, with the number of areas selected for study, and with other factors. Since not all of these factors could be known in advance of the study, it was necessary to fix the number of schedules for each city somewhat arbitrarily. * * *

It should be particularly noted that adherence to these allotments is neither necessary nor desirable. In a city where only one or two areas are studied and where standard dwellings are typical of the neighborhoods, the cost of housing and other items can be readily obtained in only a few interviews and can be checked with a comparatively small number of family visits. * * * On the other hand, in some cities, several areas may have been selected for study, two or three kinds of dwellings may be typical of the areas and these types may not meet standard specifications. In cases like this, it will be necessary to conduct many interviews and to fill many schedules in order to obtain the cost of the various types of housing demanded by the study.[26] Considerable judgment is, therefore, placed in the hands of the supervisor and of the interviewers who assume responsibility for this part of the study.

Caution to the Interviewer: The specifications * * * developed for this study are adapted to meet the *minimum* requirements for healthy and normal life under existing conditions and in no sense are they to be regarded or interpreted as general housing standards established by the F. E. R. A.

With these instructions rents were ascertained for three-, four-, five-, and six-room dwelling units.[27] Considerable nonquantitative data also were assembled. The amount allowed as rent at the maintenance level was based on fulfillment of the following particular conditions in addition to the more general ones listed in the instructions: the house or apartment must be built on a basement or piers, be in good or fair repair, have sewer and water connections or equivalent services, and a private indoor bath and toilet; it must be rented without heat, light, refrigeration, or furniture; water, stove, set washtubs, and a garage might or might not be provided by the landlord.[28] Beyond these requirements the specifications could not go, and the accommodations obtainable for the estimated rents varied widely.

Minimum housing at any level of living requires at least one room per person exclusive of bath, hall, porch, closets, attic, or basement.

[26] Housing which was either inferior or superior to standard specifications, rented or owned, was studied with other purposes in mind than computing the costs of living. The variety of room units was required as a basis for estimating the costs of living for families of other size and composition than the four-person family with which this analysis is concerned.

[27] Larger or smaller units also were priced in certain cities where they were representative of working class dwellings.

[28] Provision of these facilities by the landlord seemed to make no difference in the rent, and their presence or absence was ignored in the computations, except that the final rent estimate for each city included provision of water.

Rents of both four- and five-room dwellings were used for the four-person family of this study.[29] For the amounts thus computed, accommodations of either size could be obtained in most cities.

Hand tabulations were required because of the nature of the rent and supporting data. Complete comparability of values was not obtained in some cities, and in some there were relatively few quotations for four and five rooms. Reported rents could not be edited for reasonableness, nor could substitutions be made as with commodity quotations. Hence, the simple arithmetic mean of reported rents was not computed. Instead, an average of several quotations clustered about the median (three, four, five, or six central values) was taken.

Table 54.—Differences Between Rents Reported by Real Estate Agents and by Families, 4 or 5 Rooms and Bath, 59 Cities, March 1935

Percent difference	Number of cities
Total	59
Real estate agent higher:	
31–40.9	1
21–30.9	3
11–20.9	12
1–10.9	17
Identical or less than 1 percent difference	4
Real estate agent lower:	
1–10.9	10
11–20.9	4
21–30.9	1
31–40.9	1
No comparison possible	6

Two sets of rent averages were finally available for each city: those derived from family reports of current charges and estimates from real estate agents as to representative rents for housing meeting the specifications. The agreement of these two series was very close considering the nature of the data (table 54); in 47 of the 53 cities where comparisons were possible there was less than 21 percent difference, and in 31 cities the difference was less than 11 percent. All discrepancies in reports from the two sources were examined for explanations of observed nonagreement. Such causes appeared as differences in types of building or neighborhood, the overweighting of one sample with four rooms and the other with five in those cities where rents varied with the number of rooms, and the inclusion of water in one sample and not in the other in cities where this made a difference in rents.[30]

Several tests of the reasonableness of city rent averages were applied. Did they agree with the field supervisors' descriptions in the

[29] The composition of this family requires three sleeping rooms, one of which may be the living room in a four-room house or apartment. Two bedrooms will be sufficient for many four-person families, and there is no reason to include an additional room because of the composition of a theoretical family. On the other hand, averaging rents for units of two sizes provides for the necessity of an extra room under certain circumstances.

[30] See pp. 105–106.

neighborhood data? How did they check with the Real Property Inventory,[31] information in the files of the Bureau of Labor Statistics, and reports of rents made by other students, especially local authorities? What proportion did rent take in computed total cost of living? As a result of these comparisons reported rents were revised slightly in a few cities, where they seemed to be unrepresentative, on the basis of apparently better data.

In recognition of the fact that mathematically computed rent averages might give a semblance of exactness not warranted by the basic material, they were rounded off according to the following schedule in computing the outlay necessary for rent in each city:

1. If the modified median lay between $X.21 and $X.29 inclusive, the rent used was $X.25.

2. If the modified median lay between $X.30 and $X.70 inclusive, the rent used was $X.50.

3. If the modified median lay between $X.71 and $X.79 inclusive, the rent used was $X.75.

4. If the modified median lay between $X.80 and $X plus $1.20 inclusive, the rent used was $X plus $1.

Another problem which arose in connection with the rent estimates was what to do about the water rate. Customs with reference to paying for water used by the tenant varied among the separate cities and among landlords in the same city. For the purpose of intercity comparisons it was necessary that all rents cover the cost of water. Decision as to whether or not the water rate should be added to reported rents rested on the prevailing custom in each city. Usually two-thirds of the reports either way determined the procedure used. In a few cities where the custom was not clearly defined, decision was made on the basis of other pertinent considerations. In general, it may be said that in most cities there is a tendency for owners of low rent dwellings to supply their tenants with water,[32] and that where strictly working class housing was priced water did not constitute a separate charge. Rents for these houses often were less than for houses in the same cities where the water rate was paid by the tenant. If typical working class housing was not up to the standard specified for this investigation and city average rents were computed from charges for better accommodations, tenants usually paid for water separately and its cost was added to estimated rents. The minimum annual cost of water reported by the local water company always was

[31] United States Department of Commerce, Bureau of Foreign and Domestic Commerce, *Real Property Inventory, 1934*. There are separate reports for 64 cities, 22 of which were included in the present investigation.

[32] Table 17 shows that rents were lower in cities where water was a separate charge than where it was supplied by the landlord, and vice versa. The inclusion or exclusion of the water charge was of little, if any, importance in accounting for these differences.

used. Identical quantities were not allowed for the minimum in the separate cities, but most families interviewed seemed to find that the minimum allowance was sufficient.[33]

The plan to compute emergency level rents from quotations for dwelling units meeting all the requirements for maintenance level housing except private indoor bath proved impracticable, because in most cities houses which had a private indoor toilet also had a private indoor tub or shower; where there was no bath the toilet frequently was shared or outdoors, or the building was in poor condition and was eliminated on one or more of those counts. Where satisfactory accommodations with private indoor toilet only could be obtained, their rents averaged about 75 percent of the amounts required to obtain maintenance level housing. This ratio was used, therefore, in computing emergency level rents in all cities. The resulting figure was then rounded off as described, and the cost of water was added where water was a separate charge. Rounding off 75 percent of the modified median of maintenance level rent and adding the cost of water resulted in ratios between emergency and maintenance level rents in the separate cities which were not always exactly 75 percent, though deviations from this average were not large.

The type of dwelling to be obtained for the estimated emergency level rent cannot be specified as was maintenance level housing, but accommodations were available in every city for the rent given, which might be occupied at least temporarily without serious hazard.

Fuel

In a country where the area is as vast as the United States, with its widely varied climate and wealth of natural resources, the demand for artificial heat and the means available for supplying it form an intricate pattern. Even at one specified level of living, requirements differ in different places.[34] Anthracite consumption, in general, is confined to New England and the Middle Atlantic States. Bituminous coal is more commonly used for room warming throughout the country than any other fuel, and wood is burned in the milder climates. Gas or oil is the popular domestic heating fuel among families of small means in some cities; wood or oil occasionally is used for cooking and water heating; gas often is consumed for these purposes the year around instead of only during the summer months.

[33] In Dallas, El Paso, and Winston-Salem a necessary sewer charge paid by all tenants was also added to house rents and water rates.

[34] There are differences in the natural demand for many commodities based on temperature and other climatic influences, but the theory of substitution which is inherent in the method of cost computation used in this study implies that for the costs of living estimated by valuing a quantity budget, locally used goods and services may be obtained. For fuel, however, average allowances of specified goods or services often would be excessive in one locality and inadequate in others. In some places the items themselves could not be priced at all.

Local fuel consumption depends partly on available supply, hence on price, and partly on custom. A cost estimate which ignores these considerations may be less representative than one in which they are taken into account. On the other hand, estimates which require getting quotations for a variety of fuels and for fuels to be used under a diversity of circumstances, with a corresponding number of separate quantity allowances, would add unnecessary detail to an already complicated problem. A considerable amount of attention, however, was devoted to working out differential allowances in the quantity budgets for several kinds of fuel under a variety of climatic conditions.

The 59 cities in this study were classified in four different climate groups on the basis of their average winter temperatures and the number of months cold weather might be expected. Thirteen were in the "A" group, twenty-four were in the "B" group, thirteen were in the "C" group, and nine were in the "D" group. These groups do not conform to the usual census classification by geographic divisions but cut across them all (table 55). The cities in each climate group were as follows:

Table 55.—59 Cities Classified by 9 Geographic Divisions and 4 Separate Climate Groups

Geographic division	Number of cities in climate group				
	Total	"A"	"B"	"C"	"D"
Total	59	13	24	13	9
New England	6	2	4	—	—
Middle Atlantic	8	3	5	—	—
East North Central	8	3	5	—	—
West North Central	7	4	3	—	—
South Atlantic	9	—	3	4	2
East South Central	5	—	1	3	1
West South Central	6	—	—	3	3
Mountain	5	1	2	1	1
Pacific	5	—	1	2	2

"A" cities (winter long or cold, or long and cold): Binghamton, Buffalo, Butte, Cedar Rapids, Chicago, Detroit, Manchester, Milwaukee, Minneapolis, Omaha, Portland (Maine), Rochester, and Sioux Falls.

"B" cities (average): Baltimore, Boston, Bridgeport, Cincinnati, Clarksburg, Cleveland, Columbus, Denver, Fall River, Indianapolis, Kansas City (Mo.), Louisville, Newark, New York, Peoria, Philadelphia, Pittsburgh, Providence, St. Louis, Salt Lake City, Scranton, Spokane, Washington, and Wichita.

"C" cities (winter short or mild, or short and mild): Albuquerque, Atlanta, Birmingham, El Paso, Knoxville, Little Rock, Memphis, Norfolk, Oklahoma City, Portland (Oreg.), Richmond, Seattle, and Winston-Salem.

"D" cities (winter very short or very mild, or very short and very mild): Columbia, Dallas, Houston, Jacksonville, Los Angeles, Mobile, New Orleans, San Francisco, and Tucson.

The quantities of anthracite, bituminous coal, or wood required each winter for room warming, cooking, and water heating were determined for each climate group. Gas was included for cooking and water heating during the months when fuel for room warming is not required, and quantity allowances for these in each climate group were established (table 56). The same quantity of a given kind of fuel was allowed in each city in each climate group.[35] Though local taste

Table 56.—Fuel Allowances in 4 Separate Climate Groups [1]

Fuel allowance	Climate group			
	"A"	"B"	"C"	"D"
Number of months coal or wood is provided for room warming, cooking, and water heating	7	7	5	3
Number of months gas is provided for cooking and water heating	5	5	7	9
Relative quantity allowance of coal or wood [1]	115.4	100.0	61.5	26.9
Relative quantity allowance of gas	100.0	100.0	140.0	180.0

[1] This comparison is based on maintenance budget allowances. Emergency budget allowances show practically identical ratios. Only bituminous coal is used in all sections of the country; through establishing anthracite and wood requirements equivalent to those for bituminous coal, comparable allowances for the former were evolved.

may prefer gas or oil for room warming, coal or wood was always priced, and no substitution was made for gas as summer fuel. Costs computed from prices of fuel not in general use among families of small means undoubtedly cover the outlays necessary for the locally popular fuels, inasmuch as the substitutes had become popular because of their lower costs.

Coal or Wood

Annual quantity allowances of winter fuel in the budgets are shown in terms of tons of coal or cords of wood. Ton or cord lots could be priced everywhere, but quotations for smaller units were not obtained in some cities or were obtained for quantities not convertible into the budget units.[36] Costs were computed, therefore, from prices for tons and cords, delivered at the curb, no matter how purchases actually were made.

Whether anthracite, bituminous coal, or wood was used to compute winter fuel costs in a given city depended on local consumption.[37]

[35] Quantity allowances of wood are included in the budgets only for cities with a mild winter climate, but one average climate city in the present investigation was located in a lumber region where wood was the usual fuel, and quantity allowances for this city were estimated.

[36] Smaller quantities were bought at a time in a few localities where little fuel is required, or where storage space is limited, as in city apartments. Prices usually varied with the size of the purchase unit: the smaller the unit, the higher the price.

[37] Coke, a coal derivative, was used in one city. Both ton-lot prices of coal and cord-lot prices of wood were not always obtained in cities where coal and wood are consumed. The fuel used in cost calculations was the one for which quotations were available.

Where anthracite was priced, quotations for the chestnut size were generally obtained, but for bituminous coal or wood, the sample consisted of whatever families reported they were burning in their stoves. Heating equivalents cannot be measured exactly, and a better fuel probably was obtained in some places than in others.

Two sources of information supplied coal and wood prices: reports of what families paid and dealer quotations. The same schedule was used for both. Questions asked were: price during heating season preceding March 1935, and price of lot last purchased (sold). Reports from families were more uniform and complete than were dealers' quotations; fuel cost estimates were made from these family reports.

Prices were collected on the housing schedule.[38] They were tabulated, and averages for each city were computed as were rents: namely, modified medians were calculated from hand tabulations. City average prices in the heating season preceding March 1935 [39] as thus computed were combined with the appropriate annual quantity allowances for the particular climate group in which the city was classed.

Gas

Gas for cooking and water heating may be natural, manufactured, or a mixture of the two. The calorific value of natural gas averages nearly twice as great as that of manufactured gas, and that of mixed gas approaches one or the other. Eighty percent more manufactured gas than natural gas is provided per month in the quantity budget for a four-person family at the maintenance level, and the allowance of mixed gas is either 1,800 cubic feet or 1,000 cubic feet per month, depending on whether its B. T. U. content most nearly approaches that of manufactured or natural gas.[40] These ratios are not absolutely applicable to all cities, inasmuch as B. T. U. content is not uniform for the kind of gas specified, but they are sufficiently exact for the purpose in hand.

Gas rates for domestic cooking and water heating were obtained from the local utility companies as of March 15, 1935, and that applicable in each city to the monthly allowance in the quantity budgets was

[38] Fuel prices were collected on the housing schedule rather than on a regular commodity schedule, and reports were secured from individual families in order that something regarding consumption habits might be learned.

[39] The date to which this study of the costs of living relates is mid-March 1935. Collection of prices required a period of several months, and the last city was not completed until mid-July. The period thus covered for last sales sometimes included that of lowest fuel prices. It seemed more reasonable, therefore, to combine the price of fuel during the preceding heating season with March prices of other commodities and services than the price of fuel last purchased, which may have reflected a seasonal drop. The same practice was used with reference to certain seasonal articles of clothing.

[40] See footnote 13, p. 50, for definition of B. T. U.

used in computing costs. Minimum bills, block rates, and prompt payment discounts were taken into account. Cost per month was multiplied by the number of months' consumption allowed in the quantity budgets to determine the annual cost of gas.

To the annual cost of the maintenance budget allowance of coal or wood and gas, $5 was added in each city to provide for kindling, matches, and fuel accessories; [41] to the annual cost of the emergency budget, 75 cents was added in the "A" and "B" cities, and $3 in the "C" and "D" cities.[42]

Ice

The quantity budgets provide for ice consumption during the same months as gas for cooking and water heating: namely, those in which fuel for room warming is not required. This classification resulted in a grouping of 37 cities where ice was allowed for a period of 5 months; 13, where it was allowed for 7 months; and 9, where it was allowed for 9 months.[43] The quantity per week was the same in each group under all circumstances. Thus, multiplying the number of pounds required per week by the number of weeks ice was to be used gave necessary annual consumption in pounds. Needless to say, this is an arbitrary method of computing the annual quantity allowance of ice, but for the most part it provides a reasonable basis for calculating annual cost. The distribution of consumption throughout the year may differ, however, from that on which annual costs are computed.

Ice is purchased in units varying from 10 pounds to 100 pounds and is either called for or delivered. There may be a difference in the price per 100 pounds on the basis of either of these criteria. The unit priced for this study was 25 pounds delivered.[44] Data relating to the sale of ice and its price were obtained on the housing schedule. As in the case of rents and fuel costs, facts obtained from families appeared to be more consistent and complete than did quotations obtained from dealers. The modified median of prices reported by families who

[41] Though coal and wood are used fewer months in the "C" and "D" cities than in the "A" and "B" cities, the same amount is included in all for kindling, matches, and fuel accessories to compensate for the fact that, where gas is used for cooking 7 or 9 months a year, a gas range is likely to be used instead of the gas plate and portable oven included in the quantity budgets, which are satisfactory for 5 months' supplementary use. The cost of the surplus allowance for fuel takes the place of gas stove replacement cost.

[42] See footnote 41 above. The excessive allowance for fuel in the "C" and "D" cities will pay for the depreciation on a gas range, which is not included in the quantity budget.

[43] See p. 107 for list of cities in each climate group.

[44] If ice is called for its price may be lower than if it is delivered. Purchase of ice tickets or coupon books may reduce the cost somewhat. Such prices were not used in computing average cost, nor were deferred payment prices used.

purchased ice in 25-pound lots delivered, therefore, was taken in each city as the average price of ice.

Electricity

Electricity rates for residential service in effect March 15, 1935, in each city were obtained from the public utility companies. The main problem connected with computing electricity costs, therefore, was how to disentangle from the mass of elements frequently entering into the statement of monthly bills those applicable to the four-person family whose costs of living are measured here. As pointed out in the preliminary report on domestic rate schedules by the Federal Power Commission, "So many and such varied factors enter into the determination of electric rate structures that it is difficult to state them accurately and comprehensively even for a single community." [45] Many of the rate forms "are beyond the grasp of the average layman, and not a few [are] difficult for even an experienced rate specialist to interpret." [46]

In both maintenance and emergency budgets a house of four rooms, hall, and bath is assumed. Fifty-watt lamps are allowed for six outlets. An iron and, in the maintenance budget, a small radio are provided for. The total quantity of energy allowed per month for this service is 23 K. W. H. in the maintenance budget and 17 K. W. H. in the emergency budget.[47] Demand, minimum, and other fixed charges were considered in computing monthly costs. If there was a prompt payment discount it was deducted, and all other modifications were considered in order to ascertain the net monthly bill. This amount was multiplied by 12 to obtain the average annual cost of energy. An addition of $1.25 was made to the maintenance budget cost in all cities to cover replacement of lamps and other electrical accessories, and $1.05 was added to the emergency budget cost for the same purpose.

Household Supplies

Eleven commodities comprise the household supplies budget, as follows: kitchen soap, laundry soap, soap powder, soap flakes, starch, bluing, ammonia, scouring powder, lye, insect powder, and toilet paper. The first five of these items were separately priced in each

[45] Federal Power Commission, *Electric Rate Survey, Preliminary Report, Domestic and Residential Rates in Effect January 1, 1935, Cities of 50,000 Population and Over*, Rate Series No. 1, p. 8.

[46] *Ibid.*, p. 14.

[47] Hours of daylight vary with the seasons and with latitude of the separate cities; operation of a daylight saving program also reduces somewhat the necessary demand for artificial light. Differential allowances based on these considerations seemed unnecessary in view of the relatively small part of the total cost of living required for electricity, in comparison with the elaboration of calculation which would be required by their use.

city (table 57),[48] but the last six were assigned an identical value in all cities, based on quotations in the chain limited price variety stores combined with their respective quantity allowances. This amount, exclusive of sales tax where levied, was $5.70 per year for a four-person manual worker's family at the maintenance level of living.

Specifications for the five commodities priced separately in each city were fairly general, requiring primarily that weight or size of package and brand should be noted, except that kitchen soap was described as "white, hard milled, no caustic properties nor special cleansing agent, medium size." Multiple units as well as single units were priced where the former method of sale was common. Quotations were obtained, as for other commodities, from stores at which industrial, service, and other manual workers of small means trade.[49]

Table 57.—Number of Commodities Priced and Used in Computing Costs of Household Supplies, Furniture, Furnishings, and Household Equipment, 59 Cities, March 1935

Schedule	Number of commodities	
	Priced	Used
Total	71	[1] 54
Furniture and floor covering	17	17
Household equipment and electrical appliances	33	[2] 22
Cleaning supplies and sundries	12	[1] 6
Yard goods and textile furnishings	9	9

[1] 5 of these were household supplies; the remainder, furniture, furnishings, and household equipment. Prices of cleaning supplies and sundries not used in computing the costs of household supplies and furniture, furnishings, and household equipment were toilet soap (personal care) and kerosene (not listed in the quantity budgets). The other 4 are included in the list of commodities for which an identical amount was allowed in all cities.

[2] The 11 items of household equipment priced but not used in computing the costs of furniture, furnishings, and household equipment for the 4-person manual worker's family were commodities required for families of different size or required under different conditions, as, for example, where kerosene is used for fuel and/or light instead of coal or wood, gas, and electricity. Some of these prices can be used in studies to discover cost differentials based on size of family; others, to compute cost relatives based on local consumption habits.

All accepted quotations were reduced to a rate-per-pound basis. The arithmetic mean of these was taken as the city average for each commodity in each city, and these averages were combined with their appropriate quantity allowances in the maintenance budget. The resulting annual cost of the five commodities separately priced was added to the assigned value of nonpriced essentials to obtain the total outlay locally necessary for household supplies. An emergency budget for household supplies was not constructed, but its cost was assumed to be 90 percent of the cost of the maintenance budget.

Furniture, Furnishings, and Household Equipment

Prices of furniture, furnishings, and household equipment were collected on four schedules (table 57). Specifications described the

[48] Cleaning powder, toilet paper, bluing, lye, and kerosene were also priced, but quotations were not used in cost calculations, because identical values for the first four items are given in the quantity budgets, and kerosene is not included therein. Toilet soap (personal care) and broom (household equipment) prices were also collected on the same schedule.

[49] See pp. 95–97.

material, construction, and size of "inexpensive quality" merchandise. Stores were selected for sampling, merchandise was priced, and quotations were edited for reasonableness, according to the procedure used for other commodities.[50] In addition to the 49 commodities separately priced in each city, the furniture, furnishings, and household equipment budgets for a 4-person manual worker's family list over 100 items for which a total of $37.25 was allowed as initial cost in all cities at the maintenance level on the basis of quotations obtained in chain limited price variety stores.

The arithmetic mean of all accepted quotations for each commodity in each city was taken by machine and combined with its designated initial allowance as listed in the quantity budgets. The total of these costs, together with the identical amount allowed in all cities, constituted the outlay required to purchase a complete stock of household goods. Annual replacement cost at the maintenance level was computed as 10 percent of initial cost; emergency level cost was calculated as 6 percent of initial outlay.

Refuse Disposal

The costs of refuse disposal in the separate cities for the most part were calculated from reports by the local health officers or officials in some other departments responsible for this service. Minimum requirements were priced except in a few places where annual costs were based on specified schedules from which the allowances for a four-person manual worker's family were computed. Where monthly or weekly charges were given, annual cost was calculated from budget needs.[51] The cost of refuse disposal was the same at the maintenance and emergency levels of living.

Unspecified Essentials

The dollars and cents allowed in all cities for unspecified essentials of household operation (table 58) provide for such commodities as

Table 58.—Identical Annual Allowances[1] for Unspecified Household Essentials: Commodities and Services Not Separately Priced, 4-Person Manual Worker's Family, 59 Cities, March 1935

Item	Annual allowance[1]	
	Maintenance level	Emergency level
Total	$3.05	$2.75
Commodities	1.15	1.10
Services	1.90	1.65

[1] Sales tax to be added where levied (appendix tables 15 and 16).

[50] See pp. 95–97.

[51] The number of months' use of coal or wood, with complementary requirements for disposal of garbage.

writing materials, twine, glue, tacks, and similar odds and ends of minor importance and small cost; also such services as postage and telephone calls. No itemization of this allowance is necessary, but its desirability is obvious.

Medical Care

The annual cost of medical care was computed from prices of a small sample of the great variety of goods and services needed for this purpose. The quantity of each item allowed per year was adjusted to represent average minimum requirements per 1,000 persons. This method of cost calculation was used because only by observing the need for care among a large number of persons of different sex and all ages over a period of years could an estimate of requirements be hazarded. From cost per 1,000 persons the outlay necessary per year for the 4-person family of this study was computed, without reference to the particular needs of the sex and age of its component members.

Six sets of items listed in the medical care budget were priced (table 59). Quotations for services and for eyeglasses and frames were collected on one schedule and those for drug store commodities on another. Specifications varied in degree of exactness with the kind of items priced.

Table 59.—Number of Commodities and Services Priced and Used in Computing Costs of Medical Care, 59 Cities, March 1935

Schedule	Number of commodities and services	
	Priced	Used
Total	29	20
Medical care	14	13
Physician	6	[1] 6
Dentist	3	3
Hospital	2	1
Nurse	1	1
Eyeglasses and frame [2]	2	2
Drugs, toiletries, and drug store sundries	15	[3] 7

[1] Includes eye refraction which later was assigned to optometrists on the basis of data secured in the field, as described in the text.
[2] Though priced on the medical care service schedule, the cost of eyeglasses and frame was analyzed with the cost of commodities priced in drug stores.
[3] 7 of the 8 drug store commodities not used were not included in the quantity budgets; toothpaste was assigned an identical amount in all cities in the personal care budget.

Physicians' and dentists' charges were obtained from general practitioners and represent the usual fee asked from patients of small means. Services include physicians' office visits, day house calls, obstetrical care, appendectomies, and tonsillectomies; and dentists' filling, cleaning, and extracting teeth. The schedule called for eye refractions by physicians, specified as "simple examination for the fitting of eyeglasses." When performed by a member of the medical profession this service is usually in the field of a specialist whose fee exceeds that of general practitioners. Families of small means customarily have their eyes refracted by optometrists, and in many cities in this study only optometrists' charges were recorded. It seemed best, therefore, to use optometrists' fees for calculating costs in all cities. In those in which optometrists' fees were not obtained, $2 was uniformly allowed, as this seemed to be about the average or usual charge for eye refractions.

The hospital services priced were beds in the cheapest pay wards per day, including meals, general medical, surgical, and nursing care, and clinic visits. Clinic visits were dropped from the quantity budgets because this service is not always available, and its cost was not used in computing the cost of medical care.

The fee for nursing care was supposed to be the usual charge per visit by instructive visiting or other public health nurses. Private duty nursing was outside the scope of this study. Not all cities have a public health nursing service, however, and other provision for estimating the necessary cost of nursing care for a manual worker's family was necessary in some places. Information obtained from the National Organization for Public Health Nursing indicates that costs per visit for usual services in 34 of the 59 cities studied[52] ranged from a minimum of 57 cents to a maximum of $1.23 in 1935; the mean cost was 93 cents and the median, 91 cents. It appeared, therefore, that if $1 per visit were allowed as the fee for nursing care in cities where no amount was reported for this service, a representative figure would be provided. This would cover the outlay necessary for a public health nurse or would supply other kinds of nursing care in cities where such services are not organized.[53]

Quotations were to be obtained for inexpensive types of eyeglasses and frames, without additional specification except that toric lenses were not to be priced. One simple prescription, one antiseptic, two laxatives, aspirin, a cough syrup, and a cold ointment were used as the drug store sample. U. S. P. standard, size of container, or other recognized specification described the merchandise called for. Prices of these drug store commodities were obtained in chain, cut-rate, and neighborhood stores, according to the procedure already described for other commodities,[54] and city averages are representative of customary local charges.

Fees for physicians', dentists', optometrists', and hospital services were hand tabulated, and the modified median was calculated. In cities where services of a fairly homogeneous group of practitioners were priced, the average fee often was the usual charge; in cities where offices in both residential and downtown buildings were visited,

[52] No privately supported public health nursing service exists in 8 of the 59 cities studied, and no information regarding cost per visit was available in 17 of them.

[53] In the cities without a public health nursing service no study was made to ascertain what kind of care was available.

[54] See pp. 95–97.

a combination of the two sets of data sometimes produced an unusual figure, but one representative of a complete cross section of the cost of medical services locally available. The average price of eyeglasses and frames in each city was calculated by the same method as that used for medical services, since quotations were obtained on the same schedule and were subject to the same limitations. For the drug store commodities, machine calculated arithmetic means were the city average prices.

Charges for individual items in the medical care budget were combined with their annual quantity allowances per 1,000 persons to obtain the annual cost of a balanced list, and all intercity differences were computed from these figures. The amount a 4-person family would have to set aside each year as the cost of the maintenance medical care budget was four one-thousandths of the local cost per 1,000 persons. The allowance for medical care in the emergency budget is 90 percent of the cost of the maintenance budget and this amount was included in each city.

Transportation

The basic allowance of car or bus fare [55] in the quantity budgets for a 4-person manual worker's family provides a daily round trip to work for the man and to high school for the 13-year-old boy, plus an amount for other necessary activities equal to one-half the total of these two costs at the maintenance level, and to one-quarter, at the emergency level. A work year of 306 days and the number of school days as reported in each city were assumed.

The need for transportation is not identical in all communities. Layout of the city, location of residential areas with reference to industrial plants, schools, shopping and recreation centers, and the like, as well as transportation facilities available are responsible for customary use at any level of living. Attempts to get local estimates of patronage of public transportation systems by industrial, service, and other manual workers of small means in the cities studied were not successful, and more arbitrary means of measuring intercity differentials were necessary.

Two sets of data bearing on the need for transportation—population and land area—are available for all cities. One without the other is significant but not conclusive, and in combination they suggest a basis for local transportation differentials. This combination was made by multiplying 1930 population by land area in square miles and reducing the results to such an index as would group the 59 cities in approximately equal numbers. It is to be presumed that even in the largest cities, with the most extensive land area, some men will walk to work and some children will walk to high school, but it also is

[55] The quantity budgets do not include an automobile.

probable that the larger the population and land area the larger will be the proportion who will need an allowance for transportation.

The percentage modifiers of the basic budget allowance of transportation in the separate cities were as follows.

96 percent: Baltimore, Chicago, Cleveland, Detroit, Los Angeles, New Orleans, New York, Philadelphia, and St. Louis.

84 percent: Boston, Cincinnati, Minneapolis, Pittsburgh, San Francisco, Seattle, and Washington.

72 percent: Buffalo, Denver, Houston, Indianapolis, Kansas City (Mo.), Milwaukee, and Portland (Oreg.).

60 percent: Birmingham, Columbus, Dallas, Louisville, Memphis, Newark, and Rochester.

48 percent: Atlanta, Oklahoma City, Omaha, Providence, Richmond, Salt Lake City, and Spokane.

36 percent: Bridgeport, Fall River, Jacksonville, Knoxville, Norfolk, Scranton, Wichita, and Manchester.

24 percent: Cedar Rapids, El Paso, Little Rock, Mobile, Peoria, Portland (Maine), and Winston-Salem.

12 percent: Albuquerque, Binghamton, Butte, Clarksburg, Columbia, Sioux Falls, and Tucson.

Several public transportation systems sometimes are found in a given city, and they may charge different fares. The same system may operate on a zone basis; may issue tickets or tokens, or passes for adults or children, or both at a discount from the single cash fare; or may issue transfers free or with a charge, or may issue none at all. Thus, calculating comparable transportation costs in the separate cities becomes further complicated by the necessity for specifying a reasonable basic fare.

Were relative prices the principal consideration in this analysis, they would be computed from adult cash fares. Inasmuch as its purpose is to represent transportation requirements in the total cost of living, the appropriate charge is the lowest fare payable in each city. This appears to be the ticket or token rate, but nothing necessitating more than $1 outlay at one time was used in the calculations.[56] Where more than one transportation company operates in a city, the charge on that system which appeared to carry the greatest number of passengers was used; the existence of zones and transfers was disregarded.[57]

The fare in each city for each purpose specified was combined with its budget allowance for transportation to work, to school, and for other purposes, and the total cost of transportation was calculated. This amount then was modified by the percentage differential assigned

[56] Except that in Mobile a book of 30 tickets sold to school children for $1.05 was allowed.

[57] Except that in Los Angeles, with three street railway and bus systems operating in zones with a variety of fares, the rates used were designed to secure a representative cost picture.

to each city, as described above, to obtain the annual cost of transportation.

School Attendance

An attempt was made to ascertain average requirements and costs of public school attendance for a boy age 13 in the 9th grade and for a girl age 8 in the 3d grade. School systems are not operated on an identical plan in all cities and the 9th grade was found in both junior and senior high schools. Cost calculations for each city were made on the basis of the local plan. Technical, commercial, and other special schools were not included. Items checked were books, stationery, other supplies, and gymnasium equipment. It was assumed that laboratory and other special fees would not be required, that the cost of school lunches was taken care of in the food budget, and that social expenses must come out of the recreation allowance. Necessary car or bus fares were provided for in the cost of transportation. The same school attendance budget and prices were used for both the maintenance and the emergency levels of living; hence, costs were identical.

Information regarding school costs was collected from the boards or departments of education in the separate cities, as well as from schools in the neighborhoods where other cost data were obtained. As far as possible, initial cost of equipment which might be used longer than 1 year was prorated to measure annual cost.[58] Final figures for the most part were calculated as the modified median of separate reports, but in some cities data supplied by a central authority were accepted as representative.

Recreation

The cost of recreation was computed from costs of the quantity budgets for newspapers and motion picture theater admissions, plus identical amounts allowed in all cities for certain miscellaneous needs.

Newspapers

In the maintenance budget a newspaper is allowed every day; in the emergency budget there is no newspaper. Street sale is usual, but in some places papers are delivered to the purchaser by carrier at a weekly or monthly cost considerably below the street sale rate.[59] In many cities there is more than one newspaper. The price used in computing annual cost was the lowest at which the paper having the largest reported local circulation could be obtained each day. This

[58] Instructions for use of the schedule called for net annual cost; i. e., "obtained by deducting any refund from fees at the end of the year, sale of books, gymnasium suit, etc. If the latter is worn 4 years, only 1 year's cost should be entered."

[59] This system of carrier delivery is not to be confused with delivery by a newsdealer; in the latter case the customer pays a premium for the service instead of getting a discount from the street sale price.

was the carrier delivery charge in some places; in others, it was the street sale price; and in still a third group of cities, it was the carrier delivery charge daily and street or newsstand sale price on Sunday. In three cities where no paper was printed on Sunday, prices of Sunday editions of papers published in nearby cities were included.

Motion Picture Theater Admissions

One motion picture theater admission per week is allowed for each member of the family in the maintenance budget; in the emergency budget attendance once a month is allowed. Three different admission charges for attendance on Saturday are called for: night prices for two adults, adults' afternoon prices for the boy age 13, and children's afternoon prices for the girl age 8. Lowest prices for the performances named were used in the cost calculations, unless these rates were for special groups, such as Negroes or Mexicans, in theaters where the different races were segregated.

Admission charges were obtained from downtown and neighborhood theaters patronized by industrial, service, and other manual workers of small means. Some showed first run features; others showed pictures of later release. Some offered stage shows, others did not. Cost calculations were made from charges at neighborhood theaters and at those downtown theaters whose price scales were in line with the neighborhood theater prices. Where all theaters were centrally located, an effort was made to differentiate between them on the basis of entertainment offered, but in the smaller cities, for the most part, all necessarily were included.

The arithmetic mean of accepted quotations was computed for each admission specified above. These averages were totaled and multiplied by the number of admissions allowed per year in the budgets for the two levels of living.

Organizations, Tobacco, and Toys

To the outlay necessary in each city for newspapers and motion picture theater admissions were added the amounts specified in the budgets for a four-person family to cover organization memberships

Table 60.—Identical Annual Allowances [1] for Organizations, Tobacco, and Toys: Commodities and Services Not Separately Priced, 4-Person Manual Worker's Family, 59 Cities, March 1935

Item	Annual allowance [1]	
	Maintenance level	Emergency level
Total	$30.40	$4.80
Organizations	9.60	(2)
Tobacco and toys [1]	20.80	4.80

[1] Sales tax to be added where levied (appendix tables 15 and 16).
[2] Not included in the emergency budget.

and similar activities, tobacco, toys, and other leisure-time accessories (table 60).

Life Insurance, Church Contributions, and Other Contributions

Table 61 gives the budget allowances for life insurance, church contributions, and other contributions. Except for insurance on the life of the man at the maintenance level, which at death would leave a small surplus over funeral expenses, the provision for insurance covers the outlay necessary for burial, prorated to an annual basis.

Table 61.—Identical Annual Allowances for Life Insurance, Church Contributions, and Other Contributions, 4-Person Manual Worker's Family, 59 Cities, March 1935

Item	Annual allowance	
	Maintenance level	Emergency level
Total	$61.80	$31.20
Life insurance	46.40	20.80
Man	23.00	7.80
Woman	13.00	7.80
Boy age 13	5.20	2.60
Girl age 8	5.20	2.60
Church contributions	10.40	10.40
Other contributions	5.00	[1]

[1] Not included in the emergency budget.

Life insurance premiums depend on the character and amount of benefits, age at which the policy is taken out, sex of the insured, and frequency of premium payment. Though industrial, service, and other manual workers of small means usually buy their insurance on a weekly basis, with relatively small benefits for the premiums paid, the maintenance budget calls for an ordinary life policy on the whole life plan, with benefits of considerably greater value for the man of the family; the wife and children, however, are allowed industrial policies.

There is little difference in premiums among the recognized companies for any specified type of policy, and the $23 per year included for the man's insurance should pay for a $1,000 ordinary life policy on the whole life plan, taken out at age 35. An allowance of 25 cents per week for the woman in the family and 10 cents for each child will supply death benefits aggregating approximately $900 if the policies are taken out at their present attained ages.

In the emergency budget, both the man and the woman have industrial policies calling for payment of 15 cents per week; each child has a 5 cents per week policy. Benefits payable for these premiums average about $700 for the family.

Church contributions are included in all budgets at the rate of 5 cents per person per week regardless of sex or age; $5 per year is added in the maintenance budget for other contributions of various kinds.

Taxes

Details of tax procedure as of March 15, 1935, were obtained from local assessors and others charged with tax collection; taxes supposedly were payable in 1935. Every effort was made to get reliable reports, but there were conflicts in the data obtained from different sources in the same community, and recourse to statutes and manuals did not always clear matters completely. Data which appeared most nearly accurate as far as they could be checked were used in cost computations.

For the present study the value of taxable personal property embodied in furniture, furnishings, household equipment, and clothing was assumed to be $100 in all cities. Rates, percentages, and exemptions were applied with reference to that amount in computing personal property taxes. Capitation taxes were allowed in full for those members of the four-person manual worker's family to whom they applied.

In computing the amount of sales tax to be added to the costs of the goods and services included in the quantity budgets, it was necessary to ascertain which items were subject to tax in each city, and to apply the proper rate to their costs. No two States included or exempted the same items, and in some instances the laws were none too specific regarding their exact application. Without going into an exhaustive study, which was not warranted by the present purpose, the exact scope of some of the laws, in all details, could not be determined.

No attempt was made in this study to use the bracket system for the purpose of adding the sales tax to each dealer's price,[60] because price comparisons between cities without the tax seemed the best procedure, or at least segregation of the tax permitted an analysis which considered it as a possible causal factor in intercity cost differentials. Moreover, in the absence of universally applicable brackets in certain cities, no general rule could be applied on a bracket basis. Instead, the amount of the sales tax in each city was computed by applying the rate percent to the total cost of those groups of goods and services on which it was levied, on the assumption that if the base were large enough, the necessary consumer outlay would be accurately measured.

---

[60] See p. 89 for description of the bracket system. The tax on motion picture theater admissions was computed as levied, because all admissions are not taxed.

Chapter VIII

CONCLUSIONS

THIS STUDY was designed to find out how much a 4-person industrial, service, or other manual worker's family would need for self-support at 2 specified levels of living in each of 59 cities in the United States; to ascertain how much costs differed among the cities; to compare costs at a basic maintenance level with costs at one reduced at certain points to meet the demands of emergency conditions; and to determine what circumstances were responsible for observed intercity cost variations.

To answer these questions, new techniques were necessary. These entailed establishing the contents of the levels of living priced; maintaining their comparability under varied conditions of climate and size of community; and insuring that all the large number of persons necessarily employed in collecting prices had the same objectives in view. From construction of the budgets to analysis of the data problems were presented for the solution of which there were neither precedents nor analogies. Experimenting and testing were necessary at every stage as the work progressed. Like the results of many other investigations of social phenomena, the findings are indicative or approximate rather than exact measurements. The quantity budgets are generalized statements of average needs; judgments to some extent necessarily entered into the specifications, and into the sampling and pricing procedures used. On the other hand, the completeness of the details insures a reliability to the conclusions which might not be justified were the findings built up from a less exhaustive analysis.

How far these findings for two specified levels of living in certain cities are representative of other levels of living in the same cities or of the same levels of living in other cities cannot be stated. Though these questions were outside the scope of the present study, the limits within which ascertained costs fall and the factors which seem to account for observed variations suggest that some of the conclusions of this investigation are of wider application.

The purpose of the present chapter is to summarize the principal facts brought out in those which have preceded it, in order to work the various threads into a consistent pattern and analyze any general characteristics thus displayed. The validity of the findings is checked by comparing them with the results of other studies [1] and by comparing the cost of the maintenance budget and its distribution with expenditures by actual families of small means. Finally, certain conclusions regarding methodology are presented for the benefit of those who are interested in techniques or who may wish to make similar investigations in the future.

WHAT THE COSTS OF LIVING ARE AND HOW THEY VARY

The costs of support at a maintenance level of living for a 4-person manual worker's family in 59 cities at March 1935 prices averaged $1,261 per year, and at the emergency level comparable costs averaged $903. The average difference of 28 percent between the two did not vary greatly among the separate cities, and for all practical purposes this ratio may be considered representative. Annual costs of the two budgets were most alike for those goods and services where smallest economies are possible, and they were least similar where psychological rather than physical needs are involved or where certain commodity substitutions can be made to achieve the same purposes.

Local differences in the costs of living were found to be relatively small (appendix tables 2, 3, 8, and 9). The lowest cost of both the maintenance and emergency budgets was about 10.5 percent less and the highest was about 12 percent more than the average in the 59 cities combined. These differences amounted to $131 and $154, respectively, at the maintenance level,[2] a total excess of highest over lowest cost of 25 percent.[3] The variation between cities was $100 a year or less in more than half those studied. Nowhere did the maximum spread, $285, equal the difference between the costs of support at the maintenance and emergency levels of living.

The tendency toward similarity in the costs of the same level of living is further emphasized when the cities in the present investigation are classified by geographic division or by size (table 6). The extremes geographically at the maintenance level were found in the Middle Atlantic States, where the group average was 3 percent above

[1] No other study is exactly comparable with this in all respects, but certain comparisons can be made.

[2] All comparisons in this chapter are made with maintenance budget costs.

[3] A measure of variation from the average which takes into account every deviation plus or minus from the arithmetic mean is obtained by squaring these deviations, totaling the results, obtaining the mean of the squared totals, and extracting its square root. This so-called "standard deviation" is expressed as a percentage of the arithmetic mean to obtain the "coefficient of variation." Table 62, p. 128, shows coefficients of variation in the costs of living at the maintenance level by major budget groups and principal subgroups in the 59 cities, in geographic divisions, and in size of city classifications.

the average in the 59 cities combined, and in the 2 South Central Areas, where the averages were 6 percent below. Within the groups the costs of living for the most part were much alike, though they seemed to be more nearly uniform in certain sections than in others. For example, the spread from lowest to highest cost among the Mountain cities was less than 5 percent; in the two South Central Areas and New England it was less than 10 percent; and in the Middle Atlantic Division the range between the extreme cities did not greatly exceed 10 percent. Wider cost variations were found in the two North Central Divisions, especially among the West North Central cities, and in the South Atlantic Area. Minneapolis, with its high rent and fuel cost, ranking as the 3d most expensive city in the group of 59, is in the West North Central Division, however, and so is Wichita, where the cost of living was next to the lowest among the 59 cities. Abnormal housing conditions and high rent in Washington to a considerable extent accounted for the wide spread between lowest and highest living costs in the South Atlantic Area. The large outlays necessary for practically all necessities in San Francisco raised the average cost in the Pacific Division above the level which perhaps is more typical of that section of the country.

The average cost of living in the largest places exceeded that in the 59 cities by less than 6 percent, and in the smallest it was not 2.5 percent below the average in the 59 cities. By analyzing the size of city classifications separately, it appears that the narrowest cost range was found among the largest cities, progressing toward greater dispersion as size of city declined, except for the middle group. While the average in the middle group as a whole fell just below the average in the 59 cities combined, it was computed from extremes: Washington and Minneapolis at the top were the highest and 3d from the highest, respectively, in the array of the 59 cities; Birmingham and Columbus had lowest costs in their size of city group and ranked 6th and 7th from the lowest among the 59. These contrasts resulted in the maximum spread, 21 percent, in the costs of living among cities in any one population group. A more representative average would be in line with the range shown for the smaller cities.

The costs of all but a few essentials were high in the New England, Mountain, and Pacific cities (appendix table 5); but rents were below the average in these areas. Most costs were low in the Southern cities,[4] especially in those in the South Central States. In the Middle Atlantic and North Central States, on the other hand, a combination of low costs of some items and high costs of others served to establish the level for cities in these areas as above the average in the 59 cities combined. The most notable characteristics of the cost arrays in the

[4] Washington, in the South Atlantic Division, pushed the average for that section above its apparently more representative figure.

three last named geographic divisions were the relatively high rents and the large outlays necessary for transportation. This pattern is typical of the largest cities studied, and 13 of the 19 with a population exceeding 375,000 are in the Middle Atlantic and North Central States. It would be difficult to say, however, whether high land values often associated with large cities or the necessity for housing which is more substantial than the average accounted for above average rents. Transportation costs were higher in the largest cities because more transportation is needed.[5]

For no other budget group or subgroup except clothing upkeep could cost tendencies be completely associated with size of city (appendix table 7).[6] The outlays necessary for certain budget items, notably food, coal or wood, household supplies, medical care, and motion picture theater admissions, increased or decreased with size of city through the three or even four largest city classifications and were erratic in tendency as to the smallest places. Costs of the budget as a whole declined with size of city, except that the averages in the two largest city groups were practically identical. The inconclusive relationship between size of city and costs of certain budget items may have resulted from the choice of cities studied and may not be indicative of general tendencies. In order to cover all sections of the country properly in an investigation confined to 59 cities, it was necessary to represent some areas by small cities. These are important in their own sections of the country, but may not be typical of their size classification because most of the country's cities with comparable populations are in other areas.

All the values used in the comparisons just made include a sales tax in the 18 cities where such a tax was in operation. The maximum amount required for a sales tax was $25.20 in Louisville, or 2.1 percent of the total cost of the maintenance budget in that city.[7] The existence of a sales tax slightly increased the cost of living dispersion beyond what it would have been had there been no tax,[8] and the ranks of certain cities would be shifted up or down a few places in the scale were the tax omitted. The average cost of living in the 18 cities with a sales tax was $22.43 more than in the 41 cities without a tax,[9]

[5] See pp. 116–117.

[6] Transportation cost makes up 21.4 percent of the average total cost of miscellaneous family needs and serves to move the latter in its general direction. Personal property and capitation taxes seemed to increase as size of city decreased, but group relatives are inconclusive because only 36 of the 59 cities reported such taxes.

[7] The rate was 3 percent but not every budget item was taxed.

[8] This does not show in a comparison of highest and lowest cost cities, because neither of them had a sales tax.

[9] In New Orleans there was a tax amounting to $1.56 per year at the maintenance level of living on motion picture theater admissions exceeding 10 cents. This was not a sales tax and, for comparative purposes, New Orleans is included among the 41 cities having no sales tax.

but the cost of living in the latter group would still have been $5.67 less than in the former had there been no tax.

The sales tax, however, for families of small means in certain cities was equivalent to a large part of the amounts required for such little luxuries as motion picture theater attendance, and it was more than the cost of such necessities as clothing upkeep, gas, electricity, ice, or household supplies. Sales taxes, moreover, are State-wide except for the local excise in the city of New York and tend toward a certain geographic popularity. Hence, they constitute an element to be reckoned with as a cost of living factor in some places.

An influence toward greater cost similarity, on the other hand, lies in the inclusion of $132.33 plus sales tax where levied[10] in the maintenance budget to provide for items whose costs are known to be the same throughout the country, such as life insurance premiums, postage, and telephone calls; or whose costs are likely to be uniform because the commodities can be bought everywhere in chain limited price variety stores; or whose costs cannot be measured in terms of quantity allowances, such as church contributions, other contributions, and organization dues. These costs, which were carried as identical amounts in all cities, averaged 10.5 percent of the total cost of living in the 59 cities combined, varying from 9.4 percent in Washington to 11.7 percent in Mobile. Without this identical allowance, the range in the costs of living among the separate cities from lowest to highest averaged 28.5 percent, as contrasted with 25.2 percent when it was included. The similarity of costs which this 10.5 percent of the total is designed to measure is as real as the differences noted for items which were separately priced. The necessity for including them in the budget, in fact, does tend to hold the costs of living as a whole to a narrower range than would be found were these items not essential.

COSTS OF MAJOR BUDGET GROUPS AND PRINCIPAL SUBGROUPS

The relative similarity of total living costs in so many cities when these costs are measured by pricing one quantity budget everywhere did not appear for its constituent items (table 62). Inasmuch as all of these items are required in a balanced content of living, it is their combined cost which represents the outlay necessary for support at a specified level in each community; and all of them must be taken into account in intercity cost comparisons.

The annual cost of each group in the quantity budget is a composite of quantity allowances, specification factors, and city average prices of the goods and services of which it is made up. The first two were uniform in all cities studied for most goods and services. Average requirements for a few items were excessive in some localities and inadequate in others; hence, quantity allowances varied in designated ratios.

[10] Comparable allowances in the emergency budget totaled $62.96 in the "A" and "B" cities and $65.21 in the "C" and "D" cities, plus sales tax where levied.

Table 62.—Coefficients of Variation in the Costs [1] of Living, by Major Budget Groups and Principal Subgroups, 4-Person Manual Worker's Family, 59 Cities, March 1935

MAINTENANCE LEVEL

Budget group [1]	59 cities	Geographic division									Size of city classification, 1930				
		New England	Middle Atlantic	East North Central	West North Central	South Atlantic	East South Central	West South Central	Mountain	Pacific	1,000,000 or more	500,000 to 1,000,000	250,000 to 500,000	100,000 to 250,000	25,000 to 100,000
Total cost of living	5.3	2.8	2.8	5.0	6.4	5.2	3.0	2.9	1.8	5.1	2.2	2.8	5.1	4.2	4.5
Food	3.5	2.6	2.9	2.9	2.6	2.2	1.9	1.6	4.4	2.4	2.9	2.6	3.2	3.6	4.2
Flour, cereals, and bread [2]	5.4	3.3	4.4	4.3	4.1	2.4	3.3	6.4	10.0	3.4	6.4	4.3	4.7	5.0	5.6
Milk and cheese [2]	7.8	6.7	3.8	4.7	6.2	7.5	7.3	2.1	4.6	4.8	3.4	4.6	7.1	9.6	9.3
Fruits and vegetables [2]	6.3	3.2	5.0	5.9	3.2	7.2	3.2	6.9	7.7	4.2	9.0	3.8	5.6	5.1	7.3
Meat, fish, and eggs [2]	8.8	3.6	5.0	4.5	5.1	4.5	5.2	4.4	7.7	3.1	5.3	8.3	8.6	8.4	9.6
Fats, sugars, and accessories [2]	3.3	2.4	2.9	1.6	4.2	3.1	3.2	1.8	2.6	3.4	1.6	2.4	2.5	3.4	4.6
Clothing, clothing upkeep, and personal care	6.7	4.7	3.3	5.4	4.0	4.2	2.6	4.2	5.6	2.7	6.7	7.3	5.6	5.9	6.9
Clothing	6.9	5.2	3.6	6.4	3.9	4.8	3.3	4.1	5.0	3.4	7.5	7.2	6.2	5.8	6.4
Clothing upkeep	13.7	11.0	9.9	5.9	11.9	6.7	3.3	6.3	15.4	11.5	5.7	7.1	10.6	10.6	17.8
Personal care	7.7	3.4	3.1	5.8	4.9	3.9	4.7	7.1	8.3	4.8	5.4	9.1	5.9	8.3	7.4
Housing, including water	16.2	11.0	11.1	12.0	16.9	18.6	12.3	6.7	6.2	20.8	14.1	8.7	18.8	14.7	12.9
Household operation	13.0	5.5	9.9	10.8	18.4	6.9	3.7	8.9	8.7	5.5	5.6	12.7	14.3	8.4	14.1
Coal or wood	39.9	7.3	28.4	30.0	35.2	32.4	26.3	35.7	29.5	14.8	19.8	32.1	46.6	27.8	48.6
Gas	53.1	9.4	37.2	40.1	22.2	57.2	49.9	33.2	40.3	19.2	25.3	41.9	40.4	53.8	47.9
Ice	33.4	6.9	13.2	12.4	10.2	20.8	21.6	16.9	41.4	22.3	35.8	49.0	28.6	17.4	36.0
Coal or wood, gas, and ice combined	20.9	5.9	19.3	19.0	27.5	16.4	5.3	14.1	13.3	4.5	10.0	20.2	22.5	12.5	23.8
Electricity	17.7	12.7	16.4	16.9	10.4	15.1	5.2	18.0	9.7	8.7	13.4	17.6	20.2	12.7	10.0
Household supplies	10.3	2.8	5.4	4.9	7.6	6.5	4.2	6.4	7.2	2.6	8.0	8.7	9.2	9.1	12.1
Furniture, furnishings, and household equipment	5.9	6.0	4.4	3.4	4.2	5.1	4.8	3.1	5.4	3.4	5.3	4.8	3.7	7.4	5.5
Refuse disposal	174.7	137.1	248.2	(3)	98.6	265.7	(3)	146.9	126.2	65.3	(3)	117.4	167.4	180.3	133.7
Miscellaneous	12.2	5.4	9.2	10.9	16.6	12.8	6.2	13.5	9.7	7.9	4.2	6.8	7.4	6.1	6.2
Medical care	11.4	5.5	8.3	14.3	4.9	10.7	9.1	10.4	4.4	11.3	11.1	12.4	9.3	12.3	10.6
Services [2]	12.5	6.2	8.9	15.9	5.2	11.8	10.1	11.6	5.1	12.5	11.8	13.1	10.6	13.5	12.0
Drugs and appliances [2]	6.0	4.5	3.0	5.1	4.6	6.8	4.1	8.4	1.9	3.4	4.2	6.9	7.2	4.5	4.3
Transportation	56.9	26.0	48.7	32.4	63.5	74.6	36.4	63.1	80.6	30.8	13.9	26.0	28.1	27.7	50.3
School attendance	72.2	96.8	124.8	47.1	66.4	69.5	39.7	49.3	44.4	57.4	110.7	85.9	48.6	84.2	58.0
Newspapers	18.1	14.8	16.2	16.5	18.8	12.0	(4)	18.6	16.2	12.3	12.3	9.5	18.0	14.7	15.5
Motion picture theater admissions	14.3	14.6	12.7	10.2	13.9	14.1	12.7	10.1	8.9	17.7	6.1	11.6	13.1	12.1	16.1
Taxes [5]	82.7	54.0	177.9	88.8	70.2	68.9	40.1	51.9	55.0	(6)	180.6	75.8	84.7	64.3	57.0

[1] Include sales tax where levied except as indicated (appendix table 15).
[2] Does not include sales tax.
[3] Not a direct charge.
[4] Prices were the same in all cities in this geographic division.
[5] Exclusive of sales tax.
[6] None payable.

Some items required no direct outlay in certain cities because they were supplied from public funds; some could not be priced everywhere and substitutes were necessary; some were priced by specifications so broad that, even with the same quantity allowances, identical values were not necessarily obtained from place to place. All items priced met local needs, however, and their costs represent a satisfactory measure of requirements in the separate cities.

Widest Cost Variations

The greatest spread between lowest and highest costs among the 59 cities was found for those major budget groups and principal subgroups for which there were no quantity allowances or for which allowances differed and specifications were most general (table 62).

Refuse Disposal, School Attendance, and Taxes

Refuse disposal, school attendance, and tax costs were included as charged for a four-person manual worker's family of specified age and sex composition, without definite quantity allowances. These costs ranged from nothing per year to slightly less than 2 percent of the total budget cost (appendix table 17). The householder paid directly for his refuse disposal in some cities, and in others this service was covered by the tax rate. Expenses connected with school attendance depended largely on local policy with reference to supplying books and other equipment from public funds. Some cities levied personal property, capitation, and other direct taxes; others did not or provided exemptions sufficiently large to exclude families of small means.

Transportation, Fuel, and Ice

Wide cost dispersions for transportation, fuel, and ice were partly attributable to differential quantity allowances. The number of streetcar or bus rides provided in the budgets varies slightly with the length of the school year in the separate communities but more especially with city area and population. Eight times as many rides were allowed in the largest as in the smallest places. Cash fares on public conveyances in the 59 cities ranged from 5 cents to 10 cents per ride, but the token or ticket rate did not show such a wide spread. The combination of quantity allowances and fares payable resulted in transportation costs which were more than 12.5 times greater where most was required than where least was required. Transportation costs declined as city size decreased, regardless of fare, though the differences among size of city groups were by no means uniform. Rates themselves are subject to regulation by public authority with reference to the local situation, and competition between public carriers in most places has little to do with car or bus fares.

The budgets allow coal or wood as winter fuel and gas for cooking and water heating during the months when fuel for room warming is not necessary. As a result, several kinds of fuel had to be priced in the separate cities for the same purpose and two purposes had to be served.

The basis of gas cost differences among the 59 cities was threefold apart from rates: namely, kinds of gas, their heating values, and number of months' consumption allowed. The B. T. U. content of natural gas is much greater than that of manufactured gas.[11] Hence, less natural gas is required for a given purpose than manufactured. Natural gas rates as a rule are lower than manufactured gas rates. Differences, therefore, in monthly bills for gas to serve a specified purpose were very wide between cities where natural gas or manufactured gas was used. Annual cost dispersion was widened still farther by differential budget allowances based on climatic needs. As in the case of mass transportation facilities, supplying gas usually is a monopoly and rates are subject to public regulation.

Not so many elements contributed to the spread in the costs of fuel for room warming as of gas for cooking and water heating, and the range was correspondingly less. Budget allowances of coal or wood were adapted to the needs of four different winter climates, and specifications were so general that they were met by a number of different commodities. If, for example, wood was the popular local fuel, its price was combined with the annual quantity allowance assigned to the climate group in which the city belonged; the same procedure was followed where bituminous coal or anthracite was most frequently used for room warming.[12] Coals and woods could not be reduced to common units of heating value, however, and for each fuel priced a diversity of quality probably was obtained, depending on local consumption. This circumstance may be reflected to some extent in relative fuel prices.

Competition among fuels for the local market is perhaps more important than competition among sellers of the same kind of fuel, but for all of them distance from the supply seems to be the outstanding factor in price differentials. These differentials may be attributable partly to freight rates and partly to the fact that it does not pay to haul the lower grades of fuel far from the places where they are produced. Wood prices seldom embodied heavy shipping charges, because wood is used extensively for room warming only near the source of its supply. Anthracite, which is perhaps of a more nearly uniform grade wherever sold than either wood or bituminous coal, cost 90 percent more in some New England cities than in Scranton, the

---

[11] See footnote 13, p. 50, for definition of B. T. U.

[12] There were certain exceptions to this, in that quantity allowances were not developed for gas or oil as room warming fuels. In the few cities where either is the most popular fuel, costs were necessarily computed from the price of coal or wood, whichever most nearly represented local use.

center of the industry.[13] Gas rates also seemed to vary with distance from the supply, whether this was oil fields for natural gas or coal mines for manufactured gas, but purely local considerations also entered into the rate structure.

For gas a relatively small monthly allowance and a low rate usually were found together, and a relatively large monthly allowance and a high rate were usually combined. Prices of anthracite, bituminous coal, and wood, however, varied more nearly in inverse ratio to their respective quantity allowances. Hence, annual costs of coal and wood were less diversified among the 59 cities than annual gas costs.

The last among the budget subgroups for which differential quantity allowances were used in annual cost calculations was ice, a commodity of simple specification, locally produced, and sold for prices locally determined. Allowances of ice in the quantity budgets are complementary to allowances of coal or wood, because, in general, refrigeration is required during the months when fuel for room warming is not necessary. Ice allowances depend on whether its use is necessary during 5, 7, or 9 months per year. The largest reported annual ice cost was 3.7 times the smallest, but the highest price per 100 pounds was only double the lowest. Differential quantity allowances accounted for the discrepancy.

The combined costs of coal or wood, gas, and ice were less widely dispersed among the 59 cities than the outlays necessary for any one of them separately. In view of the arbitrary character of the quantity allowances, which are complementary as to period of use, it is perhaps unwise to attribute too much importance either to separate quantity allowances or separate costs as such.

Intermediate Cost Variations

The budget groups and subgroups whose cost dispersions were next widest were those whose quantity allowances were identical in all cities but whose specifications were general (table 62). Hence, considerable discretion was allowed in choice of the sample, local more often than universal influences entered into their price determination, or both of these circumstances played a part in establishing costs. These groups were newspapers, electricity, housing, motion picture theater admissions, clothing upkeep, and medical services. None of them varied so much as the outlays necessary for the group of items for which the dispersions were widest, but they differed considerably more than combined commodity prices which made up the narrowest cost range classification.

[13] Anthracite was cheaper in Boston and Bridgeport, where oil is much used by families of small means, than in Fall River and Providence, where alternative fuels were not reported. In Manchester anthracite prices were as high as in Fall River, though oil also was used. Bituminous coal was the most popular fuel reported in Portland (Maine), but oil, anthracite, and wood were used to some extent.

Newspapers, Electricity, Motion Picture Theater Admissions, Medical Services, and Clothing Upkeep

Annual newspaper cost was computed from the price of that daily having the largest local circulation, and price factors were local. Local considerations also largely accounted for the charges reported in each city for motion picture theater admissions, medical services, and clothing upkeep.[14] Cost differences for electricity resulted entirely from the wide range and variety of rates.[15] These are subject to public control like rates for transportation and gas; they reflect more nearly local than general price making influences.

Housing

Specifications for housing necessarily were general in order that they might be used in pricing the wide variety of dwellings which is found the country over. Hence, it cannot be said that for a given rent in one place identical accommodations could be obtained in another. Reported rents were being paid in the separate cities, however, to secure the standards of housing specified. Relative rents seemed to depend almost entirely on the prevailing balance of a combination of unmeasurable local forces. Obvious considerations of scarcity, land values, and tax policies, of desirability connected with neighborhood, type and age of structure, building material, conveniences, size of rooms, and of other circumstances which influence all rents in normal times were supplemented in this survey by factors connected with locally accepted working class housing. Where typical wage earners' dwellings in a given city met specifications for the maintenance level of living, reported rents can be explained as the result of operation of the usual forces. Where typical working class dwellings were substandard, reported rents were above the level customarily paid. Thus, high rents may have reflected local fiscal policies, a scarcity of acceptable housing, working class dwellings above the average the country over, or accomodations superior to those locally occupied by industrial, service, and other manual workers of small means. In general, high rents were found in the largest cities and in sections of the country where the most substantial housing and equipment are necessary. On the other hand, if working class dwellings meeting all specifications for standard housing were plentiful, they were obtained for less than the general average of rents. Lowest rents for standard accommodations were reported for the most part from cities with a mild climate, many of which are not far removed from the source of supply of locally popular building material.

---

[14] The allowance of an identical amount in all cities for cleaning and sewing materials served but slightly to counteract the widely varying prices of shoe repairs and cleaning and pressing services.

[15] See pp. 58 and 111.

Narrowest Cost Variations

The greatest cost uniformity was reported for those budget groups and subgroups which contain the greatest number of commodities or for which prices were the same the country over, or both (table 62). An identical quantity of each was allowed in all cities, their specifications for the most part were most definite, and their prices were local variations of wholesale costs more or less nationally determined. These groups were household supplies; personal care; clothing; drugs and appliances; furniture, furnishings, and household equipment; and food.

Household Supplies and Personal Care

Prices of trade-marked and nationally advertised household supplies, such as soap and starch, are mark-ups from wholesale prices which are identical over a wide territory. Retail quotations range all the way from resale prices established by the manufacturer to extreme cut rates, depending on individual merchandising policies. The range in costs of these commodities, most of which were priced without specifications, except that best sellers were to constitute the sample, might possibly be narrowed somewhat were only identical brands compared. Few brands have complete national distribution, however, and even these are not equally popular in all sections of the country. The cost dispersion for the household supplies group was held within a narrower range than would otherwise have been found, considering the few items separately priced, by the circumstance that three-tenths of the average group cost was an identical amount allowed in all cities. This provided for materials which can be bought for the same price everywhere at the chain limited price variety stores.

Personal care belongs in this group, from the standpoint of cost dispersion, largely because nearly one-third of the average cost was an identical amount allowed in all cities. The stabilizing effect of this common cost element counteracted to a large extent the fact that more than half the total was composed of charges for local services, and less than one-sixth for other commodities of national distribution.

Clothing; Drugs and Appliances; Furniture, Furnishings, and Household Equipment; and Food

The budget groups whose combined costs were most uniform contained no services. These groups were made up as follows: clothing, 90 separately priced commodities, identical allowance $10.25 in all cities plus sales tax where levied; drugs and appliances, 9 separately priced commodities; furniture, furnishings, and household equipment, 49 separately priced commodities, identical allowance $3.73 in all cities plus sales tax where levied; food, 44 separately priced commodities, 1 percent of their cost added for condiments. The identical allowances constituted relatively small proportions of the total costs of clothing, furniture, furnishings, and household equipment, and they served only slightly to reduce group cost dispersions.

Price variations for these commodities among the cities were as wide as, or wider than, those shown for items with differential quantity allowances; and within the separate cities articles presumably meeting identical specifications were quoted at prices of comparable diversity. Only for cough syrup was the individual commodity price range less than the cost range for the budget group in which it belongs. The relative similarity of the prices of drug store items, no matter where obtained, results probably more from control through national distribution of relatively few trade-marked articles than occurs for any other group of commodities in the quantity budgets.

Commodity prices were never all high or all low in any one city. As was pointed out earlier, combination of the prices of a large number of items permits a partial cancellation of extremes in the component parts, the extent of which determines the average cost dispersion for the group. The effect of balancing high prices for some commodities against low prices for others is particularly evident for food. Costs of this major budget group varied within narrower limits than any other. This similarity of food costs as a whole results from relative price uniformity for some commodities but a cancellation of extremes for others. The range of quotations for the different subgroups suggests that can and package foods may be standardized as to quality, meat prices may be affected by national competition and shipping costs, and prices of fresh fruits and vegetables may be dependent largely on seasonal factors. In other words, in general, the first group showed the narrowest price range the country over and the last showed the widest. Indeed, the prices of carrots, cabbage, spinach, and apples were more widely dispersed than prices of any other single commodity included in any budget group. The factor of alternative specifications used in sampling many food commodities is more or less operative in accounting for price differences.

The Budget as a Whole

Differences in service charges and other costs which for the most part are locally determined apparently are more accountable for intercity cost of living variations than differences in commodity prices. Service charges and other locally determined costs include what must be paid to the landlord and the utility companies; to physicians, dentists, and hospitals; to beauty parlors, barbers, and dry cleaning establishments; and for refuse disposal, school attendance, newspapers, motion picture theater admissions, and taxes; plus the amounts required for coal or wood and ice to obtain their budget allowances. Taken together, the outlays necessary for these items differed nearly 6 times as much between the extremes among the 59 cities included in this investigation as the amounts required for food, clothing, furniture, furnishings, and other commodities, plus allowances for items whose costs are likely to be the same wherever purchased. Costs which are determined largely by local conditions cannot be measured so accurately as commodity costs, and it is possible that in some instances their intercity range is overstated. The effect of their greater dispersion on the relative costs of the budget as a whole was reduced somewhat by the fact that they required slightly under two-fifths of the average annual cost of living. The less varied commodity costs, exclusive of coal or wood and ice, together with the outlays necessary for life insurance, postage, and other essentials whose prices are identical everywhere, required slightly over three-fifths.

Budget Cost Distributions

The proportion of the total cost of living taken by each of the major budget groups varied among the 59 cities with prices, quantity allowances, and specification factors applicable in each city (appendix tables 17, 18, 19, 20, 21, and 22). The percentages required for food and for clothing, clothing upkeep, and personal care at the same level of living were much more alike from city to city than were the percentages required for miscellaneous family needs, for household operation, or for housing, in the order named. Even for food, however, the largest share of the total maintenance budget cost required in any of the 59 cities was 28 percent more than the smallest, and the share taken by rent differed from smallest to largest by 86 percent.

Food, in general, required the smallest percentage of total budget cost where total cost was highest and increased in relative importance as the total cost of living declined. Housing required proportionally more, and clothing, clothing upkeep, and personal care proportionally less, in the higher than in the lower cost cities. The proportions of total budget cost required for household operation and for miscellaneous family needs seemed to have no relationship to the total cost of living.

As compared with the average cost of the maintenance budget in the 59 cities combined, the average emergency budget cost was so distributed that relatively more was required for food, housing, and household operation and relatively less for miscellaneous family needs, with clothing, clothing upkeep, and personal care taking a nearly identical share of both budget costs.

The largest percentages of the total cost of living required by the separate budget groups were not always found in cities where their absolute costs were high in comparison with other cities, and vice versa, but a tendency in this direction was indicated for rent, household operation, and miscellaneous family needs.

Because of the influence on budget cost distribution of circumstances peculiar to each community, it apparently is unsafe to generalize too positively with reference to the percentage each budget group requires of the total cost of living. This is particularly true with reference to local service group costs as contrasted with costs of commodities.

COMPARISONS WITH RESULTS OF OTHER STUDIES

The findings of the present investigation are not subject to absolute tests of accuracy, but they may be compared with the findings of other studies of budget costs for comparable levels of living and with expenditures by working class families to determine how closely the cost of a synthetic budget conforms with actual spending experience. The first comparison is made with the results of a survey by the National Industrial Conference Board; the second, with data collected by the Bureau of Labor Statistics. Both studies were made at practically the same time as the present investigation. The report of an investigation of relative international living costs is also available.

Quantity Budget Costs Compared

The National Industrial Conference Board studied the outlays necessary to purchase a synthetic budget for wage earners in 69 cities in February 1935.[16] The purpose of the investigation "was to measure differences in costs in the various cities and not differences in standards. For this reason the same commodities and services were used in the budget for all cities, except insofar as climatic or peculiar local housing conditions dictated a different choice. The figures resulting from the survey, therefore, show how much it would cost wage earners to live in the various cities if they lived according to the chosen standard."

Equipped with a quantity budget designed to "provide an adequate allowance of the primary necessaries, such as food, shelter, clothing, and fuel and light, as well as various miscellaneous goods and services," and questionnaires for pricing, the Conference Board secured quotations "with the aid of manufacturers and chambers of commerce and similar organizations in the cities studied." General specifications called for "inexpensive but a fair grade of merchandise" and more explicit instructions where possible described the commodities desired. "The cooperators were requested to take the questionnaires to the stores," which they themselves had previously selected as representative of working class trade, "to ask the managers to have them filled out, to collect them, and to return them to the Conference Board. In cases where information could readily be obtained by telephone,[17] it was suggested that the cooperators employ that means. * * * After all the necessary questionnaires for a city were received [by the Conference Board], they were examined for possible

[16] National Industrial Conference Board, *Conference Board Bulletin*, December 10, 1935, pp. 89–95.

[17] As, for example, motion picture theater admissions.

inaccuracies. Questionable data were followed up or rejected. The average price of each item was calculated by the arithmetic mean method" and weighted by its annual quantity allowance. These values, representative of annual use, were totaled and the sales tax was added where necessary.

The Conference Board's average for a 4-person wage earner's family in the 69 cities combined shows a cost of living in February 1935 which was 19 cents per week greater than the average in the 59 cities combined required by a 4-person manual worker's family at the maintenance level of the present investigation (table 63). The Conference Board's list includes 32 places with a population of 25,000

Table 63.—Average Costs [1] of Living, Works Progress Administration's Study, 59 Cities, March 1935, and National Industrial Conference Board's Study, 69 Cities, February 1935

Item	W. P. A. 59 cities	N. I. C. B. 69 cities
Average cost of living per week	$24.24	[2] $24.43
Percent distribution of cost		
Total	100.0	100.0
Food	35.6	34.3
Clothing	12.6	12.4
Housing	17.6	19.3
Fuel and light	6.1	7.6
Sundries [2]	28.1	26.4
Cost relatives by geographic divisions		
Average, all cities	100.0	100.0
East	—	104.3
New England	101.7	—
Middle Atlantic	103.0	—
South	—	97.6
South Atlantic	99.8	—
East South Central	93.7	—
West South Central	94.4	—
Middle West	—	97.5
East North Central	102.5	—
West North Central	100.2	—
Far West	—	100.6
Mountain	100.9	—
Pacific	101.2	—
Cost relatives by size of city		
Average, all cities	100.0	100.0
1,000,000 or more	105.6	104.5
500,000 to 1,000,000	105.7	
250,000 to 500,000	99.3	99.3
100,000 to 250,000	98.0	99.8
25,000 to 100,000	97.6	99.4
10,000 to 25,000	—	96.6

[1] Both studies measure the costs of living for a family composed of a man, a woman, and 2 children under age 14. The Works Progress Administration's figures measure the outlays necessary for basic maintenance for industrial, service, and other manual workers; the National Industrial Conference Board's figures "would provide an adequate allowance of the primary necessaries for a wage earner's family." National Industrial Conference Board, *Conference Board Bulletin*, December 10, 1935. The cities making up the Conference Board's list are only partially identical with those in the Works Progress Administration's list and include 9 with less than 25,000 population, a class not included in the Works Progress Administration's study.

[2] Do not include an automobile. The National Industrial Conference Board also computed costs to include an automobile.

Source: Works Progress Administration, table 4 and appendix tables 5, 7, and 17; National Industrial Conference Board, *Conference Board Bulletin*, December 10, 1935, p. 90.

or more which also were covered in the Works Progress Administration's study and 28 which were not covered. It contains 9 places where the population was less than 25,000. The Conference Board's figures for the separate cities have not been published. The difference between the lowest and highest costs was 29 percent as compared with 25.2 percent between extremes which the present study shows. None of the extreme cities in the two series were identical. Geographic and size of city groupings of the two sets of cost figures produced averages which were much alike. There was also close similarity of the percentage distributions of costs among the major budget groups. Considering the differences in city coverage, quantity budgets priced, and methods of collecting the data, the similarity of results is striking.

International Costs of Living Compared

An international comparison of costs of living, which as far as possible took into account "differences in national customs, consumption habits, and price systems," [18] did not show such similarity of necessary outlays as the American studies, which attempted to hold these factors constant. The International Labour Office "estimated the cost of maintaining in 1931 a standard of living approximately equivalent to that enjoyed by a certain category of Detroit worker with a family of a certain size and composition, which spent on an average a certain number of dollars during 1929." [19] It was not "a question of determining what it would cost an American worker to live in different European cities on the American standard" [20] but, rather, "how much a European worker would need to expend if his general standard of living were to be approximately equivalent to that of his Detroit counterpart." [21] The spread in the costs of living as thus estimated in 15 cities, including Detroit, was 82.5 percent from low to high.[22]

Quantity Budget Costs and Expenditures for Living Compared

In order to see how closely these estimates of necessary costs of living agree with expenditures for living by real families, comparison of the costs of the maintenance budget ascertained in the present investigation may be made with expenditures by self-supporting white families of small means in a 12-month period falling sometime within

[18] International Labour Office, *A Contribution to the Study of International Comparisons of Costs of Living*, Studies and Reports, Series N (Statistics) No. 17, second revised edition, Geneva, 1932, p. 218.

[19] *Ibid.*, p. 35.

[20] *Ibid.*, p. 7.

[21] *Ibid.*, p. 2. See also, pp. 3 and 8.

[22] *Ibid.*, pp. 30–31. See also Magnussen, Leifur, "An International Inquiry into Costs of Living: A Comparative Study of Workers' Living Costs in Detroit and Fourteen European Cities," *Journal of the American Statistical Association*, June 1933, p. 136.

the years 1933–1936, as determined by the Bureau of Labor Statistics.[23] The 2 sets of data are available for 10 cities.

The Bureau of Labor Statistics studied incomes and expenditures of wage earners and lower-salaried clerical workers without reference to the standard of living they maintained, size, or sex and age composition, except that none were on relief and the chief wage earner must have had at least 1,008 hours of employment within 36 weeks during the preceding year. Families averaged larger than the four-person group of the present investigation,[24] and treatment of certain budget items was dissimilar in the two analyses.[25]

Reported expenditures by the lowest income group [26] in each of the 10 cities under observation were similar to estimated budget costs in some respects and different in others (table 64). The average cost of living in the 10 cities combined was greater by $10 per year for a 4-person family than the average expenditure per year by a family of 4.75 members. Even allowing for possible differences in age and sex of constituent families, it is evident that the costs of the maintenance budget would provide funds equal to or greater than the

---

[23] The study was made in 55 cities. Of the reports released up to May 1937, 11 were for places where the Works Progress Administration's study was carried on, but in only 10 were expenditures classified by income groups. Williams, Faith M., "Money Disbursements of Wage Earners and Clerical Workers in Eleven New Hampshire Communities," *Monthly Labor Review*, March 1936; "Money Disbursements of Wage Earners and Clerical Workers in Richmond, Birmingham, and New Orleans," *Monthly Labor Review*, May 1936; "Money Disbursements of Wage Earners and Clerical Workers in Four Michigan Cities," *Monthly Labor Review*, June 1936; "Money Disbursements of Wage Earners and Clerical Workers in Boston and Springfield," *Monthly Labor Review*, September 1936; "Money Disbursements of Wage Earners and Clerical Workers in Rochester, Columbus, and Seattle," *Monthly Labor Review*, December 1936; "Money Disbusements of Wage Earners and Clerical Workers in New York," *Monthly Labor Review*, January 1937. For the city of Denver, see Kaplan, A. D. H., *Family Disbursements of Wage Earners and Salaried Clerical Workers in Denver*, University of Denver Reports, Business Study No. 81, April 1936. Additional studies of consumer purchases were made during 1936 by the Bureau of Labor Statistics as a Works Progress Administration project in 32 cities, and by the Bureau of Home Economics in 19 cities, 140 villages, and 66 farm counties. The results of these studies have not yet been published.

[24] Comparable "consumption units" were not calculated. "Consumption unit" is equivalent to the requirements of one adult male, computed for the purpose of eliminating size and composition of family as a factor in expenditure differentials. For method of computation in the Bureau of Labor Statistics' analysis, see *Monthly Labor Review*, March 1936, pp. 558–559.

[25] For example, life insurance was counted as investment by the Bureau, whereas the quantity budgets of the Works Progress Administration list insurance as a current charge. The Works Progress Administration's budgets make no provision for carrying debts, a current charge in the Bureau of Labor Statistics' expenditure data.

[26] Those with average annual expenditures per consumption unit of less than $400 per year.

***Table 64.*—Annual Costs of Self-Support at Maintenance Level of Living, 4-Person Manual Worker's Family, 10 Cities, March 1935, and Annual Expenditures by Wage Earners and Clerical Workers in Lowest Income Self-Supporting Groups,[1] 10 Cities, 1933–1936**

City and study	Number of families	Average number of persons per family	Annual cost of living or expenditure	Percent distribution of cost of living and family expenditure [2]										
				Total	Food	Clothing and clothing upkeep	Personal care	Housing	Household operation [3]	Furniture, furnishings, and household equipment	Medical care	Transportation	Recreation	All other [4]
Average, 10 cities: Cost of living	—	4.00	$1,267	100.0	35.8	12.6	1.9	16.9	9.8	2.4	4.1	5.0	6.0	5.5
Family expenditure	1,269	4.75	1,257	100.0	38.5	10.6	2.1	16.6	12.2	2.6	3.5	5.6	4.8	3.5
Manchester, N. H.: Cost of living	—	4.00	1,254	100.0	36.9	12.6	1.9	14.8	12.0	2.4	4.0	3.2	6.6	5.6
Family expenditure	73	4.73	1,327	100.0	38.1	13.3	1.9	12.8	13.9	3.8	3.5	3.9	4.7	4.1
Boston, Mass.: Cost of living	—	4.00	1,353	100.0	34.7	12.1	1.9	19.5	9.8	2.4	4.1	4.6	6.2	4.7
Family expenditure [5]	195	5.23	1,356	100.0	40.9	9.4	1.7	20.3	13.1	1.6	2.4	4.2	3.8	2.6
New York, N. Y.: Cost of living	—	4.00	1,375	100.0	34.7	10.8	1.8	21.8	9.3	2.0	4.1	5.2	5.7	4.6
Family expenditure [5]	194	4.96	1,407	100.0	42.1	9.1	1.8	22.6	9.5	1.2	2.5	3.7	5.3	2.2
Rochester, N. Y.: Cost of living	—	4.00	1,288	100.0	34.4	12.2	1.9	17.5	11.6	2.4	4.1	5.0	5.7	5.2
Family expenditure	96	4.51	1,286	100.0	34.5	10.3	2.0	20.8	13.6	2.7	3.0	4.2	4.9	4.0
Columbus, Ohio: Cost of living	—	4.00	1,179	100.0	37.7	13.6	2.1	16.3	8.2	2.7	3.9	3.8	5.7	6.0
Family expenditure	103	4.21	1,134	100.0	36.8	10.4	2.2	16.6	12.2	3.6	3.0	6.7	5.2	3.3
Detroit, Mich.: Cost of living	—	4.00	1,318	100.0	33.7	13.0	1.9	16.8	9.8	2.4	4.4	6.2	6.0	5.8
Family expenditure [5]	178	5.18	1,348	100.0	39.6	11.7	2.0	14.5	11.9	2.6	3.0	6.5	5.1	3.1
Richmond, Va.: Cost of living	—	4.00	1,268	100.0	35.3	13.2	1.9	18.6	9.5	2.7	4.0	3.1	5.8	5.9
Family expenditure	72	5.04	1,231	100.0	37.2	10.4	2.1	16.6	12.3	2.9	5.0	5.8	3.8	3.9
Birmingham, Ala.: Cost of living	—	4.00	1,169	100.0	38.2	12.6	2.0	14.2	8.6	2.4	4.1	5.3	6.1	6.5
Family expenditure	88	4.56	1,153	100.0	36.2	11.8	2.6	11.4	12.9	3.1	5.0	6.9	5.6	4.5
New Orleans, La.: Cost of living	—	4.00	1,233	100.0	35.0	12.1	1.9	16.1	8.3	2.4	4.3	7.9	6.4	5.6
Family expenditure	158	4.60	1,042	100.0	41.3	10.1	2.5	16.6	10.6	1.9	3.5	5.6	5.2	2.7
Seattle, Wash.: Cost of living	—	4.00	1,233	100.0	35.9	13.6	2.1	13.6	10.8	2.6	4.2	6.1	6.0	5.1
Family expenditure	112	4.49	1,290	100.0	38.1	9.9	2.0	13.5	11.6	3.0	4.5	8.6	4.6	4.2

[1] Those with average annual expenditures per consumption unit of less than $400 per year. "Consumption unit" is equivalent to the requirements of 1 adult male, computed for the purpose of eliminating size and composition of family as a factor in expenditure differentials. For method of computation in the Bureau of Labor Statistics' analysis, see *Monthly Labor Review*, March 1936, pp. 558–559.

[2] The budget groups are slightly different from those used throughout the analysis of the Works Progress Administration's figures, because the latter could be recombined to compare with the Bureau of Labor Statistics' data, but the reverse procedure could not be used. The cost of living figures include insurance, but expenditures do not; expenditures include interest on debt, but the cost of living figures do not.

[3] Exclusive of furniture, furnishings, and household equipment, shown separately.

[4] This classification includes several minor items in the 2 studies, not identical or sufficiently significant to state separately.

[5] Weighted average of families with less than $300 and $300–$400 annual expenditures per consumption unit.

Source: Cost of living figures, appendix tables 2 and 17; family expenditure figures, Manchester, *Monthly Labor Review*, March 1936; Richmond, Birmingham, and New Orleans, *Monthly Labor Review*, May 1936; Detroit, *Monthly Labor Review*, June 1936; Boston, *Monthly Labor Review*, September 1936; Rochester, Columbus, and Seattle, *Monthly Labor Review*, December 1936; New York, *Monthly Labor Review*, January 1937.

amounts spent for self-support by families of small means in 1935. The excess of estimated necessary costs of living over actual expenditures by larger families in certain cities may reflect superior purchasing habits or managerial ability, or the substandard conditions under which some families are living. Expenditures greater than estimated costs of living are accounted for in every city by families larger than the one of four persons in the present study.

The distribution of family expenditures in these 10 cities was not exactly like the distribution of maintenance budget costs. Agreement would not be expected in view of the fact that the quantity budget was designed as a balanced plan, taking all the essentials of living into account, whereas in practice families often economize on certain necessities in order to permit greater expenditures for others which meet their requirements better. Expenditure distributions vary, also, with different relationships between funds available and family needs. Thus, proportionately more of a given total must be spent for the elementary necessities as the number of persons to be provided for increases; and proportionately less must be spent for these necessities by families of the same size as the amount of their total expenditures becomes more liberal.

These relationships constitute an important consideration in any comparison of budget cost and family expenditure distributions,[27] and they serve to explain several of the observed differences between them. In each of the 10 cities, for example, families averaged larger than the 4-person group whose costs of living were measured in the present investigation. In five of the cities expenditures for living by these larger families were less than estimated costs of living.[28] Either of these circumstances may account for the fact that food required a greater share of expenditures than of living costs, if exact ratios could be worked out on the basis of comparable consumption units. In addition, however, the maintenance food budget was especially constructed to provide adequate nutriment at low cost, comparable with allowances of other necessities on a minimum basis. Hence, a smaller proportion of the total cost of living should be required for it

[27] It might be assumed, because of the period covered by the expenditure studies in certain cities and because considerably less than full time employment was required as a prerequisite for including families in the sample, that current expenditures might have been reduced somewhat below normal. Analysis of the data regarding relative financial positions at the beginning and end of the year indicates that in all the cities, except New York, more than half the lowest income families studied had increased their net assets or decreased their liabilities or both within the year. In New York 46.9 percent were financially better off at the end of the year than at the beginning and 7.7 percent reported no change. *Monthly Labor Review*, March 1936, p. 563; May 1936, p. 1464; June 1936, p. 1753; September 1936, p. 792; December 1936, pp. 1609, 1612, and 1614; January 1937, p. 240.

[28] No attempt was made to compare the results of these two studies in terms of identical consumption units.

than the proportional expenditure by families of the same size and with incomes equivalent to the estimated cost of living.

The expenditure for household operation proportionally larger than the cost of the maintenance household operation budget seems to be attributable to consumption not provided for in the cost of living estimates: domestic service, laundry out, moving, express, freight, drayage, safe deposit box, insurance on furniture, and interest on debts. The extent to which any of these services should be provided for in a basic maintenance budget for industrial, service, and other manual workers of small means obviously is a matter of opinion. Furniture insurance, for example, might be included were its cost readily determined; [29] interest on debts would hardly enter into a current cost of living estimate. Water also is accounted for as an item of household operation expense, whereas in the cost of living calculations its cost was added to rent.

For furniture, furnishings, and household equipment, personal care, and transportation the very slight excess of proportional expenditures over proportional costs shown in the average for the 10 cities appeared in varying degrees in some of the cities separately, and in some proportional costs exceeded proportional expenditures. The relatively large expenditures for transportation reported in certain places is attributable to automobile ownership.[30] The percents of families in the lowest income group owning cars in the separate cities were as follows:

City	*Percent owning automobile*
Detroit, Mich	55. 6
Seattle, Wash	55. 4
Columbus, Ohio	52. 4
Birmingham, Ala	47. 0
Rochester, N. Y	34. 4
Richmond, Va	31. 0
Manchester, N. H	27. 4
New Orleans, La	25. 0
Boston, Mass	6. 2
New York, N. Y	5. 7

Expenditures relatively greater than proportional maintenance costs for certain budget groups just shown were counterbalanced to some extent by reversed ratios for others. Average costs of the quantity budgets for clothing and its upkeep, housing, medical care, recreation,

[29] This item was omitted from the quantity budgets because its cost is fixed by numerous variables even within a given city and amounts to very little on an annual basis. Type of dwelling, its location, and the material of which it is built determine the premium to be paid for fire insurance on furniture therein. For the $100 valuation of personal property adopted in the present investigation for the purpose of estimating taxes payable (see p. 121), in houses meeting specifications for this study, premiums would be less than $1 per year.

[30] *Monthly Labor Review*, March 1936, pp. 561–563; May 1936, pp. 1457 and 1462–1463; June 1936, pp. 1744–1745, 1747, and 1749–1750; September 1936, pp. 784–786; December 1936, p. 1616; January 1937, p. 234.

and all other items,[31] for example, took more of the average total cost than comparable percentages of the average family expenditure. Though there were variations among the separate cities for these groups, comparable with those already noted for others, a larger share of budget cost than of expenditure went for recreation and all other items in every city, and for clothing and its upkeep in all of them except Manchester. In half the cities relatively more of the total expenditure was assigned to rent than quantity budget cost distribution called for. Larger families, usually with smaller total expenditures, may account for this difference in rents; counting life insurance as a current charge in budget cost and not in family expenditure explains some of the difference for all other items.

It has already been noted that family size in relation to total expenditures influences the proportion of total outlay apportioned to different needs and that exact comparisons between the results of the present study and available expenditure data are not possible. The evidence at hand suggests, however, where economies will be made when the amount required for support of a four-person family is stretched to cover the needs of a family with 4.75 members.

More than half the families whose expenditures were studied had flush toilets, running hot water inside the dwelling, electric lights, and gas or electricity as cooking fuel.[32] The proportion living in accommodations which met the superior standards specified in the cost of living study cannot be told from the data available.

Of the 10 cities only for the city of New York have expenditures for medical care been made public. They show that a much smaller volume of medical care is purchased than the maintenance budget provides and that clinic visits, at fees far below private practitioners' charges, are made as frequently as are visits to a doctor's office.[33] The small proportion of the total expenditure allotted to medical care in Boston possibly is to be explained on the same basis. Cities not so well provided with public facilities for medical services may require a larger proportional outlay for medical care from private sources.

From the comparisons just made, it is apparent that the cost of the maintenance budget in 1935 provided somewhat more than lowest income self-supporting families were spending in the 10 cities where costs of living and expenditures can be compared. Average apportionments of costs and expenditures for various essentials of living are reasonably alike, or at least their differences can be explained. The degree of similarity varied in the separate cities. These deviations

[31] "All other" in table 64 is a classification which includes several minor groups in the two lists not identical or sufficiently significant to state separately.

[32] *Monthly Labor Review,* May 1936, p. 1458; June 1936, p. 1751; September 1936, p. 790; December 1936, pp. 1610, 1612, and 1615; January 1937, p. 237.

[33] *Monthly Labor Review,* January 1937, pp. 234–235. No information is available as to the volume of medical care received by these families without money expense.

from the average reflect local peculiarities of tastes or needs which cannot be accounted for in a synthetic budget. Any of these local factors can throw the whole relationship of the separate values into changed positions. Thus, if larger than average families must spend more than the average for food and housing and if automobile ownership is not common, the entire spending pattern will be different from that in which expenditures for food and housing are less than the average, and automobiles are commonly owned by families of small means.

COMMENTS ON METHODOLOGY

The study from which the foregoing conclusions were derived was an experiment in measuring intercity differences in costs of living through pricing a definite list of goods and services by specifications which were uniform, in the main, in all places. Much was learned in the process of carrying the study to completion which may be of benefit to future students of the subject. Certain comments on methodology, therefore, are of interest.

Uniform quantity budgets in all cities as a measure of working class family needs at a given level of living, with minimum adjustments for groups of cities, for the most part afford a satisfactory basis for cost analysis. Without additional modification of a few quantity allowances to conform with prevailing local customs, some costs may prove to be too high or too low in particular communities. These adjustments seem particularly desirable for ice in certain cities, and for providing quantity allowances for gas and oil for home heating. Were it possible to differentiate between various grades of bituminous coal and wood, an improvement in cost estimates would result. That irregularities resulting from not using such procedures are smoothed out in the cost of living as a whole, and to a lesser extent perhaps in some of the major budget group costs, is apparent through such checks on the results of the present study as can be made.

It is possible that the food budget assumes too much interest on the part of the housewife to obtain an adequate diet at minimum cost, and that to supply requisite nutrition according to prevailing practice a somewhat costlier food allowance is necessary than the maintenance budget provides. At the same time, the clothing and clothing upkeep budget may be more liberal than family expenditures for these items. The household operation and transportation budgets when priced also required smaller shares of the total cost of living than the percentages which real families at a comparable economic level found necessary to spend. Increased allowances for these items, however, might require the inclusion of goods and services not called for in a basic maintenance budget. Their absence is covered by the greater budget cost of recreation and all other needs. The medical care allowance in the budget apparently should not be changed. Inasmuch as expenditures with which costs for a four-person family are compared were made by somewhat larger families, these conclusions are necessarily tentative rather than final.

If for any reason readjustments should be made in the quantity budgets for pricing purposes, the entire list of goods and services included for each level of living must be considered, because each presents a consistent picture which can easily be distorted unless adjustments are balanced at every point.

Analysis of the behavior of retail prices within a given city with reference to all the merchandising and other local elements which enter therein is no part of the present report. It is of interest, however, that despite the wide range of quotations for specified commodities, average prices in the separate cities when combined with their quantity allowances produced group costs which seemed to be representative. All commodity prices except food [34] originally were edited for specification conformity and general consistency, and the arithmetic means of accepted quotations were calculated for all except fuel and ice.[35] In six cities chosen to represent a variety of price factors, these values later were recalculated in terms of the modified medians of prices which had been edited to eliminate only articles which the field agent reported did not meet specifications. Differences in group totals calculated by these two methods varied among the separate cities, reflecting possibly a range in original editing policies, but never exceeded 3.3 percent of the costs as originally calculated, and for three cities the differences were less than 1 percent.

The use of specifications as a means of maintaining comparability of goods and services priced was an integral part of the technique of this study. Until more exact descriptions are used for some of them, however, it is not unlikely that a wide range of prices will be obtained in each city and that these will not be for identical items among the cities. Some foods are graded according to accepted specifications, but such matters as degree of freshness in fruits and vegetables are difficult to define. Pricing number of units in a range of sizes or weights does not make for uniformity of quotations. Comparing can or package and bulk sale prices results in different relationships than would be found were the sample entirely homogeneous.

Consumers demand variety and dissimilarity in clothing, furniture, furnishings, and household equipment. Merchants strive to carry goods different from their competitors' lines which may be preferable for a given purpose within the same price range. Materials, styles, colors, and construction constantly change and reorders often are not identical with original stock. The purchaser does not know how to

[34] The Bureau of Labor Statistics compiled the retail food price data.

[35] The modified median was computed for housing, coal and wood, ice, and medical services for reasons explained on p. 104. See also pp. 109, 110, and 115.

ask for many commodities in terms of precise specifications, and frequently the retailer cannot tell him exactly what he is buying. The assumption that prices obtained in this study were always for identical quality, material, construction, size, or shape, therefore, is open to question.

Some specifications were more exact than others, and some commodities had definite trade names which made identification easy. Thus, for example, when given brands of food, drugs, cosmetics, or household supplies were quoted in terms of a common size, weight, or volume, there can be little question of price comparability. Certain commodities of readily defined material, such as copper, iron, or tin, or construction, such as riveted, welded, or nailed, which were labeled in terms of linear, area, or volume measurements, could be recognized and prices of identical commodities usually were obtained. Where specifications depended largely on variations of such descriptions as "part wool," "inexpensive quality," "well made," and similar abstractions, and where commodities were priced without specification, except volume of sale or customary use, as in the case of bituminous coal or wood, some household supplies, and some drug store items, identical merchandise was not necessarily priced, though comparable values probably were obtained.

A price range of several hundred percent for a given article in any one city probably does not measure differentials for identical merchandise among stores in that place, but represents the spread of quotations for what the dealer had in stock most nearly meeting the specifications. No one quotation is necessarily typical, but the average of a group of them in a city usually can be counted on to give a fair statement of the price to be paid in the shops patronized by working class families, for a commodity of the standard specified.

In the study of the costs of living in 14 European cities compared with Detroit, the investigators attempted to maintain similarity of standard by carrying to the different places samples of certain articles of clothing for which quotations were desired.[36] It often happened, however, that nothing similar to the sample could be found in European shops; hence, no quotation could be obtained. The same situation would arise in this country were a similar method used, for even at a specified social and economic level different commodities satisfy the same needs without standardization or uniformity.

The Bureau of Labor Statistics, which has been pricing by specification since March 1935, notes that "the type of goods priced has been varied from city to city in conformity with the purchasing habits of moderate-income families in the separate cities," and that differences in the average costs of commodities from which its indexes of the costs of living

[36] International Labour Office, *op. cit.*, pp. 11 and 21.

are computed "may be due to varying standards and purchasing habits in these cities as well as to varying prices for goods of given grades." [37]

Possible variations in the kinds of commodities sold are duplicated for services. Motion picture theater admission charges furnish a case in point. Prices at the same theater vary between adults and children, with the time of the performance, the day of the week, and with seat location, but other circumstances influence prices when those factors are held constant. How long has the film been released in the city; i. e., what "run" is it? What other entertainment does the program offer? First-run features in downtown theaters command the highest admission fees in the large cities. The cheapest theaters in these cities, the so-called "grind houses," also are located downtown where, almost on a 24-hour schedule, Westerns and other films which never appear on the better known circuits cater to those with least to spend for this kind of amusement. Many residential centers have their own theaters where popular fare may be obtained for less than the first-run houses downtown. A variety of tariffs also prevails in these neighborhood theaters, depending largely on the local age of the film. With all these matters to consider in pricing, obviously the sample may vary considerably from city to city, and average admission charges in each do not necessarily indicate price differentials for identical programs, unless every qualifying factor is considered. They do measure, however, what people are paying on a certain date for a generic type of entertainment.

Rating physicians' and dentists' charges in terms of quality of services presents a similar problem. If a working class practice is consistently priced, the most comparable rates are obtained, but in some places physicians cater to persons of several economic levels, and reported fees may or may not be what they expect to collect from patients of small means. Thus, their charges showed a wide range from city to city and may not exactly represent the local situation in some of them. As previously noted, however, a combination of fees for several different services usually produced reasonable cost ratios for medical care as a whole.

The International Labour Office suggested, as a result of its efforts to measure international differences in living costs, that maximum comparability would be secured by having a single group of individuals supervise the work in all cities. This visiting commission of experts would investigate each locality, and by using the same "standards of appreciation" would be able to compare relative values.[38] Such a method is time consuming and expensive. The results of the present study suggest that it may not be necessary, if cost comparisons rather

[37] *Monthly Labor Review*, October 1936, p. 1063. The same note appears in connection with each write-up of the Bureau's quarterly index numbers.

[38] International Labour Office, *op. cit.*, p. 5.

than price comparisons are required and if standards of living in the separate cities are reasonably homogeneous. In a study of the costs of a specified level of living pricing the goods and services which families at that level buy, in stores and from service sellers that they patronize, probably will produce results sufficiently accurate for the purpose in hand even though specifications are fairly general. A large number of price quotations will have to be obtained in each community, and the local work must be done according to one plan and under one supervision. Precise measurements will not be obtained for every item which families consume, and intercity price comparisons for certain items may not be possible. For the cost of the budget as a whole, however, the results are likely to be representative.

Price comparisons present a different problem. For these, specifications cannot be too exact or refinements of sampling too minute. The more definite the specifications are, however, the fewer will be the quotations which can be obtained in any locality for commodities and services which exactly meet them, and the fewer will be the localities in which these items can be priced. Specifications will change over a period of years and probably will never be of general application. Research looking toward the improvement of specifications in price reporting has been carried on for a number of years, and changes are made as the utility of new descriptions is proved. Were measurement of the costs of a uniform level of living in different parts of the country or among cities of different sizes to await the development of universally applicable specifications for all necessary goods and services, however, it might never be made.

The schedules used in the present study could be improved, especially those on which data regarding housing and other services were collected. Such a conclusion is usual after first trial of a given method of inquiry. A larger variety of schedules, each concerned with fewer, more similar items and directed specifically to certain sources of information, would be better than the few all-inclusive schedules directed to a variety of sources which were used for some items in the present investigation.

Certain changes in sampling are advisable, especially in sampling services. With more definite descriptions of some items, prices can be confined to those goods and services which clearly comply with the specifications. This procedure will greatly reduce the work of editing the schedules and will simplify the calculation of average values. As long as enough items are priced to afford a field within which extreme quotations will largely cancel, the device of getting prices for the goods and services listed for a given level of living, in the shops and neighborhoods where persons living at this level buy, should provide a measure of costs adequate for all practical purposes in a field where exact values cannot be obtained.

Appendixes

Appendix A

LIST OF TABLES

TEXT TABLES

APPENDIX TABLES

Appendix B

BASIC TABLES

Table 1.—Cities of 25,000 or More Population, 1930, in the United States and Included in the Study of Costs of Living, Classified by Geographic Division and by Size

Geographic division and size of city classification	All cities in the United States		59 cities included in the study		Percent of population included
	Number	Population	Number	Population	
United States	376	49, 242, 877	59	30, 011, 692	[1] 60. 9
1,000,000 or more	5	15, 064, 555	5	15, 064, 555	100. 0
500,000 to 1,000,000	8	5, 763, 987	8	5, 763, 987	100. 0
250,000 to 500,000	24	7, 956, 228	19	6, 538, 086	82. 2
100,000 to 250,000	56	7, 540, 966	14	1, 927, 089	25. 6
25,000 to 100,000	283	12, 917, 141	13	717, 975	5. 6
New England	55	4, 457, 465	6	1, 443, 803	[1] 32. 4
1,000,000 or more	(2)	(2)	(2)	(2)	(2)
500,000 to 1,000,000	1	781, 188	1	781, 188	100. 0
250,000 to 500,000	1	252, 981	1	252, 981	100. 0
100,000 to 250,000	11	1, 466, 630	2	261, 990	17. 9
25,000 to 100,000	42	1, 956, 666	2	147, 644	7. 5
Middle Atlantic	76	15, 499, 658	8	11, 114, 864	[1] 71. 7
1,000,000 or more	2	8, 881, 407	2	8, 881, 407	100. 0
500,000 to 1,000,000	2	1, 242, 893	2	1, 242, 893	100. 0
250,000 to 500,000	3	1, 087, 184	2	770, 469	70. 9
100,000 to 250,000	11	1, 438, 853	1	143, 433	10. 0
25,000 to 100,000	58	2, 849, 321	1	76, 662	2. 7
East North Central	97	12, 810, 858	8	7, 634, 632	[1] 59. 6
1,000,000 or more	2	4. 945, 100	2	4, 945, 100	100. 0
500,000 to 1,000,000	2	1, 478, 678	2	1. 478, 678	100. 0
250,000 to 500,000	5	1, 651, 643	3	1, 105, 885	67. 0
100,000 to 250,000	10	1, 327, 757	1	104, 969	7. 9
25,000 to 100,000	78	3, 407, 680	(2)	(2)	(2)
West North Central	27	3, 482, 012	7	2, 100, 637	[1] 60. 3
1,000,000 or more	(2)	(2)	(2)	(2)	(2)
500,000 to 1,000,000	1	821, 960	1	821, 960	100. 0
250,000 to 500,000	3	1, 135, 708	2	864, 102	76. 1
100,000 to 250,000	5	690, 995	2	325, 116	47. 1
25,000 to 100,000	18	833, 349	2	89, 459	10. 7
South Atlantic	41	3, 826, 115	9	2, 160, 018	[1] 56. 5
1,000,000 or more	(2)	(2)	(2)	(2)	(2)
500,000 to 1,000,000	1	804, 874	1	804, 874	100. 0
250,000 to 500,000	2	757, 235	2	757, 235	100. 0
100,000 to 250,000	6	760, 583	3	442, 188	58. 1
25,000 to 100,000	32	1, 503, 423	3	155, 721	10. 4

See footnotes at end of table.

Table 1.—Cities of 25,000 or More Population, 1930, in the United States and Included in the Study of Costs of Living, Classified by Geographic Division and by Size—Con.

Geographic division and size of city classification	All cities in the United States		59 cities included in the study		Percent of population included
	Number	Population	Number	Population	
East South Central	16	1, 642, 976	5	994, 570	[1] 60. 5
1,000,000 or more	(2)	(2)	(2)	(2)	(2)
500,000 to 1,000,000	(2)	(2)	(2)	(2)	(2)
250,000 to 500,000	3	820, 566	3	820, 566	100. 0
100,000 to 250,000	3	379, 466	1	105, 802	27. 9
25,000 to 100,000	10	442, 944	1	68, 202	15. 4
West South Central	26	2, 607, 986	6	1, 381, 078	[1] 53. 0
1,000,000 or more	(2)	(2)	(2)	(2)	(2)
500,000 to 1,000,000	(2)	(2)	(2)	(2)	(2)
250,000 to 500,000	3	1, 011, 589	3	1, 011, 589	100. 0
100,000 to 250,000	5	824, 057	2	287, 810	34. 9
25,000 to 100,000	18	772, 340	1	81, 679	10. 6
Mountain	10	727, 281	5	526, 736	[1] 72. 4
1,000,000 or more	(2)	(2)	(2)	(2)	(2)
500,000 to 1,000,000	(2)	(2)	(2)	(2)	(2)
250,000 to 500,000	1	287, 861	1	287, 861	100. 0
100,000 to 250,000	1	140, 267	1	140, 267	100. 0
25,000 to 100,000	8	299, 153	3	98, 608	33. 0
Pacific	28	4, 188, 526	5	2, 655, 354	[1] 63. 4
1,000,000 or more	1	1, 238, 048	1	1, 238, 048	100. 0
500,000 to 1,000,000	1	634, 394	1	634, 394	100. 0
250,000 to 500,000	3	951, 461	2	667, 398	70. 1
100,000 to 250,000	4	512, 358	1	115, 514	22. 5
25,000 to 100,000	19	852, 265	(2)	(2)	(2)

[1] This figure represents the percent which the population in cities studied is of the population in all cities with 25,000 or more.
[2] No city in this group.

Source: *Fifteenth Census of the United States: 1930*, Population, Vol. I, pp. 14, 16, and 22–29.

Table 2.—Annual Costs[1] of Living, by Major Budget Groups and Principal Subgroups, 4-Person Manual Worker's Family, 59 Cities, March 1935

MAINTENANCE LEVEL

City	Total cost of living	Food	Clothing, clothing upkeep, and personal care				Housing, including water	Household operation							
			Total	Clothing	Clothing upkeep	Personal care		Total	Fuel			Ice	Electricity	Household supplies	Furniture, furnishings, and household equipment
									Total	Coal or wood	Gas				
Average, 59 cities	$1,260.62	$448.18	$184.35	$145.93	$13.55	$24.87	$221.89	$153.54	$57.98	$47.00	$10.98	$22.40	$18.68	$18.82	$31.10
Washington, D. C.	1,414.54	476.34	179.23	142.13	12.98	24.12	342.00	146.62	64.65	56.80	7.85	19.44	12.05	17.31	30.12
San Francisco, Calif.[1]	1,389.87	459.37	208.62	165.32	14.00	29.31	270.00	179.61	48.08	35.03	13.05	47.97	18.56	22.32	32.41
Minneapolis, Minn.	1,387.79	436.75	198.49	159.63	15.82	23.04	264.00	202.13	108.28	101.68	6.60	18.14	18.89	18.37	31.90
New York, N. Y.[1]	1,375.13	477.22	172.67	137.08	10.87	24.71	300.00	155.87	66.21	55.65	10.56	19.83	22.08	17.15	27.53
Chicago, Ill.[1]	1,356.11	462.08	193.45	153.64	12.46	27.35	240.00	162.36	73.82	68.21	5.61	19.83	17.92	17.45	30.26
Milwaukee, Wis.	1,353.34	425.66	206.15	163.61	14.29	28.25	270.00	176.48	92.85	85.10	7.75	12.96	18.29	17.15	32.18
Boston, Mass.	1,352.77	468.45	189.02	149.95	13.04	26.03	264.00	164.29	70.11	59.76	10.35	19.44	19.85	19.83	32.02
Cleveland, Ohio[1]	1,348.33	444.40	210.95	168.35	13.46	29.14	234.00	142.56	59.11	55.36	3.75	17.35	11.13	19.41	32.47
St. Louis, Mo.	1,339.55	448.46	179.50	144.08	11.46	23.97	270.00	127.27	44.26	36.01	8.25	16.85	14.33	17.36	28.42
Detroit, Mich.[1]	1,317.53	444.01	195.54	158.33	12.77	24.44	222.00	160.47	70.25	63.09	7.16	18.69	17.48	19.71	31.26
Scranton, Pa.	1,312.39	448.54	188.51	148.67	13.69	26.15	276.00	146.33	50.70	36.60	14.10	21.61	19.25	19.99	31.73
Cincinnati, Ohio[1]	1,311.74	448.74	185.37	145.25	13.51	26.61	256.80	138.90	50.21	46.46	3.75	20.02	14.37	19.39	31.83
Pittsburgh, Pa.	1,310.52	447.52	184.21	146.88	13.38	23.94	246.00	126.59	36.85	31.85	5.00	16.85	18.65	17.49	29.21
Los Angeles, Calif.[1]	1,308.11	442.07	206.36	167.23	12.43	26.70	198.00	156.73	49.63	38.12	11.52	35.98	14.48	21.33	32.23
Newark, N. J.	1,300.86	474.63	170.13	133.30	11.44	25.39	258.00	160.88	65.40	53.00	12.40	19.44	25.37	17.62	29.99
Baltimore, Md.	1,300.65	452.65	170.27	134.93	11.76	23.58	228.00	142.86	58.71	50.16	8.55	17.89	15.05	18.32	29.85
Albuquerque, N. Mex.[1]	1,299.14	485.68	192.62	147.94	16.26	28.42	232.20	173.40	48.37	37.66	10.71	35.14	24.53	23.47	34.01
Philadelphia, Pa.	1,297.69	447.68	175.62	140.11	11.64	23.87	240.00	138.15	55.62	47.52	8.10	12.96	18.05	18.93	29.54
Bridgeport, Conn.	1,296.35	487.51	181.43	143.14	12.58	25.72	234.00	157.96	72.37	59.32	13.05	19.44	15.77	18.41	28.93
Sioux Falls, S. Dak.	1,290.60	423.75	190.77	152.36	15.07	23.34	271.20	208.08	101.95	92.45	9.50	19.44	20.45	21.04	30.15
Rochester, N. Y.	1,287.63	442.76	181.09	141.56	14.88	24.65	225.00	180.99	92.75	83.75	9.00	18.14	19.85	16.79	30.41
Tucson, Ariz.[1]	1,287.25	464.09	188.98	145.25	17.17	26.56	222.00	179.73	51.69	30.62	21.08	47.50	21.89	23.93	31.64
Butte, Mont.	1,283.69	448.69	214.54	163.40	21.82	29.32	210.00	184.39	79.13	70.63	8.50	19.44	23.33	23.18	36.27
Portland, Maine	1,275.48	450.60	198.44	156.53	16.50	25.41	204.00	185.00	82.50	68.75	13.75	18.40	21.53	19.87	32.15
Peoria, Ill.[1]	1,274.30	448.89	189.21	150.91	12.73	25.58	274.28	130.76	40.69	30.49	10.20	19.83	18.41	18.12	30.63

Fall River, Mass	1,271.51	453.80	191.48	154.31	12.55	24.62	222.00	176.18	76.60	65.00	11.60	19.44	23.33	18.98	34.78
Atlanta, Ga	1,268.22	463.10	169.33	134.71	11.10	23.52	246.00	136.46	44.90	33.00	11.90	22.73	17.57	16.49	31.73
Richmond, Va	1,268.06	447.07	190.97	153.68	13.50	23.80	235.92	154.38	55.38	39.00	16.38	27.27	17.81	16.77	34.10
Buffalo, N. Y	1,261.21	441.80	184.95	147.88	13.27	23.80	210.00	150.46	65.18	61.93	3.25	19.44	13.85	17.94	31.00
Omaha, Nebr	1,258.26	443.61	184.46	145.79	14.34	24.33	238.20	150.13	68.23	60.88	7.35	14.19	16.49	18.19	28.99
Manchester, N. H	1,254.03	463.69	181.65	142.54	15.03	24.09	186.00	179.98	85.30	72.50	12.80	19.44	23.33	18.80	30.06
Norfolk, Va	1,251.38	455.96	175.46	138.70	13.57	23.19	238.00	149.70	58.52	43.40	15.12	23.63	17.81	17.29	29.39
Denver, Colo.[1]	1,246.07	434.93	182.40	144.93	13.96	23.51	204.00	142.54	52.27	43.09	9.18	15.86	18.17	19.91	31.76
Kansas City, Mo	1,245.42	448.29	180.96	147.19	11.64	22.12	198.00	132.08	47.20	40.75	6.45	15.03	18.53	16.34	28.93
Providence, R. I	1,245.26	459.55	170.82	134.47	12.67	23.69	216.00	169.12	74.50	63.00	11.50	15.94	22.85	19.49	30.29
Binghamton, N. Y	1,243.19	446.83	180.36	143.67	12.43	24.26	228.00	154.91	59.95	50.00	9.95	19.44	22.97	17.71	31.80
Salt Lake City, Utah [1]	1,243.07	432.04	199.74	159.27	15.91	24.57	195.00	165.21	60.89	51.71	9.18	22.80	22.57	20.78	35.09
Seattle, Wash	1,233.35	442.77	193.22	151.59	15.50	26.13	168.00	164.96	57.22	38.32	18.90	36.36	15.05	21.57	31.71
New Orleans, La	1,233.08	432.29	172.79	137.19	12.01	23.60	198.00	131.70	33.73	23.38	10.35	23.40	25.01	17.20	29.31
Spokane, Wash	1,228.62	426.71	206.96	160.85	17.65	28.47	174.00	180.49	69.02	50.12	18.90	22.68	16.49	22.98	34.27
Winston-Salem, N. C.[1]	1,222.18	456.34	179.29	141.16	12.47	25.66	208.92	163.13	62.85	40.17	22.68	28.09	21.09	17.30	30.72
Portland, Oreg	1,221.72	435.93	203.75	162.61	15.11	26.03	158.40	164.87	49.79	33.90	15.89	36.36	16.49	22.24	30.94
Memphis, Tenn	1,221.40	433.22	173.15	134.65	13.18	25.32	222.00	132.07	41.85	31.84	10.01	23.63	16.49	16.15	30.89
Louisville, Ky.[1]	1,220.20	443.43	178.84	142.79	12.24	23.81	209.80	133.28	50.31	46.19	4.12	16.69	15.50	17.50	30.20
Oklahoma City, Okla.[1]	1,217.80	441.03	183.20	143.25	12.58	27.37	205.20	145.46	39.54	36.36	3.18	27.54	20.78	18.25	28.29
Jacksonville, Fla	1,217.27	458.67	172.96	137.46	13.48	22.01	198.00	153.86	58.43	24.95	33.48	23.40	20.57	16.25	32.16
Houston, Tex	1,209.96	431.07	181.12	143.23	14.34	23.54	210.00	123.98	27.16	16.81	10.35	30.42	15.17	16.98	31.19
Indianapolis, Ind	1,198.08	419.64	177.45	135.41	14.44	27.60	201.00	140.09	55.48	46.93	8.55	17.37	17.09	17.79	29.32
Columbia, S. C	1,192.60	480.26	166.80	130.97	11.74	24.09	198.00	151.76	44.18	19.88	24.30	35.10	19.85	16.10	33.48
Clarksburg, W. Va.[1]	1,190.02	464.41	184.76	147.93	12.33	24.50	192.00	126.53	25.37	22.87	2.50	19.83	19.28	19.95	33.04
Dallas, Tex	1,188.97	451.62	162.09	127.61	12.42	22.05	216.00	125.49	28.18	16.93	11.25	29.02	16.49	19.79	28.97
Cedar Rapids, Iowa [1]	1,186.18	418.28	188.08	148.59	14.59	24.90	201.43	166.87	76.96	66.76	10.20	16.43	18.17	19.39	31.60
Columbus, Ohio [1]	1,178.70	444.25	186.04	148.93	12.17	24.94	192.00	128.21	41.91	39.16	2.75	20.02	12.33	18.55	32.31
Birmingham, Ala	1,168.85	446.74	170.87	134.96	12.38	23.53	167.04	128.13	38.40	28.32	10.08	22.73	17.93	17.63	28.40
Knoxville, Tenn	1,166.75	423.23	171.71	136.68	13.12	21.91	205.80	138.14	48.66	27.24	21.42	18.18	17.57	17.69	32.99
El Paso, Tex	1,153.58	441.09	167.67	132.36	12.53	22.78	195.00	156.10	54.61	42.50	12.11	22.36	23.33	20.05	30.20
Little Rock, Ark	1,139.06	443.99	172.56	135.34	13.71	23.52	174.00	125.29	32.35	25.00	7.35	18.18	23.81	18.02	29.88
Wichita, Kans	1,131.30	426.97	174.32	140.56	12.40	21.36	165.00	146.53	59.86	54.86	5.00	15.55	19.37	18.02	29.23
Mobile, Ala	1,129.81	433.40	165.00	128.79	13.21	23.01	163.44	142.22	41.76	21.96	19.80	30.42	17.57	18.39	31.03

See footnotes at end of table.

Table 2.—Annual Costs of Living, by Major Budget Groups and Principal Subgroups, 4-Person Manual Worker's Family, 59 Cities, March 1935—Continued

MAINTENANCE LEVEL—continued

City	Household operation—Continued		Miscellaneous												
							Recreation						Taxes [3]		
	Refuse disposal	Unspecified essentials [2]	Total	Medical care	Transportation	School attendance	Total	Newspapers	Motion picture theater admissions	Organizations, tobacco, and toys [2]	Life insurance [2]	Church contributions and other contributions [2]	Total	Personal property	Capitation
Average, 59 cities	[4] $1.50	$3.06	$252.67	$52.32	$53.96	[5] $6.87	$75.18	$10.84	$33.80	$30.55	$46.40	$15.40	[6] $2.54	[7] $1.10	[8] $1.44
Washington, D. C	([9])	3.05	270.34	58.91	71.44	1.35	76.84	7.80	38.64	30.40	46.40	15.40	([10])	([10])	([10])
San Francisco, Calif.[1]	7.20	3.08	272.27	64.28	50.78	8.47	86.94	13.80	42.22	30.92	46.40	15.40	([10])	([10])	([10])
Minneapolis, Minn	3.50	3.05	286.42	54.12	91.85	6.25	72.39	8.40	33.59	30.40	46.40	15.40	([10])	([10])	([10])
New York, N. Y.[1]	([9])	3.07	269.38	56.29	71.42	1.45	78.41	8.84	38.75	30.82	46.40	15.40	([10])	([10])	([10])
Chicago, Ill.[1]	([9])	3.07	298.21	57.42	93.31	3.04	80.84	11.44	38.58	30.82	46.40	15.40	1.81	1.81	([10])
Milwaukee, Wis	([9])	3.05	275.05	44.51	76.14	11.28	78.19	14.56	33.23	30.40	46.40	15.40	3.14	3.14	([10])
Boston, Mass	([9])	3.05	267.00	55.36	61.74	1.88	84.22	14.56	39.26	30.40	46.40	15.40	2.00	([10])	2.00
Cleveland, Ohio [1]	([9])	3.09	316.41	59.21	101.52	10.50	83.39	14.56	37.80	31.02	46.40	15.40	([10])	([10])	([10])
St. Louis, Mo	3.00	3.05	314.32	49.54	118.44	([9])	81.77	13.20	38.17	30.40	46.40	15.40	2.77	2.77	([10])
Detroit, Mich.[1]	([9])	3.09	295.51	58.34	82.08	14.06	79.23	13.00	35.20	31.02	46.40	15.40	([10])	([10])	([10])
Scranton, Pa	([9])	3.05	253.01	58.01	40.26	.65	83.35	11.44	41.51	30.40	46.40	15.40	8.94	([10])	8.94
Cincinnati, Ohio [1]	([9])	3.09	281.93	41.82	94.60	4.07	79.64	11.44	37.18	31.02	46.40	15.40	([10])	([10])	([10])
Pittsburgh, Pa	4.50	3.05	306.20	54.52	106.26	([9])	81.62	14.56	36.66	30.40	46.40	15.40	2.00	([10])	2.00
Los Angeles, Calif.[1]	([9])	3.08	304.95	60.08	101.30	2.49	79.27	10.60	37.75	30.92	46.40	15.40	([10])	([10])	([10])
Newark, N. J	([9])	3.05	237.22	51.94	37.75	4.00	80.74	14.56	35.78	30.40	46.40	15.40	1.00	([10])	1.00
Baltimore, Md	([9])	3.05	306.87	44.04	115.49	1.69	83.86	11.44	42.02	30.40	46.40	15.40	([10])	([10])	([10])
Albuquerque, N. Mex.[1]	4.80	3.07	215.24	57.56	12.67	9.40	73.82	7.80	35.20	30.82	46.40	15.40	([10])	([10])	([10])
Philadelphia, Pa	([9])	3.05	296.25	43.02	106.06	1.00	84.38	11.44	42.54	30.40	46.40	15.40	([10])	([10])	([10])
Bridgeport, Conn	([9])	3.05	235.45	56.15	43.74	.72	73.04	8.84	33.80	30.40	46.40	15.40	([10])	([10])	([10])
Sioux Falls, S. Dak	12.00	3.05	196.81	51.41	10.94	([9])	71.06	8.84	31.82	30.40	46.40	15.40	1.60	1.60	([10])
Rochester, N. Y	([9])	3.05	257.79	52.83	63.90	5.65	73.61	10.92	32.29	30.40	46.40	15.40	([10])	([10])	([10])
Tucson, Ariz.[1]	([9])	3.07	232.45	61.31	12.33	8.14	82.66	10.40	41.55	30.71	46.40	15.40	6.22	6.22	([10])
Butte, Mont	([9])	3.05	226.07	62.84	10.82	6.50	78.11	11.96	35.75	30.40	46.40	15.40	6.00	2.00	4.00
Portland, Maine	7.50	3.05	237.44	58.85	28.51	6.06	74.86	13.00	31.46	30.40	46.40	15.40	7.36	4.36	3.00
Peoria, Ill.[1]	([9])	3.07	231.16	43.89	29.76	18.56	73.35	10.40	32.14	30.82	46.40	15.40	3.80	3.80	([10])

Fall River, Mass.	(9)	3.05	228.05	51.24	31.46	(9)	77.36	11.44	35.52	30.40	46.40	15.40	6.20	4.20	2.00
Atlanta, Ga.	(9)	3.05	253.34	53.48	52.49	7.13	70.44	10.40	29.64	30.40	46.40	15.40	8.00	3.00	5.00
Richmond, Va.	(9)	3.05	239.72	51.23	39.92	7.75	73.82	7.80	35.62	30.40	46.40	15.40	5.20	2.20	3.00
Buffalo, N. Y.	(9)	3.05	274.00	50.75	89.28	2.04	70.13	11.44	28.29	30.40	46.40	15.40	(10)	(10)	(10)
Omaha, Nebr.	1.00	3.05	241.85	48.01	58.32	4.32	69.40	10.40	28.60	30.40	46.40	15.40	(10)	(10)	(10)
Manchester, N. H.	(9)	3.05	242.71	49.89	39.69	1.00	83.13	11.44	41.29	30.40	46.40	15.40	7.20	3.20	4.00
Norfolk, Va.	(9)	3.05	232.27	51.06	35.82	5.11	72.68	10.40	31.88	30.40	46.40	15.40	5.80	2.80	3.00
Denver, Colo.[1]	1.50	3.07	282.20	56.52	74.84	7.78	81.26	13.00	37.44	30.82	46.40	15.40	(10)	(10)	(10)
Kansas City, Mo.	3.00	3.05	286.10	51.35	95.63	11.37	62.33	7.80	24.13	30.40	46.40	15.40	3.62	3.62	(10)
Providence, R. I.	3.00	3.05	229.76	54.78	41.33	1.56	67.84	11.44	26.00	30.40	46.40	15.40	2.45	2.45	(10)
Binghamton, N. Y.	(9)	3.05	233.09	55.93	11.68	16.50	87.18	14.56	42.22	30.40	46.40	15.40	(10)	(10)	(10)
Salt Lake City, Utah[1]	(9)	3.07	251.09	56.65	53.95	1.02	73.23	10.80	31.62	30.82	46.40	15.40	4.44	4.44	(10)
Seattle, Wash.	(9)	3.05	264.40	51.82	75.47	1.63	73.67	10.20	33.07	30.40	46.40	15.40	(10)	(10)	(10)
New Orleans, La.	(9)	3.05	298.30	52.46	97.78	3.80	79.02	8.84	39.78	30.40	46.40	15.40	3.45	3.45	(10)
Spokane, Wash.	12.00	3.05	240.46	66.10	41.21	4.29	67.06	10.40	26.26	30.40	46.40	15.40	(10)	(10)	(10)
Winston-Salem, N. C.[1]	(9)	3.09	214.50	51.95	20.97	10.32	68.46	10.40	27.04	31.02	46.40	15.40	1.00	(10)	1.00
Portland, Oreg.	6.00	3.05	258.77	49.56	69.94	8.48	68.98	10.40	28.18	30.40	46.40	15.40	(10)	(10)	(10)
Memphis, Tenn.	(9)	3.05	260.97	53.29	61.24	7.50	73.14	10.40	32.34	30.40	46.40	15.40	4.00	(10)	4.00
Louisville, Ky.[1]	(9)	3.09	254.85	40.71	59.55	11.66	78.97	10.40	37.54	31.02	46.40	15.40	2.16	2.16	(10)
Oklahoma City, Okla.[1]	8.00	3.06	242.92	50.71	39.53	11.50	79.38	13.00	35.78	30.61	46.40	15.40	(10)	(10)	(10)
Jacksonville, Fla.	(9)	3.05	233.78	57.26	30.91	7.00	74.81	10.40	34.01	30.40	46.40	15.40	2.00	(10)	2.00
Houston, Tex.	(9)	3.05	263.80	52.78	66.68	9.73	69.82	9.36	30.06	30.40	46.40	15.40	3.00	(10)	3.00
Indianapolis, Ind.	(9)	3.05	259.90	43.52	65.21	9.40	74.39	13.00	30.99	30.40	46.40	15.40	5.58	2.58	3.00
Columbia, S. C.	(9)	3.05	195.79	40.94	8.75	11.14	71.17	10.40	30.37	30.40	46.40	15.40	2.00	(10)	2.00
Clarksburg, W. Va.[1]	6.00	3.07	222.32	55.32	9.20	21.19	69.82	10.40	28.60	30.82	46.40	15.40	5.00	(10)	5.00
Dallas, Tex.	(9)	3.05	233.77	49.51	35.96	12.25	70.75	7.80	32.55	30.40	46.40	15.40	3.50	(10)	3.50
Cedar Rapids, Iowa[1]	1.25	3.07	211.53	45.86	24.84	4.86	70.18	10.40	28.96	30.82	46.40	15.40	4.00	(10)	4.00
Columbus, Ohio[1]	(9)	3.09	228.20	45.78	44.46	8.94	67.22	8.32	27.87	31.02	46.40	15.40	(10)	(10)	(10)
Birmingham, Ala.	(9)	3.05	256.06	47.78	61.49	10.25	71.74	10.40	30.94	30.40	46.40	15.40	3.00	(10)	3.00
Knoxville, Tenn.	(9)	3.05	227.89	50.25	32.14	8.50	68.46	10.40	27.66	30.40	46.40	15.40	6.73	2.73	4.00
El Paso, Tex.	2.50	3.05	193.72	38.46	17.11	1.94	70.91	7.80	32.71	30.40	46.40	15.40	3.50	(10)	3.50
Little Rock, Ark.	(9)	3.05	223.22	53.55	16.46	13.17	70.11	9.60	30.11	30.40	46.40	15.40	8.13	2.13	6.00
Wichita, Kans.	1.45	3.05	218.49	50.08	26.24	14.50	65.86	7.80	27.66	30.40	46.40	15.40	(10)	(10)	(10)
Mobile, Ala.	(9)	3.05	225.75	51.84	20.93	20.51	67.22	10.40	26.42	30.40	46.40	15.40	3.45	.45	3.00

[1] Include sales tax where levied (appendix table 15).
[2] Budget allowance identical in all cities, plus sales tax where levied.
[3] Exclusive of sales tax.
[4] Though only 18 cities had a direct charge for refuse disposal, an average for 59 cities is used in order to balance the table. The 18-city average is $4.90.
[5] Though only 55 cities had a direct charge for school attendance, an average for 59 cities is used in order to balance the table. The 55-city average is $7.37.
[6] Though taxes were payable in only 36 cities, an average for 59 cities is used in order to balance the table. The 36-city average is $4.17.
[7] Though personal property taxes were payable in only 22 cities, an average for 59 cities is used in order to balance the table. The 22-city average is $2.96.
[8] Though capitation taxes were payable in only 25 cities, an average for 59 cities is used in order to balance the table. The 25-city average is $3.40.
[9] Not a direct charge. [10] None payable.

NOTE.—Owing to the necessity for rounding numbers in computing averages, there are slight discrepancies between certain totals and the sums of their component items.

Table 3.—Relative Costs [1] of Living, by Major Budget Groups and Principal Subgroups, 4-Person Manual Worker's Family, 59 Cities, March 1935

MAINTENANCE LEVEL

City	Total cost of living	Food	Clothing, clothing upkeep, and personal care				Housing, including water	Household operation							
			Total	Clothing	Clothing upkeep	Personal care		Total	Fuel			Ice	Electricity	Household supplies	Furniture, furnishings, and household equipment
									Total	Coal or wood	Gas				
Average, 59 cities:															
Amount	$1,260.62	$448.18	$184.35	$145.93	$13.55	$24.87	$221.89	$153.54	$57.98	$47.00	$10.98	$22.40	$18.68	$18.82	$31.10
Percent	100.0	100.0	100.0	100.0	100.0	100.0	100.0	100.0	100.0	100.0	100.0	100.0	100.0	100.0	100.0
Washington, D. C.	112.2	106.3	97.2	97.4	95.8	97.0	154.1	95.5	111.5	120.9	71.5	86.8	64.5	92.0	96.8
San Francisco, Calif.[1]	110.3	102.5	113.2	113.3	103.3	117.9	121.7	117.0	82.9	74.5	118.9	214.2	99.4	118.6	104.2
Minneapolis, Minn.	110.1	97.4	107.7	109.4	116.7	92.6	119.0	131.6	186.8	216.3	60.1	81.0	101.1	97.6	102.6
New York, N. Y.[1]	109.1	106.5	93.7	93.9	80.2	99.4	135.2	101.5	114.2	118.4	96.2	88.5	118.2	91.1	88.5
Chicago, Ill.[1]	107.6	103.1	104.9	105.3	92.0	110.0	108.2	105.7	127.3	145.1	51.1	88.5	95.9	92.7	97.3
Milwaukee, Wis.	107.4	95.0	111.8	112.1	105.5	113.6	121.7	114.9	160.1	181.1	70.6	57.9	97.9	91.1	103.5
Boston, Mass.	107.3	104.5	102.5	102.8	96.2	104.7	119.0	107.0	120.9	127.1	94.3	86.8	106.3	105.3	102.9
Cleveland, Ohio[1]	107.0	99.2	114.4	115.4	99.4	117.2	105.5	92.8	101.9	117.8	34.2	77.5	59.6	103.1	104.4
St. Louis, Mo.	106.3	100.1	97.4	98.7	84.5	96.4	121.7	82.9	76.3	76.6	75.1	75.2	76.7	92.2	91.4
Detroit, Mich.[1]	104.5	99.1	106.1	108.5	94.3	98.3	100.0	104.5	121.2	134.2	65.2	83.4	93.6	104.7	100.5
Scranton, Pa.	104.1	100.1	102.3	101.9	101.0	105.1	124.4	95.3	87.4	77.9	128.4	96.5	103.0	106.2	102.0
Cincinnati, Ohio[1]	104.1	100.1	100.6	99.5	99.7	107.0	115.7	90.5	86.6	98.9	34.2	89.4	76.9	103.0	102.3
Pittsburgh, Pa.	104.0	99.9	99.9	100.7	98.7	96.3	110.9	82.4	63.6	67.8	45.5	75.2	99.8	92.9	93.9
Los Angeles, Calif.[1]	103.8	98.6	111.9	114.6	91.7	107.4	89.2	102.1	85.6	81.1	104.9	160.6	77.5	113.3	103.6
Newark, N. J.	103.2	105.9	92.3	91.3	84.4	102.1	116.3	104.8	112.8	112.8	112.9	86.8	135.8	93.6	96.4
Baltimore, Md.	103.2	101.0	92.4	92.5	86.8	94.8	102.8	93.0	101.3	106.7	77.9	79.8	80.6	97.3	96.0
Albuquerque, N. Mex.[1]	103.1	108.4	104.5	101.4	120.0	114.3	104.6	112.9	83.4	80.1	97.5	156.9	131.3	124.7	109.3
Philadelphia, Pa.	102.9	99.9	95.3	96.0	85.9	96.0	108.2	90.0	95.9	101.1	73.8	57.9	96.6	100.6	95.0
Bridgeport, Conn.	102.8	108.8	98.4	98.1	92.8	103.4	105.5	102.9	124.8	126.2	118.9	86.8	84.4	97.8	93.0
Sioux Falls, S. Dak.	102.4	94.5	103.5	104.4	111.2	93.9	122.2	135.5	175.8	196.7	86.5	86.8	109.5	111.8	96.9
Rochester, N. Y.	102.1	98.8	98.2	97.0	109.8	99.1	101.4	117.9	160.0	178.2	82.0	81.0	106.3	89.2	97.8
Tucson, Ariz.[1]	102.1	103.5	102.5	99.5	126.7	106.8	100.0	117.1	89.2	65.1	192.0	212.1	117.2	127.2	101.7
Butte, Mont.	101.8	100.1	116.4	112.0	161.0	117.9	94.6	120.1	136.5	150.3	77.4	86.8	124.9	123.1	116.6
Portland, Maine	101.2	100.5	107.6	107.3	121.8	102.2	91.9	120.5	142.3	146.3	125.2	82.2	115.2	105.6	103.4
Peoria, Ill.[1]	101.1	100.2	102.6	103.4	93.9	102.9	123.6	85.2	70.2	64.9	92.9	88.5	98.5	96.3	98.5

Fall River, Mass	100.9	101.3	103.9	105.7	92.6	99.0	100.0	114.7	132.1	138.3	105.6	86.8	124.9	100.8	111.8
Atlanta, Ga	100.6	103.3	91.9	92.3	81.9	94.6	110.9	88.9	77.4	70.2	108.4	101.5	94.0	87.6	102.0
Richmond, Va	100.6	99.8	103.6	105.3	99.6	95.7	106.3	100.5	95.5	83.0	149.2	121.7	95.3	89.1	109.6
Buffalo, N. Y	100.0	98.6	100.3	101.3	97.9	95.7	94.6	98.0	112.4	131.8	29.6	86.8	74.1	95.3	99.7
Omaha, Nebr	99.8	99.0	100.1	99.9	105.8	97.8	107.3	97.8	117.7	129.5	66.9	63.4	88.3	96.6	93.2
Manchester, N. H	99.5	103.5	98.5	97.7	110.9	96.9	83.8	117.2	147.1	154.3	116.6	86.8	124.9	99.9	96.6
Norfolk, Va	99.3	101.7	95.2	95.1	100.1	93.2	107.3	97.5	100.9	92.3	137.7	105.5	95.3	91.9	94.5
Denver, Colo.[1]	98.8	97.0	98.9	99.3	103.0	94.5	91.9	92.8	90.2	91.7	83.6	70.8	97.2	105.8	102.1
Kansas City, Mo	98.8	100.0	98.2	100.9	85.9	89.0	89.2	86.0	81.4	86.7	58.7	67.1	99.2	86.8	93.0
Providence, R. I	98.8	102.5	92.7	92.1	93.5	95.2	97.3	110.1	128.5	134.0	104.7	71.2	122.3	103.6	97.4
Binghamton, N. Y	98.6	99.7	97.8	98.5	91.7	97.6	102.8	100.9	103.4	106.4	90.6	86.8	123.0	94.1	102.2
Salt Lake City, Utah[1]	98.6	96.4	108.4	109.1	117.4	98.8	87.9	107.6	105.0	110.0	83.6	101.8	120.8	110.4	112.8
Seattle, Wash	97.8	98.8	104.8	103.9	114.4	105.1	75.7	107.4	98.7	81.5	172.1	162.3	80.6	114.6	101.9
New Orleans, La	97.8	96.5	93.7	94.0	88.6	94.9	89.2	85.8	58.2	49.7	94.3	104.5	133.9	91.4	94.2
Spokane, Wash	97.5	95.2	112.3	110.2	130.2	114.5	78.4	117.6	119.0	106.6	172.1	101.3	88.3	122.1	110.2
Winston-Salem, N. C.[1]	97.0	101.8	97.3	96.7	92.0	103.2	94.2	106.2	108.4	85.5	206.6	125.4	112.9	91.9	98.8
Portland, Oreg	96.9	97.3	110.5	111.4	111.5	104.7	71.4	107.4	85.9	72.1	144.7	162.3	88.3	118.2	99.5
Memphis, Tenn	96.9	96.7	93.9	92.3	97.2	101.8	100.0	86.0	72.2	67.7	91.2	105.5	88.3	85.8	99.3
Louisville, Ky.[1]	96.8	98.9	97.0	97.9	90.3	95.8	94.5	86.8	86.8	98.3	37.5	74.5	83.0	93.0	97.1
Oklahoma City, Okla.[1]	96.6	98.4	99.4	98.2	92.8	110.0	92.5	94.7	68.2	77.4	29.0	123.0	111.2	97.0	90.9
Jacksonville, Fla	96.6	102.3	93.8	94.2	99.5	88.5	89.2	100.2	100.8	53.1	304.9	104.5	110.1	86.3	103.4
Houston, Tex	96.0	96.2	98.2	98.2	105.8	94.7	94.6	80.7	46.8	35.8	94.3	135.8	81.2	90.2	100.3
Indianapolis, Ind	95.0	93.6	96.3	92.8	106.6	111.0	90.6	91.2	95.7	99.9	77.9	77.5	91.5	94.5	94.3
Columbia, S. C	94.6	107.2	90.5	89.8	86.6	96.9	89.2	98.8	76.2	42.3	221.3	156.7	106.3	85.6	107.6
Clarksburg, W. Va.[1]	94.4	103.6	100.2	101.4	91.0	98.5	86.5	82.4	43.8	48.7	22.8	88.5	103.2	106.0	106.2
Dallas, Tex	94.3	100.8	87.9	87.4	91.7	88.7	97.3	81.7	48.6	36.0	102.5	129.5	88.3	105.2	93.1
Cedar Rapids, Iowa[1]	94.1	93.3	102.0	101.8	107.7	100.1	90.8	108.7	132.7	142.0	92.9	73.3	97.2	103.0	101.6
Columbus, Ohio[1]	93.5	99.1	100.9	102.1	89.8	100.3	86.5	83.5	72.3	83.3	25.0	89.4	66.0	98.6	103.9
Birmingham, Ala	92.7	99.7	92.7	92.5	91.4	94.6	75.3	83.5	66.2	60.3	91.8	101.5	96.0	93.7	91.3
Knoxville, Tenn	92.6	94.4	93.1	93.7	96.8	88.1	92.7	90.0	83.9	58.0	195.1	81.2	94.0	94.0	106.1
El Paso, Tex	91.5	98.4	91.0	90.7	92.4	91.6	87.9	101.7	94.2	90.4	110.3	99.8	124.9	106.5	97.1
Little Rock, Ark	90.4	99.1	93.6	92.7	101.2	94.6	78.4	81.6	55.8	53.2	66.9	81.2	127.4	95.8	96.1
Wichita, Kans	89.7	95.3	94.6	96.3	91.5	85.9	74.4	95.4	103.2	116.7	45.5	69.4	103.7	95.8	94.0
Mobile, Ala	89.6	96.7	89.5	88.3	97.5	92.5	73.7	92.6	72.0	46.7	180.3	135.8	94.0	97.7	99.8

See footnotes at end of table.

Table 3.—Relative Costs of Living, by Major Budget Groups and Principal Subgroups, 4-Person Manual Worker's Family, 59 Cities, March 1935—Continued

MAINTENANCE LEVEL—continued

City	Household operation—Continued		Miscellaneous												
							Recreation						Taxes [3]		
	Refuse disposal	Unspecified essentials [2]	Total	Medical care	Transportation	School attendance	Total	Newspapers	Motion picture theater admissions	Organizations, tobacco, and toys [2]	Life insurance [2]	Church contributions and other contributions [2]	Total	Personal property	Capitation
Average, 59 cities:															
Amount	[4] $1.50	$3.06	$252.67	$52.32	$53.96	[5] $6.87	$75.18	$10.84	$33.80	$30.55	$46.40	$15.40	[6] $2.54	[7] $1.10	[8] $1.44
Percent	100.0	100.0	100.0	100.0	100.0	100.0	100.0	100.0	100.0	100.0	100.0	100.0	100.0	100.0	100.0
Washington, D. C.	[9]	99.7	107.0	112.6	132.4	19.7	102.2	72.0	114.3	99.5	100.0	100.0	[10]	[10]	[10]
San Francisco, Calif.[1]	480.0	100.7	107.8	122.9	94.1	123.3	115.7	127.4	124.9	101.2	100.0	100.0	[10]	[10]	[10]
Minneapolis, Minn.	233.3	99.7	113.4	103.5	170.2	91.0	96.3	77.5	99.4	99.5	100.0	100.0	[10]	[10]	[10]
New York, N. Y.[1]	[9]	100.3	106.6	107.6	132.4	21.2	104.3	81.6	114.6	100.9	100.0	100.0	[10]	[10]	[10]
Chicago, Ill.[1]	[9]	100.3	118.0	109.8	172.9	44.2	107.5	105.6	114.1	100.9	100.6	100.0	71.3	164.5	[10]
Milwaukee, Wis.	[9]	99.7	108.9	85.1	141.1	164.1	104.0	134.4	98.3	99.5	100.0	100.0	123.6	285.5	[10]
Boston, Mass.	[9]	99.7	105.7	105.8	114.4	27.4	112.0	134.4	116.2	99.5	100.0	100.0	78.7	[10]	138.9
Cleveland, Ohio [1]	[9]	101.0	125.2	113.2	188.1	152.7	110.9	134.4	111.8	101.5	100.0	100.0	[10]	[10]	[10]
St. Louis, Mo.	200.0	99.7	124.4	94.7	219.5	[9]	108.8	121.8	112.9	99.5	100.0	100.0	109.1	251.8	[10]
Detroit, Mich.[1]	[9]	101.0	117.0	111.5	152.1	204.7	105.4	120.0	104.1	101.5	100.0	100.0	[10]	[10]	[10]
Scranton, Pa.	[9]	99.7	100.1	110.9	74.6	9.5	110.9	105.6	122.8	99.5	100.0	100.0	352.0	[10]	620.8
Cincinnati, Ohio [1]	[9]	101.0	111.6	79.9	175.3	59.2	105.9	105.6	110.0	101.5	100.0	100.0	[10]	[10]	[10]
Pittsburgh, Pa.	300.0	99.7	121.2	104.2	196.9	[9]	108.6	134.4	108.5	99.5	100.0	100.0	78.7	[10]	138.9
Los Angeles, Calif.[1]	[9]	100.7	120.7	114.8	187.7	36.3	105.4	97.8	111.7	101.2	100.0	100.0	[10]	[10]	[10]
Newark, N. J.	[9]	99.7	93.9	99.3	70.0	58.2	107.4	134.4	105.9	99.5	100.0	100.0	39.4	[10]	69.4
Baltimore, Md.	[9]	99.7	121.5	84.2	214.0	24.6	111.5	105.6	124.3	99.5	100.0	100.0	[10]	[10]	[10]
Albuquerque, N. Mex.[1]	320.0	100.3	85.2	110.0	23.5	136.8	98.2	72.0	104.1	100.9	100.0	100.0	[10]	[10]	[10]
Philadelphia, Pa.	[9]	99.7	117.2	82.2	196.6	14.6	112.2	105.6	125.9	99.5	100.0	100.0	[10]	[10]	[10]
Bridgeport, Conn.	[9]	99.7	93.2	107.3	81.1	10.5	97.2	81.6	100.0	99.5	100.0	100.0	[10]	[10]	[10]
Sioux Falls, S. Dak.	800.0	99.7	77.9	98.3	20.3	[9]	94.5	81.6	94.1	99.5	100.0	100.0	63.0	145.5	[10]
Rochester, N. Y.	[9]	99.7	102.0	101.0	118.4	82.2	97.9	100.8	95.5	99.5	100.0	100.0	[10]	[10]	[10]
Tucson, Ariz.[1]	[9]	100.3	92.0	117.2	22.9	118.4	110.0	96.0	122.9	100.5	100.0	100.0	244.9	565.5	[10]
Butte, Mont.	[9]	99.7	89.5	120.1	20.1	94.6	103.9	110.4	105.8	99.5	100.0	100.0	236.2	181.8	277.8
Portland, Maine	500.0	99.7	94.0	112.5	52.8	88.2	99.6	120.0	93.1	99.5	100.0	100.0	289.8	396.4	208.3
Peoria, Ill.[1]	[9]	100.3	91.5	83.9	55.2	270.2	97.6	96.0	95.1	100.9	100.0	100.0	149.6	345.5	[10]

Fall River, Mass.	(9)	99.7	90.3	97.9	58.3	(9)	102.9	105.6	105.1	99.5	100.0	100.0	244.1	381.8	138.9
Atlanta, Ga.	(9)	99.7	100.3	102.2	97.3	103.8	93.7	96.0	87.7	99.5	100.0	100.0	315.0	272.7	347.2
Richmond, Va.	(9)	99.7	94.9	97.9	74.0	112.8	98.2	72.0	105.4	99.5	100.0	100.0	204.7	200.0	208.3
Buffalo, N. Y.	(9)	99.7	108.4	97.0	165.5	29.7	93.3	105.6	83.7	99.5	100.0	100.0	(10)	(10)	(10)
Omaha, Nebr.	66.7	99.7	95.7	91.8	108.1	62.9	92.3	96.0	84.6	99.5	100.0	100.0	(10)	(10)	(10)
Manchester, N. H.	(9)	99.7	96.1	95.4	73.6	14.6	110.6	105.6	122.2	99.5	100.0	100.0	283.5	290.9	277.8
Norfolk, Va.	(9)	99.7	91.9	97.6	66.4	74.4	96.7	96.0	94.3	99.5	100.0	100.0	228.3	254.5	208.3
Denver, Colo.[1]	100.0	100.3	111.7	108.0	138.7	113.2	108.1	120.0	110.8	100.9	100.0	100.0	(10)	(10)	(10)
Kansas City, Mo.	200.0	99.7	113.2	98.1	177.2	165.5	82.9	72.0	71.4	99.5	100.0	100.0	142.5	329.1	(10)
Providence, R. I.	200.0	99.7	90.9	104.7	76.6	22.7	90.2	105.6	76.9	99.5	100.0	100.0	96.5	222.7	(10)
Binghamton, N. Y.	(9)	99.7	92.3	106.9	21.6	240.2	116.0	134.4	124.9	99.5	100.0	100.0	(10)	(10)	(10)
Salt Lake City, Utah[1]	(9)	100.3	99.4	108.3	100.0	14.8	97.4	99.7	93.6	100.9	100.0	100.0	174.8	403.6	(10)
Seattle, Wash.	(9)	99.7	104.6	99.1	139.9	23.7	98.0	94.1	97.8	99.5	100.0	100.0	(10)	(10)	(10)
New Orleans, La.	(9)	99.7	118.1	100.3	181.2	55.3	105.1	81.6	117.7	99.5	100.0	100.0	135.8	313.6	(10)
Spokane, Wash.	800.0	99.7	95.2	126.3	76.4	62.4	89.2	96.0	77.7	99.5	100.0	100.0	(10)	(10)	(10)
Winston-Salem, N. C.[1]	(9)	101.0	84.9	99.3	38.9	150.2	91.1	96.0	80.0	101.5	100.0	100.0	39.4	(10)	69.4
Portland, Oreg.	400.0	99.7	102.4	94.7	129.6	123.5	91.8	96.0	83.4	99.5	100.0	100.0	(10)	(10)	(10)
Memphis, Tenn.	(9)	99.7	103.3	101.9	113.5	109.2	97.3	96.0	95.7	99.5	100.0	100.0	157.5	(10)	277.8
Louisville, Ky.[1]	(9)	101.0	100.9	77.8	110.4	169.7	105.0	96.0	111.1	101.5	100.0	100.0	85.0	196.4	(10)
Oklahoma City, Okla.[1]	533.3	100.0	96.1	96.9	73.3	167.4	105.6	120.0	105.9	100.2	100.0	100.0	(10)	(10)	(10)
Jacksonville, Fla.	(9)	99.7	92.5	109.5	57.3	101.9	99.5	96.0	100.6	99.5	100.0	100.0	78.7	(10)	138.9
Houston, Tex.	(9)	99.7	104.4	100.9	123.6	141.6	92.9	86.4	88.9	99.5	100.0	100.0	118.1	(10)	208.3
Indianapolis, Ind.	(9)	99.7	102.9	83.2	120.8	136.8	99.0	120.0	91.7	99.5	100.0	100.0	219.7	234.5	208.3
Columbia, S. C.	(9)	99.7	77.5	78.2	16.2	162.1	94.7	96.0	89.9	99.5	100.0	100.0	78.7	(10)	138.9
Clarksburg, W. Va.[1]	400.0	100.3	88.0	105.7	17.0	308.4	92.9	96.0	84.6	100.9	100.0	100.0	196.9	(10)	347.2
Dallas, Tex.	(9)	99.7	92.5	94.6	66.6	178.3	94.1	72.0	96.3	99.5	100.0	100.0	137.8	(10)	243.1
Cedar Rapids, Iowa[1]	83.3	100.3	83.7	87.6	46.0	70.7	93.4	96.0	85.7	100.9	100.0	100.0	157.5	(10)	277.8
Columbus, Ohio[1]	(9)	101.0	90.3	87.5	82.4	130.2	89.4	76.8	82.5	101.5	100.0	100.0	(10)	(10)	(10)
Birmingham, Ala.	(9)	99.7	101.3	91.3	114.0	149.2	95.4	96.0	91.5	99.5	100.0	100.0	118.1	(10)	208.3
Knoxville, Tenn.	(9)	99.7	90.2	96.1	59.6	123.7	91.1	96.0	81.8	99.5	100.0	100.0	265.0	248.2	277.8
El Paso, Tex.	166.7	99.7	76.7	73.5	31.7	28.2	94.3	72.0	96.8	99.5	100.0	100.0	137.8	(10)	243.1
Little Rock, Ark.	(9)	99.7	88.3	102.4	30.5	191.7	93.3	88.6	89.1	99.5	100.0	100.0	320.1	193.6	416.7
Wichita, Kans.	96.7	99.7	86.5	95.7	48.6	211.1	87.6	72.0	81.8	99.5	100.0	100.0	(10)	(10)	(10)
Mobile, Ala.	(9)	99.7	89.3	99.1	38.8	298.5	89.4	96.0	78.2	99.5	100.0	100.0	135.8	40.9	208.3

[1] Include sales tax where levied (appendix table 15).
[2] Budget allowance identical in all cities, plus sales tax where levied.
[3] Exclusive of sales tax.
[4] Though only 18 cities had a direct charge for refuse disposal, an average for 59 cities is used in order to balance the table. The 18-city average is $4.90.
[5] Though only 55 cities had a direct charge for school attendance, an average for 59 cities is used in order to balance the table. The 55-city average is $7.37.
[6] Though taxes were payable in only 36 cities, an average for 59 cities is used in order to balance the table. The 36-city average is $4.17.
[7] Though personal property taxes were payable in only 22 cities, an average for 59 cities is used in order to balance the table. The 22-city average is $2.96.
[8] Though capitation taxes were payable in only 25 cities, an average for 59 cities is used in order to balance the table. The 25-city average is $3.40.
[9] Not a direct charge.
[10] None payable.

NOTE.—Owing to the necessity for rounding numbers in computing averages, there are slight discrepancies between certain totals and the sums of their component items.

Table 4.—Annual Costs[1] of Living, by Major Budget Groups and Principal Subgroups, in 9 Geographic Divisions, 4-Person Manual Worker's Family, 59 Cities, March 1935

MAINTENANCE LEVEL

Budget group	Average, 59 cities	Geographic division								
		New England	Middle Atlantic	East North Central	West North Central	South Atlantic	East South Central	West South Central	Mountain	Pacific
Total cost of living	$1, 260. 62	$1, 282. 57	$1, 298. 58	$1, 292. 27	$1, 262. 73	$1, 258. 32	$1, 181. 40	$1, 190. 41	$1, 271. 84	$1, 276. 33
Food	448. 18	463. 93	453. 37	442. 21	435. 16	461. 65	436. 00	440. 18	453. 08	441. 37
Clothing, clothing upkeep, and personal care	184. 35	185. 48	179. 69	193. 02	185. 23	176. 56	171. 91	173. 24	195. 66	203. 78
Clothing	145. 93	146. 82	142. 39	153. 05	148. 31	140. 19	135. 57	136. 50	152. 16	161. 52
Clothing upkeep	13. 55	13. 73	12. 70	13. 23	13. 62	12. 55	12. 82	12. 93	17. 02	14. 94
Personal care	24. 87	24. 93	24. 60	26. 74	23. 29	23. 83	23. 52	23. 81	26. 48	27. 33
Housing, including water	221. 89	221. 00	247. 88	236. 26	229. 69	231. 87	193. 62	199. 70	212. 64	193. 68
Household operation	153. 54	172. 09	151. 77	147. 48	161. 87	147. 26	134. 77	134. 67	169. 05	169. 33
Fuel	57. 98	76. 90	61. 58	60. 54	72. 39	52. 55	44. 20	35. 93	58. 47	54. 75
Coal or wood	47. 00	64. 72	52. 54	54. 35	64. 77	36. 69	31. 11	26. 83	46. 74	39. 10
Gas	10. 98	12. 18	9. 05	6. 19	7. 62	15. 86	13. 09	9. 10	11. 73	15. 65
Ice	22. 40	18. 68	18. 46	18. 26	16. 52	24. 15	22. 33	25. 15	28. 15	35. 87
Electricity	18. 68	21. 11	20. 01	15. 88	18. 03	17. 90	17. 01	20. 76	22. 10	16. 21
Household supplies	18. 82	19. 23	17. 95	18. 45	18. 39	17. 31	17. 47	18. 38	22. 25	22. 09
Furniture, furnishings, and household equipment	31. 10	31. 37	30. 15	31. 28	29. 89	31. 62	30. 70	29. 64	33. 75	32. 31
Refuse disposal	[2] 1. 50	1. 75	. 56	(3)	3. 60	. 67	(3)	1. 75	1. 26	5. 04
Unspecified essentials [4]	3. 06	3. 05	3. 05	3. 07	3. 05	3. 06	3. 06	3. 05	3. 07	3. 06
Miscellaneous	252. 67	240. 07	265. 88	273. 30	250. 79	240. 99	245. 10	242. 62	241. 41	268. 17
Medical care	52. 32	54. 38	52. 91	49. 31	50. 05	51. 58	48. 78	49. 58	58. 97	58. 37
Transportation	53. 96	41. 08	65. 83	73. 39	60. 90	42. 78	47. 07	45. 59	32. 92	67. 74
School attendance	[5] 6. 87	1. 87	3. 91	9. 98	5. 90	8. 08	11. 68	8. 73	6. 57	5. 07
Recreation	75. 18	76. 74	79. 93	77. 03	70. 43	73. 54	71. 91	73. 33	77. 82	75. 18
Newspapers	10. 84	11. 79	12. 22	12. 09	9. 55	9. 94	10. 40	9. 40	10. 79	11. 08
Motion picture theater admissions	33. 80	34. 55	37. 26	34. 13	30. 42	33. 09	30. 98	33. 50	36. 31	33. 50
Organizations, tobacco, and toys [4]	30. 55	30. 40	30. 45	30. 82	30. 46	30. 52	30. 53	30. 44	30. 71	30. 61
Life insurance [4]	46. 40	46. 40	46. 40	46. 40	46. 40	46. 40	46. 40	46. 40	46. 40	46. 40
Church contributions and other contributions [4]	15. 40	15. 40	15. 40	15. 40	15. 40	15. 40	15. 40	15. 40	15. 40	15. 40
Taxes [6]	[7] 2. 54	4. 20	1. 49	1. 79	1. 71	3. 22	3. 87	3. 60	3. 33	(8)
Personal property	[9] 1. 10	2. 37	(8)	1. 41	1. 14	. 89	1. 07	. 93	2. 53	(8)
Capitation	[10] 1. 44	1. 83	1. 49	. 38	. 57	2. 33	2. 80	2. 67	. 80	(8)

[1] Include sales tax where levied (appendix table 15).

[2] Though only 18 cities had a direct charge for refuse disposal, an average for 59 cities is used in order to balance the table. The 18-city average is $4.90. The averages for the geographic divisions are based on the total number of cities in each division included in this study.

[3] Not a direct charge.

[4] Budget allowance identical in all cities, plus sales tax where levied.

[5] Though only 55 cities had a direct charge for school attendance, an average for 59 cities is used in order to balance the table. The 55-city average is $7.37. The averages for the geographic divisions are based on the total number of cities in each division included in this study.

[6] Exclusive of sales tax.

[7] Though taxes were payable in only 36 cities, an average for 59 cities is used in order to balance the table. The 36-city average is $4.17. The averages for the geographic divisions are based on the total number of cities in each division included in this study.

[8] None payable.

[9] Though personal property taxes were payable in only 22 cities, an average for 59 cities is used in order to balance the table. The 22-city average is $2.96. The averages for the geographic divisions are based on the total number of cities in each division included in this study.

[10] Though capitation taxes were payable in only 25 cities, an average for 59 cities is used in order to balance the table. The 25-city average is $3.40. The averages for the geographic divisions are based on the total number of cities in each division included in this study.

NOTE.—Owing to the necessity for rounding numbers in computing averages, there are slight discrepancies between certain totals and the sums of their component items.

Table 5.—Relative Costs [1] of Living, by Major Budget Groups and Principal Subgroups, in 9 Geographic Divisions, 4-Person Manual Worker's Family, 59 Cities, March 1935

MAINTENANCE LEVEL

Budget group	Average, 59 cities		Geographic division								
	Amount	Percent	New England	Middle Atlantic	East North Central	West North Central	South Atlantic	East South Central	West South Central	Mountain	Pacific
Total cost of living	$1,260.62	100.0	101.7	103.0	102.5	100.2	99.8	93.7	94.4	100.9	101.2
Food	448.18	100.0	103.5	101.2	98.7	97.1	103.0	97.3	98.2	101.1	98.5
Clothing, clothing upkeep, and personal care	184.35	100.0	100.6	97.5	104.7	100.5	95.8	93.3	94.0	106.1	110.5
Clothing	145.93	100.0	100.6	97.6	104.9	101.6	96.1	92.9	93.5	104.3	110.7
Clothing upkeep	13.55	100.0	101.3	93.7	97.6	100.5	92.6	94.6	95.4	125.6	110.2
Personal care	24.87	100.0	100.2	98.9	107.5	93.7	95.8	94.6	95.7	106.5	109.9
Housing, including water	221.89	100.0	99.6	111.7	106.5	103.5	104.5	87.3	90.0	95.8	87.3
Household operation	153.54	100.0	112.1	98.8	96.1	105.4	95.9	87.8	87.7	110.1	110.3
Fuel	57.98	100.0	132.6	106.2	104.4	124.9	90.6	76.2	62.0	100.8	94.4
Coal or wood	47.00	100.0	137.7	111.8	115.6	137.8	78.1	66.2	57.1	99.4	83.2
Gas	10.98	100.0	110.9	82.4	56.4	69.4	144.4	119.2	82.9	106.8	142.5
Ice	22.40	100.0	83.4	82.4	81.5	73.7	107.8	99.7	112.3	125.7	160.1
Electricity	18.68	100.0	113.0	107.1	85.0	96.5	95.8	91.1	111.1	118.3	86.8
Household supplies	18.82	100.0	102.2	95.4	98.0	97.7	92.0	92.8	97.7	118.2	117.4
Furniture, furnishings, and household equipment	31.10	100.0	100.9	96.9	100.6	96.1	101.7	98.7	95.3	108.5	103.9
Refuse disposal	[2] 1.50	100.0	116.7	37.3	(3)	240.0	44.7	(3)	116.7	84.0	336.0
Unspecified essentials [4]	3.06	100.0	99.7	99.7	100.3	99.7	100.0	100.0	99.7	100.3	100.0
Miscellaneous	252.67	100.0	95.0	105.2	108.2	99.3	95.4	97.0	96.0	95.5	106.1
Medical care	52.32	100.0	103.9	101.1	94.3	95.7	98.6	93.2	94.8	112.7	111.6
Transportation	53.96	100.0	76.1	122.0	136.0	112.9	79.3	87.2	84.5	61.0	125.6
School attendance	[5] 6.87	100.0	27.2	56.9	145.3	85.9	117.5	170.1	127.1	95.6	73.8
Recreation	75.18	100.0	102.1	106.3	102.5	93.7	97.8	95.6	97.5	103.5	100.0
Newspapers	10.84	100.0	108.8	112.8	111.6	88.1	91.7	96.0	86.8	99.6	102.3
Motion picture theater admissions	33.80	100.0	102.2	110.2	100.9	90.0	97.9	91.7	99.1	107.4	99.1
Organizations, tobacco, and toys [4]	30.55	100.0	99.5	99.7	100.9	99.7	99.9	99.9	99.6	100.5	100.2
Life insurance [4]	46.40	100.0	100.0	100.0	100.0	100.0	100.0	100.0	100.0	100.0	100.0
Church contributions and other contributions [4]	15.40	100.0	100.0	100.0	100.0	100.0	100.0	100.0	100.0	100.0	100.0
Taxes [6]	[7] 2.54	100.0	165.4	58.7	70.5	67.3	126.8	152.4	141.7	131.1	(8)
Personal property	[9] 1.10	100.0	215.5	(8)	128.2	103.6	80.9	97.3	84.5	230.0	(8)
Capitation	[10] 1.44	100.0	127.1	103.5	26.4	39.6	161.8	194.4	185.4	55.6	(8)

[1] Include sales tax where levied (appendix table 15).

[2] Though only 18 cities had a direct charge for refuse disposal, an average for 59 cities is used in order to balance the table. The 18-city average is $4.90. The averages for the geographic divisions are based on the total number of cities in each division included in this study.

[3] Not a direct charge.

[4] Budget allowance identical in all cities, plus sales tax where levied.

[5] Though only 55 cities had a direct charge for school attendance, an average for 59 cities is used in order to balance the table. The 55-city average is $7.37. The averages for the geographic divisions are based on the total number of cities in each division included in this study.

[6] Exclusive of sales tax.

[7] Though taxes were payable in only 36 cities, an average for 59 cities is used in order to balance the table. The 36-city average is $4.17. The averages for the geographic divisions are based on the total number of cities in each division included in this study.

[8] None payable.

[9] Though personal property taxes were payable in only 22 cities, an average for 59 cities is used in order to balance the table. The 22-city average is $2.96. The averages for the geographic divisions are based on the total number of cities in each division included in this study.

[10] Though capitation taxes were payable in only 25 cities, an average for 59 cities is used in order to balance the table. The 25-city average is $3.40. The averages for the geographic divisions are based on the total number of cities in each division included in this study.

NOTE.—Owing to the necessity for rounding numbers in computing averages, there are slight discrepancies between certain totals and the sums of their component items.

***Table 6.*—Annual Costs [1] of Living, by Major Budget Groups and Principal Subgroups, in 5 Size of City Classifications, 4-Person Manual Worker's Family, 59 Cities, March 1935**

MAINTENANCE LEVEL

Budget group	Average, 59 cities	Size of city classification				
		1,000,000 or more	500,000 to 1,000,000	250,000 to 500,000	100,000 to 250,000	25,000 to 100,000
Total cost of living	$1,260.62	$1,330.92	$1,332.03	$1,251.68	$1,235.05	$1,230.25
Food	448.18	454.61	448.54	445.58	445.37	452.31
Clothing, clothing upkeep, and personal care	184.35	188.73	191.71	179.85	184.15	184.91
Clothing	145.93	151.28	152.63	142.22	146.12	144.96
Clothing upkeep	13.55	12.04	13.08	13.25	13.62	14.79
Personal care	24.87	25.42	26.00	24.38	24.42	25.16
Housing, including water	221.89	240.00	249.00	218.53	218.32	207.01
Household operation	153.54	154.72	151.27	146.45	153.66	164.71
Fuel	57.98	63.11	59.39	53.90	58.11	60.95
Coal or wood	47.00	54.52	51.90	44.38	44.46	47.63
Gas	10.98	8.59	7.49	9.52	13.65	13.32
Ice	22.40	21.46	21.09	22.14	21.28	25.14
Electricity	18.68	18.00	16.21	17.64	19.25	21.37
Household supplies	18.82	18.91	18.73	18.27	18.70	19.78
Furniture, furnishings, and household equipment	31.10	30.16	30.95	30.54	31.48	31.99
Refuse disposal	[2] 1.50	([3])	1.84	.90	1.78	2.43
Unspecified essentials [4]	3.06	3.07	3.06	3.06	3.05	3.06
Miscellaneous	252.67	292.86	291.52	261.27	233.56	221.30
Medical care	52.32	55.03	52.78	50.68	52.08	53.63
Transportation	53.96	90.84	89.96	66.40	37.17	17.52
School attendance	[5] 6.87	4.41	4.48	6.99	6.13	9.91
Recreation	75.18	80.42	81.26	73.31	73.05	74.44
Newspapers	10.84	11.06	13.52	10.26	10.09	10.74
Motion picture theater admissions	33.80	38.56	37.21	32.53	32.48	33.14
Organizations, tobacco, and toys [4]	30.55	30.80	30.54	30.52	30.47	30.57
Life insurance [4]	46.40	46.40	46.40	46.40	46.40	46.40
Church contributions and other contributions [4]	15.40	15.40	15.40	15.40	15.40	15.40
Taxes [6]	[7] 2.54	.36	1.24	2.09	3.33	4.00
Personal property	[8] 1.10	.36	.74	.91	1.44	1.54
Capitation	[9] 1.44	([10])	.50	1.18	1.89	2.46

[1] Include sales tax where levied (appendix table 15).

[2] Though only 18 cities had a direct charge for refuse disposal, an average for 59 cities is used in order to balance the table. The 18-city average is $4.90. The averages for the size of city groups are based on the total number of cities in each group included in this study.

[3] Not a direct charge.

[4] Budget allowance identical in all cities, plus sales tax where levied.

[5] Though only 55 cities had a direct charge for school attendance, an average for 59 cities is used in order to balance the table. The 55-city average is $7.37. The averages for the size of city groups are based on the total number of cities in each group included in this study.

[6] Exclusive of sales tax.

[7] Though taxes were payable in only 36 cities, an average for 59 cities is used in order to balance the table. The 36-city average is $4.17. The averages for the size of city groups are based on the total number of cities in each group included in this study.

[8] Though personal property taxes were payable in only 22 cities, an average for 59 cities is used in order to balance the table. The 22-city average is $2.96. The averages for the size of city groups are based on the total number of cities in each group included in this study.

[9] Though capitation taxes were payable in only 25 cities, an average for 59 cities is used in order to balance the table. The 25-city average is $3.40. The averages for the size of city groups are based on the total number of cities in each group included in this study.

[10] None payable.

NOTE.—Owing to the necessity for rounding numbers in computing averages, there are slight discrepancies between certain totals and the sums of their component items.

Table 7.—Relative Costs[1] of Living, by Major Budget Groups and Principal Subgroups, in 5 Size of City Classifications, 4-Person Manual Worker's Family, 59 Cities, March 1935

MAINTENANCE LEVEL

Budget group	Average, 59 cities		Size of city classification				
	Amount	Percent	1,000,000 or more	500,000 to 1,000,000	250,000 to 500,000	100,000 to 250,000	25,000 to 100,000
Total cost of living	$1,260.62	100.0	105.6	105.7	99.3	98.0	97.6
Food	448.18	100.0	101.4	100.1	99.4	99.4	100.9
Clothing, clothing upkeep, and personal care	184.35	100.0	102.4	104.0	97.6	99.9	100.3
Clothing	145.93	100.0	103.7	104.6	97.5	100.1	99.3
Clothing upkeep	13.55	100.0	88.8	96.5	97.8	100.5	109.2
Personal care	24.87	100.0	102.2	104.6	98.0	98.2	101.2
Housing, including water	221.89	100.0	108.2	112.2	98.5	98.4	93.3
Household operation	153.54	100.0	100.8	98.5	95.4	100.1	107.3
Fuel	57.98	100.0	108.8	102.4	93.0	100.2	105.1
Coal or wood	47.00	100.0	116.0	110.4	94.4	94.6	101.3
Gas	10.98	100.0	78.2	68.2	86.7	124.3	121.3
Ice	22.40	100.0	95.8	94.2	98.9	95.0	112.2
Electricity	18.68	100.0	96.4	86.8	94.4	103.1	114.4
Household supplies	18.82	100.0	100.5	99.5	97.1	99 3	105.1
Furniture, furnishings, and household equipment	31.10	100.0	97.0	99.5	98.2	101.2	102.8
Refuse disposal	[2] 1.50	100.0	([3])	122.7	60.0	118.7	162.0
Unspecified essentials [4]	3.06	100.0	100.3	100.0	100.0	99.7	100.0
Miscellaneous	252.67	100.0	115.9	115.4	103.4	92.4	87.6
Medical care	52.32	100.0	105.2	100.9	96.9	99.5	102.5
Transportation	53.96	100.0	168.4	166.7	123.1	68.9	32.5
School attendance	[5] 6.87	100.0	64.2	65.2	101.7	89.2	144.2
Recreation	75.18	100.0	107.0	108.1	97.5	97.2	99.0
Newspapers	10.84	100.0	102.1	124.7	94.7	93.2	99.1
Motion picture theater admissions	33.80	100.0	114.1	110.1	96.2	96.1	98.0
Organizations, tobacco, and toys [4]	30.55	100.0	100.8	100.0	99.9	99.7	100.1
Life insurance [4]	46.40	100.0	100.0	100.0	100.0	100.0	100.0
Church contributions and other contributions [4]	15.40	100.0	100.0	100.0	100.0	100.0	100.0
Taxes [6]	[7] 2.54	100.0	14.2	48.8	82.3	131.1	157.5
Personal property	[8] 1.10	100.0	32.7	67.3	82.7	130.9	140.0
Capitation	[9] 1.44	100.0	([10])	34.7	81.9	131.2	170.8

[1] Include sales tax where levied (appendix table 15).

[2] Though only 18 cities had a direct charge for refuse disposal, an average for 59 cities is used in order to balance the table. The 18-city average is $4.90. The averages for the size of city groups are based on the total number of cities in each group included in this study.

[3] Not a direct charge.

[4] Budget allowance identical in all cities, plus sales tax where levied.

[5] Though only 55 cities had a direct charge for school attendance, an average for 59 cities is used in order to balance the table. The 55-city average is $7.37. The averages for the size of city groups are based on the total number of cities in each group included in this study.

[6] Exclusive of sales tax.

[7] Though taxes were payable in only 36 cities, an average for 59 cities is used in order to balance the table. The 36-city average is $4.17. The averages for the size of city groups are based on the total number of cities in each group included in this study.

[8] Though personal property taxes were payable in only 22 cities, an average for 59 cities is used in order to balance the table. The 22-city average is $2.96. The averages for the size of city groups are based on the total number of cities in each group included in this study.

[9] Though capitation taxes were payable in only 25 cities, an average for 59 cities is used in order to balance the table. The 25-city average is $3.40. The averages for the size of city groups are based on the total number of cities in each group included in this study.

[10] None payable.

NOTE.—Owing to the necessity for rounding numbers in computing averages, there are slight discrepancies between certain totals and the sums of their component items.

***Table* 8.—Annual Costs[1] of Living, by Major Budget Groups and Principal Subgroups, 4-Person Manual Worker's Family, 59 Cities, March 1935**

EMERGENCY LEVEL

City	Total cost of living	Food	Clothing, clothing upkeep, and personal care				Housing, including water	Household operation							
			Total	Clothing	Clothing upkeep	Personal care		Total	Fuel			Ice	Electricity	Household supplies	Furniture, furnishings, and household equipment
									Total	Coal or wood	Gas				
Average, 59 cities	$903.27	$340.30	$128.05	$100.23	$11.88	$15.93	$167.79	$121.84	$48.80	$38.66	$10.14	$18.67	$14.52	$16.94	$18.66
Washington, D. C.	1,013.98	356.94	124.24	97.51	11.44	15.29	258.00	115.98	53.33	46.08	7.25	16.20	10.05	15.58	18.07
Minneapolis, Minn.	1,013.88	334.77	139.52	110.49	13.81	15.23	198.00	166.33	93.96	87.76	6.20	15.12	15.33	16.53	19.14
San Francisco, Calif.[1]	1,001.12	352.21	144.78	114.71	12.17	17.90	204.00	145.63	41.04	28.71	12.33	39.98	15.12	20.08	19.45
New York, N. Y.[1]	982.11	359.24	120.06	94.25	9.58	16.23	222.00	124.14	54.69	45.00	9.69	16.52	18.21	15.43	16.52
Chicago, Ill.[1]	972.59	349.16	134.17	105.88	10.72	17.57	180.00	129.98	62.77	57.57	5.20	16.52	14.05	15.71	18.16
Milwaukee, Wis.	970.64	321.54	141.53	111.90	12.13	17.50	204.00	141.98	80.04	72.84	7.20	10.80	13.65	15.44	19.31
Cleveland, Ohio[1]	964.71	337.59	144.97	115.96	11.26	17.74	177.00	111.90	48.94	45.19	3.75	14.46	8.76	17.47	19.48
Boston, Mass.	958.45	349.43	131.30	102.60	11.80	16.89	198.00	129.51	58.17	48.67	9.50	16.20	15.33	17.84	19.22
St. Louis, Mo.	956.48	337.93	124.61	99.11	10.06	15.44	204.00	99.07	35.83	28.18	7.65	14.04	10.77	15.63	17.05
Albuquerque, N. Mex.[1]	947.57	376.86	134.91	102.63	14.14	18.14	181.20	138.63	41.55	31.55	10.00	29.28	18.70	21.13	20.41
Detroit, Mich.[1]	944.00	332.05	135.72	108.69	10.85	16.18	168.00	128.99	59.46	52.92	6.54	15.57	14.68	17.74	18.76
Sioux Falls, S. Dak.	938.27	329.30	133.29	104.53	13.51	15.24	205.20	170.16	85.66	79.46	6.20	16.20	16.53	18.93	18.09
Los Angeles, Calif.[1]	935.85	336.11	142.47	114.75	11.00	16.72	147.00	124.45	42.24	31.35	10.89	29.98	10.92	19.19	19.34
Cincinnati, Ohio[1]	935.54	339.61	128.52	100.05	11.67	16.80	193.80	108.36	41.07	37.32	3.75	16.69	11.28	17.45	19.10
Scranton, Pa.	932.21	341.42	129.06	101.23	11.44	16.38	207.00	113.80	41.65	28.40	13.25	18.01	14.37	17.99	19.04
Butte, Mont.	932.11	347.07	150.66	114.13	18.91	17.62	165.00	147.05	68.11	59.81	8.30	16.20	17.37	20.86	21.76
Pittsburgh, Pa.	930.45	336.73	127.74	100.68	11.53	15.53	183.00	98.91	29.50	24.50	5.00	14.04	14.85	15.74	17.53
Baltimore, Md.	926.71	340.77	117.27	91.92	10.21	15.15	174.00	111.41	48.12	40.27	7.85	14.90	11.25	16.49	17.91
Rochester, N. Y.	925.16	333.12	126.99	97.41	13.51	16.07	168.00	147.15	79.88	71.63	8.25	15.12	16.05	15.11	18.24
Philadelphia, Pa.	924.56	340.87	121.81	96.04	10.23	15.55	180.00	107.97	45.41	37.96	7.45	10.80	14.25	17.04	17.72
Portland, Maine	921.94	343.46	138.03	106.87	14.90	16.25	156.00	151.05	70.93	58.13	12.80	15.34	17.37	17.88	19.29
Newark, N. J.	920.54	356.38	118.04	92.09	9.77	16.18	192.00	126.67	54.45	42.75	11.70	16.20	19.41	15.86	18.00
Bridgeport, Conn.	920.39	363.25	125.49	97.95	11.02	16.53	174.00	126.15	60.23	48.28	11.95	16.20	13.05	16.57	17.36
Tucson, Ariz.[1]	920.05	356.83	131.14	99.52	15.27	16.35	165.00	141.62	42.13	24.94	17.19	39.59	16.62	21.54	18.99
Peoria, Ill.[1]	913.39	342.08	131.93	104.21	11.25	16.47	208.28	100.92	32.41	23.23	9.18	16.52	14.54	16.31	18.38

Atlanta, Ga	911.25	347.39	116.70	92.10	9.79	14.81	189.00	108.32	38.63	27.50	11.13	18.94	14.13	14.84	19.04
Richmond, Va	910.36	337.88	131.90	104.84	11.93	15.13	181.92	122.12	47.80	32.75	15.05	22.73	13.29	15.10	20.46
Omaha, Nebr	908.71	339.97	129.21	100.78	12.61	15.82	181.20	119.60	57.94	51.04	6.90	11.83	12.33	16.37	17.39
Buffalo, N. Y	901.72	333.11	128.96	101.55	11.74	15.67	156.00	119.01	54.30	51.35	2.95	16.20	11.01	16.15	18.60
Kansas City, Mo	899.85	338.88	125.43	100.60	10.21	14.62	150.00	103.08	38.38	32.38	6.00	12.53	14.37	14.70	17.36
Fall River, Mass	898.09	337.15	131.85	104.30	11.21	16.34	168.00	138.37	64.10	53.25	10.85	16.20	17.37	17.08	20.87
Spokane, Wash	894.02	333.17	143.51	110.88	15.36	17.28	132.00	145.16	57.93	40.23	17.70	18.90	12.33	20.69	20.56
Norfolk, Va	891.57	342.02	122.09	94.88	12.16	15.05	178.00	119.39	50.46	36.60	13.86	19.70	13.29	15.56	17.64
Salt Lake City, Utah [1]	890.84	331.89	140.99	110.67	14.04	16.28	144.00	129.17	50.41	42.00	8.42	19.00	17.23	18.70	21.05
Manchester, N. H	889.61	348.25	127.78	98.90	13.36	15.52	138.00	143.87	72.60	60.75	11.85	16.20	17.37	16.92	18.03
Seattle, Wash	886.58	339.91	133.62	104.09	13.16	16.38	126.00	132.25	49.52	32.16	17.36	30.30	11.25	19.41	19.03
Denver, Colo.[1]	885.24	331.04	127.64	99.95	12.46	15.24	150.00	110.81	42.79	34.37	8.42	13.22	13.56	17.92	19.06
Providence, R. I	885.17	340.75	117.69	91.22	11.40	15.07	162.00	134.97	62.25	51.50	10.75	13.28	17.97	17.54	18.17
Portland, Oreg	884.81	334.97	143.48	113.23	13.44	16.82	119.40	133.08	42.41	27.57	14.84	30.30	13.05	20.02	18.56
New Orleans, La	882.80	331.30	120.37	93.94	10.76	15.66	147.00	103.02	28.29	18.75	9.54	19.50	19.41	15.48	17.59
Binghamton, N. Y	878.10	335.71	124.81	98.50	10.70	15.61	171.00	124.26	50.05	40.75	9.30	16.20	20.25	15.94	19.08
Memphis, Tenn	877.27	332.53	119.15	92.11	11.38	15.66	168.00	103.64	35.80	26.49	9.31	19.70	12.33	14.54	18.53
Oklahoma City, Okla.[1]	874.17	339.00	127.68	98.43	11.22	18.03	157.20	115.92	33.33	30.43	2.90	22.95	15.48	16.42	16.97
Winston-Salem, N. C.[1]	873.04	342.05	124.23	97.20	11.10	15.93	157.92	130.92	54.52	33.73	20.79	23.41	16.20	15.57	18.44
Louisville, Ky.[1]	871.62	337.98	123.87	97.61	10.66	15.61	161.80	103.09	40.94	37.08	3.86	13.91	11.59	15.75	18.12
Houston, Tex	869.23	327.94	126.06	98.13	12.78	15.15	159.00	97.50	23.31	13.50	9.81	25.35	12.09	15.28	18.71
Jacksonville, Fla	868.57	344.87	120.74	93.94	11.89	14.90	150.00	122.83	51.33	20.10	31.23	19.50	15.33	14.63	19.29
Indianapolis, Ind	859.04	319.30	122.82	93.05	12.62	17.16	156.00	109.27	45.64	37.84	7.80	14.47	12.81	16.01	17.59
Dallas, Tex	853.98	343.11	113.32	87.96	10.81	14.55	165.00	98.77	24.31	13.60	10.71	24.18	12.33	17.82	17.38
Clarksburg, W. Va.[1]	852.87	355.40	127.68	102.00	9.97	15.71	147.00	96.45	18.98	16.48	2.50	16.52	14.39	17.95	19.83
Cedar Rapids, Iowa [1]	849.35	318.56	130.64	102.02	12.77	15.85	153.43	133.12	65.44	56.26	9.18	13.69	13.56	17.45	18.96
Columbia, S. C	844.92	360.21	114.46	89.26	10.44	14.76	150.00	119.98	38.07	15.75	22.32	29.25	15.33	14.49	20.09
Knoxville, Tenn	844.37	326.74	119.35	93.37	11.75	14.23	157.80	110.85	43.11	22.46	20.65	15.15	14.13	15.92	19.79
Columbus, Ohio [1]	840.68	340.95	127.81	101.25	10.46	16.10	144.00	98.15	33.36	30.86	2.50	16.69	9.24	16.70	19.39
Birmingham, Ala	835.81	336.88	118.89	92.67	10.80	15.42	128.04	101.37	32.65	23.41	9.24	18.94	14.13	15.87	17.04
El Paso, Tex	832.05	340.31	117.52	91.47	10.86	15.19	153.00	123.36	45.94	34.88	11.06	18.64	17.37	18.04	18.12
Little Rock, Ark	819.97	340.15	120.32	93.29	12.50	14.53	135.00	98.34	27.00	20.00	7.00	15.15	19.29	16.22	17.93
Mobile, Ala	814.92	330.35	113.50	87.12	11.57	14.81	127.44	113.47	36.08	17.54	18.54	25.35	14.13	16.55	18.62
Wichita, Kans	809.64	323.17	122.46	97.20	10.98	14.28	123.00	117.18	49.85	44.85	5.00	12.96	16.41	16.22	17.54

See footnotes at end of table.

Table 8.—Annual Costs of Living, by Major Budget Groups and Principal Subgroups, 4-Person Manual Worker's Family, 59 Cities, March 1935—Continued

EMERGENCY LEVEL—continued

City	Household operation—Continued		Miscellaneous											
							Recreation					Taxes [3]		
	Refuse disposal	Unspecified essentials [2]	Total	Medical care	Transportation	School attendance	Total	Motion picture theater admissions	Tobacco and toys [2]	Life insurance [2]	Church contributions [2]	Total	Personal property	Capitation
Average, 59 cities	[4] $1.50	$2.76	$145.30	$47.08	$44.97	[5] $6.87	$12.63	$7.80	$4.83	$20.80	$10.40	[6] $2.54	[7] $1.10	[8] $1.44
Washington, D. C.	(9)	2.75	158.83	53.02	59.54	1.35	13.72	8.92	4.80	20.80	10.40	(10)	(10)	(10)
Minneapolis, Minn.	3.50	2.75	175.26	48.71	76.55	6.25	12.55	7.75	4.80	20.80	10.40	(10)	(10)	(10)
San Francisco, Calif.[1]	7.20	2.78	154.50	57.85	42.32	8.47	14.66	9.74	4.92	20.80	10.40	(10)	(10)	(10)
New York, N. Y.[1]	(9)	2.77	156.68	50.66	59.52	1.45	13.84	8.94	4.90	20.80	10.40	(10)	(10)	(10)
Chicago, Ill.[1]	(9)	2.77	179.28	51.67	77.76	3.04	13.80	8.90	4.90	20.80	10.40	1.81	1.81	(10)
Milwaukee, Wis.	(9)	2.75	161.59	40.06	63.45	11.28	12.47	7.67	4.80	20.80	10.40	3.14	3.14	(10)
Cleveland, Ohio [1]	(9)	2.78	193.25	53.29	84.60	10.50	13.67	8.72	4.94	20.80	10.40	(10)	(10)	(10)
Boston, Mass.	(9)	2.75	150.21	49.82	51.45	1.88	13.86	9.06	4.80	20.80	10.40	2.00	(10)	2.00
St. Louis, Mo.	3.00	2.75	190.87	44.59	98.70	(9)	13.61	8.81	4.80	20.80	10.40	2.77	2.77	(10)
Albuquerque, N. Mex.[1]	4.80	2.77	115.98	51.80	10.56	9.40	13.02	8.12	4.90	20.80	10.40	(10)	(10)	(10)
Detroit, Mich.[1]	(9)	2.78	179.23	52.51	68.40	14.06	13.07	8.12	4.94	20.80	10.40	(10)	(10)	(10)
Sioux Falls, S. Dak.	12.00	2.75	100.33	46.27	9.11	(9)	12.14	7.34	4.80	20.80	10.40	1.60	1.60	(10)
Los Angeles, Calif.[1]	(9)	2.78	185.82	54.08	84.42	2.49	13.63	8.71	4.92	20.80	10.40	(10)	(10)	(10)
Cincinnati, Ohio [1]	(9)	2.78	165.26	37.63	78.83	4.07	13.52	8.58	4.94	20.80	10.40	(10)	(10)	(10)
Scranton, Pa.	(9)	2.75	140.93	52.21	33.55	.65	14.38	9.58	4.80	20.80	10.40	8.94	(10)	8.94
Butte, Mont.	(9)	2.75	122.33	56.56	9.02	6.50	13.05	8.25	4.80	20.80	10.40	6.00	2.00	4.00
Pittsburgh, Pa.	4.50	2.75	184.08	49.07	88.55	(9)	13.26	8.46	4.80	20.80	10.40	2.00	(10)	2.00
Baltimore, Md.	(9)	2.75	183.26	39.63	96.24	1.69	14.50	9.70	4.80	20.80	10.40	(10)	(10)	(10)
Rochester, N. Y.	(9)	2.75	149.90	47.55	53.25	5.65	12.25	7.45	4.80	20.80	10.40	(10)	(10)	(10)
Philadelphia, Pa.	(9)	2.75	173.91	38.71	88.38	1.00	14.62	9.82	4.80	20.80	10.40	(10)	(10)	(10)
Portland, Maine	7.50	2.75	133.40	52.96	23.76	6.06	12.06	7.26	4.80	20.80	10.40	7.36	4.36	3.00
Newark, N. J.	(9)	2.75	127.46	46.75	31.46	4.00	13.06	8.26	4.80	20.80	10.40	1.00	(10)	1.00
Bridgeport, Conn.	(9)	2.75	131.50	50.53	36.45	.72	12.60	7.80	4.80	20.80	10.40	(10)	(10)	(10)
Tucson, Ariz.[1]	(9)	2.77	125.47	55.18	10.28	8.14	14.46	9.59	4.87	20.80	10.40	6.22	6.22	(10)
Peoria, Ill.[1]	(9)	2.77	130.17	39.50	24.80	18.56	12.31	7.42	4.90	20.80	10.40	3.80	3.80	(10)

Atlanta, Ga	(9)	2.75	149.85	48.14	43.74	7.13	11.64	6.84	4.80	20.80	10.40	8.00	3.00	5.00
Richmond, Va	(9)	2.75	136.54	46.11	33.26	7.75	13.02	8.22	4.80	20.80	10.40	5.20	2.20	3.00
Omaha, Nebr	1.00	2.75	138.73	43.21	48.60	4.32	11.40	6.60	4.80	20.80	10.40	(10)	(10)	(10)
Buffalo, N. Y	(9)	2.75	164.65	45.68	74.40	2.04	11.33	6.53	4.80	20.80	10.40	(10)	(10)	(10)
Kansas City, Mo	3.00	2.75	182.47	46.21	79.70	11.37	10.37	5.57	4.80	20.80	10.40	3.62	3.62	(10)
Fall River, Mass	(9)	2.75	122.72	46.11	26.21	(9)	13.00	8.20	4.80	20.80	10.40	6.20	4.20	2.00
Spokane, Wash	12.00	2.75	140.18	59.49	34.34	4.29	10.86	6.06	4.80	20.80	10.40	(10)	(10)	(10)
Norfolk, Va	(9)	2.75	130.07	45.95	29.85	5.11	12.16	7.36	4.80	20.80	10.40	5.80	2.80	3.00
Salt Lake City, Utah [1]	(9)	2.77	144.79	50.98	44.95	1.02	12.19	7.30	4.90	20.80	10.40	4.44	4.44	(10)
Manchester, N. H	(9)	2.75	131.71	44.90	33.08	1.00	14.33	9.53	4.80	20.80	10.40	7.20	3.20	4.00
Seattle, Wash	(9)	2.75	154.80	46.64	62.90	1.63	12.43	7.63	4.80	20.80	10.40	(10)	(10)	(10)
Denver, Colo. [1]	1.50	2.77	165.75	50.86	62.37	7.78	13.54	8.64	4.90	20.80	10.40	(10)	(10)	(10)
Providence, R. I	3.00	2.75	129.75	49.30	34.44	1.56	10.80	6.00	4.80	20.80	10.40	2.45	2.45	(10)
Portland, Oreg	6.00	2.75	153.88	44.61	58.28	8.48	11.30	6.50	4.80	20.80	10.40	(10)	(10)	(10)
New Orleans, La	(9)	2.75	181.12	47.21	81.48	3.80	13.98	9.18	4.80	20.80	10.40	3.45	3.45	(10)
Binghamton, N. Y	(9)	2.75	122.31	50.34	9.74	16.50	14.54	9.74	4.80	20.80	10.40	(10)	(10)	(10)
Memphis, Tenn	(9)	2.75	153.95	47.96	51.03	7.50	12.26	7.46	4.80	20.80	10.40	4.00	(10)	4.00
Oklahoma City, Okla. [1]	8.00	2.76	134.38	45.64	32.94	11.50	13.10	8.26	4.85	20.80	10.40	(10)	(10)	(10)
Winston-Salem, N. C. [1]	(9)	2.78	117.93	46.75	17.48	10.32	11.18	6.24	4.94	20.80	10.40	1.00	(10)	1.00
Louisville, Ky. [1]	(9)	2.78	144.89	36.64	49.63	11.66	13.61	8.66	4.94	20.80	10.40	2.16	2.16	(10)
Houston, Tex	(9)	2.75	158.73	47.50	55.57	9.73	11.74	6.94	4.80	20.80	10.40	3.00	(10)	3.00
Jacksonville, Fla	(9)	2.75	130.14	51.53	25.76	7.00	12.65	7.85	4.80	20.80	10.40	2.00	(10)	2.00
Indianapolis, Ind	(9)	2.75	151.64	39.17	54.34	9.40	11.95	7.15	4.80	20.80	10.40	5.58	2.58	3.00
Dallas, Tex	(9)	2.75	133.79	44.56	29.97	12.25	12.31	7.51	4.80	20.80	10.40	3.50	(10)	3.50
Clarksburg, W. Va. [1]	6.00	2.77	126.34	49.78	7.67	21.19	11.50	6.60	4.90	20.80	10.40	5.00	(10)	5.00
Cedar Rapids, Iowa [1]	1.25	2.77	113.61	41.27	20.70	4.86	11.58	6.68	4.90	20.80	10.40	4.00	(10)	4.00
Columbia, S. C	(9)	2.75	100.28	36.84	7.29	11.14	11.81	7.01	4.80	20.80	10.40	2.00	(10)	2.00
Knoxville, Tenn	(9)	2.75	129.63	45.23	26.78	8.50	11.18	6.38	4.80	20.80	10.40	6.73	2.73	4.00
Columbus, Ohio [1]	(9)	2.78	129.78	41.21	37.05	8.94	11.38	6.43	4.94	20.80	10.40	(10)	(10)	(10)
Birmingham, Ala	(9)	2.75	150.64	43.01	51.24	10.25	11.94	7.14	4.80	20.80	10.40	3.00	(10)	3.00
El Paso, Tex	2.50	2.75	97.86	34.62	14.26	1.94	12.35	7.55	4.80	20.80	10.40	3.50	(10)	3.50
Little Rock, Ark	(9)	2.75	126.16	48.20	13.72	13.17	11.75	6.95	4.80	20.80	10.40	8.13	2.13	6.00
Mobile, Ala	(9)	2.75	130.16	46.66	17.45	20.51	10.90	6.10	4.80	20.80	10.40	3.45	.45	3.00
Wichita, Kans	1.45	2.75	123.83	45.07	21.87	14.50	11.18	6.38	4.80	20.80	10.40	(10)	(10)	(10)

1 Include sales tax where levied (appendix table 16).
2 Budget allowance identical in all cities, plus sales tax where levied.
3 Exclusive of sales tax.
4 Though only 18 cities had a direct charge for refuse disposal, an average for 59 cities is used in order to balance the table. The 18-city average is $4.90.
5 Though only 55 cities had a direct charge for school attendance, an average for 59 cities is used in order to balance the table. The 55-city average is $7.37.
6 Though taxes were payable in only 36 cities, an average for 59 cities is used in order to balance the table. The 36-city average is $4.17.
7 Though personal property taxes were payable in only 22 cities, an average for 59 cities is used in order to balance the table. The 22-city average is $2.96.
8 Though capitation taxes were payable in only 25 cities, an average for 59 cities is used in order to balance the table. The 25-city average is $3.40.
9 Not a direct charge.
10 None payable.

NOTE.—Owing to the necessity for rounding numbers in computing averages, there are slight discrepancies between certain totals and the sums of their component items.

Table 9.—Relative Costs [1] of Living, by Major Budget Groups and Principal Subgroups, 4-Person Manual Worker's Family, 59 Cities, March 1935

EMERGENCY LEVEL

City	Total cost of living	Food	Clothing, clothing upkeep, and personal care				Housing, including water	Household operation							
			Total	Clothing	Clothing upkeep	Personal care		Total	Fuel			Ice	Electricity	Household supplies	Furniture, furnishings, and household equipment
									Total	Coal or wood	Gas				
Average, 59 cities:															
Amount	$903.27	$340.30	$128.05	$100.23	$11.88	$15.93	$167.79	$121.84	$48.80	$38.66	$10.14	$18.67	$14.52	$16.94	$18.66
Percent	100.0	100.0	100.0	100.0	100.0	100.0	100.0	100.0	100.0	100.0	100.0	100.0	100.0	100.0	100.0
Washington, D. C.	112.3	104.9	97.0	97.3	96.3	96.0	153.8	95.2	109.3	119.2	71.5	86.8	69.2	92.0	96.8
Minneapolis, Minn.	112.2	98.4	109.0	110.2	116.2	95.6	118.0	136.5	192.5	227.0	61.1	81.0	105.6	97.6	102.6
San Francisco, Calif.[1]	110.8	103.5	113.1	114.4	102.4	112.4	121.6	119.5	84.1	74.3	121.6	214.2	104.1	118.6	104.2
New York, N. Y.[1]	108.7	105.6	93.8	94.0	80.6	101.9	132.3	101.9	112.1	116.4	95.6	88.5	125.4	91.1	88.5
Chicago, Ill.[1]	107.7	102.6	104.8	105.6	90.2	110.3	107.3	106.7	128.6	148.9	51.3	88.5	96.7	92.7	97.3
Milwaukee, Wis.	107.5	94.5	110.5	111.6	102.1	109.8	121.6	116.5	164.0	188.4	71.0	57.9	94.0	91.1	103.5
Cleveland, Ohio [1]	106.8	99.2	113.2	115.7	94.8	111.4	105.5	91.8	100.3	116.9	37.0	77.5	60.3	103.1	104.4
Boston, Mass.	106.1	102.7	102.5	102.4	99.3	106.0	118.0	106.3	119.2	125.9	93.7	86.8	105.6	105.3	102.9
St. Louis, Mo.	105.9	99.3	97.3	98.9	84.7	96.9	121.6	81.3	73.4	72.9	75.4	75.2	74.2	92.2	91.4
Albuquerque, N. Mex.[1]	104.9	110.7	105.4	102.4	119.0	113.8	108.0	113.8	85.1	81.6	98.6	156.9	128.7	124.7	109.3
Detroit, Mich.[1]	104.5	97.6	106.0	108.4	91.3	101.5	100.1	105.9	121.8	136.9	64.5	83.4	101.1	104.7	100.5
Sioux Falls, S. Dak.	103.9	96.8	104.1	104.3	113.7	95.7	122.3	139.7	175.5	205.5	61.1	86.8	113.8	111.8	96.9
Los Angeles, Calif.[1]	103.6	98.8	111.3	114.5	92.6	104.9	87.6	102.1	86.6	81.1	107.4	160.6	75.2	113.3	103.6
Cincinnati, Ohio [1]	103.6	99.8	100.4	99.8	98.2	105.4	115.5	88.9	84.2	96.5	37.0	89.4	77.7	103.0	102.3
Scranton, Pa.	103.2	100.3	100.8	101.0	96.3	102.8	123.4	93.4	85.3	73.5	130.7	96.5	98.9	106.2	102.0
Butte, Mont.	103.2	102.0	117.7	113.9	159.2	110.6	98.3	120.7	139.6	154.7	81.9	86.8	119.6	123.1	116.6
Pittsburgh, Pa.	103.0	99.0	99.8	100.5	97.0	97.5	109.1	81.2	60.5	63.4	49.3	75.2	102.3	92.9	93.9
Baltimore, Md.	102.6	100.1	91.6	91.7	85.9	95.1	103.7	91.4	98.6	104.2	77.4	79.8	77.5	97.3	96.0
Rochester, N. Y.	102.4	97.9	99.2	97.2	113.7	100.9	100.1	120.8	163.7	185.3	81.4	81.0	110.5	89.2	97.8
Philadelphia, Pa.	102.4	100.2	95.1	95.8	86.1	97.6	107.3	88.6	93.1	98.2	73.5	57.9	98.1	100.6	95.0
Portland, Maine	102.1	100.9	107.8	106.6	125.4	102.0	93.0	124.0	145.3	150.4	126.2	82.2	119.6	105.6	103.4
Newark, N. J.	101.9	104.7	92.2	91.9	82.3	101.6	114.4	104.0	111.6	110.6	115.4	86.8	133.7	93.6	96.4
Bridgeport, Conn.	101.9	106.7	98.0	97.7	92.7	103.7	103.7	103.5	123.4	124.9	117.9	86.8	89.9	97.8	93.0
Tucson, Ariz.[1]	101.9	104.9	102.4	99.3	128.5	102.6	98.3	116.2	86.3	64.5	169.5	212.1	114.5	127.2	101.7
Peoria, Ill.[1]	101.1	100.5	103.0	104.0	94.6	103.4	124.1	82.8	66.4	60.1	90.5	88.5	100.1	96.3	98.5

Atlanta, Ga	100.9	102.1	91.1	91.9	82.4	92.9	112.6	88.9	79.2	71.1	109.8	101.5	97.3	87.6	102.0
Richmond, Va	100.8	99.3	103.0	104.6	100.4	95.0	108.4	100.2	98.0	84.7	148.4	121.7	91.5	89.1	109.6
Omaha, Nebr	100.6	99.9	100.9	100.6	106.2	99.3	108.0	98.2	118.7	132.0	68.0	63.4	84.9	96.6	93.2
Buffalo, N. Y	99.8	97.9	100.7	101.3	98.8	98.4	93.0	97.7	111.3	132.8	29.1	86.8	75.8	95.3	99.7
Kansas City, Mo	99.6	99.6	98.0	100.4	85.9	91.8	89.4	84.6	78.6	83.8	59.2	67.1	98.9	86.8	93.0
Fall River, Mass	99.4	99.1	103.0	104.1	94.3	102.6	100.1	113.6	131.4	137.7	107.0	86.8	119.6	100.8	111.8
Spokane, Wash	99.0	97.9	112.1	110.6	129.2	108.5	78.7	119.1	118.7	104.1	174.6	101.3	84.9	122.1	110.2
Norfolk, Va	98.7	100.5	95.4	94.7	102.3	94.5	106.1	98.0	103.4	94.7	136.7	105.5	91.5	91.9	94.5
Salt Lake City, Utah [1]	98.6	97.5	110.1	110.4	118.1	102.2	85.8	106.0	103.3	108.6	83.0	101.8	118.6	110.4	112.8
Manchester, N. H	98.5	102.3	99.8	98.7	112.4	97.4	82.2	118.1	148.8	157.1	116.9	86.8	119.6	99.9	96.6
Seattle, Wash	98.2	99.9	104.4	103.8	110.7	102.8	75.1	108.5	101.5	83.2	171.2	162.3	77.5	114.6	101.9
Denver, Colo.[1]	98.0	97.3	99.7	99.7	104.8	95.6	89.4	90.9	87.7	88.9	83.0	70.8	93.3	105.8	102.1
Providence, R. I	98.0	100.1	91.9	91.0	96.0	94.6	96.5	110.8	127.6	133.2	106.0	71.2	123.7	103.6	97.4
Portland, Oreg	98.0	98.4	112.1	113.0	113.1	105.5	71.2	109.2	86.9	71.3	146.4	162.3	89.9	118.2	99.5
New Orleans, La	97.7	97.4	94.0	93.7	90.5	98.3	87.6	84.6	58.0	48.5	94.1	104.5	133.7	91.4	94.2
Binghamton, N. Y	97.2	98.7	97.5	98.3	90.1	97.9	101.9	102.0	102.6	105.4	91.7	86.8	139.4	94.1	102.2
Memphis, Tenn	97.1	97.7	93.1	91.9	95.8	98.3	100.1	85.1	73.4	68.5	91.8	105.5	84.9	85.8	99.3
Oklahoma City, Okla.[1]	96.8	99.6	99.7	98.2	94.4	113.1	93.7	95.1	68.3	78.7	28.6	123.0	106.6	97.0	90.9
Winston-Salem, N. C.[1]	96.7	100.5	97.0	97.0	93.4	100.0	94.1	107.5	111.7	87.2	205.0	125.4	111.6	91.9	98.8
Louisville, Ky.[1]	96.5	99.3	96.7	97.4	89.7	97.9	96.4	84.6	83.9	95.9	38.1	74.5	79.8	93.0	97.1
Houston, Tex	96.2	96.4	98.5	97.9	107.6	95.1	94.8	80.0	47.8	34.9	96.7	135.8	83.2	90.2	100.3
Jacksonville, Fla	96.2	101.3	94.3	93.7	100.1	93.5	89.4	100.8	105.2	52.0	308.0	104.5	105.6	86.3	103.4
Indianapolis, Ind	95.1	93.8	95.9	92.8	106.2	107.7	93.0	89.7	93.5	97.9	76.9	77.5	88.2	94.5	94.3
Dallas, Tex	94.5	100.8	88.5	87.8	91.0	91.3	98.3	81.1	49.8	35.2	105.6	129.5	84.9	105.2	93.1
Clarksburg, W. Va.[1]	94.4	104.4	99.7	101.8	83.9	98.6	87.6	79.2	38.9	42.6	24.7	88.5	99.1	106.0	106.2
Cedar Rapids, Iowa [1]	94.0	93.6	102.0	101.8	107.5	99.5	91.4	109.3	134.1	145.5	90.5	73.3	93.3	103.0	101.6
Columbia, S. C	93.5	105.9	89.4	89.1	87.9	92.6	89.4	98.5	78.0	40.7	220.1	156.7	105.6	85.6	107.6
Knoxville, Tenn	93.5	96.0	93.2	93.2	98.8	89.3	94.0	91.0	88.3	58.1	203.6	81.2	97.3	94.0	106.1
Columbus, Ohio [1]	93.1	100.2	99.8	101.0	88.1	101.0	85.8	80.6	68.4	79.8	24.7	89.4	63.6	98.6	103.9
Birmingham, Ala	92.5	99.0	92.8	92.5	90.9	96.7	76.3	83.2	66.9	60.6	91.1	101.5	97.3	93.7	91.3
El Paso, Tex	92.1	100.0	91.8	91.3	91.4	95.3	91.2	101.2	94.1	90.2	109.1	99.8	119.6	106.5	97.1
Little Rock, Ark	90.8	100.0	94.0	93.1	105.2	91.2	80.5	80.7	55.3	51.7	69.0	81.2	132.8	95.8	96.1
Mobile, Ala	90.2	97.1	88.6	86.9	97.3	92.9	76.0	93.1	73.9	45.4	182.8	135.8	97.3	97.7	99.8
Wichita, Kans	89.6	95.0	95.6	97.0	92.4	89.6	73.3	96.2	102.2	116.0	49.3	69.4	113.0	95.8	94.0

See footnotes at end of table.

Table 9.—Relative Costs of Living, by Major Budget Groups and Principal Subgroups, 4-Person Manual Worker's Family, 59 Cities, March 1935—Continued

EMERGENCY LEVEL—continued

City	Household operation—Continued: Refuse disposal	Household operation—Continued: Unspecified essentials [2]	Miscellaneous: Total	Miscellaneous: Medical care	Miscellaneous: Transportation	Miscellaneous: School attendance	Recreation: Total	Recreation: Motion picture theater admissions	Recreation: Tobacco and toys [2]	Life insurance [2]	Church contributions [2]	Taxes [3]: Total	Taxes [3]: Personal property	Taxes [3]: Capitation
Average, 59 cities:														
Amount	[4] $1.50	$2.76	$145.30	$47.08	$44.97	[5] $6.87	$12.63	$7.80	$4.83	$20.80	$10.40	[6] $2.54	[7] $1.10	[8] $1.44
Percent	100.0	100.0	100.0	100.0	100.0	100.0	100.0	100.0	100.0	100.0	100.0	100.0	100.0	100.0
Washington, D. C.	(9)	99.6	109.3	112.6	132.4	19.7	108.6	114.3	99.4	100.0	100.0	(10)	(10)	(10)
Minneapolis, Minn.	233.3	99.6	120.6	103.5	170.2	91.0	99.4	99.4	99.4	100.0	100.0	(10)	(10)	(10)
San Francisco, Calif.[1]	480.0	100.7	106.3	122.9	94.1	123.3	116.1	124.9	101.9	100.0	100.0	(10)	(10)	(10)
New York, N. Y.[1]	(9)	100.4	107.8	107.6	132.4	21.2	109.5	114.6	101.4	100.0	100.0	(10)	(10)	(10)
Chicago, Ill.[1]	(9)	100.4	123.4	109.8	172.9	44.2	109.2	114.1	101.4	100.0	100.0	71.3	164.5	(10)
Milwaukee, Wis.	(9)	99.6	111.2	85.1	141.1	164.1	98.7	98.3	99.4	100.0	100.0	123.6	285.5	(10)
Cleveland, Ohio [1]	(9)	100.7	133.0	113.2	188.1	152.7	108.2	111.8	102.3	100.0	100.0	(10)	(10)	(10)
Boston, Mass.	(9)	99.6	103.4	105.8	114.4	27.4	109.7	116.2	99.4	100.0	100.0	78.7	(10)	138.9
St. Louis, Mo.	200.0	99.6	131.4	94.7	219.5	(9)	107.7	112.9	99.4	100.0	100.0	109.1	251.8	(10)
Albuquerque, N. Mex. [1]	320.0	100.4	79.8	110.0	23.5	136.8	103.1	104.1	101.4	100.0	100.0	(10)	(10)	(10)
Detroit, Mich.[1]	(9)	100.7	123.4	111.5	152.1	204.7	103.4	104.1	102.3	100.0	100.0	(10)	(10)	(10)
Sioux Falls, S. Dak.	800.0	99.6	69.0	98.3	20.3	(9)	96.1	94.1	99.4	100.0	100.0	63.0	145.5	(10)
Los Angeles, Calif.[1]	(9)	100.7	127.9	114.8	187.7	36.3	107.9	111.7	101.9	100.0	100.0	(10)	(10)	(10)
Cincinnati, Ohio [1]	(9)	100.7	113.7	79.9	175.3	59.2	107.1	110.0	102.3	100.0	100.0	(10)	(10)	(10)
Scranton, Pa.	(9)	99.6	97.0	110.9	74.6	9.5	113.8	122.8	99.4	100.0	100.0	352.0	(10)	620.8
Butte, Mont.	(9)	99.6	84.2	120.1	20.1	94.6	103.3	105.8	99.4	100.0	100.0	236.2	181.8	277.8
Pittsburgh, Pa.	300.0	99.6	126.7	104.2	196.9	(9)	105.0	108.5	99.4	100.0	100.0	78.7	(10)	138.9
Baltimore, Md.	(9)	99.6	126.1	84.2	214.0	24.6	114.7	124.3	99.4	100.0	100.0	(10)	(10)	(10)
Rochester, N. Y.	(9)	99.6	103.2	101.0	118.4	82.2	97.0	95.5	99.4	100.0	100.0	(10)	(10)	(10)
Philadelphia, Pa.	(9)	99.6	119.7	82.2	196.6	14.6	115.7	125.9	99.4	100.0	100.0	(10)	(10)	(10)
Portland, Maine	500.0	99.6	91.8	112.5	52.8	88.2	95.5	93.1	99.4	100.0	100.0	289.8	396.4	208.3
Newark, N. J.	(9)	99.6	87.7	99.3	70.0	58.2	103.3	105.9	99.4	100.0	100.0	39.4	(10)	69.4
Bridgeport, Conn.	(9)	99.6	90.5	107.3	81.1	10.5	99.7	100.0	99.4	100.0	100.0	(10)	(10)	(10)
Tucson, Ariz.[1]	(9)	100.4	86.4	117.2	22.9	118.4	114.5	122.9	100.8	100.0	100.0	244.9	565.5	(10)
Peoria, Ill.[1]	(9)	100.4	89.6	83.9	55.2	270.2	97.5	95.1	101.4	100.0	100.0	149.6	345.5	(10)

Atlanta, Ga.	(9)	99.6	103.1	102.2	97.3	103.8	92.1	87.7	99.4	100.0	100.0	315.0	272.7	347.2
Richmond, Va.	(9)	99.6	94.0	97.9	74.0	112.8	103.1	105.4	99.4	100.0	100.0	204.7	200.0	208.3
Omaha, Nebr.	66.7	99.6	95.5	91.8	108.1	62.9	90.2	84.6	99.4	100.0	100.0	(10)	(10)	(10)
Buffalo, N. Y.	(9)	99.6	113.3	97.0	165.5	29.7	89.7	83.7	99.4	100.0	100.0	(10)	(10)	(10)
Kansas City, Mo.	200.0	99.6	125.6	98.1	177.2	165.5	82.1	71.4	99.4	100.0	100.0	142.5	329.1	(10)
Fall River, Mass.	(9)	99.6	84.5	97.9	58.3	(9)	102.9	105.1	99.4	100.0	100.0	244.1	381.8	138.9
Spokane, Wash.	800.0	99.6	96.5	126.3	76.4	62.4	86.0	77.7	99.4	100.0	100.0	(10)	(10)	(10)
Norfolk, Va.	(9)	99.6	89.5	97.6	66.4	74.4	96.2	94.3	99.4	100.0	100.0	228.3	254.5	208.3
Salt Lake City, Utah [1]	(9)	100.4	99.7	108.3	100.0	14.8	96.5	93.6	101.4	100.0	100.0	174.8	403.6	(10)
Manchester, N. H.	(9)	99.6	90.6	95.4	73.6	14.6	113.4	122.2	99.4	100.0	100.0	283.5	290.9	277.8
Seattle, Wash.	(9)	99.6	106.5	99.1	139.9	23.7	98.4	97.8	99.4	100.0	100.0	(10)	(10)	(10)
Denver, Colo. [1]	100.0	100.4	114.1	108.0	138.7	113.2	107.1	110.8	101.4	100.0	100.0	(10)	(10)	(10)
Providence, R. I.	200.0	99.6	89.3	104.7	76.6	22.7	85.5	76.9	99.4	100.0	100.0	96.5	222.7	(10)
Portland, Oreg.	400.0	99.6	105.9	94.7	129.6	123.5	89.5	83.4	99.4	100.0	100.0	(10)	(10)	(10)
New Orleans, La.	(9)	99.6	124.7	100.3	181.2	55.3	110.7	117.7	99.4	100.0	100.0	135.8	313.6	(10)
Binghamton, N. Y.	(9)	99.6	84.2	106.9	21.6	240.2	115.1	124.9	99.4	100.0	100.0	(10)	(10)	(10)
Memphis, Tenn.	(9)	99.6	106.0	101.9	113.5	109.2	97.1	95.7	99.4	100.0	100.0	157.5	(10)	277.8
Oklahoma City, Okla. [1]	533.3	100.0	92.5	96.9	73.3	167.4	103.7	105.9	100.4	100.0	100.0	(10)	(10)	(10)
Winston-Salem, N. C. [1]	(9)	100.7	81.2	99.3	38.9	150.2	88.5	80.0	102.3	100.0	100.0	39.4	(10)	69.4
Louisville, Ky. [1]	(9)	100.7	99.7	77.8	110.4	169.7	107.7	111.1	102.3	100.0	100.0	85.0	196.4	(10)
Houston, Tex.	(9)	99.6	109.2	100.9	123.6	141.6	92.9	88.9	99.4	100.0	100.0	118.1	(10)	208.3
Jacksonville, Fla.	(9)	99.6	89.6	109.5	57.3	101.9	100.1	100.6	99.4	100.0	100.0	78.7	(10)	138.9
Indianapolis, Ind.	(9)	99.6	104.4	83.2	120.8	136.8	94.6	91.7	99.4	100.0	100.0	219.7	234.5	208.3
Dallas, Tex.	(9)	99.6	92.1	94.6	66.6	178.3	97.5	96.3	99.4	100.0	100.0	137.8	(10)	243.1
Clarksburg, W. Va. [1]	400.0	100.4	87.0	105.7	17.0	308.4	91.0	84.6	101.4	100.0	100.0	196.9	(10)	347.2
Cedar Rapids, Iowa [1]	83.3	100.4	78.2	87.6	46.0	70.7	91.7	85.7	101.4	100.0	100.0	157.5	(10)	277.8
Columbia, S. C.	(9)	99.6	69.0	78.2	16.2	162.1	93.5	89.9	99.4	100.0	100.0	78.7	(10)	138.9
Knoxville, Tenn.	(9)	99.6	89.2	96.1	59.6	123.7	88.5	81.8	99.4	100.0	100.0	265.0	248.2	277.8
Columbus, Ohio [1]	(9)	100.7	89.3	87.5	82.4	130.2	90.0	82.5	102.3	100.0	100.0	(10)	(10)	(10)
Birmingham, Ala.	(9)	99.6	103.7	91.3	114.0	149.2	94.5	91.5	99.4	100.0	100.0	118.1	(10)	208.3
El Paso, Tex.	166.7	99.6	67.4	73.5	31.7	28.2	97.7	96.8	99.4	100.0	100.0	137.8	(10)	243.1
Little Rock, Ark.	(9)	99.6	86.8	102.4	30.5	191.7	93.0	89.1	99.4	100.0	100.0	320.1	193.6	416.7
Mobile, Ala.	(9)	99.6	89.6	99.1	38.8	298.5	86.3	78.2	99.4	100.0	100.0	135.8	40.9	208.3
Wichita, Kans.	96.7	99.6	85.2	95.7	48.6	211.1	88.5	81.8	99.4	100.0	100.0	(10)	(10)	(10)

1 Include sales tax where levied (appendix table 16).
2 Budget allowance identical in all cities, plus sales tax where levied.
3 Exclusive of sales tax.
4 Though only 18 cities had a direct charge for refuse disposal, an average for 59 cities is used in order to balance the table. The 18-city average is $4.90.
5 Though only 55 cities had a direct charge for school attendance, an average for 59 cities is used in order to balance the table. The 55-city average is $7.37.
6 Though taxes were payable in only 36 cities, an average for 59 cities is used in order to balance the table. The 36-city average is $4.17.
7 Though personal property taxes were payable in only 22 cities, an average for 59 cities is used in order to balance the table. The 22-city average is $2.96.
8 Though capitation taxes were payable in only 25 cities, an average for 59 cities is used in order to balance the table. The 25-city average is $3.40.
9 Not a direct charge.
10 None payable.

NOTE.—Owing to the necessity for rounding numbers in computing averages, there are slight discrepancies between certain totals and the sums of their component items.

Table 10.—Annual Costs [1] of Living, by Major Budget Groups and Principal Subgroups, in 9 Geographic Divisions, 4-Person Manual Worker's Family, 59 Cities, March 1935

EMERGENCY LEVEL

Budget group	Average, 59 cities	Geographic division								
		New England	Middle Atlantic	East North Central	West North Central	South Atlantic	East South Central	West South Central	Mountain	Pacific
Total cost of living	$903.27	$912.27	$924.36	$925.07	$910.88	$899.25	$848.80	$855.37	$915.16	$920.48
Food	340.30	347.05	342.07	335.29	331.80	347.50	332.89	336.97	348.74	339.27
Clothing, clothing upkeep, and personal care	128.05	128.69	124.68	133.43	129.31	122.15	118.95	120.88	137.07	141.57
Clothing	100.23	100.31	97.72	105.12	102.10	95.96	92.58	93.87	105.38	111.53
Clothing upkeep	11.88	12.28	11.06	11.37	11.99	10.99	11.23	11.49	14.96	13.02
Personal care	15.93	16.10	15.90	16.94	15.21	15.19	15.15	15.52	16.73	17.02
Housing, including water	167.79	166.00	184.88	178.89	173.55	176.20	148.62	152.70	161.04	145.68
Household operation	121.84	137.32	120.24	116.20	129.79	116.38	106.48	106.15	133.46	136.11
Fuel	48.80	64.71	51.24	50.46	61.01	44.58	37.71	30.36	49.00	46.63
Coal or wood	38.66	53.43	42.79	44.72	54.28	29.92	25.40	21.86	38.53	32.00
Gas	10.14	11.28	8.45	5.74	6.73	14.66	12.32	8.50	10.47	14.62
Ice	18.67	15.57	15.39	15.22	13.77	20.13	18.61	20.96	23.46	29.89
Electricity	14.52	16.41	16.05	12.38	14.19	13.70	13.26	16.00	16.70	12.53
Household supplies	16.94	17.31	16.16	16.60	16.55	15.58	15.73	16.54	20.03	19.88
Furniture, furnishings, and household equipment	18.66	18.82	18.09	18.77	17.93	18.97	18.42	17.78	20.25	19.39
Refuse disposal	[2] 1.50	1.75	.56	(3)	3.60	.67	(3)	1.75	1.26	5.04
Unspecified essentials [4]	2.76	2.75	2.75	2.77	2.75	2.76	2.76	2.75	2.76	2.76
Miscellaneous	145.30	133.22	152.49	161.28	146.44	137.02	141.85	138.67	134.86	157.84
Medical care	47.08	48.94	47.62	44.38	45.05	46.42	43.90	44.62	53.07	52.53
Transportation	44.97	34.23	54.86	61.15	50.75	35.65	39.23	37.99	27.44	56.45
School attendance	[5] 6.87	1.87	3.91	9.98	5.90	8.08	11.68	8.73	6.57	5.07
Recreation	12.63	12.77	13.41	12.77	11.83	12.46	11.98	12.54	13.25	12.58
Motion picture theater admissions	7.80	7.97	8.60	7.88	7.02	7.64	7.15	7.73	8.38	7.73
Tobacco and toys [4]	4.83	4.80	4.81	4.90	4.81	4.83	4.83	4.81	4.87	4.85
Life insurance [4]	20.80	20.80	20.80	20.80	20.80	20.80	20.80	20.80	20.80	20.80
Church contributions [4]	10.40	10.40	10.40	10.40	10.40	10.40	10.40	10.40	10.40	10.40
Taxes [6]	[7] 2.54	4.20	1.49	1.79	1.71	3.22	3.87	3.60	3.33	(8)
Personal property	[9] 1.10	2.37	(8)	1.41	1.14	.89	1.07	.93	2.53	(8)
Capitation	[10] 1.44	1.83	1.49	.38	.57	2.33	2.80	2.67	.80	(8)

[1] Include sales tax where levied (appendix table 16).

[2] Though only 18 cities had a direct charge for refuse disposal, an average for 59 cities is used in order to balance the table. The 18-city average is $4.90. The averages for the geographic divisions are based on the total number of cities in each division included in this study.

[3] Not a direct charge.

[4] Budget allowance identical in all cities, plus sales tax where levied.

[5] Though only 55 cities had a direct charge for school attendance, an average for 59 cities is used in order to balance the table. The 55-city average is $7.37. The averages for the geographic divisions are based on the total number of cities in each division included in this study.

[6] Exclusive of sales tax.

[7] Though taxes were payable in only 36 cities, an average for 59 cities is used in order to balance the table. The 36-city average is $4.17. The averages for the geographic divisions are based on the total number of cities in each division included in this study.

[8] None payable.

[9] Though personal property taxes were payable in only 22 cities, an average for 59 cities is used in order to balance the table. The 22-city average is $2.96. The averages for the geographic divisions are based on the total number of cities in each division included in this study.

[10] Though capitation taxes were payable in only 25 cities, an average for 59 cities is used in order to balance the table. The 25-city average is $3.40. The averages for the geographic divisions are based on the total number of cities in each division included in this study.

NOTE.—Owing to the necessity for rounding numbers in computing averages, there are slight discrepancies between certain totals and the sums of their component items.

Table 11.—Relative Costs[1] of Living, by Major Budget Groups and Principal Subgroups, in 9 Geographic Divisions, 4-Person Manual Worker's Family, 59 Cities, March 1935

EMERGENCY LEVEL

Budget group	Average, 59 cities		Geographic division								
	Amount	Percent	New England	Middle Atlantic	East North Central	West North Central	South Atlantic	East South Central	West South Central	Mountain	Pacific
Total cost of living	$903.27	100.0	101.0	102.3	102.4	100.8	99.6	94.0	94.7	101.3	101.9
Food	340.30	100.0	102.0	100.5	98.5	97.5	102.1	97.8	99.0	102.5	99.7
Clothing, clothing upkeep, and personal care	128.05	100.0	100.5	97.4	104.2	101.0	95.4	92.9	94.4	107.0	110.6
Clothing	100.23	100.0	100.1	97.5	104.9	101.9	95.7	92.4	93.7	105.1	111.3
Clothing upkeep	11.88	100.0	103.4	93.1	95.7	100.9	92.5	94.5	96.7	125.9	109.6
Personal care	15.93	100.0	101.0	99.8	106.3	95.5	95.3	95.0	97.4	105.0	106.8
Housing, including water	167.79	100.0	98.9	110.2	106.6	103.4	105.0	88.6	91.0	96.0	86.8
Household operation	121.84	100.0	112.7	98.7	95.4	106.5	95.5	87.4	87.1	109.5	111.7
Fuel	48.80	100.0	132.6	105.0	103.4	125.0	91.4	77.3	62.2	100.4	95.6
Coal or wood	38.66	100.0	138.2	110.7	115.7	140.4	77.4	65.7	56.5	99.7	82.8
Gas	10.14	100.0	111.2	83.3	56.6	66.4	144.6	121.5	83.8	103.3	144.2
Ice	18.67	100.0	83.4	82.4	81.5	73.7	107.8	99.7	112.3	125.7	160.1
Electricity	14.52	100.0	113.0	110.5	85.2	97.7	94.3	91.3	110.1	115.0	86.3
Household supplies	16.94	100.0	102.2	95.4	98.0	97.7	92.0	92.8	97.7	118.2	117.4
Furniture, furnishings, and household equipment	18.66	100.0	100.9	96.9	100.6	96.1	101.7	98.7	95.3	108.5	103.9
Refuse disposal	[2] 1.50	100.0	116.7	37.3	(3)	240.0	44.7	(3)	116.7	84.0	336.0
Unspecified essentials [4]	2.76	100.0	99.6	99.6	100.4	99.6	100.0	100.0	99.6	100.0	100.0
Miscellaneous	145.30	100.0	91.7	104.9	111.0	100.8	94.3	97.6	95.4	92.8	108.6
Medical care	47.08	100.0	103.9	101.1	94.3	95.7	98.6	93.2	94.8	112.7	111.6
Transportation	44.97	100.0	76.1	122.0	136.0	112.9	79.3	87.2	84.5	61.0	125.6
School attendance	[5] 6.87	100.0	27.2	56.9	145.3	85.9	117.5	170.1	127.1	95.6	73.8
Recreation	12.63	100.0	101.1	106.1	101.1	93.7	98.7	94.8	99.2	104.9	99.6
Motion picture theater admissions	7.80	100.0	102.2	110.2	100.9	90.0	97.9	91.7	99.1	107.4	99.1
Tobacco and toys [4]	4.83	100.0	99.4	99.6	101.4	99.6	100.0	100.0	99.6	100.8	100.4
Life insurance [4]	20.80	100.0	100.0	100.0	100.0	100.0	100.0	100.0	100.0	100.0	100.0
Church contributions [4]	10.40	100.0	100.0	100.0	100.0	100.0	100.0	100.0	100.0	100.0	100.0
Taxes [6]	[7] 2.54	100.0	165.4	58.7	70.5	67.3	126.8	152.4	141.7	131.1	(8)
Personal property	[9] 1.10	100.0	215.5	(8)	128.2	103.6	80.9	97.3	84.5	230.0	(8)
Capitation	[10] 1.44	100.0	127.1	103.5	26.4	39.6	161.8	194.4	185.4	55.6	(9)

[1] Include sales tax where levied (appendix table 16).

[2] Though only 18 cities had a direct charge for refuse disposal, an average for 59 cities is used in order to balance the table. The 18-city average is $4.90. The averages for the geographic divisions are based on the total number of cities in each division included in this study.

[3] Not a direct charge.

[4] Budget allowance identical in all cities, plus sales tax where levied.

[5] Though only 55 cities had a direct charge for school attendance, an average for 59 cities is used in order to balance the table. The 55-city average is $7.37. The averages for the geographic divisions are based on the total number of cities in each division included in this study.

[6] Exclusive of sales tax.

[7] Though taxes were payable in only 36 cities, an average for 59 cities is used in order to balance the table. The 36-city average is $4.17. The averages for the geographic divisions are based on the total number of cities in each division included in this study.

[8] None payable.

[9] Though personal property taxes were payable in only 22 cities, an average for 59 cities is used in order to balance the table. The 22-city average is $2.96. The averages for the geographic divisions are based on the total number of cities in each division included in this study.

[10] Though capitation taxes were payable in only 25 cities, an average for 59 cities is used in order to balance the table. The 25-city average is $3.40. The averages for the geographic divisions are based on the total number of cities in each division included in this study.

NOTE.—Owing to the necessity for rounding numbers in computing averages, there are slight discrepancies between certain totals and the sums of their component items.

Table 12.—Annual Costs[1] of Living, by Major Budget Groups and Principal Subgroups, in 5 Size of City Classifications, 4-Person Manual Worker's Family, 59 Cities, March 1935

EMERGENCY LEVEL

Budget group	Average, 59 cities	Size of city classification				
		1,000,000 or more	500,000 to 1,000,000	250,000 to 500,000	100,000 to 250,000	25,000 to 100,000
Total cost of living	$903.27	$951.82	$951.29	$897.50	$884.88	$883.29
Food	340.30	343.49	338.66	338.09	338.78	344.94
Clothing, clothing upkeep, and personal care	128.05	130.85	132.64	124.96	128.13	128.57
Clothing	100.23	103.92	104.80	97.65	100.30	99.69
Clothing upkeep	11.88	10.48	11.36	11.63	11.98	13.01
Personal care	15.93	16.45	16.48	15.67	15.85	15.87
Housing, including water	167.79	179.40	187.50	165.00	165.39	157.86
Household operation	121.84	123.10	119.68	115.89	121.77	131.46
Fuel	48.80	52.91	49.49	45.31	49.04	51.62
Coal or wood	38.66	44.96	42.46	36.45	36.32	39.63
Gas	10.14	7.95	7.03	8.86	12.71	12.00
Ice	18.67	17.88	17.58	18.45	17.73	20.95
Electricity	14.52	14.42	12.59	13.70	14.75	16.70
Household supplies	16.94	17.02	16.86	16.44	16.83	17.80
Furniture, furnishings, and household equipment	18.66	18.10	18.57	18.32	18.89	19.19
Refuse disposal	[2] 1.50	(3)	1.84	.90	1.78	2.43
Unspecified essentials [4]	2.76	2.77	2.76	2.76	2.75	2.76
Miscellaneous	145.30	174.98	172.80	153.57	130.82	120.46
Medical care	47.08	49.53	47.50	45.61	46.87	48.27
Transportation	44.97	75.70	74.96	55.33	30.97	14.60
School attendance	[5] 6.87	4.41	4.48	6.99	6.13	9.91
Recreation	12.63	13.79	13.42	12.33	12.31	12.49
Motion picture theater admissions	7.80	8.90	8.59	7.51	7.50	7.65
Tobacco and toys [4]	4.83	4.89	4.83	4.83	4.82	4.84
Life insurance [4]	20.80	20.80	20.80	20.80	20.80	20.80
Church contributions [4]	10.40	10.40	10.40	10.40	10.40	10.40
Taxes [6]	[7] 2.54	.36	1.24	2.09	3.33	4.00
Personal property	[8] 1.10	.36	.74	.91	1.44	1.54
Capitation	[9] 1.44	(10)	.50	1.18	1.89	2.46

[1] Include sales tax where levied (appendix table 16).

[2] Though only 18 cities had a direct charge for refuse disposal, an average for 59 cities is used in order to balance the table. The 18-city average is $4.90. The averages for the size of city groups are based on the total number of cities in each group included in this study.

[3] Not a direct charge.

[4] Budget allowance identical in all cities, plus sales tax where levied.

[5] Though only 55 cities had a direct charge for school attendance, an average for 59 cities is used in order to balance the table. The 55-city average is $7.37. The averages for the size of city groups are based on the total number of cities in each group included in this study.

[6] Exclusive of sales tax.

[7] Though taxes were payable in only 36 cities, an average for 59 cities is used in order to balance the table. The 36-city average is $4.17. The averages for the size of city groups are based on the total number of cities in each group included in this study.

[8] Though personal property taxes were payable in only 22 cities, an average for 59 cities is used in order to balance the table. The 22-city average is $2.96. The averages for the size of city groups are based on the total number of cities in each group included in this study.

[9] Though capitation taxes were payable in only 25 cities, an average for 59 cities is used in order to balance the table. The 25-city average is $3.40. The averages for the size of city groups are based on the total number of cities in each group included in this study.

[10] None payable.

NOTE.—Owing to the necessity for rounding numbers in computing averages, there are slight discrepancies between certain totals and the sums of their component items.

Table 13.—Relative Costs[1] of Living, by Major Budget Groups and Principal Sub groups, in 5 Size of City Classifications, 4-Person Manual Worker's Family, 59 Cities, March 1935

EMERGENCY LEVEL

Budget group	Average, 59 cities		Size of city classification				
	Amount	Percent	1,000,000 or more	500,000 to 1,000,000	250,000 to 500,000	100,000 to 250,000	25,000 to 100,000
Total cost of living	$903.27	100.0	105.4	105.3	99.4	98.0	97.8
Food	340.30	100.0	100.9	99.5	99.4	99.6	101.4
Clothing, clothing upkeep, and personal care	128.05	100.0	102.2	103.6	97.6	100.1	100.4
Clothing	100.23	100.0	103.7	104.6	97.4	100.1	99.5
Clothing upkeep	11.88	100.0	88.2	95.6	97.9	100.8	109.5
Personal care	15.93	100.0	103.2	103.4	98.4	99.5	99.6
Housing, including water	167.79	100.0	106.9	111.7	98.3	98.6	94.1
Household operation	121.84	100.0	101.0	98.2	95.1	99.9	107.9
Fuel	48.80	100.0	108.4	101.4	92.8	100.5	105.8
Coal or wood	38.66	100.0	116.3	109.8	94.3	93.9	102.5
Gas	10.14	100.0	78.4	69.3	87.4	125.3	118.3
Ice	18.67	100.0	95.8	94.2	98.9	95.0	112.2
Electricity	14.52	100.0	99.3	86.7	94.4	101.6	115.0
Household supplies	16.94	100.0	100.5	99.5	97.1	99.3	105.1
Furniture, furnishings, and household equipment	18.66	100.0	97.0	99.5	98.2	101.2	102.8
Refuse disposal	[2] 1.50	100.0	(3)	122.7	60.0	118.7	162.0
Unspecified essentials [4]	2.76	100.0	100.4	100.0	100.0	99.6	100.0
Miscellaneous	145.30	100.0	120.4	118.9	105.7	90.0	82.9
Medical care	47.08	100.0	105.2	100.9	96.9	99.5	102.5
Transportation	44.97	100.0	168.4	166.7	123.1	68.9	32.5
School attendance	[5] 6.87	100.0	64.2	65.2	101.7	89.2	144.2
Recreation	12.63	100.0	109.2	106.2	97.6	97.5	98.8
Motion picture theater admissions	7.80	100.0	114.1	110.1	96.2	96.1	98.0
Tobacco and toys [4]	4.83	100.0	101.2	100.0	100.0	99.8	100.2
Life insurance [4]	20.80	100.0	100.0	100.0	100.0	100.0	100.0
Church contributions [4]	10.40	100.0	100.0	100.0	100.0	100.0	100.0
Taxes [6]	[7] 2.54	100.0	14.2	48.8	82.3	131.1	157.5
Personal property	[8] 1.10	100.0	32.7	67.3	82.7	130.9	140.0
Capitation	[9] 1.44	100.0	(10)	34.7	81.9	131.2	170.8

[1] Include sales tax where levied (appendix table 16).

[2] Though only 18 cities had a direct charge for refuse disposal, an average for 59 cities is used in order to balance the table. The 18-city average is $4.90. The averages for the size of city groups are based on the total number of cities in each group included in this study.

[3] Not a direct charge.

[4] Budget allowance identical in all cities, plus sales tax where levied.

[5] Though only 55 cities had a direct charge for school attendance, an average for 59 cities is used in order to balance the table. The 55-city average is $7.37. The averages for the size of city groups are based on the total number of cities in each group included in this study.

[6] Exclusive of sales tax.

[7] Though taxes were payable in only 36 cities, an average for 59 cities is used in order to balance the table. The 36-city average is $4.17. The averages for the size of city groups are based on the total number of cities in each group included in this study.

[8] Though personal property taxes were payable in only 22 cities, an average for 59 cities is used in order to balance the table. The 22-city average is $2.96. The averages for the size of city groups are based on the total number of cities in each group included in this study.

[9] Though capitation taxes were payable in only 25 cities, an average for 59 cities is used in order to balance the table. The 25-city average is $3.40. The averages for the size of city groups are based on the total number of cities in each group included in this study.

[10] None payable.

NOTE.—Owing to the necessity for rounding numbers in computing averages, there are slight discrepancies between certain totals and the sums of their component items.

Table 14.—Annual Costs[1] of Minimum Medical Care per 1,000 Persons, 59 Cities, March 1935

City	Total	Services[2]	Drugs and appliances[3]
Average, 59 cities	$13,079.01	$11,831.67	$1,247.34
Spokane, Wash	16,524.49	15,257.24	1,267.25
San Francisco, Calif.[1]	16,069.47	14,783.61	1,285.86
Butte, Mont	15,709.50	14,429.25	1,280.25
Tucson, Ariz.[1]	15,327.21	13,976.75	1,350.46
Los Angeles, Calif.[1]	15,020.86	13,806.75	1,214.11
Cleveland, Ohio[1]	14,802.74	13,393.44	1,409.30
Washington, D. C	14,727.93	13,618.68	1,109.25
Portland, Maine	14,711.83	13,525.08	1,186.75
Detroit, Mich.[1]	14,585.49	13,264.00	1,321.49
Scranton, Pa	14,502.50	13,256.25	1,246.25
Albuquerque, N. Mex.[1]	14,389.16	13,061.38	1,327.79
Chicago, Ill.[1]	14,354.46	13,120.00	1,234.46
Jacksonville, Fla	14,315.00	13,137.00	1,178.00
Salt Lake City, Utah[1]	14,161.75	12,836.00	1,325.75
Denver, Colo.[1]	14,129.40	12,841.14	1,288.26
New York, N. Y.[1]	14,072.76	12,864.36	1,208.41
Bridgeport, Conn	14,036.96	12,861.96	1,175.00
Binghamton, N. Y	13,981.50	12,846.00	1,135.50
Boston, Mass	13,839.00	12,620.00	1,219.00
Clarksburg, W. Va.[1]	13,829.03	12,540.00	1,289.03
Providence, R. I	13,694.44	12,442.44	1,252.00
Pittsburgh, Pa	13,630.11	12,463.36	1,166.75
Minneapolis, Minn	13,530.75	12,150.00	1,380.75
Little Rock, Ark	13,387.75	12,158.00	1,229.75
Atlanta, Ga	13,370.91	12,095.16	1,275.75
Memphis, Tenn	13,322.25	12,120.00	1,202.25
Rochester, N. Y	13,208.25	12,053.00	1,155.25
Houston, Tex	13,193.75	11,964.00	1,229.75
New Orleans, La	13,113.89	12,036.64	1,077.25
Winston-Salem, N. C.[1]	12,987.25	11,633.06	1,354.19
Newark, N. J	12,985.14	11,787.39	1,197.75
Mobile, Ala	12,960.50	11,670.00	1,290.50
Seattle, Wash	12,956.00	11,700.00	1,256.00
Sioux Falls, S. Dak	12,852.19	11,506.19	1,346.00
Kansas City, Mo	12,836.65	11,498.40	1,338.25
Fall River, Mass	12,809.25	11,667.50	1,141.75
Richmond, Va	12,807.36	11,609.36	1,198.00
Norfolk, Va	12,765.40	11,603.40	1,162.00
Buffalo, N. Y	12,688.39	11,536.64	1,151.75
Oklahoma City, Okla.[1]	12,677.61	11,377.00	1,300.61
Knoxville, Tenn	12,562.75	11,280.00	1,282.75
Wichita, Kans	12,519.89	11,225.64	1,294.25
Manchester, N. H	12,472.67	11,170.92	1,301.75
Portland, Oreg	12,391.31	11,071.56	1,319.75
St. Louis, Mo	12,386.46	11,193.21	1,193.25
Dallas, Tex	12,376.56	10,944.56	1,432.00
Omaha, Nebr	12,001.75	10,770.00	1,231.75
Birmingham, Ala	11,945.61	10,777.36	1,168.25
Cedar Rapids, Iowa[1]	11,463.64	10,148.35	1,315.29
Columbus, Ohio[1]	11,445.52	10,166.00	1,279.52
Milwaukee, Wis	11,127.66	9,915.66	1,212.00
Baltimore, Md	11,008.67	9,954.92	1,053.75
Peoria, Ill.[1]	10,972.00	9,770.44	1,201.56
Indianapolis, Ind	10,881.25	9,521.00	1,360.25
Philadelphia, Pa	10,754.44	9,633.44	1,121.00
Cincinnati, Ohio[1]	10,454.49	9,116.00	1,338.49
Columbia, S. C	10,233.54	8,955.04	1,278.50
Louisville, Ky.[1]	10,178.42	8,934.44	1,243.98
El Paso, Tex	9,616.30	8,409.80	1,206.50

[1] Include sales tax where levied. Medical care costs for a 4-person manual worker's family at the maintenance level of living were computed as 4/1000 of the costs shown in this table. By definition, emergency budget medical care cost is 90 percent of maintenance budget cost. See appendix tables 15 and 16 for amount of sales tax for a 4-person family.

[2] Includes physicians, dentists, optometrists, hospitals, and nurses.

[3] Includes eyeglasses and frames, proprietary medicines, and prescriptions.

NOTE.—Owing to the necessity for rounding numbers in computing averages, there are slight discrepancies between certain totals and the sums of their component items.

Table 15.—Annual Sales Tax on Costs of Living, by Major Budget Groups and Principal Subgroups, 4-Person Manual Worker's Family, 18 Cities,[1] March 1935

MAINTENANCE LEVEL

City	Total cost of living	Food	Clothing, clothing upkeep, and personal care				Water	Household operation										Miscellaneous					
									Fuel													Recreation	
			Total	Clothing	Clothing upkeep	Personal care		Total	Total	Coal or wood	Gas	Ice	Electricity	Household supplies	Furniture, furnishings, and household equipment	Unspecified essentials	Total	Medical care	Transportation	School attendance	Total	Motion picture theater admissions	Tobacco and toys
Average,[2] 59 cities	$5.14	$2.66	$1.16	$1.04	$0.02	$0.10	$0.01	$0.94	$0.34	$0.31	$0.03	$0.17	$0.07	$0.13	$0.22	$0.01	$0.37	$0.05	*	$0.05	$0.27	$0.12	$0.15
Louisville, Ky	25.20	12.92	5.17	4.16	.32	.69	.52	3.83	1.47	1.35	.12	.49	.45	.51	.88	.04	2.77	.14	(3)	.34	2.29	1.66	.62
Detroit, Mich	23.76	12.93	5.03	4.61	.05	.37	(3)	4.62	2.05	1.83	.21	.54	.51	.57	.91	.04	1.19	.15	(3)	.41	.62	(3)	.62
Albuquerque, N. Mex	20.25	9.52	3.78	2.90	.32	.56	(3)	3.27	.95	.74	.21	.69	.48	.46	.67	.02	3.68	.86	$0.25	.08	2.50	2.08	.42
Cleveland, Ohio	20.08	9.97	5.32	4.90	.05	.36	(3)	3.70	1.61	1.61	(3)	.51	[4].04	.57	.95	.04	1.09	.16	(3)	.31	.62	(3)	.62
San Francisco, Calif	19.85	11.20	4.37	4.03	.04	.30	(3)	3.42	.86	.86	(3)	1.17	[4].03	.54	.79	.03	.85	.12	(3)	.21	.52	(3)	.52
Columbus, Ohio	19.15	10.09	4.75	4.34	.05	.37	(3)	3.28	1.14	1.14	(3)	.58	[4].04	.54	.94	.04	1.04	.15	(3)	.26	.62	(3)	.62
Los Angeles, Calif	19.08	10.78	4.42	4.08	.04	.30	(3)	3.17	.93	.93	(3)	.88	[4].03	.52	.79	.03	.70	.12	(3)	.06	.52	(3)	.52
Cincinnati, Ohio	18.88	9.85	4.64	4.23	.05	.36	(3)	3.50	1.35	1.35	(3)	.58	[4].04	.57	.93	.04	.90	.15	(3)	.12	.62	(3)	.62
Winston-Salem, N. C	17.25	8.41	4.51	4.11	.05	.35	(3)	3.46	1.17	1.17	(3)	.82	[4].04	.50	.90	.04	.87	.16	(3)	.09	.62	(3)	.62
Cedar Rapids, Iowa	16.95	8.20	3.18	2.91	.03	.24	.19	3.21	1.51	1.31	.20	.32	.36	.38	.62	.02	2.18	.10	(3)	.10	1.98	1.56	.42
Chicago, Ill	16.06	9.06	3.28	3.01	.03	.24	(3)	3.15	1.45	1.34	.11	.39	.35	.34	.59	.02	.57	.10	(3)	.06	.42	(3)	.42
Salt Lake City, Utah	15.52	8.38	3.40	3.12	.03	.24	(3)	3.20	1.19	1.01	.18	.45	.44	.41	.69	.02	.54	.10	(3)	.02	.42	(3)	.42
Peoria, Ill	15.52	8.80	3.23	2.96	.03	.24	.08	2.53	.80	.60	.20	.39	.36	.36	.60	.02	.88	.10	(3)	.36	.42	(3)	.42
Clarksburg, W. Va	15.08	9.11	3.39	2.90	.24	.25	(3)	1.92	.45	.45	(3)	.39	[4].03	.39	.65	.02	.66	.10	(3)	.14	.42	(3)	.42
Denver, Colo	13.06	6.56	3.11	2.84	.03	.24	(3)	2.73	1.03	.85	.18	.31	.36	.39	.62	.02	.67	.10	(3)	.15	.42	(3)	.42
Tucson, Ariz	11.95	6.86	2.36	2.15	.02	.19	(3)	2.22	.56	.46	.11	.70	.12	.35	.47	.02	.51	.08	(3)	.12	.31	(3)	.31
Oklahoma City, Okla	7.60	4.37	1.56	1.42	.02	.13	(3)	1.34	.39	.36	.03	.27	.21	.18	.28	.01	.33	.01	(3)	.11	.21	(3)	.21
New York, N. Y	6.49	(1)	2.96	2.69	.03	.24	(3)	3.02	1.30	1.09	.21	.39	.43	.34	.54	.02	.51	.06	(3)	.03	.42	(3)	.42

* Less than $0.005.

[1] In addition, New Orleans had a local tax of 1 cent on motion picture theater admissions exceeding 10 cents. It amounted to $1.56 per year. Though this tax was not a sales tax, it is included in the average for the total cost of living and for motion picture theater admissions.

[2] All averages in this table are based on 59 cities rather than on the number in which the tax was levied, in order to account for the tax in the 59-city average total cost of living and averages for the separate budget groups.

[3] No tax.

[4] Includes sales tax on accessories only; energy is not taxed.

NOTE.—Owing to the necessity for rounding numbers in computing averages, there are slight discrepancies between certain totals and the sums of their component items.

Table 16.—Annual Sales Tax on Costs of Living, by Major Budget Groups and Principal Subgroups, 4-Person Manual Worker's Family, 18 Cities,[1] March 1935

EMERGENCY LEVEL

City	Total cost of living	Food	Clothing, clothing upkeep, and personal care				Water	Household operation									Miscellaneous						
									Fuel												Recreation		
			Total	Clothing	Clothing upkeep	Personal care		Total	Total	Coal or wood	Gas	Ice	Electricity	Household supplies	Furniture, furnishings, and household equipment	Unspecified essentials	Total	Medical care	Transportation	School attendance	Total	Motion picture theater admissions	Tobacco and toys
Average,[2] 59 cities	$3.78	$2.06	$0.82	$0.72	$0.02	$0.08	$0.01	$0.74	$0.28	$0.26	$0.03	$0.14	$0.06	$0.12	$0.13	$0.01	$0.16	$0.04	*	$0.05	$0.06	$0.03	$0.03
Louisville, Ky	17.92	9.84	3.61	2.84	.31	.46	.52	2.96	1.19	1.08	.11	.41	.34	.46	.53	.03	1.00	.13	(3)	.34	.53	.38	.14
Detroit, Mich	17.61	9.67	3.54	3.17	.04	.33	(3)	3.71	1.73	1.54	.19	.45	.43	.52	.55	.03	.69	.14	(3)	.41	.14	(3)	.14
Cleveland, Ohio	15.12	7.89	3.75	3.38	.04	.33	(3)	2.88	1.32	1.32	(3)	.42	[4].03	.51	.57	.03	.60	.15	(3)	.31	.14	(3)	.14
San Francisco, Calif	14.82	8.59	3.10	2.80	.03	.27	(3)	2.69	.70	.70	(3)	.98	[4].03	.49	.47	.03	.44	.11	(3)	.21	.12	(3)	.12
Columbus, Ohio	14.37	8.01	3.32	2.95	.04	.33	(3)	2.50	.90	.90	(3)	.49	[4].03	.49	.57	.03	.54	.14	(3)	.26	.14	(3)	.14
Albuquerque, N. Mex	14.26	7.39	2.65	2.01	.28	.36	(3)	2.59	.82	.62	.20	.57	.37	.41	.40	.02	1.64	.77	$0.21	.08	.58	.48	.10
Cincinnati, Ohio	14.18	7.80	3.28	2.91	.04	.32	(3)	2.70	1.09	1.09	(3)	.49	[4].03	.51	.56	.03	.40	.14	(3)	.12	.14	(3)	.14
Los Angeles, Calif	14.08	8.20	3.10	2.80	.03	.27	(3)	2.49	.77	.77	(3)	.73	[4].03	.47	.47	.03	.29	.11	(3)	.06	.12	(3)	.12
Winston-Salem, N. C	13.26	6.98	3.19	2.83	.04	.31	(3)	2.72	.98	.98	(3)	.68	[4].03	.45	.54	.03	.37	.14	(3)	.09	.14	(3)	.14
Chicago, Ill	11.92	6.85	2.32	2.08	.03	.22	(3)	2.52	1.23	1.13	.10	.32	.28	.31	.36	.02	.24	.09	(3)	.06	.10	(3)	.10
Cedar Rapids, Iowa	11.87	6.25	2.24	2.00	.03	.21	.19	2.55	1.28	1.10	.18	.27	.27	.34	.37	.02	.64	.09	(3)	.10	.46	.36	.10
Peoria, Ill	11.57	6.71	2.28	2.04	.03	.21	.08	1.95	.64	.46	.18	.32	.29	.32	.36	.02	.55	.09	(3)	.36	.10	(3)	.10
Salt Lake City, Utah	11.54	6.42	2.42	2.17	.03	.22	(3)	2.50	.99	.82	.17	.37	.34	.37	.41	.02	.21	.09	(3)	.02	.10	(3)	.10
Clarksburg, W. Va	11.15	6.97	2.42	2.00	.20	.22	(3)	1.43	.32	.32	(3)	.32	[4].02	.35	.39	.02	.33	.09	(3)	.14	.10	(3)	.10
Denver, Colo	9.86	5.22	2.20	1.96	.03	.21	(3)	2.11	.84	.67	.17	.26	.27	.35	.37	.02	.34	.09	(3)	.15	.10	(3)	.10
Tucson, Ariz	8.95	5.27	1.66	1.47	.02	.17	(3)	1.75	.46	.37	.09	.59	.09	.32	.28	.02	.26	.07	(3)	.12	.07	(3)	.07
Oklahoma City, Okla	5.68	3.36	1.10	.97	.01	.11	(3)	1.05	.33	.30	.03	.23	.15	.16	.17	.01	.17	.01	(3)	.11	.05	(3)	.05
New York, N. Y	4.68	(3)	2.09	1.85	.03	.22	(3)	2.40	1.07	.88	.19	.32	.36	.30	.32	.02	.18	.06	(3)	.03	.10	(3)	.10

* Less than $0.005.

[1] In addition, New Orleans had a local tax of 1 cent on motion picture theater admissions exceeding 10 cents. It amounted to 36 cents per year. Though this tax was not a sales tax, it is included in the average for the total cost of living and for motion picture theater admissions.

[2] All averages in this table are based on 59 cities rather than on the number in which the tax was levied, in order to account for the tax in the 59-city average total cost of living and averages for the separate budget groups.

[3] No tax.

[4] Includes sales tax on accessories only; energy is not taxed.

NOTE.—Owing to the necessity for rounding numbers in computing averages, there are slight discrepancies between certain totals and the sums of their component items.

***Table 17.*—Percent Distribution of the Costs[1] of Living Among Major Budget Groups and Principal Subgroups, 4-Person Manual Worker's Family, 59 Cities, March 1935**

MAINTENANCE LEVEL

City	Total cost of living		Food	Clothing, clothing upkeep, and personal care				Housing, including water	Household operation							
										Fuel						
	Amount	Percent		Total	Clothing	Clothing upkeep	Personal care		Total	Total	Coal or wood	Gas	Ice	Electricity	Household supplies	Furniture, furnishings, and household equipment
Average, 59 cities	$1, 260. 62	100. 0	35. 6	14. 6	11. 5	1. 1	2. 0	17. 6	12. 2	4. 6	3. 7	0. 9	1. 8	1. 5	1. 5	2. 5
Washington, D. C	1, 414. 54	100. 0	33. 7	12. 6	10. 0	0. 9	1. 7	24. 2	10. 3	4. 5	3. 9	0. 6	1. 4	0. 9	1. 2	2. 1
San Francisco, Calif.[1]	1, 389. 87	100. 0	33. 1	15. 0	11. 9	1. 0	2. 1	19. 4	12. 9	3. 5	2. 6	0. 9	3. 5	1. 3	1. 6	2. 3
Minneapolis, Minn	1, 387. 79	100. 0	31. 5	14. 3	11. 5	1. 1	1. 7	19. 0	14. 6	7. 8	7. 3	0. 5	1. 3	1. 4	1. 3	2. 3
New York, N. Y.[1]	1, 375. 13	100. 0	34. 7	12. 6	10. 0	0. 8	1. 8	21. 8	11. 3	4. 9	4. 1	0. 8	1. 4	1. 6	1. 2	2. 0
Chicago, Ill.[1]	1, 356. 11	100. 0	34. 2	14. 3	11. 4	0. 9	2. 0	17. 7	11. 9	5. 4	5. 0	0. 4	1. 5	1. 3	1. 3	2. 2
Milwaukee, Wis	1, 353. 34	100. 0	31. 5	15. 2	12. 0	1. 1	2. 1	20. 0	13. 1	6. 8	6. 2	0. 6	1. 0	1. 4	1. 3	2. 4
Boston, Mass	1, 352. 77	100. 0	34. 7	14. 0	11. 1	1. 0	1. 9	19. 5	12. 2	5. 2	4. 4	0. 8	1. 4	1. 5	1. 5	2. 4
Cleveland, Ohio[1]	1, 348. 33	100. 0	33. 0	15. 6	12. 4	1. 0	2. 2	17. 4	10. 6	4. 5	4. 2	0. 3	1. 3	0. 8	1. 4	2. 4
St. Louis, Mo	1, 339. 55	100. 0	33. 5	13. 4	10. 7	0. 9	1. 8	20. 2	9. 5	3. 3	2. 7	0. 6	1. 3	1. 1	1. 3	2. 1
Detroit, Mich.[1]	1, 317. 53	100. 0	33. 7	14. 9	12. 0	1. 0	1. 9	16. 8	12. 2	5. 4	4. 9	0. 5	1. 4	1. 3	1. 5	2. 4
Scranton, Pa	1, 312. 39	100. 0	34. 2	14. 4	11. 4	1. 0	2. 0	21. 0	11. 1	3. 9	2. 8	1. 1	1. 6	1. 5	1. 5	2. 4
Cincinnati, Ohio[1]	1, 311. 74	100. 0	34. 3	14. 1	11. 1	1. 0	2. 0	19. 6	10. 5	3. 8	3. 5	0. 3	1. 5	1. 1	1. 5	2. 4
Pittsburgh, Pa	1, 310. 52	100. 0	34. 1	14. 1	11. 3	1. 0	1. 8	18. 8	9. 6	2. 9	2. 5	0. 4	1. 3	1. 4	1. 3	2. 2
Los Angeles, Calif.[1]	1, 308. 11	100. 0	33. 8	15. 8	12. 8	1. 0	2. 0	15. 1	12. 0	3. 8	2. 9	0. 9	2. 8	1. 1	1. 6	2. 5
Newark, N. J	1, 300. 86	100. 0	36. 4	13. 1	10. 2	0. 9	2. 0	19. 8	12. 4	5. 0	4. 0	1. 0	1. 5	2. 0	1. 4	2. 3
Baltimore, Md	1, 300. 65	100. 0	34. 8	13. 1	10. 4	0. 9	1. 8	17. 5	11. 0	4. 5	3. 8	0. 7	1. 4	1. 2	1. 4	2. 3
Albuquerque, N. Mex.[1]	1, 299. 14	100. 0	37. 4	14. 8	11. 3	1. 3	2. 2	17. 9	13. 3	3. 7	2. 9	0. 8	2. 7	1. 9	1. 8	2. 6
Philadelphia, Pa	1, 297. 69	100. 0	34. 4	13. 5	10. 8	0. 9	1. 8	18. 5	10. 7	4. 3	3. 7	0. 6	1. 0	1. 4	1. 5	2. 3
Bridgeport, Conn	1, 296. 35	100. 0	37. 5	14. 0	11. 0	1. 0	2. 0	18. 1	12. 2	5. 7	4. 7	1. 0	1. 5	1. 2	1. 4	2. 2
Sioux Falls, S. Dak	1, 290. 60	100. 0	32. 9	14. 8	11. 8	1. 2	1. 8	21. 1	16. 0	7. 9	7. 2	0. 7	1. 5	1. 6	1. 6	2. 3
Rochester, N. Y	1, 287. 63	100. 0	34. 4	14. 1	11. 0	1. 2	1. 9	17. 5	14. 0	7. 2	6. 5	0. 7	1. 4	1. 5	1. 3	2. 4
Tucson, Ariz.[1]	1, 287. 25	100. 0	36. 1	14. 7	11. 3	1. 3	2. 1	17. 2	14. 0	4. 0	2. 4	1. 6	3. 7	1. 7	1. 9	2. 5
Butte, Mont	1, 283. 69	100. 0	35. 0	16. 7	12. 7	1. 7	2. 3	16. 4	14. 3	6. 2	5. 5	0. 7	1. 5	1. 8	1. 8	2. 8
Portland, Maine	1, 275. 48	100. 0	35. 3	15. 6	12. 3	1. 3	2. 0	16. 0	14. 5	6. 5	5. 4	1. 1	1. 4	1. 7	1. 6	2. 5
Peoria, Ill.[1]	1, 274. 30	100. 0	35. 3	14. 8	11. 8	1. 0	2. 0	21. 5	10. 3	3. 3	2. 5	0. 8	1. 6	1. 4	1. 4	2. 4

See footnotes at end of table.

Table 17.—Percent Distribution of the Costs of Living Among Major Budget Groups and Principal Subgroups, 4-Person Manual Worker's Family, 59 Cities, March 1935—Continued

MAINTENANCE LEVEL—continued

City	Total cost of living		Food	Clothing, clothing upkeep, and personal care				Housing, including water	Household operation							
										Fuel						
	Amount	Percent		Total	Clothing	Clothing upkeep	Personal care		Total	Total	Coal or wood	Gas	Ice	Electricity	Household supplies	Furniture, furnishings, and household equipment
Fall River, Mass	$1,271.51	100.0	35.7	15.1	12.2	1.0	1.9	17.5	13.8	6.1	5.2	0.9	1.5	1.8	1.5	2.7
Atlanta, Ga	1,268.22	100.0	36.5	13.4	10.6	0.9	1.9	19.4	10.7	3.5	2.6	0.9	1.8	1.4	1.3	2.5
Richmond, Va	1,268.06	100.0	35.3	15.1	12.1	1.1	1.9	18.6	12.2	4.4	3.1	1.3	2.2	1.4	1.3	2.7
Buffalo, N. Y	1,261.21	100.0	34.9	14.7	11.7	1.1	1.9	16.7	12.0	5.2	4.9	0.3	1.5	1.1	1.4	2.5
Omaha, Nebr	1,258.26	100.0	35.3	14.7	11.7	1.1	1.9	18.9	12.0	5.5	4.9	0.6	1.1	1.3	1.4	2.3
Manchester, N. H	1,254.03	100.0	36.9	14.5	11.4	1.2	1.9	14.8	14.4	6.7	5.7	1.0	1.6	1.9	1.5	2.4
Norfolk, Va	1,251.38	100.0	36.4	14.0	11.0	1.1	1.9	19.0	12.0	4.7	3.5	1.2	1.9	1.4	1.4	2.3
Denver, Colo.[1]	1,246.07	100.0	35.0	14.6	11.6	1.1	1.9	16.4	11.5	4.2	3.5	0.7	1.3	1.5	1.6	2.5
Kansas City, Mo	1,245.42	100.0	36.1	14.5	11.8	0.9	1.8	15.9	10.6	3.8	3.3	0.5	1.2	1.5	1.3	2.3
Providence, R. I	1,245.26	100.0	36.9	13.7	10.8	1.0	1.9	17.4	13.6	6.0	5.1	0.9	1.3	1.8	1.6	2.4
Binghamton, N. Y	1,243.19	100.0	36.0	14.6	11.6	1.0	2.0	18.3	12.5	4.8	4.0	0.8	1.6	1.8	1.4	2.6
Salt Lake City, Utah [1]	1,243.07	100.0	34.7	16.1	12.8	1.3	2.0	15.7	13.3	4.9	4.2	0.7	1.8	1.8	1.7	2.8
Seattle, Wash	1,233.35	100.0	35.9	15.7	12.3	1.3	2.1	13.6	13.4	4.7	3.2	1.5	2.9	1.2	1.7	2.6
New Orleans, La	1,233.08	100.0	35.0	14.0	11.1	1.0	1.9	16.1	10.7	2.7	1.9	0.8	1.9	2.0	1.4	2.4
Spokane, Wash	1,228.62	100.0	34.7	16.8	13.1	1.4	2.3	14.2	14.7	5.6	4.1	1.5	1.8	1.3	1.9	2.8
Winston-Salem, N. C.[1]	1,222.18	100.0	37.3	14.7	11.6	1.0	2.1	17.0	13.4	5.2	3.3	1.9	2.3	1.7	1.4	2.5
Portland, Oreg	1,221.72	100.0	35.7	16.7	13.4	1.2	2.1	13.0	13.4	4.0	2.7	1.3	3.0	1.3	1.8	2.5
Memphis, Tenn	1,221.40	100.0	35.4	14.2	11.0	1.1	2.1	18.2	10.8	3.4	2.6	0.8	1.9	1.4	1.3	2.5
Louisville, Ky.[1]	1,220.20	100.0	36.2	14.7	11.7	1.0	2.0	17.2	10.9	4.0	3.7	0.3	1.4	1.3	1.4	2.5
Oklahoma City, Okla.[1]	1,217.80	100.0	36.2	15.0	11.8	1.0	2.2	16.9	12.0	3.2	2.9	0.3	2.3	1.7	1.5	2.3
Jacksonville, Fla	1,217.27	100.0	37.6	14.2	11.3	1.1	1.8	16.3	12.6	4.8	2.0	2.8	1.9	1.7	1.3	2.6
Houston, Tex	1,209.96	100.0	35.6	14.9	11.8	1.2	1.9	17.4	10.3	2.2	1.3	0.9	2.5	1.3	1.4	2.6
Indianapolis, Ind	1,198.08	100.0	35.1	14.8	11.3	1.2	2.3	16.8	11.6	4.6	3.9	0.7	1.4	1.4	1.5	2.4
Columbia, S. C	1,192.60	100.0	40.3	14.0	11.0	1.0	2.0	16.6	12.7	3.6	1.7	1.9	2.9	1.7	1.4	2.8
Clarksburg, W. Va[1]	1,190.02	100.0	39.0	15.5	12.4	1.0	2.1	16.1	10.7	2.1	1.9	0.2	1.7	1.6	1.7	2.8

Dallas, Tex	1,188.97	100.0	38.0	13.6	10.7	1.0	1.9	18.2	10.5	2.3	1.4	0.9	2.4	1.4	1.7	2.4
Cedar Rapids, Iowa [1]	1,186.18	100.0	35.2	15.9	12.6	1.2	2.1	17.0	14.1	6.5	5.6	0.9	1.4	1.5	1.6	2.7
Columbus, Ohio [1]	1,178.70	100.0	37.7	15.7	12.6	1.0	2.1	16.3	10.9	3.6	3.4	0.2	1.7	1.0	1.6	2.7
Birmingham, Ala	1,168.85	100.0	38.2	14.6	11.5	1.1	2.0	14.2	11.0	3.4	2.5	0.9	1.9	1.5	1.5	2.4
Knoxville, Tenn	1,166.75	100.0	36.2	14.7	11.7	1.1	1.9	17.7	11.8	4.1	2.3	1.8	1.6	1.5	1.5	2.8
El Paso, Tex	1,153.58	100.0	38.3	14.6	11.5	1.1	2.0	16.9	13.5	4.8	3.8	1.0	1.9	2.0	1.7	2.6
Little Rock, Ark	1,139.06	100.0	39.0	15.2	11.9	1.2	2.1	15.3	11.0	2.8	2.2	0.6	1.6	2.1	1.6	2.6
Wichita, Kans	1,131.30	100.0	37.7	15.4	12.4	1.1	1.9	14.6	13.0	5.3	4.9	0.4	1.4	1.7	1.6	2.6
Mobile, Ala	1,129.81	100.0	38.4	14.6	11.4	1.2	2.0	14.5	12.5	3.6	1.8	1.8	2.7	1.6	1.6	2.7

See footnotes at end of table.

Table 17.—Percent Distribution of the Costs of Living Among Major Budget Groups and Principal Subgroups, 4-Person Manual Worker's Family, 59 Cities, March 1935—Continued

MAINTENANCE LEVEL—continued

City	Household operation—Continued		Miscellaneous												
	Refuse disposal	Unspecified essentials [2]	Total	Medical care	Transportation	School attendance	Recreation				Life insurance [2]	Church contributions and other contributions [2]	Taxes [3]		
							Total	Newspapers	Motion picture theater admissions	Organizations, tobacco, and toys [2]			Total	Personal property	Capitation
Average, 59 cities	[4] 0.1	0.2	20.0	4.2	4.3	[5] 0.5	5.9	0.9	2.6	2.4	3.7	1.2	[6] 0.2	[7] 0.1	[8] 0.1
Washington, D. C.	(9)	0.2	19.2	4.2	5.1	0.1	5.4	0.6	2.7	2.1	3.3	1.1	(10)	(10)	(10)
San Francisco, Calif.[1]	0.5	0.2	19.6	4.6	3.7	0.6	6.3	1.0	3.1	2.2	3.3	1.1	(10)	(10)	(10)
Minneapolis, Minn.	0.3	0.2	20.6	3.9	6.6	0.5	5.2	0.6	2.4	2.2	3.3	1.1	(10)	(10)	(10)
New York, N. Y.[1]	(9)	0.2	19.6	4.1	5.2	0.1	5.7	0.6	2.9	2.2	3.4	1.1	(10)	(10)	(10)
Chicago, Ill.[1]	(9)	0.2	21.9	4.2	6.9	0.2	6.0	0.8	2.9	2.3	3.4	1.1	0.1	0.1	(10)
Milwaukee, Wis.	(9)	0.2	20.2	3.3	5.6	0.8	5.8	1.1	2.5	2.2	3.4	1.1	0.2	0.2	(10)
Boston, Mass.	(9)	0.2	19.6	4.1	4.6	0.1	6.2	1.1	2.9	2.2	3.4	1.1	0.1	(10)	0.1
Cleveland, Ohio [1]	(9)	0.2	23.4	4.4	7.5	0.8	6.2	1.1	2.8	2.3	3.4	1.1	(10)	(10)	(10)
St. Louis, Mo.	0.2	0.2	23.4	3.7	8.8	(9)	6.1	1.0	2.8	2.3	3.5	1.1	0.2	0.2	(10)
Detroit, Mich.[1]	(9)	0.2	22.4	4.4	6.2	1.1	6.0	1.0	2.6	2.4	3.5	1.2	(10)	(10)	(10)
Scranton, Pa.	(9)	0.2	19.3	4.4	3.1	*	6.4	0.9	3.2	2.3	3.5	1.2	0.7	(10)	0.7
Cincinnati, Ohio [1]	(9)	0.2	21.5	3.2	7.2	0.3	6.1	0.9	2.8	2.4	3.5	1.2	(10)	(10)	(10)
Pittsburgh, Pa.	0.3	0.2	23.4	4.2	8.1	(9)	6.2	1.1	2.8	2.3	3.5	1.2	0.2	(10)	0.2
Los Angeles, Calif.[1]	(9)	0.2	23.3	4.6	7.7	0.2	6.1	0.8	2.9	2.4	3.5	1.2	(10)	(10)	(10)
Newark, N. J.	(9)	0.2	18.3	4.0	2.9	0.3	6.2	1.1	2.8	2.3	3.6	1.2	0.1	(10)	0.1
Baltimore, Md.	(9)	0.2	23.6	3.4	8.9	0.1	6.4	0.9	3.2	2.3	3.6	1.2	(10)	(10)	(10)
Albuquerque, N. Mex.[1]	0.4	0.2	16.6	4.4	1.0	0.7	5.7	0.6	2.7	2.4	3.6	1.2	(10)	(10)	(10)
Philadelphia, Pa.	(9)	0.2	22.9	3.3	8.2	0.1	6.5	0.9	3.3	2.3	3.6	1.2	(10)	(10)	(10)
Bridgeport, Conn.	(9)	0.2	18.2	4.3	3.4	0.1	5.6	0.7	2.6	2.3	3.6	1.2	(10)	(10)	(10)
Sioux Falls, S. Dak.	0.9	0.2	15.2	4.0	0.8	(9)	5.5	0.7	2.4	2.4	3.6	1.2	0.1	0.1	(10)
Rochester, N. Y.	(9)	0.2	20.0	4.1	5.0	0.4	5.7	0.8	2.5	2.4	3.6	1.2	(10)	(10)	(10)
Tucson, Ariz.[1]	(9)	0.2	18.0	4.8	1.0	0.6	6.3	0.8	3.1	2.4	3.6	1.2	0.5	0.5	(10)
Butte, Mont.	(9)	0.2	17.6	4.9	0.8	0.5	6.1	0.9	2.8	2.4	3.6	1.2	0.5	0.2	0.3
Portland, Maine	0.6	0.2	18.6	4.6	2.2	0.5	5.9	1.0	2.5	2.4	3.6	1.2	0.6	0.4	0.2
Peoria, Ill.[1]	(9)	0.2	18.1	3.4	2.3	1.5	5.8	0.8	2.6	2.4	3.6	1.2	0.3	0.3	(10)

Fall River, Mass.	(9)	0.2	17.9	4.0	2.5	(9)	6.1	0.9	2.8	2.4	3.6	1.2	0.5	0.3	0.2
Atlanta, Ga.	(9)	0.2	20.0	4.2	4.1	0.6	5.6	0.8	2.3	2.5	3.7	1.2	0.6	0.2	0.4
Richmond, Va.	(9)	0.2	18.8	4.0	3.1	0.6	5.8	0.6	2.8	2.4	3.7	1.2	0.4	0.2	0.2
Buffalo, N. Y.	(9)	0.3	21.7	4.0	7.1	0.2	5.5	0.9	2.2	2.4	3.7	1.2	(10)	(10)	(10)
Omaha, Nebr.	0.1	0.3	19.1	3.8	4.6	0.3	5.5	0.8	2.3	2.4	3.7	1.2	(10)	(10)	(10)
Manchester, N. H.	(9)	0.3	19.4	4.0	3.2	0.1	6.6	0.9	3.3	2.4	3.7	1.2	0.6	0.3	0.3
Norfolk, Va.	(9)	0.3	18.6	4.1	2.9	0.4	5.8	0.8	2.6	2.4	3.7	1.2	0.5	0.2	0.3
Denver, Colo.[1]	0.1	0.3	22.5	4.5	6.0	0.6	6.5	1.0	3.0	2.5	3.7	1.2	(10)	(10)	(10)
Kansas City, Mo.	0.2	0.3	22.9	4.1	7.7	0.9	5.0	0.6	1.9	2.5	3.7	1.2	0.3	0.3	(10)
Providence, R. I.	0.2	0.3	18.4	4.4	3.3	0.1	5.5	0.9	2.1	2.5	3.7	1.2	0.2	0.2	(10)
Binghamton, N. Y.	(9)	0.3	18.6	4.5	0.9	1.3	7.0	1.2	3.4	2.4	3.7	1.2	(10)	(10)	(10)
Salt Lake City, Utah [1]	(9)	0.3	20.2	4.6	4.3	0.1	5.9	0.9	2.5	2.5	3.7	1.2	0.4	0.4	(10)
Seattle, Wash.	(9)	0.3	21.4	4.2	6.1	0.1	6.0	0.8	2.7	2.5	3.8	1.2	(10)	(10)	(10)
New Orleans, La.	(9)	0.3	24.2	4.3	7.9	0.3	6.4	0.7	3.2	2.5	3.8	1.2	0.3	0.3	(10)
Spokane, Wash.	1.0	0.3	19.6	5.4	3.4	0.3	5.4	0.8	2.1	2.5	3.8	1.3	(10)	(10)	(10)
Winston-Salem, N. C.[1]	(9)	0.3	17.6	4.3	1.7	0.8	5.6	0.9	2.2	2.5	3.8	1.3	0.1	(10)	0.1
Portland, Oreg.	0.5	0.3	21.2	4.1	5.7	0.7	5.6	0.9	2.3	2.4	3.8	1.3	(10)	(10)	(10)
Memphis, Tenn.	(9)	0.3	21.4	4.4	5.0	0.6	6.0	0.9	2.6	2.5	3.8	1.3	0.3	(10)	0.3
Louisville, Ky.[1]	(9)	0.3	21.0	3.3	4.9	1.0	6.5	0.9	3.1	2.5	3.8	1.3	0.2	0.2	(10)
Oklahoma City, Okla.[1]	0.7	0.3	19.9	4.2	3.2	0.9	6.5	1.1	2.9	2.5	3.8	1.3	(10)	(10)	(10)
Jacksonville, Fla.	(9)	0.3	19.3	4.7	2.5	0.6	6.2	0.9	2.8	2.5	3.8	1.3	0.2	(10)	0.2
Houston, Tex.	(9)	0.3	21.8	4.4	5.5	0.8	5.8	0.8	2.5	2.5	3.8	1.3	0.2	(10)	0.2
Indianapolis, Ind.	(9)	0.3	21.7	3.6	5.4	0.8	6.2	1.1	2.6	2.5	3.9	1.3	0.5	0.2	0.3
Columbia, S. C.	(9)	0.3	16.4	3.4	0.7	0.9	6.0	0.9	2.5	2.6	3.9	1.3	0.2	(10)	0.2
Clarksburg, W. Va.[1]	0.5	0.3	18.7	4.6	0.8	1.8	5.9	0.9	2.4	2.6	3.9	1.3	0.4	(10)	0.4
Dallas, Tex.	(9)	0.3	19.7	4.2	3.0	1.0	6.0	0.7	2.7	2.6	3.9	1.3	0.3	(10)	0.3
Cedar Rapids, Iowa [1]	0.1	0.3	17.8	3.9	2.1	0.4	5.9	0.9	2.4	2.6	3.9	1.3	0.3	(10)	0.3
Columbus, Ohio [1]	(9)	0.3	19.4	3.9	3.8	0.8	5.7	0.7	2.4	2.6	3.9	1.3	(10)	(10)	(10)
Birmingham, Ala.	(9)	0.3	22.0	4.1	5.3	0.9	6.1	0.9	2.6	2.6	4.0	1.3	0.3	(10)	0.3
Knoxville, Tenn.	(9)	0.3	19.6	4.3	2.8	0.7	5.9	0.9	2.4	2.6	4.0	1.3	0.6	0.2	0.4
El Paso, Tex.	0.2	0.3	16.7	3.3	1.5	0.2	6.1	0.7	2.8	2.6	4.0	1.3	0.3	(10)	0.3
Little Rock, Ark.	(9)	0.3	19.5	4.7	1.4	1.2	6.0	0.8	2.6	2.6	4.1	1.4	0.7	0.2	0.5
Wichita, Kans.	0.1	0.3	19.3	4.4	2.3	1.3	5.8	0.7	2.4	2.7	4.1	1.4	(10)	(10)	(10)
Mobile, Ala.	(9)	0.3	20.0	4.6	1.9	1.8	5.9	0.9	2.3	2.7	4.1	1.4	0.3	*	0.3

*Less than 0.05 percent.

[1] Include sales tax where levied (appendix table 15).
[2] Budget allowance identical in all cities, plus sales tax where levied.
[3] Exclusive of sales tax.
[4] Though only 18 cities had a direct charge for refuse disposal, an average for 59 cities is used in order to balance the table.
[5] Though only 55 cities had a direct charge for school attendance, an average for 59 cities is used in order to balance the table.
[6] Though taxes were payable in only 36 cities, an average for 59 cities is used in order to balance the table.
[7] Though personal property taxes were payable in only 22 cities, an average for 59 cities is used in order to balance the table.
[8] Though capitation taxes were payable in only 25 cities, an average for 59 cities is used in order to balance the table.
[9] Not a direct charge.
[10] None payable.

Table 18.—Percent Distribution of the Costs[1] of Living Among Major Budget Groups and Principal Subgroups, in 9 Geographic Divisions, 4-Person Manual Worker's Family, 59 Cities, March 1935

MAINTENANCE LEVEL

Budget group	Average, 59 cities	Geographic division								
		New England	Middle Atlantic	East North Central	West North Central	South Atlantic	East South Central	West South Central	Mountain	Pacific
Total cost of living: Amount	$1, 260. 62	$1, 282. 57	$1, 298. 58	$1, 292. 27	$1, 262. 73	$1, 258. 32	$1, 181. 40	$1, 190. 41	$1, 271. 84	$1, 276. 33
Percent	100. 0	100. 0	100. 0	100. 0	100. 0	100. 0	100. 0	100. 0	100. 0	100. 0
Food	35. 6	36. 2	34. 9	34. 3	34. 4	36. 7	36. 9	36. 9	35. 6	34. 5
Clothing, clothing upkeep, and personal care	14. 6	14. 5	13. 8	14. 9	14. 7	14. 0	14. 6	14. 6	15. 4	16. 0
Clothing	11. 5	11. 5	10. 9	11. 8	11. 8	11. 1	11. 5	11. 5	12. 0	12. 7
Clothing upkeep	1. 1	1. 1	1. 0	1. 0	1. 1	1. 0	1. 1	1. 1	1. 3	1. 2
Personal care	2. 0	1. 9	1. 9	2. 1	1. 8	1. 9	2. 0	2. 0	2. 1	2. 1
Housing, including water	17. 6	17. 2	19. 1	18. 3	18. 2	18. 4	16. 4	16. 8	16. 7	15. 2
Household operation	12. 2	13. 4	11. 7	11. 4	12. 8	11. 7	11. 4	11. 3	13. 3	13. 3
Fuel	4. 6	6. 1	4. 8	4. 8	5. 7	4. 2	3. 7	3. 1	4. 7	4. 4
Coal or wood	3. 7	5. 2	4. 1	4. 3	5. 1	2. 9	2. 6	2. 3	3. 8	3. 2
Gas	0. 9	0. 9	0. 7	0. 5	0. 6	1. 3	1. 1	0. 8	0. 9	1. 2
Ice	1. 8	1. 5	1. 4	1. 4	1. 3	1. 9	1. 9	2. 1	2. 2	2. 8
Electricity	1. 5	1. 6	1. 5	1. 2	1. 4	1. 4	1. 4	1. 7	1. 7	1. 3
Household supplies	1. 5	1. 5	1. 4	1. 4	1. 5	1. 4	1. 5	1. 5	1. 7	1. 7
Furniture, furnishings, and household equipment	2. 5	2. 4	2. 3	2. 4	2. 4	2. 5	2. 6	2. 5	2. 7	2. 5
Refuse disposal[2]	0. 1	0. 1		(3)	0. 3	0. 1	(3)	0. 1	0. 1	0. 4
Unspecified essentials[4]	0. 2	0. 2	0. 2	0. 2	0. 2	0. 2	0. 3	0. 3	0. 2	0. 2
Miscellaneous	20. 0	18. 7	20. 5	21. 1	19. 9	19. 2	20. 7	20. 4	19. 0	21. 0
Medical care	4. 2	4. 2	4. 1	3. 8	4. 0	4. 1	4. 1	4. 2	4. 7	4. 6
Transportation	4. 3	3. 2	5. 0	5. 7	4. 8	3. 4	4. 0	3. 8	2. 6	5. 3
School attendance[5]	0. 5	0. 1	0. 3	0. 8	0. 5	0. 6	1. 0	0. 7	0. 5	0. 4
Recreation	5. 9	6. 1	6. 2	5. 9	5. 6	5. 9	6. 1	6. 2	6. 1	5. 9
Newspapers	0. 9	0. 9	0. 9	0. 9	0. 8	0. 8	0. 9	0. 8	0. 8	0. 9
Motion picture theater admissions	2. 6	2. 8	3. 0	2. 6	2. 4	2. 7	2. 6	2. 8	2. 9	2. 6
Organizations, tobacco, and toys[4]	2. 4	2. 4	2. 3	2. 4	2. 4	2. 4	2. 6	2. 6	2. 4	2. 4
Life insurance[4]	3. 7	3. 6	3. 6	3. 6	3. 7	3. 7	3. 9	3. 9	3. 6	3. 6
Church contributions and other contributions[4]	1. 2	1. 2	1. 2	1. 2	1. 2	1. 2	1. 3	1. 3	1. 2	1. 2
Taxes[6 7]	0. 2	0. 3	0. 1	0. 1	0. 1	0. 3	0. 3	0. 3	0. 3	(8)
Personal property[9]	0. 1	0. 2	(8)	0. 1	0. 1	0. 1	0. 1	0. 1	0. 2	(8)
Capitation[10]	0. 1	0. 1	0. 1	*	*	0. 2	0. 2	0. 2	0. 1	(8)

*Less than 0.05 percent.

[1] Include sales tax where levied (appendix table 15).

[2] Though only 18 cities had a direct charge for refuse disposal, an average for 59 cities is used in order to balance the table. The percents for the geographic divisions are averages for the cities in each division included in this study.

[3] Not a direct charge.

[4] Budget allowance identical in all cities, plus sales tax where levied.

[5] Though only 55 cities had a direct charge for school attendance, an average for 59 cities is used in order to balance the table. The percents for the geographic divisions are averages for the cities in each division included in this study.

[6] Exclusive of sales tax.

[7] Though taxes were payable in only 36 cities, an average for 59 cities is used in order to balance the table. The percents for the geographic divisions are averages for the cities in each division included in this study.

[8] None payable.

[9] Though personal property taxes were payable in only 22 cities, an average for 59 cities is used in order to balance the table. The percents for the geographic divisions are averages for the cities in each division included in this study.

[10] Though capitation taxes were payable in only 25 cities, an average for 59 cities is used in order to balance the table. The percents for the geographic divisions are averages for the cities in each division included in this study.

Table 19.—Percent Distribution of the Costs[1] of Living Among Major Budget Groups and Principal Subgroups, in 5 Size of City Classifications, 4-Person Manual Worker's Family, 59 Cities, March 1935

MAINTENANCE LEVEL

Budget group	Average, 59 cities	Size of city classification				
		1,000,000 or more	500,000 to 1,000,000	250,000 to 500,000	100,000 to 250,000	25,000 to 100,000
Total cost of living: Amount	$1, 260. 62	$1, 330. 92	$1, 332. 03	$1, 251. 68	1, 235. 05	$1, 230. 25
Percent	100. 0	100. 0	100. 0	100. 0	100. 0	100. 0
Food	35. 6	34. 2	33. 7	35. 5	36. 1	36. 8
Clothing, clothing upkeep, and personal care	14. 6	14. 2	14. 4	14. 4	14. 9	15. 0
Clothing	11. 5	11. 4	11. 4	11. 4	11. 8	11. 8
Clothing upkeep	1. 1	0. 9	1. 0	1. 1	1. 1	1. 2
Personal care	2. 0	1. 9	2. 0	1. 9	2. 0	2. 0
Housing, including water	17. 6	18. 0	18. 7	17. 5	17. 7	16. 8
Household operation	12. 2	11. 6	11. 3	11. 7	12. 4	13. 4
Fuel	4. 6	4. 7	4. 5	4. 3	4. 8	5. 0
Coal or wood	3. 7	4. 1	3. 9	3. 5	3. 7	3. 9
Gas	0. 9	0. 6	0. 6	0. 8	1. 1	1. 1
Ice	1. 8	1. 6	1. 6	1. 8	1. 7	2. 1
Electricity	1. 5	1. 4	1. 2	1. 4	1. 6	1. 7
Household supplies	1. 5	1. 4	1. 4	1. 5	1. 5	1. 6
Furniture, furnishings, and household equipment	2. 5	2. 3	2. 3	2. 4	2. 5	2. 6
Refuse disposal [2]	0. 1	(3)	0. 1	0. 1	0. 1	0. 2
Unspecified essentials [4]	0. 2	0. 2	0. 2	0. 2	0. 2	0. 2
Miscellaneous	20. 0	22. 0	21. 9	20. 9	18. 9	18. 0
Medical care	4. 2	4. 1	4. 0	4. 0	4. 2	4. 4
Transportation	4. 3	6. 8	6. 7	5. 3	3. 0	1. 4
School attendance [5]	0. 5	0. 3	0. 3	0. 6	0. 5	0. 8
Recreation	5. 9	6. 0	6. 1	5. 9	5. 9	6. 0
Newspapers	0. 9	0. 8	1. 0	0. 8	0. 8	0. 9
Motion picture theater admissions	2. 6	2. 9	2. 8	2. 7	2. 6	2. 6
Organizations, tobacco, and toys [4]	2. 4	2. 3	2. 3	2. 4	2. 5	2. 5
Life insurance [4]	3. 7	3. 5	3. 5	3. 7	3. 8	3. 8
Church contributions and other contributions [4]	1. 2	1. 2	1. 2	1. 2	1. 2	1. 3
Taxes [6 7]	0. 2	*	0. 1	0. 2	0. 3	0. 3
Personal property [8]	0. 1	*	0. 1	0. 1	0. 1	0. 1
Capitation [9]	0. 1	(10)	*	0. 1	0. 2	0. 2

*Less than 0.05 percent.

[1] Include sales tax where levied (appendix table 15).

[2] Though only 18 cities had a direct charge for refuse disposal, an average for 59 cities is used in order to balance the table. The percents for the size of city groups are averages for the cities in each group included in this study.

[3] Not a direct charge.

[4] Budget allowance identical in all cities, plus sales tax where levied.

[5] Though only 55 cities had a direct charge for school attendance, an average for 59 cities is used in order to balance the table. The percents for the size of city groups are averages for the cities in each group included in this study.

[6] Exclusive of sales tax.

[7] Though taxes were payable in only 36 cities, an average for 59 cities is used in order to balance the table. The percents for the size of city groups are averages for the cities in each group included in this study.

[8] Though personal property taxes were payable in only 22 cities, an average for 59 cities is used in order to balance the table. The percents for the size of city groups are averages for the cities in each group included in this study.

[9] Though capitation taxes were payable in only 25 cities, an average for 59 cities is used in order to balance the table. The percents for the size of city groups are averages for the cities in each group included in this study.

[10] None payable.

Table 20.—Percent Distribution of the Costs[1] of Living Among Major Budget Groups and Principal Subgroups, 4-Person Manual Worker's Family, 59 Cities, March 1935

EMERGENCY LEVEL

City	Total cost of living		Food	Clothing, clothing upkeep, and personal care				Housing, including water	Household operation						
										Fuel					
	Amount	Percent		Total	Clothing	Clothing upkeep	Personal care		Total	Total	Coal or wood	Gas	Ice	Electricity	Household supplies
Average, 59 cities	$903.27	100.0	37.6	14.2	11.1	1.3	1.8	18.6	13.5	5.3	4.2	1.1	2.1	1.6	1.9
Washington, D. C.	1,013.98	100.0	35.2	12.2	9.6	1.1	1.5	25.4	11.5	5.3	4.6	0.7	1.6	1.0	1.5
Minneapolis, Minn.	1,013.88	100.0	33.1	13.8	10.9	1.4	1.5	19.5	16.4	9.3	8.7	0.6	1.5	1.5	1.6
San Francisco, Calif.[1]	1,001.12	100.0	35.2	14.5	11.5	1.2	1.8	20.4	14.5	4.1	2.9	1.2	4.0	1.5	2.0
New York, N. Y.[1]	982.11	100.0	36.5	12.2	9.5	1.0	1.7	22.6	12.7	5.5	4.5	1.0	1.7	1.9	1.6
Chicago, Ill.[1]	972.59	100.0	35.9	13.8	10.9	1.1	1.8	18.5	13.4	6.5	6.0	0.5	1.7	1.4	1.6
Milwaukee, Wis.	970.64	100.0	33.2	14.6	11.6	1.2	1.8	21.0	14.6	8.2	7.5	0.7	1.1	1.4	1.6
Cleveland, Ohio[1]	964.71	100.0	35.0	15.0	12.0	1.2	1.8	18.3	11.6	5.1	4.7	0.4	1.5	0.9	1.8
Boston, Mass.	958.45	100.0	36.4	13.7	10.7	1.2	1.8	20.7	13.5	6.0	5.0	1.0	1.7	1.6	1.9
St. Louis, Mo.	956.48	100.0	35.3	13.0	10.3	1.1	1.6	21.3	10.4	3.8	3.0	0.8	1.5	1.1	1.6
Albuquerque, N. Mex.[1]	947.57	100.0	39.7	14.2	10.8	1.5	1.9	19.1	14.7	4.4	3.3	1.1	3.1	2.0	2.2
Detroit, Mich.[1]	944.00	100.0	35.2	14.3	11.5	1.1	1.7	17.8	13.7	6.3	5.6	0.7	1.6	1.6	1.9
Sioux Falls, S. Dak.	938.27	100.0	35.1	14.2	11.2	1.4	1.6	21.9	18.1	9.1	8.4	0.7	1.7	1.8	2.0
Los Angeles, Calif.[1]	935.85	100.0	35.9	15.2	12.2	1.2	1.8	15.7	13.3	4.4	3.2	1.2	3.2	1.2	2.1
Cincinnati, Ohio[1]	935.54	100.0	36.5	13.7	10.7	1.2	1.8	20.7	11.6	4.4	4.0	0.4	1.8	1.2	1.9
Scranton, Pa.	932.21	100.0	36.7	13.8	10.8	1.2	1.8	22.2	12.2	4.6	3.2	1.4	1.9	1.5	1.9
Butte, Mont.	932.11	100.0	37.3	16.2	12.3	2.0	1.9	17.7	15.7	7.3	6.4	0.9	1.7	1.9	2.2
Pittsburgh, Pa.	930.45	100.0	36.3	13.7	10.8	1.2	1.7	19.7	10.6	3.1	2.6	0.5	1.5	1.6	1.7
Baltimore, Md.	926.71	100.0	36.7	12.7	10.0	1.1	1.6	18.8	12.0	5.2	4.4	0.8	1.6	1.2	1.8
Rochester, N. Y.	925.16	100.0	36.1	13.7	10.5	1.5	1.7	18.2	15.9	8.7	7.8	0.9	1.6	1.7	1.6
Philadelphia, Pa.	924.56	100.0	36.8	13.2	10.4	1.1	1.7	19.5	11.7	5.0	4.2	0.8	1.2	1.5	1.8
Portland, Maine	921.94	100.0	37.2	15.0	11.6	1.6	1.8	16.9	16.4	7.7	6.3	1.4	1.7	1.9	1.9
Newark, N. J.	920.54	100.0	38.7	12.8	9.9	1.1	1.8	20.9	13.8	5.9	4.6	1.3	1.8	2.1	1.7
Bridgeport, Conn.	920.39	100.0	39.4	13.6	10.6	1.2	1.8	18.9	13.7	6.5	5.2	1.3	1.8	1.4	1.8
Tucson, Ariz.[1]	920.05	100.0	38.7	14.3	10.8	1.7	1.8	17.9	15.4	4.6	2.7	1.9	4.3	1.8	2.3
Peoria, Ill.[1]	913.39	100.0	37.7	14.4	11.4	1.2	1.8	22.8	11.0	3.5	2.5	1.0	1.8	1.6	1.8

See footnotes at end of table.

Table 20.—Percent Distribution of the Costs of Living Among Major Budget Groups and Principal Subgroups, 4-Person Manual Worker's Family, 59 Cities, March 1935—Continued

EMERGENCY LEVEL—continued

City	Total cost of living		Food	Clothing, clothing upkeep, and personal care				Housing, including water	Household operation						
	Amount	Percent		Total	Clothing	Clothing upkeep	Personal care		Total	Fuel			Ice	Electricity	Household supplies
										Total	Coal or wood	Gas			
Atlanta, Ga	$911.25	100.0	38.1	12.8	10.1	1.1	1.6	20.7	11.9	4.2	3.0	1.2	2.1	1.6	1.6
Richmond, Va	910.36	100.0	37.1	14.5	11.5	1.3	1.7	20.0	13.3	5.1	3.4	1.7	2.5	1.5	1.7
Omaha, Nebr	908.71	100.0	37.4	14.2	11.1	1.4	1.7	20.0	13.1	6.3	5.5	0.8	1.3	1.4	1.8
Buffalo, N. Y	901.72	100.0	36.8	14.3	11.3	1.3	1.7	17.3	13.2	6.0	5.7	0.3	1.8	1.2	1.8
Kansas City, Mo	899.85	100.0	37.6	13.9	11.2	1.1	1.6	16.7	11.4	4.3	3.6	0.7	1.4	1.6	1.6
Fall River, Mass	898.09	100.0	37.6	14.7	11.7	1.2	1.8	18.7	15.4	7.2	6.0	1.2	1.8	1.9	1.9
Spokane, Wash	894.02	100.0	37.2	16.1	12.5	1.7	1.9	14.8	16.2	6.5	4.5	2.0	2.1	1.4	2.3
Norfolk, Va	891.57	100.0	38.3	13.7	10.6	1.4	1.7	19.9	13.4	5.7	4.1	1.6	2.2	1.5	1.7
Salt Lake City, Utah [1]	890.84	100.0	37.3	15.8	12.4	1.6	1.8	16.2	14.5	5.7	4.8	0.9	2.1	1.9	2.1
Manchester, N. H	889.61	100.0	39.3	14.4	11.2	1.5	1.7	15.5	16.1	8.1	6.8	1.3	1.8	2.0	1.9
Seattle, Wash	886.58	100.0	38.3	15.1	11.8	1.5	1.8	14.2	14.9	5.6	3.6	2.0	3.4	1.3	2.2
Denver, Colo.[1]	885.24	100.0	37.5	14.4	11.3	1.4	1.7	16.9	12.6	4.9	3.9	1.0	1.5	1.5	2.0
Providence, R. I	885.17	100.0	38.4	13.3	10.3	1.3	1.7	18.3	15.3	7.1	5.9	1.2	1.5	2.0	2.0
Portland, Oreg	884.81	100.0	37.8	16.2	12.8	1.5	1.9	13.4	15.1	4.8	3.1	1.7	3.4	1.5	2.3
New Orleans, La	882.80	100.0	37.5	13.6	10.6	1.2	1.8	16.7	11.7	3.2	2.1	1.1	2.2	2.2	1.8
Binghamton, N. Y	878.10	100.0	38.1	14.2	11.2	1.2	1.8	19.5	14.2	5.8	4.7	1.1	1.8	2.3	1.8
Memphis, Tenn	877.27	100.0	37.7	13.6	10.5	1.3	1.8	19.2	11.8	4.1	3.0	1.1	2.2	1.4	1.7
Oklahoma City, Okla.[1]	874.17	100.0	38.8	14.6	11.2	1.3	2.1	18.0	13.2	3.8	3.5	0.3	2.6	1.8	1.9
Winston-Salem, N. C.[1]	873.04	100.0	39.1	14.2	11.1	1.3	1.8	18.1	15.0	6.2	3.8	2.4	2.7	1.9	1.8
Louisville, Ky.[1]	871.62	100.0	38.8	14.2	11.2	1.2	1.8	18.5	11.9	4.8	4.4	0.4	1.6	1.3	1.8
Houston, Tex	869.23	100.0	37.6	14.5	11.3	1.5	1.7	18.3	11.3	2.7	1.6	1.1	2.9	1.4	1.8
Jacksonville, Fla	868.57	100.0	39.7	13.9	10.8	1.4	1.7	17.3	14.1	5.9	2.3	3.6	2.2	1.8	1.7
Indianapolis, Ind	859.04	100.0	37.3	14.3	10.8	1.5	2.0	18.1	12.7	5.3	4.4	0.9	1.7	1.5	1.9
Dallas, Tex	853.98	100.0	40.3	13.3	10.3	1.3	1.7	19.4	11.5	2.9	1.6	1.3	2.8	1.4	2.1
Clarksburg, W. Va.[1]	852.87	100.0	41.8	15.0	12.0	1.2	1.8	17.2	11.3	2.3	2.0	0.3	1.9	1.7	2.1

Cedar Rapids, Iowa [1]	849.35	100.0	37.5	15.4	12.0	1.5	1.9	18.1	15.6	7.7	6.6	1.1	1.6	1.6	2.1
Columbia, S. C.	844.92	100.0	42.6	13.5	10.6	1.2	1.7	17.8	14.2	4.5	1.9	2.6	3.5	1.8	1.7
Knoxville, Tenn.	844.37	100.0	38.7	14.1	11.0	1.4	1.7	18.7	13.1	5.1	2.7	2.4	1.8	1.7	1.9
Columbus, Ohio [1]	840.68	100.0	40.5	15.2	12.1	1.2	1.9	17.1	11.7	4.0	3.7	0.3	2.0	1.1	2.0
Birmingham, Ala.	835.81	100.0	40.5	14.2	11.1	1.3	1.8	15.3	12.1	3.9	2.8	1.1	2.3	1.7	1.9
El Paso, Tex.	832.05	100.0	40.9	14.1	11.0	1.3	1.8	18.4	14.9	5.6	4.3	1.3	2.2	2.1	2.2
Little Rock, Ark.	819.97	100.0	41.5	14.7	11.4	1.5	1.8	16.4	12.0	3.3	2.4	0.9	1.8	2.4	2.0
Mobile, Ala.	814.92	100.0	40.7	13.9	10.7	1.4	1.8	15.6	13.9	4.5	2.2	2.3	3.1	1.7	2.0
Wichita, Kans.	809.64	100.0	39.8	15.1	11.9	1.4	1.8	15.2	14.5	6.2	5.6	0.6	1.6	2.0	2.0

See footnotes at end of table.

***Table* 20.**—Percent Distribution of the Costs of Living Among Major Budget Groups and Principal Subgroups, 4-Person Manual Worker's Family, 59 Cities, March 1935—Continued

EMERGENCY LEVEL—continued

City	Household operation—Con.			Miscellaneous											
	Furniture, furnishings, and household equipment	Refuse disposal	Unspecified essentials [2]	Total	Medical care	Transportation	School attendance	Recreation			Life insurance [2]	Church contributions [2]	Taxes [3]		
								Total	Motion picture theater admissions	Tobacco and toys [2]			Total	Personal property	Capitation
Average, 59 cities	2.1	[4] 0.2	0.3	16.1	5.1	5.0	[5] 0.8	1.4	0.9	0.5	2.3	1.2	[6] 0.3	[7] 0.1	[8] 0.2
Washington, D. C.	1.8	[9]	0.3	15.7	5.2	5.9	0.1	1.4	0.9	0.5	2.1	1.0	[10]	[10]	[10]
Minneapolis, Minn.	1.9	0.3	0.3	17.2	4.8	7.5	0.6	1.2	0.7	0.5	2.1	1.0	[10]	[10]	[10]
San Francisco, Calif.[1]	1.9	0.7	0.3	15.4	5.8	4.2	0.8	1.5	1.0	0.5	2.1	1.0	[10]	[10]	[10]
New York, N. Y.[1]	1.7	[9]	0.3	16.0	5.2	6.1	0.1	1.4	0.9	0.5	2.1	1.1	[10]	[10]	[10]
Chicago, Ill.[1]	1.9	[9]	0.3	18.4	5.3	8.0	0.3	1.4	0.9	0.5	2.1	1.1	0.2	0.2	[10]
Milwaukee, Wis.	2.0	[9]	0.3	16.6	4.1	6.5	1.2	1.3	0.8	0.5	2.1	1.1	0.3	0.3	[10]
Cleveland, Ohio[1]	2.0	[9]	0.3	20.1	5.5	8.8	1.1	1.4	0.9	0.5	2.2	1.1	[10]	[10]	[10]
Boston, Mass.	2.0	[9]	0.3	15.7	5.2	5.4	0.2	1.4	0.9	0.5	2.2	1.1	0.2	[10]	0.2
St. Louis, Mo.	1.8	0.3	0.3	20.0	4.7	10.3	[9]	1.4	0.9	0.5	2.2	1.1	0.3	0.3	[10]
Albuquerque, N. Mex.[1]	2.2	0.5	0.3	12.3	5.5	1.1	1.0	1.4	0.9	0.5	2.2	1.1	[10]	[10]	[10]
Detroit, Mich.[1]	2.0	[9]	0.3	19.0	5.6	7.2	1.5	1.4	0.9	0.5	2.2	1.1	[10]	[10]	[10]
Sioux Falls, S. Dak.	1.9	1.3	0.3	10.7	4.9	1.0	[9]	1.3	0.8	0.5	2.2	1.1	0.2	0.2	[10]
Los Angeles, Calif.[1]	2.1	[9]	0.3	19.9	5.8	9.0	0.3	1.5	1.0	0.5	2.2	1.1	[10]	[10]	[10]
Cincinnati, Ohio[1]	2.0	[9]	0.3	17.5	4.0	8.4	0.4	1.4	0.9	0.5	2.2	1.1	[10]	[10]	[10]
Scranton, Pa.	2.0	[9]	0.3	15.1	5.6	3.6	0.1	1.5	1.0	0.5	2.2	1.1	1.0	[10]	1.0
Butte, Mont.	2.3	[9]	0.3	13.1	6.1	1.0	0.7	1.4	0.9	0.5	2.2	1.1	0.6	0.2	0.4
Pittsburgh, Pa.	1.9	0.5	0.3	19.7	5.3	9.5	[9]	1.4	0.9	0.5	2.2	1.1	0.2	[10]	0.2
Baltimore, Md.	1.9	[9]	0.3	19.8	4.3	10.4	0.2	1.6	1.1	0.5	2.2	1.1	[10]	[10]	[10]
Rochester, N. Y.	2.0	[9]	0.3	16.1	5.1	5.8	0.6	1.3	0.8	0.5	2.2	1.1	[10]	[10]	[10]
Philadelphia, Pa.	1.9	[9]	0.3	18.8	4.2	9.6	0.1	1.6	1.1	0.5	2.2	1.1	[10]	[10]	[10]
Portland, Maine	2.1	0.8	0.3	14.5	5.7	2.6	0.7	1.3	0.8	0.5	2.3	1.1	0.8	0.5	0.3
Newark, N. J.	2.0	[9]	0.3	13.8	5.1	3.4	0.4	1.4	0.9	0.5	2.3	1.1	0.1	[10]	0.1
Bridgeport, Conn.	1.9	[9]	0.3	14.4	5.5	4.0	0.1	1.4	0.9	0.5	2.3	1.1	[10]	[10]	[10]
Tucson, Ariz.[1]	2.1	[9]	0.3	13.7	6.0	1.1	0.9	1.6	1.1	0.5	2.3	1.1	0.7	0.7	[10]
Peoria, Ill.[1]	2.0	[9]	0.3	14.1	4.3	2.7	2.0	1.3	0.8	0.5	2.3	1.1	0.4	0.4	[10]

Atlanta, Ga	2.1	[9]	0.3	16.5	5.3	4.8	0.8	1.3	0.8	0.5	2.3	1.1	0.9	0.4	0.5
Richmond, Va	2.2	[9]	0.3	15.1	5.1	3.7	0.9	1.4	0.9	0.5	2.3	1.1	0.6	0.2	0.4
Omaha, Nebr	1.9	0.1	0.3	15.3	4.8	5.3	0.5	1.3	0.8	0.5	2.3	1.1	[10]	[10]	[10]
Buffalo, N. Y	2.1	[9]	0.3	18.4	5.1	8.3	0.2	1.3	0.8	0.5	2.3	1.2	[10]	[10]	[10]
Kansas City, Mo	1.9	0.3	0.3	20.4	5.1	8.9	1.3	1.2	0.7	0.5	2.3	1.2	0.4	0.4	[10]
Fall River, Mass	2.3	[9]	0.3	13.6	5.1	2.9	[9]	1.4	0.9	0.5	2.3	1.2	0.7	0.5	0.2
Spokane, Wash	2.3	1.3	0.3	15.7	6.7	3.8	0.5	1.2	0.7	0.5	2.3	1.2	[10]	[10]	[10]
Norfolk, Va	2.0	[9]	0.3	14.7	5.2	3.3	0.6	1.4	0.9	0.5	2.3	1.2	0.7	0.3	0.4
Salt Lake City, Utah [1]	2.4	[9]	0.3	16.2	5.7	5.0	0.1	1.4	0.8	0.6	2.3	1.2	0.5	0.5	[10]
Manchester, N. H	2.0	[9]	0.3	14.7	5.0	3.7	0.1	1.6	1.1	0.5	2.3	1.2	0.8	0.4	0.4
Seattle, Wash	2.1	[9]	0.3	17.5	5.3	7.1	0.2	1.4	0.9	0.5	2.3	1.2	[10]	[10]	[10]
Denver, Colo.[1]	2.2	0.2	0.3	18.6	5.7	7.0	0.9	1.5	0.9	0.6	2.3	1.2	[10]	[10]	[10]
Providence, R. I	2.1	0.3	0.3	14.7	5.6	3.9	0.2	1.2	0.7	0.5	2.3	1.2	0.3	0.3	[10]
Portland, Oreg	2.1	0.7	0.3	17.5	5.0	6.6	1.0	1.3	0.8	0.5	2.4	1.2	[10]	[10]	[10]
New Orleans, La	2.0	[9]	0.3	20.5	5.3	9.2	0.4	1.6	1.1	0.5	2.4	1.2	0.4	0.4	[10]
Binghamton, N. Y	2.2	[9]	0.3	14.0	5.7	1.1	1.9	1.7	1.2	0.5	2.4	1.2	[10]	[10]	[10]
Memphis, Tenn	2.1	[9]	0.3	17.7	5.5	5.8	0.9	1.4	0.9	0.5	2.4	1.2	0.5	[10]	0.5
Oklahoma City, Okla.[1]	1.9	0.9	0.3	15.4	5.2	3.8	1.3	1.5	0.9	0.6	2.4	1.2	[10]	[10]	[10]
Winston-Salem, N. C.[1]	2.1	[9]	0.3	13.6	5.4	2.0	1.2	1.3	0.7	0.6	2.4	1.2	0.1	[10]	0.1
Louisville, Ky.[1]	2.1	[9]	0.3	16.6	4.2	5.7	1.3	1.6	1.0	0.6	2.4	1.2	0.2	0.2	[10]
Houston, Tex	2.2	[9]	0.3	18.3	5.5	6.4	1.1	1.4	0.8	0.6	2.4	1.2	0.3	[10]	0.3
Jacksonville, Fla	2.2	[9]	0.3	15.0	5.9	3.0	0.8	1.5	0.9	0.6	2.4	1.2	0.2	[10]	0.2
Indianapolis, Ind	2.0	[9]	0.3	17.6	4.6	6.3	1.1	1.4	0.8	0.6	2.4	1.2	0.6	0.3	0.3
Dallas, Tex	2.0	[9]	0.3	15.5	5.2	3.5	1.4	1.4	0.8	0.6	2.4	1.2	0.4	[10]	0.4
Clarksburg, W. Va.[1]	2.3	0.7	0.3	14.7	5.8	0.9	2.5	1.3	0.7	0.6	2.4	1.2	0.6	[10]	0.6
Cedar Rapids, Iowa [1]	2.2	0.1	0.3	13.4	4.9	2.4	0.6	1.4	0.8	0.6	2.4	1.2	0.5	[10]	0.5
Columbia, S. C	2.4	[9]	0.3	11.9	4.4	0.9	1.3	1.4	0.8	0.6	2.5	1.2	0.2	[10]	0.2
Knoxville, Tenn	2.3	[9]	0.3	15.4	5.4	3.2	1.0	1.3	0.7	0.6	2.5	1.2	0.8	0.3	0.5
Columbus, Ohio [1]	2.3	[9]	0.3	15.5	4.9	4.4	1.1	1.4	0.8	0.6	2.5	1.2	[10]	[10]	[10]
Birmingham, Ala	2.0	[9]	0.3	17.9	5.1	6.1	1.2	1.4	0.8	0.6	2.5	1.2	0.4	[10]	0.4
El Paso, Tex	2.2	0.3	0.3	11.7	4.2	1.7	0.2	1.5	0.9	0.6	2.5	1.2	0.4	[10]	0.4
Little Rock, Ark	2.2	[9]	0.3	15.4	5.9	1.7	1.6	1.4	0.8	0.6	2.5	1.3	1.0	0.3	0.7
Mobile, Ala	2.3	[9]	0.3	15.9	5.7	2.1	2.5	1.3	0.7	0.6	2.6	1.3	0.4	*	0.4
Wichita, Kans	2.2	0.2	0.3	15.4	5.6	2.7	1.8	1.4	0.8	0.6	2.6	1.3	[10]	[10]	[10]

*Less than 0.05 percent.

[1] Include sales tax where levied (appendix table 16).
[2] Budget allowance identical in all cities, plus sales tax where levied.
[3] Exclusive of sales tax.
[4] Though only 18 cities had a direct charge for refuse disposal, an average for 59 cities is used in order to balance the table.
[5] Though only 55 cities had a direct charge for school attendance, an average for 59 cities is used in order to balance the table.
[6] Though taxes were payable in only 36 cities, an average for 59 cities is used in order to balance the table.
[7] Though personal property taxes were payable in only 22 cities, an average for 59 cities is used in order to balance the table.
[8] Though capitation taxes were payable in only 25 cities, an average for 59 cities is used in order to balance the table.
[9] Not a direct charge
[10] None payable.

Table 21.—Percent Distribution of the Costs[1] of Living Among Major Budget Groups and Principal Subgroups, in 9 Geographic Divisions, 4-Person Manual Worker's Family, 59 Cities, March 1935

EMERGENCY LEVEL

Budget group	Average, 59 cities	Geographic division								
		New England	Middle Atlantic	East North Central	West North Central	South Atlantic	East South Central	West South Central	Mountain	Pacific
Total cost of living: Amount	$903.27	$912.27	$924.36	$925.07	$910.88	$899.25	$848.80	$855.37	$915.16	$920.48
Percent	100.0	100.0	100.0	100.0	100.0	100.0	100.0	100.0	100.0	100.0
Food	37.6	38.0	37.0	36.3	36.4	38.6	39.2	39.4	38.1	36.9
Clothing, clothing upkeep, and personal care	14.2	14.1	13.5	14.4	14.2	13.6	14.0	14.1	15.0	15.4
Clothing	11.1	11.0	10.6	11.4	11.2	10.7	10.9	11.0	11.6	12.2
Clothing upkeep	1.3	1.3	1.2	1.2	1.3	1.2	1.3	1.3	1.6	1.4
Personal care	1.8	1.8	1.7	1.8	1.7	1.7	1.8	1.8	1.8	1.8
Housing, including water	18.6	18.2	20.0	19.3	19.1	19.6	17.5	17.9	17.6	15.8
Household operation	13.5	15.1	13.0	12.6	14.2	12.9	12.5	12.4	14.6	14.8
Fuel	5.3	7.1	5.5	5.6	6.6	5.0	4.3	3.5	5.4	5.1
Coal or wood	4.2	5.9	4.6	5.0	5.9	3.4	2.8	2.5	4.3	3.5
Gas	1.1	1.2	0.9	0.6	0.7	1.6	1.5	1.0	1.1	1.6
Ice	2.1	1.7	1.7	1.6	1.5	2.2	2.2	2.5	2.6	3.2
Electricity	1.6	1.8	1.7	1.3	1.6	1.5	1.6	1.9	1.8	1.4
Household supplies	1.9	1.9	1.7	1.8	1.8	1.7	1.9	1.9	2.2	2.2
Furniture, furnishings, and household equipment	2.1	2.1	2.0	2.0	2.0	2.1	2.2	2.1	2.2	2.1
Refuse disposal[2]	0.2	0.2	0.1	(3)	0.4	0.1	(3)	0.2	0.1	0.5
Unspecified essentials[4]	0.3	0.3	0.3	0.3	0.3	0.3	0.3	0.3	0.3	0.3
Miscellaneous	16.1	14.6	16.5	17.4	16.1	15.3	16.8	16.2	14.7	17.1
Medical care	5.1	5.3	5.1	4.8	4.9	5.1	5.2	5.3	5.8	5.7
Transportation	5.0	3.8	5.9	6.6	5.7	4.0	4.6	4.4	3.0	6.0
School attendance[5]	0.8	0.2	0.4	1.1	0.6	0.9	1.4	1.0	0.7	0.6
Recreation	1.4	1.4	1.5	1.4	1.3	1.4	1.4	1.5	1.4	1.4
Motion picture theater admissions	0.9	0.9	1.0	0.9	0.8	0.9	0.8	0.9	0.9	0.9
Tobacco and toys[4]	0.5	0.5	0.5	0.5	0.5	0.5	0.6	0.6	0.5	0.5
Life insurance[4]	2.3	2.3	2.3	2.2	2.3	2.3	2.5	2.4	2.3	2.3
Church contributions[4]	1.2	1.1	1.1	1.1	1.1	1.2	1.2	1.2	1.1	1.1
Taxes[6 7]	0.3	0.5	0.2	0.2	0.2	0.4	0.5	0.4	0.4	(8)
Personal property[9]	0.1	0.3	(8)	0.2	0.1	0.1	0.1	0.1	0.3	(8)
Capitation[10]	0.2	0.2	0.2	*	0.1	0.3	0.3	0.3	0.1	(8)

* Less than 0.05 percent.

1 Include sales tax where levied (appendix table 16).

2 Though only 18 cities had a direct charge for refuse disposal, an average for 59 cities is used in order to balance the table. The percents for the geographic divisions are averages for the cities in each division included in this study.

3 Not a direct charge.

4 Budget allowance identical in all cities, plus sales tax where levied.

5 Though only 55 cities had a direct charge for school attendance, an average for 59 cities is used in order to balance the table. The percents for the geographic divisions are averages for the cities in each division included in this study.

6 Exclusive of sales tax.

7 Though taxes were payable in only 36 cities, an average for 59 cities is used in order to balance the table. The percents for the geographic divisions are averages for the cities in each division included in this study.

8 None payable.

9 Though personal property taxes were payable in only 22 cities, an average for 59 cities is used in order to balance the table. The percents for the geographic divisions are averages for the cities in each division included in this study.

10 Though capitation taxes were payable in only 25 cities, an average for 59 cities is used in order to balance the table. The percents for the geographic divisions are averages for the cities in each division included in this study.

Table 22.—Percent Distribution of the Costs[1] of Living Among Major Budget Groups and Principal Subgroups, in 5 Size of City Classifications, 4-Person Manual Worker's Family, 59 Cities, March 1935

EMERGENCY LEVEL

Budget group	Average, 59 cities	Size of city classification				
		1,000,000 or more	500,000 to 1,000,000	250,000 to 500,000	100,000 to 250,000	25,000 to 100,000
Total cost of living: Amount	$903.27	$951.82	$951.29	$897.50	$884.88	$883.29
Percent	100.0	100.0	100.0	100.0	100.0	100.0
Food	37.6	36.1	35.6	37.7	38.2	39.0
Clothing, clothing upkeep, and personal care	14.2	13.7	13.9	13.9	14.5	14.6
Clothing	11.1	10.9	11.0	10.9	11.3	11.3
Clothing upkeep	1.3	1.1	1.2	1.3	1.4	1.5
Personal care	1.8	1.7	1.7	1.7	1.8	1.8
Housing, including water	18.6	18.8	19.7	18.4	18.7	17.9
Household operation	13.5	13.0	12.6	12.9	13.8	14.9
Fuel	5.3	5.6	5.2	5.1	5.6	5.8
Coal or wood	4.2	4.8	4.5	4.1	4.2	4.4
Gas	1.1	0.8	0.7	1.0	1.4	1.4
Ice	2.1	1.9	1.8	2.1	2.0	2.4
Electricity	1.6	1.5	1.3	1.5	1.7	1.9
Household supplies	1.9	1.8	1.8	1.8	1.9	2.0
Furniture, furnishings, and household equipment	2.1	1.9	2.0	2.0	2.1	2.2
Refuse disposal[2]	0.2	(3)	0.2	0.1	0.2	0.3
Unspecified essentials[4]	0.3	0.3	0.3	0.3	0.3	0.3
Miscellaneous	16.1	18.4	18.2	17.1	14.8	13.6
Medical care	5.1	5.2	5.0	5.1	5.2	5.3
Transportation	5.0	8.0	7.9	6.1	3.5	1.7
School attendance[5]	0.8	0.5	0.5	0.8	0.7	1.1
Recreation	1.4	1.4	1.4	1.4	1.4	1.4
Motion picture theater admissions	0.9	0.9	0.9	0.9	0.9	0.9
Tobacco and toys[4]	0.5	0.5	0.5	0.5	0.5	0.5
Life insurance[4]	2.3	2.2	2.2	2.3	2.4	2.4
Church contributions[4]	1.2	1.1	1.1	1.2	1.2	1.2
Taxes[6 7]	0.3	*	0.1	0.2	0.4	0.5
Personal property[8]	0.1	*	0.1	0.1	0.2	0.2
Capitation[9]	0.2	(10)	*	0.1	0.2	0.3

*Less than 0.05 percent.

[1] Include sales tax where levied (appendix table 16).

[2] Though only 18 cities had a direct charge for refuse disposal, an average for 59 cities is used in order to balance the table. The percents for the size of city groups are averages for the cities in each group included in this study.

[3] Not a direct charge.

[4] Budget allowance identical in all cities, plus sales tax where levied.

[5] Though only 55 cities had a direct charge for school attendance, an average for 59 cities is used in order to balance the table. The percents for the size of city groups are averages for the cities in each group included in this study.

[6] Exclusive of sales tax.

[7] Though taxes were payable in only 36 cities, an average for 59 cities is used in order to balance the table. The percents for the size of city groups are averages for the cities in each group included in this study.

[8] Though personal property taxes were payable in only 22 cities, an average for 59 cities is used in order to balance the table. The percents for the size of city groups are averages for the cities in each group included in this study.

[9] Though capitation taxes were payable in only 25 cities, an average for 59 cities is used in order to balance the table. The percents for the size of city groups are averages for the cities in each group included in this study.

[10] None payable.

Index

INDEX

32592°—38——16

○